May Agnes Fleming

A Changed Heart

A Novel

May Agnes Fleming

A Changed Heart
A Novel

ISBN/EAN: 9783744692564

Printed in Europe, USA, Canada, Australia, Japan

Cover: Foto ©Thomas Meinert / pixelio.de

More available books at **www.hansebooks.com**

A
CHANGED HEART

A Novel.

BY

MAY AGNES FLEMING,

AUTHOR OF

"GUY EARSLCOURT'S WIFE,"   "A TERRIBLE SECRET,"
"A WONDERFUL WOMAN," "ONE NIGHT'S MYSTERY,"
"SILENT AND TRUE,"   "A MAD MARRIAGE,"
"LOST FOR A WOMAN,"
ETC., ETC.

"If Fortune, with a smiling face,
    Strew roses on our way,
When shall we stoop to pick them up?
    To-day, my love, to-day."

Stereotyped by
SAMUEL STODDER,
ELECTROTYPER & STEREOTYPER,
90 ANN STREET, N. Y.

TROW
PRINTING AND BOOK-BINDING CO.
N. Y.

CONTENTS.

A CHANGED HEART.

.

CHAPTER I.

MISS M'GREGOR AT HOME.

T was a foggy night in Speckport. There was nothing uncommon in its being foggy this close May evening; but it was rather provoking and ungallant of the clerk of the weather, seeing that Miss McGregor particularly desired it to be fine. Miss Jeannette (she had been christened plain Jane, but scorned to answer to anything so unromantic)—Miss Jeannette McGregor was at home to-night to all the élite of Speckport; and as a good many of the élite owned no other conveyance than that which Nature had given them, it was particularly desirable the weather should be fine. But it wasn't fine; it was nasty and drizzly, and sultry and foggy; and sky and sea were blotted out; and the gas-lamps sprinkled through the sloppy streets of Speckport blinked feebly through the gloom; and people buttoned up to the chin and wrapped in cloaks flitted by each other like phantoms, in the pale blank of wet and fog. And half the year round that is the sort of weather they enjoy in Speckport.

You don't know Speckport! There I have the advantage of you; for I know its whole history, past, present, and—future, I was going to say, though I don't set up for a prophet; but the future of Speckport does not seem hard to foretell. The Union-jack floats over it, the State of Maine is its next-door neighbor, and fish and fog are its principal productions. It also had the honor of producing Miss McGregor, who was born one other foggy night, just two-and-twenty years previous to this "At Home," to which you and I are going presently, in a dirty little black street, which she scorns to know even by name now. Two-and-twenty years ago, Sandy McGregor worked as a day-laborer in a shipyard, at three and six-pence per day. Now, Mr. Alexander McGregor is a ship-builder, and has an income of ten thousand gold dollars per year. Not a millionaire, you know; but very well off, and very comfortable, and very contented; living in a nice house, nicely furnished, keeping horses and carriage, and very much looked up to, and very much respected in Speckport.

Speckport has its Fifth Avenue as well as New York. Not that they call it Fifth Avenue, you understand; its name is Golden Row, and the abiders therein are made of the porcelain of human clay. Great people, magnates and aristocrats to their finger-tips, scorning the pigmies who move in second and third society and have only the happiness of walking through Golden Row, never of dwelling there. The houses were not brown-stone fronts. Oh, no! there were half-a-dozen brick buildings, some pretty, little Gothic cottages, with green vines, and bee-hives, and bird-houses, about them, and all the rest were great painted palaces of wood. Some had green shutters, and some had not; some were painted white, and some brown, and some stone-color and drab, and they all had a glittering air of spickspan-newness about them, as if their owners had them painted every other week. And in one of these palaces Mr. McGregor lived.

You drove down Golden Row through the fog and drizzle, between the blinking lamps, and you stop at a stone-colored house with a brown hall-door, and steps going up to it. The hall is brilliant with gas, so is the drawing-room, so are the two parlors, so is the dining-room, so are the dressing-rooms; and the élite of Speck-port are bustling and jostling one another about, and making considerable noise, and up in the gallery the band is in full blast at the "Lancers"—for they know how to dance the Lancers in Speckport—and the young ladies dipping and bowing through the intricacies of the dance, wear their dresses just as low in the neck and as short in the sleeves as any Fifth avenue belle dare to do.

Very pretty girls they are, floating about in all the colors of the rainbow. There are no diamonds, perhaps, except glass ones; but there are gold chains and crosses, and bracelets, and lockets and things; and some of the young ladies have rings right up to the middle joint of their fingers. The young gentlemen wear rings, too, and glittering shirt studs and bosom-pins, and are good looking and gentlemanly. While the young folks dance, the old folks play wallflower or cards, or take snuff or punch, or talk politics. All the juvenile rag-tag and bobtail of Speckport are out side, gaping up with open-mouthed admiration at the blazing front of the McGregor mansion, and swallowing the music that floats through the open windows.

Sailing along Golden Row, with an umbrella up to protect her bonnet from the fog, comes a tall lady, unprotected and alone, and "There's Miss Jo, hurrah!" yells a shrill voice; and the tall lady receives her ovation with a gratified face, and bows as she steps over the McGregor threshold. Ten minutes later, she enters the drawing-room, divested of her wrappings; and you see she is elderly and angular, and prim and precise, and withal good-natured. She is sharp at the joints and shoulder-blades, and her black silk dress is hooked up behind in the fashion of twenty years ago. She wears no crinoline, and looks about as graceful as a lamp-post; but she is fearfully and wonderfully fine, with a massive gold chain about her neck that would have made a ship's cable easily, and a cross and a locket clattering from it, and beating time to her movements on a cameo brooch the size of a dinner-plate. Eardrops, a finger-length long, dangle from her ears; cameo bracelets adorn her skinny wrists; and her hair, of which she has nothing to speak of, is worn in little corkscrew curls about her sallow face.

Miss Johanna Blake is an old maid, and looks like it; she is also an exile of Erin, and the most inveterate gossip in Speckport.

1*

A tremendous uproar greets her as she enters the drawing-room, and she stops in considerable consternation.

In a recess near the door was a card-table, round which four elderly ladies and four elderly gentlemen sat, with a laughing crowd looking on from behind. The card-party were in a violently agitated and excited state, all screaming out together at the top of the gamut.

Miss Jo swept on in majestic silence, nodding right and left as she streamed down the apartment to where Mrs. McGregor stood, with a little knot of matrons around her—a lady as tall as Miss Jo herself, and ever so much stouter, her fat face hot and flushed, and wielding a fan ponderously, as if it were a ton weight. Mrs. McGregor, during forty years of her life, had been a good deal more familiar with scrubbing-brushes than fans; but you would not think so now, maybe, if you saw her in that purple-satin dress and gold watch, her fat hands flashing with rings, and that bewildering combination of white lace and ribbons on her head. Her voice was as loud as her style of dress, and she shook Miss Jo's hand as if it had been a pump-handle.

"And how do you do, Miss Blake, and whatever on earth kept you till this hour? I was just saying to Jeannette, a while ago, I didn't believe you were going to come at all."

·"I could not help it," said Miss Jo. "Val didn't come home till late, and then I had to stop and find him his things. You know, my dear, what a trouble men are, and that Val beats them all. Has everybody come?"

"I think so; everybody but your Val and the Marshes. Maybe my lady is in one of her tantrums, and won't let Natty come at all. Jeannette is all but distracted. Natty's got lots of parts in them things they're having—tablets—no; tableaux, that's the name, and they never can get on without her. Jeannette's gone to look for Sandy to send him up to Redmon to see."

"I say, Miss Jo, how do you find yourself this evening?" exclaimed a spirited voice behind her; and Mrs. McGregor gave a little yelp of delight as she saw who it was—a young man, not more than twenty, perhaps, very good-looking, with bright gray eyes, fair hair, and a sunny smile. He was holding out a hand, small and fair as a lady's, to Miss Blake, who took it and shook it heartily.

"Jo's very well, thank you, Mr. Charles. How is your mamma this evening?"

"She was all right when I left home. Is Val here?"

"Not yet. Have you just come?"

The young gentleman nodded, and was turning away, but Mrs. McGregor recalled him.

"Isn't your mother coming, Charley?"

"No, she can't," said Charley. "The new teacher's come, and she's got to stay with her. She told me to bring her apologies."

The ladies were all animation directly. The new teacher! What was she like? When did she come? Was she young? Was she pretty? Did she seem nice?

"I didn't see her," said Charley, lounging against a sofa and flapping his gloves about.

"Didn't see her! I thought you said she was in your house?" cried Mrs. McGregor.

"So she is. I mean I didn't see her face. She had a thick vail on, and kept it down, and I left two or three minutes after she came."

"She came to Speckport in this evening's boat, then?" said Miss Jo. "What did she wear?"

Charley was bowing and smiling to a pretty girl passing on her partner's arm.

Mrs. McGregor nodded, and Charley sauntered off. The two ladies looked after him.

"What a nice young man that Charley Marsh is!" exclaimed Miss Jo, admiringly, "and so good-looking, and so steady, and so good to his mamma. You won't find many like him nowadays."

Mrs. McGregor lowered her voice to a mysterious whisper.

"Do you know, Miss Jo, they say he goes after that Cherrie Nettleby. Did you hear it?"

"Fiddlestick!" said Miss Jo, politely. "Speckport's got that story out, has it? I don't believe a word of it!"

"Here's Val!" cried Mrs. McGregor, off on a new tack; "and, my patience! what a swell he's got with him!"

Miss Jo looked round. Coming down the long room together were two young men, whose appearance created a visible sensation—one of them, preposterously tall and thin, with uncommonly long legs and arms—a veritable Shanghai—was Mr. Valentine Blake, Miss Jo's brother and sole earthly relative. He looked seven-and-twenty, was carelessly dressed, his clothes hanging about him any way—not handsome, but with a droll look of good humor about his face, and a roguish twinkle in his eyes that would have redeemed a plainer countenance.

His companion was a stranger, and it was he who created the sensation, not easy Val. Mrs. McGregor had called him a "swell," but Mrs. McGregor was not a very refined judge. He was dressed well, but not overdressed, as the slang term would imply, and he looked a thorough gentleman. A very handsome one, too, with dark curling hair, dark, bright, handsome eyes, a jetty mustache on his lip, and a flashing diamond ring on his finger. There was a certain air militaire about him that bespoke his profession, though he wore civilian's clothes, and he and Val looked about the same age. No wonder the apparition of so distinguished-looking a stranger in Mrs. McGregor's drawing-room should create a buzzing among the Speckport bon ton.

"My goodness!" cried Mrs. McGregor, all in a flutter. "Whoever can he be? He looks like a soldier, don't he?"

"There came a regiment from Halifax this morning," said Miss Jo. "Here's Val bringing him up."

Mr. Val was presenting him even while she spoke. "Captain Cavendish, Mrs. McGregor, of the —th," and then the captain was bowing profoundly; and the lady of the mansion was returning it, in a violent trepidation and tremor, not knowing in the least what she was expected to say to so distinguished a visitor. But relief was at hand. Charley Marsh was beside them with a young lady on his arm—a young lady best described by that odious word "genteel." She was not pretty; she was sandy-haired and freckled, but she was the daughter of the house, and, as such, demanding attention. Val introduced the captain directly, and Mrs. McGregor breathed freely again.

"Look here, Val!" she whispered, catching him by the button, "who is he, anyway?"

Val lowered his voice and looked round him cautiously.

"Did you ever hear of the Marquis of Carrabas, Mrs. McGregor?"

"No—yes—I don't remember. Is he an English nobleman?"

"A very great nobleman, Ma'am; famous in history as connected with the cat-trade, and Captain Cavendish is next heir to the title. Mrs. Marsh can tell you all about the Marquis; can't she, Charley?"

Charley, who was ready to burst into a fit of laughter at Mrs. McGregor's open-mouthed awe, took hold of the arm of a feeble-minded-looking young gentleman, whose freckled features, sandy hair, and general resemblance to the family, proclaimed him to be Mr. Alexander McGregor, Junior, and walked him off.

"And he came from Halifax this evening, Val?" Mrs. McGregor asked, gazing at the young Englishman in the same state of awe and delight.

"Yes," said Val, "it was there I got acquainted with him first. I met him on my way here, and thought you would not be offended at the liberty I took in fetching him along."

"Offended! My dear Val, you couldn't have pleased me better if you had been trying for a week. A Markis and a Captain in the Army! Why, it's the greatest honor, and I'm ever so much obliged to you. I am, indeed!"

"All right," said Val. "Speckport will be envious enough, I dare say, for it's not every place he'll go to, and all will want him. You'll lose Jane if you're not careful, though—see how he's talking to her."

Mrs. McGregor's eyes were dancing in her head. A

dazzling vision rose before her—her daughter a Marchioness, living in a castle, dressed in satin and diamonds the year round! She could have hugged Val in her rapture; and Val reading some such idea in her beaming face, backed a little, in some alarm.

"I say, though, wasn't there to be tableaux or something?" he inquired. "When are they coming off?"

"As soon as Natty Marsh gets here; they can't get on without her."

"What keeps her?" asked Val.

"The new teacher's come to Mrs. Marsh's, Charley says, and Natty is stopping in to see her. There's the captain asking Jeannette to dance."

So he was; and Miss Jeannette, with a gratified simper, was just laying her kidded fingers inside his coat-sleeve, when her brother came breathlessly up.

"Look here, Janie! you'd better not go off dancing," was his cry, "if you mean to have those tableaux to-night. Natty's come!"

CHAPTER II.

NATHALIE.

RS. McGREGOR'S drawing-room was empty. Everybody had flocked into the front parlor and arranged themselves on seats there to witness the performance; that is to say, everybody who had no part in the proceedings. Most of the young people of both sexes were behind the solemn green curtain, with its row of footlights, that separated the two rooms, dressing for their parts. The old people were as much interested in the proceedings as the young people, for their sons and daughters were the actors and actresses.

Captain Cavendish and Mr. Val Blake occupied a front

seat. Val had a part assigned him; but it did not come on for some time, so he was playing spectator now.

"I saw you making up to little Jane, Cavendish," Val was saying, sotto voce, for Miss Janie's mamma sat near. "Was it a case of love at first sight?"

"Miss McGregor is not very pretty," said Captain Cavendish, moderately. "Who was that young lady with the red cheeks and bright eyes I saw you speaking to, just before we came here?"

"Red cheeks and bright eyes!" repeated Val, putting on his considering-cap, "that description applies to half the girls in Speckport. What had she on?"

Captain Cavendish laughed.

"Would any one in the world but Val Blake ask such a question? She had on a pink dress, and had pink and white flowers in her hair, and looked saucy."

"Oh, I know now!" Val cried, with a flash of recollection; "that was Laura Blair, one of the nicest little girls that ever sported crinoline! Such a girl to laugh, you know!"

"She looks it! Ah! up you go!"

This apostrophe was addressed to the curtain, which was rising as he spoke. There was a general flutter, and settling in seats to look; the orchestra pealed forth and the first tableau was revealed.

It was very pretty, but very common—"Rebecca and Rowena." Miss Laura Blair was Rowena, and a tall brunette, Rebecca. The audience applauded, as in duty bound, and the curtain fell. The second was "Patience" —"Patience on a monument smiling at Grief." On a high pedestal stood Miss Laura Blair, again, draped in a white sheet, like a ghost, her hair all loose about her, and an azure girdle all over spangles clasping her waist.

At the foot of the pedestal crouched Grief, in a strange, distorted attitude of pain. The face of the performer was hidden in her hands; her black garments falling heavily around her, her hair unbound, too, her whole manner expressing despair, as fully as attitude could express it. The music seemed changing to a wail; the effect of the whole was perfect.

"What do you think of that?" said Val.

"Very good," said Captain Cavendish. "It goes considerably ahead of anything I had expected. Patience is very nice-looking girl."

"And isn't she jolly? She's dying to shout out this minute! I should think 'the glare of these footlights would force her eyelids open."

"Who is Grief?"

"Miss Catty Clowrie—isn't there music in that name? She makes a very good Grief—looks as if she had supped sorrow in spoonfuls."

"Is she pretty? She won't let us see her face."

"Beauty's a matter of taste," said Val, "perhaps you'll think her pretty. If you do, you will be the only one who ever thought the like. She is a nice little girl though, is Catty — the double-distilled essence of good-nature. Down goes the curtain!"

It rose next on a totally different scene, and to music solemn and sad. The stage was darkened, and made as much as possible to resemble a convent-cell. The walls were hung with religious pictures and statues, a coverless deal table held a crucifix, an open missal, and a candle which flared and guttered in the draft. On a prie-dieu before the table a figure knelt—a nun, eyes uplifted, the young face, quite colorless, raised, the hands holding her rosary, clasped in prayer. It was Evangeline—beautiful, broken-hearted Evangeline—the white face, the great dark lustrous eyes full of unspeakable woe. Fainter, sweeter and sadder the music wailed out; dimmer and dimmer paled the lights; all hushed their breathing to watch. The kneeling figure never moved, the face looked deadly pale by the flickering candle-gleam, and slowly the curtain began to descend. It was down; the tableau was over; the music closed, but for a second or two not a sound was to be heard. Then a tumult of applause broke out rapturously, and "Encore, encore!" twenty voices cried, in an ecstasy.

Captain Cavendish turned to Val with an enthusiastic face.

"By George, Blake! what a beautiful girl! Evangeline herself never was half so lovely. Who is she?"

"That's Natty," said Val, with composure. "Charley Marsh's sister."

"I never saw a lovelier face in all my life! Blake, you must give me an introduction as soon as these tableaux are over."

"All right! But you needn't fall in love with her—it's of no use."

"Why isn't it?"

"Because the cantankerous old toad who owns her will never let her get married."

"Do you mean her mother?"

"No, I don't, she doesn't live with her mother. And, besides, she has no room in her heart for any one but Charley. She idolizes him!"

"Happy fellow! That Evangeline was perfect. I never saw anything more exquisite."

"I don't believe Longfellow's Evangeline was half as good-looking as Natty," said Val. "Oh! there she is again!"

Val stopped talking. The curtain had arisen on an old scene—"Rebecca at the well." Evangeline had transformed herself into a Jewish maiden in an incredibly short space of time, and stood with her pitcher on her shoulder, looking down on Eleazer at her feet. Sandy McGregor was Eleazer, and a sorry Jew he made, but nobody except his mother looked at him. Like a young queen Rebecca stood, her eyes fixed on the bracelets and rings, her hair falling in a shower of golden bronze ripples over her bare white shoulders. One would have expected black hair with those luminous dark eyes, but no ebon tresses could have been half so magnificent as that waving mass of darkened gold.

"Nice hair, isn't it?" whispered Val. "Natty's proud of her hair and her voice beyond anything. You ought to hear her sing!"

"She sings well?" Captain Cavendish asked, his eyes fixed as if fascinated on the beautiful face.

"Like another Jenny Lind! She leads the choir up there in the cathedral, and plays the organ besides."

Captain Cavendish had a pretty pink half-blown rose in his button-hole. He took it out and flung it at her feet as the curtain was going down. He had time to see her bright dark eye turn upon it, then with a little pleased smile over the spectators in quest of the donor, and then that envious green curtain hid all again.

"Very neat and appropriate," criticised Val. "You're not going to wait for the introduction to begin your love-passage, I see, Captain Cavendish."

The captain laughed.

"Nothing like taking time by the forelock, my dear fellow. I will never be able to thank you sufficiently for bringing me here to-night!"

"You don't say so!" exclaimed Val, opening his eyes, "you never mean to say you're in love already, do you?"

"It's something very like it, then. Where are you going?"

"Behind the scenes. The next is 'Jack and the Beanstalk,' and they want me for the beanstalk," said Val, complacently, as his long legs strode over the carpet on his way to the back parlor.

There were ever so many tableaux after that—Captain Cavendish, impatient and fidgety, wondered if they would ever end. Perhaps you don't believe in love at first sight, dear reader mine; perhaps I don't myself; but Captain Cavendish, of Her Most Gracious Majesty's —th Regiment of Artillery did, and had fallen in love at first sight at least a dozen times within quarter that number of years.

Captain Cavendish had to exercise the virtue of patience for another half-hour, and then the end came.

In flocked the performers, in laughing commotion, to find themselves surrounded by the rest, and showered with congratulations. Captain Cavendish stood apart, leaning against a fauteuil, stroking his mustache thoughtfully, and looking on. Looking on one face and form only of all the dozens before him; a form tall, taller than the average height, slender, graceful, and girlish as became its owner's eighteen years; and a face inexpressibly lovely in the garish gaslight. There was nobility as well as beauty in that classic profile, that broad brow; fire in those laughing blue eyes, so dark that you nearly mistook them for black; resolution in those molded lips, the sweetest that ever were kissed. The hair alone of Nathalie Marsh would have made a plain face pretty; it hung loose over her shoulders as it had done on the stage, reaching to her waist, a cloud of spun gold, half waves, half curls, half yellow ripples.

Few could have worn this hair like that, but it was eminently becoming to Nathalie, whom everything became. Her dress was of rose color, of a tint just deeper than the rose color in her cheeks, thin and flouting, and she was entirely without ornament. A half-blown rose was fastened in the snowy lace of her corsage, a rose that had decked the buttonhole of Captain Cavendish half an hour before.

Val espied him at last and came over. "Are you making a tableau of yourself," he asked, "for a certain pair of bright eyes to admire? I saw them wandering curiously this way two or three times since we came in."

"Whose were they?"

"Miss Nathalie Marsh's. Come and be introduced."

"But she is surrounded."

"Never mind, they'll make way for you. Stand out of the way, Sandy. Lo! the conquering hero comes! Miss Marsh, let me present Captain Cavendish, of the —th; Miss Marsh, Captain Cavendish."

The music at that instant struck up a delicious waltz. Mr. Val Blake, without ceremony, laid hold of the nearest young lady he could grab.

"Come, Catty! let's take a twist or two. That's it, Cavendish! follow in our wake!"

For Captain Cavendish, having asked Miss Marsh to waltz, was leading her off, and received the encouraging nod of Val with an amused smile.

"What a character he is!" he said, looking after Val, spinning around with considerable more energy than grace; "the most unceremonious and best-natured fellow in existence."

The young lady laughed.

"Oh, everybody likes Val! Have you known him long?"

"About a year. I have seen him in Halifax frequently, and we are the greatest friends, I assure you. Damon and Pythias were nothing to us!"

"It is something new for Mr. Blake to be so enthusiastic, then. Pythias is a new rôle for him. I hope he played it better than he did Robert Bruce in that horrid tableau awhile ago."

They both laughed at the recollection. Natty scented her rose.

"Some one threw me this. Gallant, wasn't it? I love roses."

"Sweets to the sweet! I am only sorry I had not something more worthy 'Evangeline,' than that poor little flower."

"Then it it was you. I thought so! Thank you for the rose and the compliment. One is as pretty as the other."

She laughed saucily, her bright eyes flashing a dangerous glance at him. Next instant they were floating round, and round, and round; and Captain Cavendish began to think the world must be a great rose garden, and Speckport Eden, since in it he had found his Eve. Not quite his yet, though, for the moment the waltz concluded, a dashing and dangerously good-looking young fellow stepped coolly up and bore her off.

Val having given his partner a finishing whirl into a seat, left her there, and came up, wiping his face.

"By jingo, 'tis hard work, and Catty Clowrie goes the pace with a vengeance. How do you like Natty?"

"'Like' is not the word. Who is that gentleman she is walking with?"

"That—where are they? Oh, I see—that is Captain Locksley, of the merchant-service. The army and navy forever, eh! Where are you going?"

"Out of this hot room a moment. I'll be back directly."

Mrs. McGregor came up and asked Val to join a whist-party she was getting up. "And be my partner, Val," she enjoined, as she led him off, "because you're the best cheat I know of."

Val was soon completely absorbed in the fascinations of whist, at a penny a game, but the announcement of supper soon broke up both card-playing and dancing; and as he rose from the table he caught sight of Captain Cavendish just entering. His long legs crossed the room in three strides.

"You've got back, have you? What have you been about all this time?"

"I was smoking a cigar out there on the steps, and getting a little fresh air—no, fog, for I'll take my oath its thick enough to be cut with a knife. When I was in London, I thought I knew something of fog, but Speckport beats it all to nothing."

"Yes," said Val, gravely, "it's one of the institutions of the country, and we're proud of it. Did you see Charley Marsh anywhere in your travels. I heard Natty just now asking for him."

"Oh, yes, I've seen him," said Captain Cavendish, significantly.

There was that in his tone which made Val look at him. "Where was he and what was he doing?" he inquired.

"Making love, to your first question; sitting in a recess of the tall window, to your second. He did not see me, but I saw him."

"Who was he with?"

"Something very pretty—prettier than anything in this room, excepting Miss Natty. Black eyes, black curls, rosy cheeks, and the dearest little waist! Who is she?"

Val gave a long, low whistle.

"Do you know her?" persisted Captain Cavendish.

"Oh, don't I though? Was she little, and was she laughing?"

"Yes, to both questions. Now, who is she?"

Val's answer was a shower of mysterious nods.

"I heard the story before, but I didn't think the boy was such a fool. Speckport is such a place for gossip, you know; but it seems the gossips were right for once. What will Natty say, I wonder?"

"Will you tell me who she is?" cried Captain Cavendish, impatiently.

"Come to supper," was Val's answer; "I'm too hungry to talk now. I'll tell you about it by-and-by."

Charley was before them at the table, helping all the young ladies right and left, and keeping up a running fire of jokes, old and new, stale and original, and setting the table in a roar. Everybody was talking and laughing at the top of their lungs; glass and china, and knives and forks, rattled and jingled until the uproar became deafening, and people shouted with laughter, without in the least knowing what they were laughing at. The mustached lip of Captain Cavendish curled with a little contemptuous smile at the whole thing, and Miss Jeannette McGregor, who had managed to get him beside her, saw it, and felt fit to die with mortification.

"What a dreadful noise they do keep up. It makes my head ache to listen to them!" she said, resentfully.

Captain Cavendish, who had been listening to her tattle-tittle for the last half-hour, answering yes and no at random, started into consciousness that she was talking again.

"I beg your pardon, Miss McGregor. What was it you said? I am afraid I was not attending."

"I am afraid you were not," said Miss McGregor, forcing a laugh, while biting her lips. "They are going back to the drawing-room—*Dieu merci!* It is like Babel being here."

"Let us wait," said Captain Cavendish, eying the crowd, and beginning to be gallant. "I am not going to have you jostled to death. One would think it was for life or death they were pushing."

It was fully ten minutes before the coast was clear, and then the captain drew Miss Jeannette's arm within his, and led her to the drawing-room. Mrs. McGregor, sitting there among her satellites, saw them, and the maternal bosom glowed with pride. It was the future Marquis and Marchioness of Carrabas!

Some one was singing. A splendid soprano voice was ringing through the room, singing, "Hear me, Norma." It finished as they drew near, and the singer, Miss Natty Marsh, glancing over her shoulder, flashed one of her bright bewitching glances at them.

She rose up from the piano, flirting out her gauze skirts, and laughing at the shower of entreaties to sing again.

"I am going to see some engravings Alick has promised to show me," she said; "so spare your eloquence, Mesdames et Messieurs. I am inexorable."

"I think I will go over and have a look at the engravings, too," said Captain Cavendish.

She was sitting at a little stand, all her bright hair loose around her, and shading the pictures. Young McGregor was bending devoutly near her, but not talking, only too happy to be just there, and talking was not the young gentleman's forte.

"Captain Cavendish," said the clear voice, as, without turning round, she held the engraving over her shoulder, "look at this—is it not pretty?"

How had she seen him? Had she eyes in the back of her head? He took the engraving, wondering inwardly, and sat down beside her.

It was a strange picture she had given him. A black and wrathful sky, a black and heaving sea, and a long strip of black and desolate coast. A full moon flickered ghastly through the scudding clouds, and wan in its light you saw a girl standing on a high rock, straining her eyes out to sea. Her hair and dress fluttered in the wind; her face was wild, spectral, and agonized. Captain Cavendish gazed on it as if fascinated.

"What a story it tells!" Nathalie cried. "It makes one think of Charles Kingsley's weird song of the 'Three Fishers.' Well, Charley, what is it?"

"It is the carryall from Redmon come for you," said

Charley, who had sauntered up. " If you are done looking at the pictures you had better go home."

Natty pushed the portfolio away pettishly, and rose,
half-poutingly.

"What a nuisance, to go so soon !"

Then, catching Captain Cavendish's eye, she laughed
good-naturedly.

"What can't be cured—you know the proverb, Captain Cavendish. Charley, wait for me in the hall, I will
be there directly."

She crossed the room with the airy elegance peculiar
to her light swinging tread, made her adieux quietly to
the hostess, and sought her wrappings and the dressing-
room.

As she ran down into the hall in a large shawl, gracefully worn, and a white cloud round her pretty face, she
found Captain Cavendish waiting with Charley. It was
he who offered her his arm, and Charley ran down the
steps before them. Through the wet fog they saw an
old-fashioned two-seated buggy waiting, and the driver
looking impatiently down.

"I wish you would drive up with me, Charley," said
Natty, settling herself in her seat.

"Can't," said Charley. "I am going to see somebody else's sister home. I'll take a run up to-morrow
evening."

"Miss Marsh," Captain Cavendish lazily began, "if
you will permit me to——" but Natty cut him short with
a gay laugh.

"And make all the young ladies in there miserable
for the rest of the evening ! No, thank you ! I am not
quite so heartless. Good night !"

She leaned forward to say it, the next moment she
was lost in the fog. He caught one glimpse of a white
hand waved, of the half-saucy, half-wicked, wholly-be-
witching smile, of the dancing blue eyes and golden hair,
and then there was nothing but a pale blank of mist and
wet, and Charley was speaking :

"Hang the fog! it goes through one like a knife!
Come along in, captain, they are going to dance."

Captain Cavendish went in, but not to dance. He had come from curiosity to see what the Speckportonians were like, not intending to remain over an hour or so. Now that Natty was gone, there was no inducement to stay. He sought out Mrs. McGregor, to say good-night. ·

"What's your hurry?" said Val, following him out.

"It is growing late, and I am ashamed to say I am sleepy. Will you be in the office to-morrow morning?"

"From eight till two," said Val.

"Then I'll drop in. Good night!"

The cathedral clock struck three as he came out into the drizzly morning, and all the other clocks in the town took it up. The streets were empty, as he walked rapidly to his lodgings, with buttoned-up overcoat, and hat drawn over his eyes. But a "dancing shape, an image gay" were with him, flashing on him through the fog; hunting him all the way home, through the smur and mist of the dismal day-dawn.

CHAPTER III.

MISS ROSE.

IGHT was striking by every clock in the town, as down Queen Street—the Broadway of Speck-port—a tall female streamed, with a step that rang and resounded on the wooden pavement. The tall female, nodding to her acquaintances right and left, and holding up her bombazine skirts out of the slop, was Miss Jo Blake, as bright as a new penny, though she had not had a wink of sleep the night before. Early as the hour was, Miss Jo was going to make a morning call, and strode on through the fog with her head up, and a nod for nearly every one she passed.

Down Queen Street Miss Jo turned to the left, and kept straight on, facing the bay, all blurred and misty, so

that you could hardly tell where the fog ended and the
sun began. The business part of the town, with its noise
and rattle and bustle, was left half a mile behind, and
Miss Jo turned into a pretty and quiet street, right down
on the sea-shore. It was called Cottage Street, very ap-
propriately, too; for all the houses in it were cozy little
cottages, a story and a half high, all as much alike as 'f
turned out of a mold. They were all painted white, had
a red door in the center, and two windows on either side
of the door, decorated with green shutters. They had
little grass-plots and flower-beds in front, with white pal-
ings, and white gate, and a little graveled path, and behind they had vegetable-yards sloping right down to the
very water. If you leaned over the fences at the lower
end of these gardens, on a stormy day, and at high tide,
you could feel the salt spray dashing up in your face,
from the waves below. At low water, there was a long,
smooth, sandy beach, delightful to walk over on hot summer days.

Before one of the cottages Miss Jo drew rein, and
rapped.' While waiting for the door to open, the flutter
of a skirt in the back garden caught her eye; and, peering
round the corner of the house, she had a full view of it
and its wearer.

And Miss Jo set herself to contemplate the view with
keenest interest. To see the wearer of that fluttering
skirt it was that had brought Miss Jo all the way from
her own home so early in the morning, though she had
never set eyes on her before.

Uncommonly friendly, perhaps you are thinking. Not
at all: Miss Jo was a woman, consequently curious; and
curiosity, not kindness, had brought her out.

The sight was very well worth looking at. You might
have gazed for a week, steadily, and not grown tired of
the prospect. A figure, slender and small, wearing a
black dress, white linen cuffs at the wrists, a white linen
collar, fastened with a knot of crape, a profusion of pretty
brown hair, worn in braids, and low in the neck, hands
like a child's, small and white. She was leaning against
a tree, a gnarled old rowan tree, with her face turned sea-

ward, watching the fishing-boats gliding in and out
through the fog; but presently, at some noise in the
street, she glanced around, and Miss Jo saw her face. A
small, pale face, very pale, with pretty features, and lit
with large, soft eyes. A face that was a history, could
Miss Jo have read it; pale and patient, gentle and sweet,
and in the brown eye a look of settled melancholy.
This young lady in black had been learning the great lesson of life, that most of us poor mortals must learn,
sooner or later, endurance —the lesson One too sublime
to name came on earth to teach.

Miss Jo dodged back, the door swung open, and a fat
girl, bursting out of her hooks and eyes, and with a head
like a tow mop, opened the door. Miss Jo strode in without ceremony.

"Good morning, Betsy Ann! Is Mrs. Marsh at home
this morning?"

"Yes, Miss Jo," said Betsy Ann, opening a door to
the left, for there was a door on either hand; that to the
right, leading to the drawing-room of the cottage, and a
staircase at the end leading to the sleeping-room above;
the door to the left admitted you to the sitting-room and
dining-room, for it was both in one—a pleasant little room
enough, with a red and green ingrain carpet, cane-seated
chairs, red moreen window-curtains on the two windows,
one looking on the bay, the other on the street. There
was a little upright piano in one corner, a lounge in another; pictures on the papered walls; a Dutch clock and
some china cats and dogs and shepherdesses on the man-
telpiece; a coal-fire in the Franklin, and a table laid for
breakfast.

The room had but one occupant, a faded and feeble-
looking woman, who sat in a low rocking-chair, her feet
crossed on the fender, a shawl around her, and a book in
her hand. She looked up in her surprise at her early
visitor.

"Law! Miss Blake, is it you? Who'd have thought
it? Betsy Ann, give Miss Blake a chair."

"It's quite a piece from our house here, and I feel
kind of tired," said Miss Jo, seating herself. "Your fire

feels comfortable, Mrs. Marsh; these foggy days are chilly. Ain't you had breakfast yet?"

"It's all Charley's fault; he hasn't come down stairs yet. How did you enjoy yourself at the party last night?"

"First-rate. Never went home till six this morning, and then I had to turn to and make Val his breakfast. Charley left early."

"Early!" retorted Mrs. Marsh; "I don't know what you call early. It was after six when he came here, Betsy Ann says."

"Well, that's odd," said Miss Jo. "He left McGregor's about half past three, anyway. Did you hear they had an officer there last night?"

"An officer! No. Who is it?"

"His name is Captain Cavendish, and a beautiful man he is, with a diamond ring on his finger, my dear, and the look of a real gentleman. His folks are very great in England. His brother's the Marquis of Cabbage—Carraways—no, I forget it; but Val knows all about him."

"Law!" exclaimed Mrs. Marsh, opening her light-blue eyes, "a Marquis! Who brought him?"

"Val did. Val knows every one, I believe, and got acquainted with him in Halifax. You never saw any one so proud as Mr. McGregor. I didn't say anything, my dear; but I thought of the time when lords and marquises, and dukes and captains without end, used to be entertained at Castle Blake," said Miss Jo, sighing.

"And what does he look like? Is he handsome?" asked Mrs. Marsh, with interest; for Castle Blake and its melancholy reminiscences were an old story to her.

"Uncommon," said Miss Jo; "and I believe Mrs. McGregor thinks her Jane will get him. You never saw any one so tickled in your life. Why weren't you up?—I expected you."

"I couldn't go. Miss Rose came just as I was getting ready, and of course I had to stay with her."

"Oh, the new teacher! I saw a young woman in black standing in the background as I came in; was that her?" said Miss Jo, who did not always choose to be confined to the rules of severe grammar.

"Yes," said Mrs. Marsh; "and what do you think, Miss Blake, if she wasn't up this morning before six o'clock? Betsy Ann always rises at six, and when she was rolling up the blind Miss Rose came down-stairs already dressed, and has been out in the garden ever since. Betsy Ann says she was weeding the flowers most of the time."

"She's a little thing, isn't she?" said Miss Jo; "and so delicate-looking! I don't believe she'll ever be able to manage them big rough girls in the school. What's her other name besides Miss Rose?"

"I don't know. She looks as if she had seen trouble," said Mrs. Marsh, pensively.

"Who is she in mourning for?"

"I don't know. I didn't like to ask, and she doesn't talk much herself."

"Where did she come from? Montreal, wasn't it?"

"I forget. Natty knows. Natty was here last night before she went up to McGregor's. She said she would come back this morning, and go with Miss Rose to the school. Here's Charley at last." Miss Jo faced round, and confronted that young gentleman sauntering in.

"Well, Sleeping Beauty, you've got up now, have you?" was her salute. "How do you feel after all you danced last night?"

"Never better. You're out betimes this morning, Miss Jo."

"Yes," said Miss Jo; "the sun don't catch me simmering in bed like it does some folks. Did it take you from half-past three till six to get home this morning, Mr. Charles?"

"Who says it was six?" said Charley.

"Betsy Ann does," replied his mother. "Where were you all the time?"

"Betsy Ann's eyes were a couple of hours too fast. I say, mother, is the breakfast ready? It's nearly time I was off."

"It's been ready this half-hour. Betsy Ann!"

That maiden appeared.

"Go and ask Miss Rose to please come in to breakfast, and then fetch the coffee."

Betsy Ann fled off, and Charley glanced out of the window.

"Miss Rose is taking a constitutional, is she? What is she like, mother—pretty? I didn't see her last night, you know."

"What odds is it to you?" demanded Miss Jo; "she's not as pretty as Cherrie Nettleby, anyhow."

Charley turned scarlet, and Miss Jo's eyes twinkled at the success of her random shaft. The door opened at that instant, and the small, slender black figure glided in. Glided was the word for that swift, light motion, so noiseless and fleet.

"Good morning," said Mrs. Marsh, rising smiling to shake hands; "you are an early bird, I find. Miss Blake, Miss Rose—Miss Rose, my son Charles."

My son Charles and Miss Blake both shook hands with the new teacher, and welcomed her to Speckport. A faint smile, a shy fluttering color coming and going in her delicate cheeks, and a few low-murmured words, and then Miss Rose sat down on the chair Charley had placed for her, her pretty eyes fixed on the coals, her small childlike hands fluttering still one over the other. Betsy Ann came in with the coffee-pot and rolls and eggs, and Mrs. Marsh invited Miss Jo to sit over and have some breakfast.

"I don't care if I do," said Miss Jo, untying her bonnet promptly. "I didn't feel like taking anything when Val had his this morning, and your coffee smells good. Are you fond of coffee, Miss Rose?"

Miss Rose smiled a little as they all took their places.

"Yes, I like it very well."

"Some folks like tea best," said Miss Jo, pensively, stirring in a third teaspoonful of sugar in her cup, "but I don't. What sort of a journey had you, Miss Rose?"

"Very pleasant, indeed."

"You arrived yesterday?"

Miss Rose assented.

"Was it from Halifax you came?"

"No, ma'am; from Montreal."

"Oh, from Montreal! You were born in Montreal, I suppose?"

"No, I was born in New York."

"Law!" cried Mrs. Marsh, "then, you're a Yankee, Miss Rose?"

"Do your folks live in Montreal, Miss Rose?" recommenced the persevering Miss Jo.

The faint, rosy light flickered and faded again in the face of Miss Rose.

"I have no relatives," she said, without lifting her eyes.

"None at all! Father, nor mother, nor brothers, nor sisters, nor nothing."

"I have none at all."

"Dear me, that's a pity! Who are you in black for?"

There was a pause—then Miss Rose answered, still without looking up:

"For my father."

"Oh, for your father! Has he been long dead? Another cup, if you please. Betsy Ann knows how to make nice coffee."

"He has been dead ten months," said Miss Rose, a flush of intolerable pain dyeing her pale cheeks at this questioning.

"How do you think you'll like Speckport?" went on the dauntless Miss Jo. "It's not equal to Montreal or New York, they tell me, but the Bluenoses think there's no place like it. Poor things! if they once saw Dublin, it's little they'd think of such a place as this is."

"Halte là!" cried Charley; "please to remember, Miss Jo, I am a native, to the manner born, an out-and-out Bluenose, and will stand no nonsense about Speckport! There's no place like it. See Speckport and die! Mother, I'll trouble you for some of that toast."

"Won't you have some, Miss Rose?" said Mrs. Marsh. "You ain't eating anything."

"Not any more, thank you. I like Speckport very much, Miss Blake; all I have seen of it."

"That's right, Miss Rose!" exclaimed Charley; "say you like fog and all. Are you going to commence teaching to-day?"

"I should prefer commencing at once. Miss Marsh said she was coming this morning, did she not?" Miss Rose asked, lifting her shy brown eyes to Mrs. Marsh.

"Yes, dear. Charley, what time did Natty go home last night?"

"She didn't go home last night; it was half-past two this morning."

"Did she walk?"

"No; the old lady sent that wheelbarrow of hers after her."

"Wheelbarrow!" cried his mother, aghast. "Why, Charley, what do you mean?"

"It's the same thing," said Charley. "I'd as soon go in a wheelbarrow as that carryall. Such a shabby old rattle-trap! It's like nothing but the old dame herself."

"Charley, you ought to be ashamed of yourself. Did you go with her?"

"Not I! I was better engaged. Another gentleman offered his services, but she declined."

"Who was it? Captain Locksley?"

"No, another captain—Captain Cavendish."

"Did he want to go home with Natty?" asked Miss Jo, with interest. "I thought he was more attentive to her than to Jane McGregor! Why wouldn't she have him?"

"She would look fine having him—an utter stranger! If it had been Locksley, it would have been different. See here, Miss Rose," Charley cried, springing up in alarm, "what is the matter?"

"She is going to faint!" exclaimed Miss Jo, in consternation. "Charley, run for a glass of water."

Miss Rose had fallen suddenly back in her seat, her face growing so dreadfully white that they might well be startled. It was nothing for Miss Rose to look pale, only this was like the pallor of death. Charley made a rush for the water, and was back in a twinkling, holding it to her lips. She drank a portion, pushed it away, and sat up, trying to smile.

"I am afraid I have startled you," she said, as it necessary to apologize, "but I am not very strong, and——"

Her voice, faltering throughout, died entirely away; and, leaning her elbows on the table, she bowed her forehead on her hands. Miss Jo looked at her with compressed lips and prophetic eye.

"You'll never stand that school, Miss Rose, and I thought so from the first. Them girls would try a constitution of iron, let alone yours."

Miss Rose lifted her white face, and arose from the table.

"It is nothing," she said, faintly. "I do not often get weak, like this. Thank you!"

She had gone to the window, as if for air, and Charley had sprung forward and opened it.

"Does the air revive you, or shall I fetch you some more water?" inquired Charley, with a face full of concern.

"Oh, no! indeed, it is nothing. I am quite well now."

"You don't look like it," said Miss Jo; "you are as white as a sheet yet. Don't you go near that school to-day, mind."

Miss Rose essayed a smile.

"The school will do me no harm, Miss Blake—thank you for your kindness all the same."

Miss Jo shook her head.

"You ain't fit for it, and that you'll find. Are you off, Charley?"

"Very hard, isn't it, Miss Jo?" said Charley, drawing on his gloves. "But I must tear myself away. Old Pestle and Mortar will be fit to bastinado me for staying till this time of day."

"Look here, then," said Miss Jo, "have you any engagement particular for this evening?"

"Particular? no, not very. I promised Natty to spend the evening up at Redmon, that's all."

2*

"Oh, that's nothing, then. I want you and your mother, and Miss Rose, to come over to our house this evening, and take a cup of tea. I'll get Natty to come, too."

"All right," said Charley, boyishly, taking his wide-awake. "I'll take two or three cups if you like. Good morning, all. Miss Rose, don't you go and use yourself up in that hot school-room to-day."

Off went Charley, whistling "Cheer, boys, cheer!" and his hands rammed down in his coat-pockets; and Miss Jo got up and took her bonnet.

"You'll be sure to come, Mrs. Marsh, you and Miss Rose, and come nice and early, so as we can have a chat."

"Certainly," said Mrs. Marsh, "if Miss Rose has no objection."

Miss Rose hesitated a little, and glanced at her mourning dress, and from it to Miss Jo, with her soft, wistful eyes.

"I have not gone out at all since—since——"

"Yes, dear, I know," said Miss Jo, kindly, interrupting. "But it isn't a party or anything, only just two or three friends to spend a few hours. Now, don't make any objection. I shall expect you both, without fail, so good-bye."

With one of her familiar nods, Miss Jo strode out, and nearly ran against a young lady, who was opening the gate.

"Is it you, Miss Jo? You nearly knocked me down! You must have been up with the birds this morning, to get here so soon."

The speaker was a young lady who had been at Mrs. McGregor's the previous night; a small, wiry damsel, with sallow face, thin lips, dull, yellow, lusterless hair, and light, faded-looking eyes. She was not pretty, but she looked pleasant—that is, if incessant smiles can make a face pleasant—and she had the softest and sweetest of voices—you could liken it to nothing but the purring of a cat; and her hands were limp and velvety, and catlike too.

Miss Jo nodded her recognition.

"How d'ye do, Catty? How do you feel after last night?"

"Very well."

"Well enough to spend this evening with me?"

Miss Catty Clowrie laughed.

"I am always well enough for that, Miss Jo! Are you going to eclipse Mrs. McGregor?"

"Nonsense! Mrs. Marsh and Miss Rose are coming to take tea with me, that's all, and I want you to come up."

"I shall be very happy to. Are Natty and—Charley coming?"

Miss Jo nodded again, and without further parley walked away. As she turned the corner of Cottage Street into a more busy thoroughfare, known as Park Lane, she saw a lady and gentleman taking the sidewalk in dashing style. Everybody looked after them, and everybody might have gone a long way without finding anything better worth looking after. The young lady's tall, slight, willowy figure was set off by a close-fitting black cloth basque, and a little, coquettish, black velvet cap was placed above one of the most bewitching faces that ever turned a man's head. Rosette, smiling, sunshiny, the bright blue eyes flashing laughing light everywhere they fell. Her gloved hands daintily uplifting her skirts, and displaying the pretty high-heeled boots, as she sailed along with a very peculiar, jaunty, swinging gait.

And quite as well worth looking at, in his way, was her cavalier, gallant and handsome, with an unmistakable military stride, and an unmistakable military air generally, although dressed in civilian's clothes. As they swept past Miss Jo, the young lady made a dashing bow; and the young gentleman lifted his hat. Miss Jo stood, with her mouth open, gazing after them.

"A splendid couple, ain't they, Miss Blake?" said a man, passing. It was Mr. Clowrie, on his way to his office, and Miss Jo, just deigning to acknowledge him, walked on.

"My patience!" was her mental ejaculation, "what

a swell they cut! He's as handsome as a lord, that young man; and she's every bit as good-looking! I must go up to Redmon this afternoon, and ask her down. Wouldn't it be great now, if that should turn out to be a match!"

CHAPTER IV.

VAL'S OFFICE.

AMONG the many tall, dingy brick buildings, fronting on that busy thoroughfare of Speckport, Queen Street, there stood one to the right as you went up, taller and dingier, if possible, than its neighbors, and bearing this legend along its grimy front, "Office of Speckport Spouter." There were a dozen newspapers, more or less, published in Speckport, weekly, semi-weekly, and daily; but the Spouter went ahead of them all, and distanced all competitors.

At about half-past seven o'clock, this foggy spring morning, two individuals of the manly sex occupied the principal apartment of the printing establishment. A dirty, nasty, noisy place it generally was; and dirty and nasty, though not very noisy, it was this morning, for the only sound to be heard was the voice of one of its occupants, chattering incessantly, and the scratching of the other's pen, as he wrote, perched up on a high stool.

The writer was foreman in the office, a sober-looking, middle-aged man, who wore spectacles, and wrote away as mechanically as if he was doing it by steam. The speaker was a lively youth of twelve, office-boy, printer's devil, and errand-runner, and gossiper-in-chief to the place. His name was in the baptismal register of Speckport cathedral, William Blair; but in every-day life he was Bill Blair, brother to pretty Laura, whom Val Blake had eulogized as "such a girl to laugh."

Laughter seemed to be a weakness in the family, for Master Bill's mouth was generally stretched in a steady grin from one week's end to the other, and was, just at this present moment. He was perched up on another high stool, swinging his legs about, chewing gum, looking out of the window, and talking.

"And there goes Old Leach in his gig, tearing along as if Old Nick was after him," went on Master Bill, criticising the passers-by. "Somebody's kicking the bucket in Speckport! And there's Sim Tod hobbling along on his stick! Now, I should admire to know how long that old codger's going to live; he must be as old as Methuselah's cat by this time. And there, I vow, if there ain't Miss Jo, streaking along as tall as a grenadier, and as spry as if she hadn't been up all night at that rout in Golden Row. What a frisky old girl it is!"

"I tell you what, Bill Blair," said the foreman, Mr. Gilcase, "if you don't take yourself down out of that, and get to work, I'll report you to Mr. Blake as soon as he comes in!"

"No, you won't!" said Bill, snapping his gum between his teeth like a pistol-shot. "There ain't nothing to do. I swept the office, and sprinkled this floor, and I want a rest now, I should think. I feel as if I should drop!"

"The office looks as if it had been swept," said Mr. Gilcase, contemptuously; "there's the addresses to write on those wrappers; go and do that!"

"That's time enough," said Bill; "Blake won't be here for an hour or two yet; he's snoozing, I'll bet you, after being up all night. Look here, Mr. Gilcase, did you know the new teacher was come?"

"No," said the foreman, looking somewhat interested; "has she?"

"Came last night," nodded Bill; "our Laury heard so last night at the party. Her name's Miss Rose. Did you know they had an officer last night at McGregor's?"

"I didn't think the officers visited McGregor's?"

"None of 'em ever did before; but one of them was there last night, a captain, by the same token; and, I ex pect, old McGregor's as proud as a pig with two tails. As for Jane, there'll be no standing her now, and she was stuck-up enough before. Oh, here's Clowrie, and about as pleasant-looking as a wild cat with the whooping-cough!"

A heavy, lumbering foot was ascending the steep dark stairs, and the door opened presently to admit a young gentleman in a pea-jacket and glazed cap. A short and thick-set young gentleman, with a sulky face, who was never known to laugh, and whose life it was the delight of Master Bill Blair to torment and make a misery of. The young gentleman was Mr. Jacob Clowrie, eldest son and hope of Peter Clowrie, Esq., attorney-at-law.

"How are you, Jake?" began Mr. Blair, in a friendly tone, knocking his heels about on the stool. "You look kind of sour this morning. Was the milk at breakfast curdled, or didn't Catty get up to make you any breakfast at all?"

Mr. Clowrie's reply to this was a growl, as he hung up his cap.

"I say, Jake, you weren't at McGregor's tea-splash last night, were you? I know the old man and Catty were there. Scaly lot not to ask you and me!"

Mr. Clowrie growled again, and sat down at a desk.

"I say, Jake," resumed that young demon, Bill, grinning from ear to ear, "how's our Cherrie, eh?—seen her lately?"

"What would you give to know?" snapped Mr. Clowrie, condescending to retort.

"But I do know, though, without giving nothing! and I know your cake's dough, my boy! Lor, I think I see 'em now!" cried Bill, going off in a shout of laughter at some lively recollection.

Mr. Clowrie glared at him over the top of his desk, with savage inquiry.

"Oh, you're cut out, old fellow! you're dished, you are! Cherrie's got a new beau, and you're left in the lurch!"

"What do you mean, you young imp?" inquired Mr.

Clowrie, growing very red in the face. "I'll go over and twist your neck for you, if you don't look sharp!"

Mr. Blair winked.

"Don't you think you see yourself doing it, Jakey? I tell you it's as true as preaching! Cherrie's got a new fellow, and the chap's name is Charley Marsh."

There was a pause. Bill looked triumphant, Mr. Clowrie black as a thunderbolt, and the foreman amused in spite of himself. Bill crunched his gum and waited for his announcement to have proper effect, and then resumed, in an explanatory tone:

"You see, Jake, I had heard Charley was after her, but I didn't believe it till last night, when I see them with my own two blessed eyes. My governor and Laury were off to McGregor's, so I cut over to Jim Tod's, to see a lot of terrier-pups he's got—me and Tom Smith—and he promised us a pup apiece. Jim's folks were at the junketing, too; so we had the house to ourselves. And Jim, he stole in the pantry through the window and hooked a lot of pies and cakes, and raspberry wine, and Tom had a pack of cards in his trowsers pocket. And we went up to Jim's room, and, crackey! hadn't we a time! There was no hurry neither; for we knew the old folks wouldn't be home till all hours, so we staid till after three in the morning, and by this time Jim and me had lost three shillings in pennies each, and the three of us were about ready to burst with all we had eat and drank! It was foggy and misty coming home, and me and Tom cut across them fields and waste lots between Tod's and Park Lane, when just as we turned into Golden Row, who should we meet but Charley Marsh and Cherrie. There they were, coming along as large as life, linking together, and Charley's head down, listening to her, till their noses were nearly touching. Me and Tom laughed till we were fit to split!"

Mr. Blair laughed again at the recollection, but Mr. Clowrie, scowling more darkly than ever, replied not save by scornful silence. Bill had his laugh out, and recommenced.

"So you see, Jake, it's no go! You can't get the beautifulest mug that ever was looked at, and you haven't the

shadow of a chance against such a fellow as Charley Marsh!
O Lor!"

With the last ejaculation of alarm, Bill sprang down
from his perch in consternation, as the door opened and
Mr. Val Blake entered. He had been so absorbed chaffing
Mr. Clowrie that he had not heard Val coming up-stairs,
and now made a desperate dash at the nearest desk. Val
stretched out his long arm and pinned him.

"You young vagabond! is this the way you spend
your time in my absence? What's that about Charley
Marsh?"

"Nothing, sir," said Bill, grinning a malicious grin
over at Mr. Clowrie. "I was only telling Jake how he
was being cut out!"

"Cut out! What do you mean?"

"Why, with that Cherrie Nettleby! Charley Marsh's
got her now!"

"What!" said Val, shortly; "what are you talking
about, you little rascal?"

"I can't help it, sir," said Bill, with an injured look,
"if I am a rascal. I saw him seeing her home this morning between three and four o'clock, and if that don't look
like cutting Jake out, I don't know what does!"

"And what were you doing out at three o'clock in the
morning, Master Blair?"

"I was over to Tod's spending the evening, me and a
lot more fellows, and that was the time we were getting
home. I don't see," said Bill, with a still more aggrieved
air, "why we shouldn't stop out a while, if all the old
codgers in the town set us the example!"

Val released him, and strode on to an inner room.

"See if you can attend to your business for one morning, sir, and give your tongue a holiday. Mr. Gilcase,
was the postman here?"

"Yes, sir. The letters and papers are on your table."

Val disappeared, closing the door behind him, and
Master Blair turned a somersault of delight and cut a
pigeon-wing afterward.

"Get to work, sir!" shouted Mr. Gilcase, "or I'll make
Mr. Blake turn you out of the office!"

"Mr. Blake knows better," retorted the incorrigible. "I rather think the Spouter would be nowhere if I left; Do you know, Mr. Gilcase, I think Blake has some notion of taking me into partnership shortly! He has to work like a horse now."

Val had to work hard—no mistake about it, for he was sole editor and proprietor of the Sunday and Weekly Speckport Spouter. He is sitting in his room now—and a dusty, grimy, littered, disordered room it is—before a table heaped with papers, letters, books, and manuscript of all kinds, busily tearing the envelopes off sundry overgrown letters, and disgorging their contents.

"What's this? a private note from Miss Incognita. 'Would I be so kind as to speak to the printers; they made such frightful mistakes in her last sketch, filled her heroine's eyes with tars, instead of tears, and in the battle-scene defeated Cromwell and his soldiers with wildest laughter, instead of slaughter!' Humph.

"It's her own fault; why don't she write decently? Very well, Miss Laura, I'll stick you in; you think I don't know you, I suppose. Come in."

Val looked up from his literary labors to answer a tap at the door. Mr. Gilcase put in his head.

"There's a gentleman here wants to see you, sir. Captain Cavendish."

Val got up and went out. Captain Cavendish, in a loose overcoat, and smoking a cigar, was lounging against a desk, and being stared at by Messrs. Clowrie and Blair, took out his cigar and extended his hand languidly to Val.

"Good morning! Are you very busy? Am I an intruder? If so, I'll go away again."

"I'm no busier than common," said Val. Come in, this is my sanctum, and here's the editorial chair; sit down."

"Is it any harm to smoke?" inquired the Captain, looking rather doubtful.

"Not the least. I'll blow a cloud myself. How did you find your way here through the clouds of fog?"

"Not very easily. Does the sun ever shine at all in Speckport?"

"Occasionally—when it cannot help itself. But when did you take to early rising, pray? You used to be lounging over your breakfast about this hour when I knew you in Halifax."

"Yes, I know—I'm a reformed character. Apropos, early rising seems to be the style here. I met two ladies of my acquaintance figuring through the streets ever so long ago."

"Who were they?"

"Your sister was one; Miss Marsh, the other."

"Natty, eh? Oh, she always was an early bird. Were you speaking to her?"

"I had the pleasure of escorting her to her mother's. By the way, she does not live with her mother, does she?"

"No; she lives with old Lady Leroy, up at Redmon."

"Where is Redmon?"

"About a mile from Speckport. Natty walks it two or three times a day, and thinks it's only a hen's jump. Redmon's a fine place."

"Indeed."

"Not the house exactly—it's a great barn—but the property. It's worth eight thousand pounds."

"So much?" said Captain Cavendish, looking interested. "And who is Lady Leroy?"

"The wife—the widow of a dead Jew. Don't stare, she only gets the title as a nickname, for she's the greatest old oddity the sun ever shone on. She's a cousin of Natty's mother, and Natty is to be her heiress."

Captain Cavendish's eyes lightened vividly.

"Her heiress! Is she very rich, then?"

"Immensely! Worth thirty thousand pounds or more, and the stingiest old skinflint that ever breathed. Natty has been with her over a year now, as a sort of companion, and a fine time she has with the old toad, I know."

"And there is no doubt Miss Marsh is to be her heiress?"

"None at all—the will is made and in the hands of Darcy, her lawyer. She has no children, and no relatives that ever I heard of nearer than Miss Marsh. She was old Leroy's servant when he married her—it happened in New

York, where he made his money. This place, Redmon,
was to be sold for debt; Leroy bid it in dirt cheap, and
rented it, employing Darcy as his agent to collect rents,
for there is quite a village attached to it. After the old
fellow's death, a year and a half ago, his venerable relict
came here, took up her abode at Redmon, with as great an
oddity as herself for a servant. She took a great fancy to
pretty Natty after awhile, and got her to go up there and
reside as companion."

"And those Marshes—what are they? like the rest of
Speckport—begging your pardon !—nobody ?"

"Family, you mean? That question is so like an
Englishman. The father was a gentleman. His profession
was that of engineer, and his family, I have heard, was
something extra in England ; but he made a low marriage
over here, and they would have nothing more to do with
him. Mrs. Marsh was pretty, and as insipid as a mug of
milk and water, caring for nothing in the world wide but
sitting in a rocking-chair reading novels. He married her,
though ; and they lived quite in style until Charley was
fourteen and Natty twelve years old. Then Mr. Marsh
had a stroke of paralysis which left him altogether incapa-
ble of attending to his business, of doing anything, in fact,
but teaching. He started a school, and got a salary for
playing the organ in the cathedral, but he only lived two
years after. Before he died they had to give up their fine
house, dismiss their servants, auction their furniture, and
rent the cottage they live in now. Miss Natty, sir, kept
the school, gave music-lessons after hours, took the organ
Sundays, and supported the family for the next three
years ; in point of fact, does to this day."

"How is that ?' said Captain Cavendish. "Mrs. Leroy
pays her a salary as companion, I suppose ?"

"She does; but that's only a pittance, wouldn't pay
her mother's bills in the circulating library. Natty refused
to go to Redmon unless under certain conditions. She
would retain the school, the organ, and her music-pupils
as usual, only she would engage another teacher for the
school, coming there one hour a day to superintend. That
would take about four hours a day, the rest was at the

service of Lady Leroy. Her ladyship grumbled, but had to consent; so Natty went to live up at Redmon, and between all has her hands full."

"She is indeed a brave girl! What are her duties at the old lady's?"

"No trifle! She reads to her, retails all the news of the town, writes her letters, keeps her accounts, receives the rents, makes out the receipts, oversees the household—does a thousand things besides. If she had as many hands as what's his name, the fellow in the mythology,—Briareus, wasn't it?—the old vixen would keep them all occupied. By the way, did you see Charley this morning when you were in?"

"I wasn't in, I left Miss Natty at the door. I say, Val, you didn't tell me last night who that pretty girl was I saw him with in the window. She was not a guest, though I'll take my oath there wasn't a young lady present half so pretty, save the belle of Speckport herself. Who was she?"

"Cherrie, otherwise Miss Charlotte Nettleby. A little flirting piece of conceit. She has had the young men of Speckport tagging after her. Rumor set Charley down lately as one of her killed or wounded; but Speckport is always gossiping, and I paid no attention to it. It seems it's true though, for that young scamp Blair in the next room saw him escorting her home this morning."

"What was she doing at the house if not invited!"

"How should I know? Cherrie is everywhere—she knows the servants, I suppose."

"Oh, is that it? Then she is nobody."

"I wish she heard you! If ever any one thought themselves somebody it's the same Miss Cherrie. She aspires to be a lady—bless your heart!—and that foolish boy is to be entrapped into marrying her."

Val stopped to knock the ashes off his cigar.

"Well; and what then?" asked the captain.

"Why, Natty will go frantic, that is all. She thinks the Princess Royal not half good enough for Charley."

"Is Miss Cherrie's position in life so low, then?"

"It's not that. Her father is a gardener, a poor man,

but honest and respectable enough. It's Cherrie herself; she's a shallow, vain, silly little beauty, as ever made fools of men, and her vanity, and her idleness, and her dress, and her flirtations are the scandal of the town. Not that anything worse can be said of little Cherrie, mind; but she is not the girl for Charley Marsh to marry."

"Charley is a gentleman; perhaps he isn't going to marry her," suggested Captain Cavendish, with a light laugh, that told more of his character than folios could have done.

"Being a gentleman," said Val, with emphasis, "he means to marry her if he means anything at all."

And the young officer shrugged his shoulders.

"*Chacun à son goût.* I must be going, I believe. Here I have been trespassing on your time these two hours."

"The day's young yet," said Val; "have you any engagement for this evening?"

"I believe not, except a dinner at the mess-room, which can be shirked."

"Then come up to Redmon. If you are a student of character, Mrs. Leroy will amply repay the trouble."

"I'm there! but not," said Captain Cavendish, laughing, "to see Mrs. Leroy."

"I understand. Well, good morning."

"Until then, *au revoir.*"

Mr. Bill Blair, perched on his high stool, his elbows spread out on the desk, stared at him as he went out.

"Cracky, what a rum swell them officer chaps are? I say, Clowrie, wouldn't Cherrie like that cove for a beau? He would be safe to win if he tried it on, and Charley Marsh would be where you are now—nowhere."

And little did Mr. William Blair or his hearers think he was uttering a prophecy.

CHAPTER V.

KILLING TWO BIRDS WITH ONE STONE.

APTAIN CAVENDISH, looking very handsome and distinguished in the admiring eyes of Speckport, lounged down Queen Street, and down half a dozen other streets, toward the sea-shore. The tide was ebbing as he descended to the beach, and the long, lazy swell breaking on the strand was singing the old everlasting song it has sung through all time. Its mysterious music was lost on Captain Cavendish; his thoughts were hundreds of miles away. Not very pleasant thoughts, either, judging by his contracted brow and compressed lips, as he leaned against a tall rock, his eyes looking out to sea. He started up after awhile, with a gesture of impatience.

"Pshaw!" he said; "what's the use of thinking of it now? it's all past and gone. It is Fate, I suppose; and if Fate has ordained I must marry a rich wife or none, where is the good of my puny struggles? But poor little Winnie! I have been the greatest villain that ever was known to you."

He walked along the beach, sending pebbles skimming over the waves as he went. Two fishermen in oilcloth trowsers, very scaly and rattling, were drawing up their boat, laden to the water's edge with gaspereaux, all alive and kicking. Captain Cavendish stopped and looked at them.

"Your freight looks lively, my men. You have got a fine boatload there."

The two young men looked at him. They were tall, strapping, sunburnt, black-eyed, good-looking fellows both, and the one hauling up the boat answered; the other, pulling the fish out of the nets, went on with his work in silence.

"Yes, sir, we had a good haul last night. The

freshet's been strong this spring, and has made the fishing good."

" Were you out all night ?"

" Yes; we have to go when the tide suits."

" You had a foggy night for it, then. Can you tell me which is the road to Redmon ?"

The young fisherman turned and pointed to a path going up the hillside from the shore.

"Do you see that path ? Well, follow it ; cut across the field, and let down the bars t'other side. There's a road there; keep straight on and it will fetch you to Redmon. You can't miss the house when you get to it; it's a big brick building on a sort of hill, with lots of trees around it."

" Thank you. I'll find it, I think."

He sauntered lazily up the hillside-path, cut across the fields, and let down the bars as he had been directed, putting them conscientiously up again.

The road was a very quiet one ; green meadows on either hand, and clumps of cedar and spruce wood sparsely dotting it here and there. The breeze swept up cool and fresh from the sea; the town with its bustle and noise was out of sight and hearing.

He was walking so slowly that it was nearly half an hour before Redmon came in sight—a large weather-beaten brick house on the summit of a hill, with bleak corners and reedy marshes, and dark trees all around it, the whole inclosed by a high wooden fence. The place took its name from these marshes or moors about it, sown in some time with crimson cranberries and pigeonberries, like fields of red stars. But Captain Cavendish only glanced once at Redmon; for the instant it had come in sight something else had come in sight, too, a thousand times better worth looking at. Just outside the extremity of the fence nearest him there stood a cottage—a little whitewashed affair, standing out in dazzling contrast to the black cedar woods beside it, hop-vines clustering round its door and windows, and a tall gate at one side opening into a well-cultivated vegetable garden.

Swinging back and forward on this gate was a young

girl, whom Captain Cavendish recognized in a moment. It was a face that few young men forgot easily, for its owner was a beauty born; the figure was petite and plump, delightfully rounded and ripe indeed, with no nasty sharp curves or harsh angles; the complexion dark and clear, the forehead low, with black, arching brows; the eyes like black beads; the cheeks like June roses; the lips as red, and ripe, and sweet as summer strawberries, the teeth they parted to disclose, literally like pearls, and they parted very often, indeed, to disclose them. The hair was black as hair can be, and all clustering in little short, shining rings and kinks about the forehead and neck. Captain Cavendish had seen that face for the first time last night, in the window with Charley Marsh, but he was a sufficiently good judge of physiognomy to know it was not necessary to be very ceremonious with Miss Cherrie Nettleby. He therefore advanced at once, with a neat little fiction at the top of his tongue.

"I beg your pardon," he said politely, "but I am very thirsty. Will you be kind enough to give me a drink?"

Miss Cherrie, though but nineteen in years, was forty at least in penetration where handsome men were concerned, and saw through the ruse at once. She sprang down from the gate and held it open, with the prettiest affectation of timidity in the world.

"Yes, sir. Will you please to walk in."

"Thank you," said the captain, languidly, "I believe I will. My walk has completely used me up."

Miss Cherrie led the way into the cottage. The front door opened directly into the parlor of the dwelling, a neat little room, the floor covered with mats; a table, with books and knicknacks in the center; a lounge and a rocking-chair, and some common colored prints on the walls. It had an occupant as they came in, a sallow, dark-eyed girl of sixteen, whose hands fairly flew as she sat at the window, netting on a fisherman's net, already some twenty fathoms long.

"Ann," said Cherrie, placing a chair for their distinguished visitor, "go and fetch the gentleman a drink."

The girl turned her sallow but somewhat sullen face, without rising.

"There ain't no water in," she said, curtly.

"Go for some now," said Cherrie. "I'll knit till you come back."

"No, no!" hastily interposed Captain Cavendish. "I beg you will give yourself no such trouble. I am not so thirsty as I thought I was."

"Oh, we'll want the water anyhow to get the boys' dinner," said Cherrie, throwing off her scarlet shawl. "Go, Ann, and make haste."

Ann got up crossly, and strolled out of the room at a snail's pace, and Miss Cherrie took her place, and went to work industriously.

"Is that your sister?" he asked, watching Cherrie's hand flying as swiftly in and out as Ann's had done.

"Yes, that's our Ann," replied the young lady, as if every one should know Ann, as a matter of course.

"And do you and Ann live here alone together?"

Cherrie giggled at the idea.

"Oh dear, no. There's father and the boys."

"The boys, and are they——"

"My brothers," said Cherrie. "Two of 'em, Rob and Eddie. They fish, you know, and Ann, she knits the nets."

"Are those you are now making for them?"

"Yes, these are shad-nets. I hate to knit, but the boys pay Ann for doing it, and she does them all. I guess you'll be pretty thirsty," said Cherrie, laughing as easily as if she had known him for the past ten years, "before Ann gets back with the water. She's horrid slow."

"Never mind. The longer she is away, the better I shall like it, Miss Cherrie."

Miss Cherrie dropped her needle and mesh-block, and opened her black eyes.

"Why, how did you find out my name? You don't know me, do you?"

"A little. I trust we shall be very well acquainted before long."

. 8

Cherrie smiled graciously.

"Everybody knows me, I think. How did you find out who I was?"

"I saw you last night."

"No! did you, though? What time? where was I?"

"Sitting in a window, breaking a young gentleman's heart."

Cherrie giggled again.

"I'm sure I wasn't doing any such thing. That was only Charley Marsh."

"Only Charley Marsh. Had you and he a pleasant walk home this morning?"

"Now, I never. How did you know he saw me home?"

"A little bird told me. I only wish it had been my good fortune."

"Oh, what a story!" cried Cherrie, her wicked black eyes dancing in her head; "I wonder you ain't ashamed! Didn't I hear you wanting to ride home with Miss Natty. I was peeking out through the dining-room door, and I heard you as plain as could be."

"Well, I wanted to be polite, you know. Not having the honor of your acquaintance, Cherrie, I knew there was no hope of escorting you; so I made the offer to Miss Marsh in sheer despair. Now, Cherrie, I don't want you to get too fond of that brother of hers."

Cherrie tittered once more.

"Now, how can you! I'm sure I don't care nothing about him; but I can't help his talking to me, and seeing me home, can I?"

"I don't know. I wouldn't talk too much to him, if I were you; and as for seeing you home, I'd rather do it myself. There is no telling what nonsense he may get talking! Does he come here often?"

"Pretty often; but all the young fellows come! Sandy McGregor, Jake Clowrie, Mr. Blake, Charley Marsh, and the whole lot of 'em!"

"What time do they come?"

"Evenings, mostly. Then, there's a whole lot of Bob

and Eddie's friends come, too, and the house is full most
every night!"

"And what do you all do?"

"Oh, ever so many things! Play cards, sing songs,
and carry on, and dance, sometimes."

"May I come, too, Cherrie?"

"You may, if you like," said Cherrie, with coquettish
indifference. "But the young ladies in Speckport won't
like that!"

"What do I care for the young ladies in Speckport!
Oh, here's the water!"

Ann came in with a glass, and the captain drank it
without being the least thirsty.

"Bob and Eddie's coming up the road," said Ann
to her sister; "you knit while I peel the potatoes for
dinner."

"I am afraid I must go," said Captain Cavendish, rising, having no desire to make the acquaintance of the
Messrs. Nettleby. "I have been here nearly half an
hour."

"That ain't long, I'm sure," said Cherrie; "what's
your hurry?"

"I have a call to make. May I come again, Miss
Cherrie?"

"Oh, of course!" said Miss Cherrie, with perfect
coolness; "we always like to see our friends. Are you
going to Redmon?"

Captain Cavendish nodded, and took his hat. Pretty
Cherrie got up to escort him to the gate.

"Good-bye, Miss Cherrie," he said, making her a
flourishing bow. "I will have the pleasure of calling on
you to-morrow."

Cherrie smiled most gracious consent.

As he turned out of the gate he encountered the two
young fishermen who had directed him to Redmon. They
were Cherrie's brothers, then; and, laughing inwardly at
the memory of the late interview with that young lady,
he entered the grounds of Redmon.

"She's a deuced pretty girl!" he said, slapping his
boot with a rattan he carried; "and, faith, she's free and

easy! No nonsensical prudery about Miss Cherrie. I only hope I may get on as well with the golden-haired heiress as I seem to have done with the black-eyed grisette!"

He opened the wooden gate, and sauntered along a bleak avenue, the grounds on either hand overrun with rank weeds, and spruce, and tamarack, and fir trees, casting somber gloom around.

The house, a great red barn, as Val had said, looked like a black, grimy jail; the shutters were closed on every window, the hall-door seemed hermetically sealed, and swallows flew about it, and built their nests in security on the eaves and down the chimneys. There was a great, grim iron knocker on the door, and the young man's knock reverberated with a hollow and ghostly echo through the weird house.

"What a place for such a girl to live in!" he thought, looking up at it. "Her desire for wealth must be strong to tempt her to bury herself alive in such an old tomb. The riches of the Rothschilds would not induce me."

A rusty key grated in a lock, the door swung open with a creaking sound, and the bright face of Nathalie Marsh looked out.

She smiled when she saw who it was, and frankly held out her hand.

"You have lost no time, Monsieur. Walk in, and please to excuse me a few moments. I must go back to Mrs. Leroy."

They were in a long and dismal hall, flanked with doors, and with a great, wide, old-fashioned staircase sweeping up and losing itself somehow in the upper gloom. Natty opened one of the doors, ushered him into the reception parlor of the establishment, and then flew swiftly up the stairs and was gone.

Captain Cavendish looked about him, that is, as well as he could for the gloom. The parlor of Redmon was furnished after the style of the cabin of a certain "fine ould Irish g'ntleman," immortalized in song, "with nothing at all for show." No carpet on the dreary Sahara of floor; no curtains on the gloomy windows; no pictures

on the dead, blank waste of whitewashed walls; a few
chairs, a black, old mahogany table, a dreary horsehair
sofa, about as soft as if cushioned with bricks; and that
was all. The silence of the place was something blood-
chilling; not the squeak of a mouse relieved its deathlike
quiet.

Five, ten, fifteen, twenty minutes passed, and the captain, getting desperate, was seriously thinking of making
his escape, when a light step came tripping down the
stairs, and Natty, all breathless and laughing, came breezily
in.

"Are you tired to death waiting?" she laughed gayly.
"Mrs. Leroy is dreadfully tiresome over her toilet, and I
am femme de chambre, if you please! It is over now,
and she desires me to escort you to her presence, and
be introduced. I hope you may make a favorable im-
pression!"

"But what am I to do?" said Captain Cavendish,
with an appalled face. "How am I to insinuate myself
into her good graces? Where is the key to her
heart?"

"The key was lost years ago, and her heart is now
closed. Don't contradict her, whatever you do. Hush!
here we are!"

They had ascended to a hall like the one below;
flanked, like it, by doors. Natty, with a glance of wicked
delight at his dolorous face, opened the first door to the
right, and ushered him at once into the presence of the
awful Lady Leroy.

Something—it certainly looked more like an Egyptian
mummy than anything else—swathed in shawls and
swaddling-clothes, was stuck up in a vast Sleepy Hollow
open arm-chair, and had its face turned to the door. That
face, and a very yellow, and scared, and wrinkled, and unlovely face it was, buried in the flapping obscurity of a
deeply-frilled white cap, was lit by a pair of little, twinkling eyes, bright and keen as two stilettos.

"Mrs. Leroy," said Natty, her tone demure, but her
mischievous eyes dancing under their lashes, "this is Captain Cavendish."

"How d'ye do, Captain Cavendish?" said Mrs. Leroy, in a shrill, squeaking voice, like a penny whistle out of tune; "sit down—do! Natty, can't you give the young man a cheer?"

Natty did not cheer, but she placed a chair for him, whispering, as she did so, "Speak loud, or she won't hear you."

"What's the weather like out o' doors?" inquired the old lady, scanning him from head to foot with her little piercing eyes; "be the sun a-shining, hey?"

"No, Madam," said Captain Cavendish, in a loud key, "it is foggy."

She had paid no attention to his reply; she had been staring at him all the time, until even he, cool as any man of the world could be, got a trifle disconcerted. Natty, sitting demurely near, was enjoying it all with silent but intense delight.

"So you're the young English captain Natty was telling me about. You're not so handsome as she said you were; leastways, you ain't to my taste!"

It was Natty's turn now to look disconcerted, which she did with a vengeance, as the dark, laughing eyes of the young officer turned upon her.

"Miss Marsh does me too much honor to mention me at all," he said, speaking more at the young lady than to the old one.

"Hey?" inquired Lady Leroy, shrilly. "What's that? What did you say?"

"I was saying how remarkably well you were looking, ma'am," said the captain, raising his voice, "and that this Redmon is a very fine old place."

"It's not!" screamed Lady Leroy, viciously; "it's the hatefulest, daftest, uncomfortablest hole ever anybody set foot in! Natty!"

"Yes, ma'am!" said Natty. "What is it?"

"Is old Nettleby planting them potatoes to-day?"

"Yes, of course he is."

"He'll plant Carters where he ought to plant Early Blues! I know he will!" cried the old lady in an ecstasy of alarm; "run out as fast as you can, Natty, and tell him not to plant any Carters in the three-cornered field. Run, run, run!"

Natty knew Lady Leroy a great deal too well to expostulate. "I will be back directly," she said, in a low voice, the laughing light in her eyes still, as she passed her visitor; "do not get into trouble if you can help it, in my absence."

She was gone, and Lady Leroy, with her eyes fixed on the opposite wall, seemed to have gone off into a fit of musing. Captain Cavendish tried to look about him, which he had not ventured to do before, under those basilisk eyes. It was a large square room, like all the rest in the house, and stiflingly close and warm. No wonder, for a small cooking-stove was burning away, and every window was closed and shuttered. A bed stood in one corner, an old-fashioned clock ticked in a loud hoarse voice on the mantel-piece, a small round table stood at the old lady's elbow, and the floor was covered with a carpet that had been Brussels once, but which was dirty, and colorless, and ragged now. There was an open cupboard with dishes, and a sort of pantry with a half glass door, through which he could see boxes and barrels, hams and dried beef, and other commissary stores. The chair matched the flinty sofa down stairs, and the only thing to attract attention in the room was a green cabinet of covered wood that stood beside the bed. While he was looking at it, the old-fashioned clock began striking twelve in a gruff and surly way, as if it did it against its better judgment. The sound woke the old lady up from her brown study—woke her up with a sharp jerk.

"It's twelve o'clock!" she exclaimed shrilly, "and I want my dinner! Call Midge!"

This was addressed to Captain Cavendish, and in so peremptory a tone that that gallant young officer looked alarmed and disconcerted.

"Call Midge, I tell you! Call her quick!" yelped Lady Leroy in an excited way. "Call Midge, will you!"

"Where is she? Where will I call her?" said the young man, in considerable consternation.

"Open that door, stupid, and call Midge!" cried the old woman, violently excited; "call her quick, I tell you!"

Thus ordered, Captain Cavendish opened the door and began calling loudly on the unknown lady bearing the name of Midge.

Out of the gloom and dismalness below a hoarse voice shouted in reply, "I'm a coming;" and Captain Cavendish went back to his seat. The voice was that of a man, and of a man with a shocking bad cold, too; and the step lumbering up stairs was a man's step; but for all that, Midge wasn't a man, but a woman. Such a woman! the Egyptian mummy in the arm-chair was a Parisian belle compared to her. Between three and four feet high, and between four and five feet broad, Midge was just able to waddle under the weight of her own fair person, and no more. A shock of hair, very like a tar-mop, stood, bristling defiance at combs and brushes, up on end, like "quills upon the fretful porcupine." To say she had no forehead, and only two pinholes for eyes, and a little round lump of flesh in lieu of a decent nose, would be doing no sort of justice to the subject; for the face, with its fat, puffy cheeks, was altogether indescribable. The costume of the lady was scant, her dress displaying to the best advantage a pair of ankles some fifteen inches in circumference, and a pair of powerful arms, bare to the shoulders, were rolled up in a cotton apron. With the airy tread of an elephant inclined to embonpoint, this sylph-like being crossed the hall and stood in the doorway awaiting orders, while Captain Cavendish stared aghast, and backed a few paces with a feeble "By Jove!"

"What do you want, ma'am?" inquired the damsel in the doorway, who might have been anywhere in the vale of years between twenty and fifty.

"Get my dinner! It's after twelve! Don't I always tell you to come and get my dinner when you hear the clock strike twelve?"

"And how do you suppose I can hear that there clock half a mile off, down in that kitchen!" retorted Midge, sharply. "I ain't jest got ears as sharp as lancets, I'd have you know. I'll take the key!"

Mrs. Leroy produced a key from a pocket somewhere about her; and Midge, rather jerking it out of her hands than otherwise, unlocked the pantry, and began busying herself among the forage there. Mrs. Leroy's keen eyes followed every motion as a cat follows its prey, and Captain Cavendish gazed too, as if fascinated, on the fairy form of Miss Midge. In passing to and fro, Midge had more than once caught his eye, and at last her feelings got the better of her, and, pausing abruptly before him, with her arms akimbo, burst out, "Look here, sir! I don't know who you are, but if you're a doggertype-man, come to take my picter, I'd jest thank you to be quick about it, and not sit there gaping like——"

"Midge!" called a ringing voice in the doorway. It was Nathalie, her face stern, her voice imperative. "Midge, how dare you speak so?"

"Oh, never mind!" said Captain Cavendish, who, in the main, was a good-natured young officer. "I deserve it, I dare say. I have made an unpardonably long call, I believe. Mrs. Leroy, I wish you good morning."

"Good morning!" said Mrs. Leroy, without looking at him, all her eyes being absorbed in the doings of Midge in the culinary department. "Natty, you let him out."

Natty did so, and they both laughed when at a safe distance.

"What did you do to Midge?" she inquired, "to tempt her to pour the vials of her wrath on your head, as she was doing when I came in."

"Staring very hard, I am afraid! Where is Barnum, that he does not get hold of that domestic monstrosity?"

"Oh, hush!" said Natty. But the warning came too late. Midge, descending the stairs, had heard the speech, and gave the speaker a look so baleful and vindictive, that, had he been troubled with those feminine miseries, nerves, might have haunted him many a day. He smiled at it then, but he remembered that look long after.

"She is acutely sensitive, dull as she seems," said Natty, with a pained look. "I am sorry she heard you."

"I am sincerely sorry for my thoughtless words, then, Miss Marsh, if they pain you."

8*

"She saved Charley's life once," said Natty, "when he was a little fellow. I have always liked Midge since, and I believe she loves me with the faithful and blind fidelity of—but no irreverence—a dog. A slighting word rankles in her memory long."

"I shall fetch her a peace-offering the next time I come, which, by the way," he said, coolly, "is to be this evening, with your permission. Blake is to be my chaperon on the occasion."

"I regret I shall not see either of you then; but," said Natty, with a funny look, "no doubt Mrs. Leroy will be delighted to entertain you till her bedtime comes, which is precisely nine o'clock."

"Not see us? Are you——"

"I have promised to spend the evening out. When I was with the gardener a few moments ago, Miss Blake came in and asked me to spend the evening with her. Mamma and Miss Rose, the new teacher, are to be there, and I could not refuse."

"Then I shall postpone my call. Oh, there is a summons for you! How impatient your old lady is!"

They shook hands, and parted. Captain Cavendish lit a cigar, and went smoking, meditatingly, down the dreary avenue, and out into the highroad. Standing near the gate was pretty Cherrie, and a refulgent smile greeted him from the rosy lips. He lifted his hat, and passed on; for standing in the doorway was the stalwart young fishermen of the beach.

"Two very pretty girls!" he mused, over his Havana; "*belle blonde, et jolie brunette.* It's extremely convenient their living so near together; one journey does for both. I think I understand now what is meant by the old adage of killing two birds with one stone."

CHAPTER VI.

AN EVENING AT MISS BLAKE'S.

HE establishment of Miss Joanna Blake was not on a scale of magnificence. Miss Jo's only parlor being about ten feet square, was not too grandly vast at any time, and not exactly adapted for the mirthful throng to disport themselves in. The style of furniture, too, was, some people might think, on a trifle too grand a scale for its dimensions. When Val, and his fourteen or fifteen friends aforesaid, lit their cigars, tilted back their chairs, elevated the heels of their boots on the piano or table, and all puffed away together, the parlor became rather obscure, and a stranger suddenly entering might have conceived the idea that the house was in flames; and that, perhaps, was the reason the parlor always smelt like a tobacconist's shop. Besides the parlor, Miss Jo had a dining-room and a kitchen, and two bedrooms, in the floor, though, and she did her own work.

In the parlor of No. 16 Great St. Peter's Street, the lamp was lit, the drab moreen curtains let down, and the table set for tea. There was a snowy cloth on the mahogany which hid the marks of the bootheels and the stains of the punch-tumblers, and the china cups and saucers, and the glass preserve-plates and butter-dish, and spoon-holder, not to speak of the spoons themselves, which were of real silver, and had cost a dollar a piece, and had a big capital "B" engraven thereon, glittered and flashed in the light. There was buttered toast, and hot biscuit, and pound-cake, and fruit-cake, and mince-pie, and quince-jelly, and cold chicken, and coffee and tea—all the work of Miss Jo's own fair hands; and Miss Jo herself, rather flushed with the heat, but very imposing and stately to look at in a green poplin dress—real Irish poplin at that—and a worked collar a finger-length deep, presided at the tea-tray, and dispensed the hospitalities of the festive board. Val, sitting opposite, did his part, which consisted chiefly in attempting to pass the cake-plates. and spilling their contents, of upsetting everything he touched, and looking mildly but reproachfully at the refractory object afterward. Mrs. Marsh was there, placid, and insipid, and faded, and feeble, as usual; and Miss Rose was there, pale and pretty; and Miss Clowrie was there, smiling and soft of voice, and deft of touch, and purring more than ever; and Miss Blair was there, laughing at all the funny things, and rosy as Hebe herself; and Charley Marsh was there, making a martyr of himself in the attempt to be fascinating to three young ladies at once; and everybody had eaten and drank, forced thereto by Miss Blake, until they were, as Charley forcibly put it, "a misery to themselves." So a move was made to adjourn, which just consisted of pushing their chairs about five inches from the table, not being able to push them any further, and Miss Jo began rattling among the tea-things, which she called clearing them off. Miss Catty, always sweet and obliging, and that sort of a thing, insisted on helping her, and Charley opening the upright, clattered a "Fisher's Hornpipe" in spirited style.

"Come and sing us a song, Laura—that's a good girl," he said, while Val, making an apology, slipped out. "Come and sing 'The Laird o' Cockpen.'"

Miss Blair, all smiles, took her seat, and sung not only "The Laird o' Cockpen," but a dozen others of the same kidney.

"What do you think of that?" inquired Miss Blair, triumphantly rising up, with a finishing bang. "Who says I can't sing? Now, Miss Rose, you sing, I know."

"Of course she does," said Charley. "Miss Rose, permit me to lead you to the instrument."

Miss Rose looked as though she were about to excuse herself, but that impulsive Laura Blair ran over and caught her by both hands.

"Up with you! We won't take any excuses. Charley, the young lady is at your mercy, lead her off."

Charley promptly did so. Miss Rose, smiling gra

ciously, ran her white fingers over the yellow keys, and looked up at him.

" What shall I sing, Monsieur ?"

" Anything you please, Mademoiselle. I am prepared to be delighted with ' Old Dan Tucker,' if you chose it."

The white fingers still ran idly over the keys, breaking into a plaintive prelude at last, and in a voice, " low and sweet " as Annie Laurie's own, the song began. The words were those of a gifted young American poetess ; the melody, a low sweet air, in a melancholy minor key— Miss Rose's own, perhaps.

The sweet voice faltered a little toward the close ; but as a buzz of congratulation ran around the circle she arose hastily. Arose to find herself face to face with two gentlemen who had entered as she began her song, and who had stood silently listening with the rest. It was Captain Cavendish and Val ; and the young officer's face wore a look no one in that room had ever seen it wear before—a pale and startled look of anxiety, almost of fear—and as she faced them he .backed a few paces involuntarily. Miss Rose, evidently taken completely by surprise. started visibly, growing white and red by turns. But Val was introducing them, and only he and one other present saw the changing faces of the twain. That other was Miss Catty Clowrie, whose eyes were as keen as any other cat's, and who watched them furtively, with vividest interest. Miss Catty was enough of a mathematician to know there is no effect without a cause. What, then, was the cause of this ? It was easily enough answered. Captain Cavendish and Miss Rose had met before, and had known each other well, though they were now bowing as perfect strangers. The elegant officer had recovered all his highbred sangfroid, and was smooth and bland as sweet oil ; but Miss Rose's face had settled into so deadly a pallor that Mrs. Marsh, albeit not the most eagle-sighted in the world, noticed it.

" Dear me, Miss Rose, how pale you are ! Aren't you well ?"

Miss Rose murmured something about the heat, and subsided into the most shadowy corner she could find ;

and Charley created a diversion by sitting down to the piano himself and rattling off a jingling symphony.

In the midst of it carriage wheels rolled up to the door of No. 16, and the first-floor bell rang loudly a minute after.

"That's Natty," said Charley.

Miss Jo met her in the hall and escorted her to her bedroom, which was the dressing-room for the evening; and presently Miss Nathalie came in, dressed in black silk, trimmed with black lace, and all her beautiful golden hair falling in glittering ringlets over her shoulders, her cheeks glowing with the rapid ride through the night air. Brilliant she looked; and Captain Cavendish's heart, or whatever the thing is that does duty for a heart with men of the world, quickened its beating a little, as he shook hands. Nathalie kissed Miss Rose, sitting so very still in her quiet corner.

"My pale little girl! Here you sit like a white shadow, all by yourself. Charley, what on earth are you shouting there?"

"Now, Natty, it's your turn," said Miss Jo.

"Here's the cards," said Charley, laying hold of a pack. "While Natty's singing we'll play 'Muggins.' Does anybody here know 'Muggins'?"

Nobody did.

"What a disgrace! Then I'll teach you. Miss Jo, I'll sit beside you. Come along, captain; here Laura, Catty, Val, mother; Miss Rose, won't you join us?"

"Don't, Miss Rose," said Natty, who was playing a waltz. "They're nothing but a noisy set. Come here and sing with me."

Natty sung everything—Italian arias, French chansonettes, German and Scotch ballads; her full, rich soprano voice filling the room with melody, as on Sundays it filled the long cathedral aisles. Natty's voice was superb.—Miss Rose listened like one entranced. So did another, Captain Cavendish, who made all sorts of blunders in the game, and could not learn it at all, for watching the two black figures at the piano—the little pale girl with the modest brown braids, and the stately heiress with her shining yellow curls. Catty Clowrie watched them and the captain, and the game too, noting everything, and making no mistakes. A very noisy party they were, every one laughing, expostulating, and straining their voices together, and Charley winning everything right and left.

"I say, Cavendish, old fellow! what are you thinking of?" cried Val. "This is the third time I've told you to play."

Captain Cavendish started into recollection, and began playing with the wildest rapidity, utterly at random.

"Look here, Natty," called Charley, as the card-party, more noisy than ever, broke up; "I say it's not fair of you to monopolize Miss Rose all the evening. Here's Captain Cavendish has lost all his spare change, because he couldn't watch the game for watching that piano."

Miss Rose retreated hastily to her corner; Natty wheeled round on the piano-stool.

"What noise you have been making. Have you finished your game?"

Charley jingled a pocketful of pennies—Speckport pennies at that—as large as quoits.

"Yes, we have finished, for the simple reason I have cleaned the whole party completely out, and I have won small change enough to keep me in cigars for the next two months. Who's this?"

"It's somebody for me," said Natty, starting up; "that's Rob Nettleby's knock."

"Don't go yet, Natty," said Val, "it is too early."

"It is half-past ten; I should have been off half an hour ago. Miss Blake, my things, please."

Miss Jo produced a white cloud and large cloak, and Natty's move was a signal for all to depart. Catty, Laura, Miss Rose, and Mrs. Marsh's mufflings had to be got, and the little parlor was a scene of "confusion worse confounded."

Val strolled over to where Captain Cavendish was making himself useful, helping Miss Marsh on with her cloak.

"Natty, I'll go home with you, if you like," said polite

Val; "it will be rather a dismal drive up there with no one but Rob Nettleby."

"Mr. Blake is forestalled," said Captain Cavendish, coolly. "Miss Marsh has accorded the honor to me."

"All right," said Val, "I'll go home with Laura Blair, then. Charley can take care of the other three, for Catty lives next door."

Lady Leroy's carryall, with Cherrie Nettleby's elder brother for driver, was waiting at the door. Good-byes were said, Natty kissed her mamma, Laura and Miss Rose, but only shook hands with Miss Clowrie. Captain Cavendish noticed the omission as he seated himself beside her, and they drove off.

"I don't like her," said Natty; "I never did, since I was a child. She was such a crafty, cunning little thing in those days—a sort of spy on the rest of us—a sort of female Uriah Heep."

"Is she so still?"

"Oh, no; she is well enough now; but old prejudices cling to one, you know. I don't like her, because I don't like her—an excellent female reason, you understand."

"Does your brother share your prejudices, Miss Marsh?" asked the young officer, with a meaning smile.

"Charley? I don't know. Why?"

"Because I fancy the young lady is rather disposed to regard him with favor. I may be mistaken, though."

Natty suddenly drew herself up.

"I think you are mistaken, Captain Cavendish. Catty Clowrie has sense, whatever else she may lack, and never would dream of so preposterous a thing."

"Pardon! it has been my mistake, then. You seem to be all old friends in this place."

"Oh," said Natty, with her gay laugh, "every one knows every one else in Speckport, and a stranger is a marked being at once. Apropos of strangers, what a perfect darling that Miss Rose is."

"How very young-ladylike! Miss Rose does not sound like a family name; has she no other cognomen?"

"Her letter to me was signed W. Rose. I don't know

what the 'W' is for. I think she has the sweetest face I ever saw."

"What a lovely night it is?" was Captain Cavendish's somewhat irrelevant answer; and had the moon been shining, Natty might have seen the flush his face wore. Perhaps it was the sea-breeze, though; for it was blowing up fresh and bracing, and a host of stars spangled a sky of cloudless blue. The monotonous plash of the waves on the shore came dully booming over the rattle of their own carriage-wheels.

"What are the wild waves saying? Miss Rose and I have a bond of sympathy between us: we both love the sea. I suppose," said Natty, going off into another subject, "Mrs. Leroy will read me a lecture for my long stay, when I get back."

"Will she not be asleep?"

"Asleep? No, indeed; I believe if I staid out for a week she would never close an eye until I got back."

"Is she so very fond of you, then?"

"It is not that; though I think she is as fond of me as it is in her nature to be of anything, except," with another laugh, "eating and money. It is fear that keeps her awake; she dreads being left alone."

"Why? Not from an evil conscience, I trust."

"For shame, sir. No, she always keeps a large sum of money in her chamber—you saw that queer cabinet—well, in that; and she is terribly scared of robbers, in spite of all our bolts and bars."

"She should not keep it about her, then."

"Very true; but she will. I sleep in the room next hers, and I presume she feels my presence there a sort of safeguard against burglars. In Midge she has no confidence whatever."

"And yet I should consider Midge the greatest possible safeguard. The sight of her might scare away an army of robbers."

"Now, now!" cried Natty. "I shall not have Midge abused. She is the most faithful and trustworthy creature that ever lived."

"Perhaps so; but you will own that she is not the most lovely. When I was a boy at Eton, I used to read

German legends of beautiful princesses guarded by malignant spirits, in uncouth human forms. I thought of the
stories this morning when I was at Redmon."

"That's a compliment, I suppose," said Natty, "but I
don't-relish compliments, I can tell you, at Midge's expense. Here we are at the cottage."

"What cottage is it?" Captain Cavendish asked, forgetting suddenly that he had spent half an hour there that
very morning.

"The Nettlebys. The father is our gardener; the sons,
the whole family, make themselves useful about the place,
all but Cherrie, who is more for ornament than use. Here
we are at Redmon, and there is the light burning in Mrs.
Leroy's window."

"Does it burn all night?" he asked, looking up at it.

"No; it is a beacon for me. I must go to her room
the first thing now, give an account of myself, and extin-
guish it. Good-night; I hope you will enjoy your soli-
tary journey back."

"I shall have pleasant thoughts of a lady fair to keep
me company. Are you sure you can get in?"

"Midge is opening the door now; once more, good-
night."

Waving her hand to him, she was gone while she
spoke. Midge stood blinking in the doorway, holding a
candle above her head, which tar-mop was now tied up in
a red flannel petticoat.

She shaded her eyes with her hand, peering out at the
tall figure in the loose overcoat; and when she made sure
of his identity, slamming the door to with a bang that left
no doubt of her feelings toward him.

"Midge, why did you do that?" Natty said, reprov-
ingly.

"Because I never want to see his wicked face here,
Miss Natty; that's why!" cried Midge, shrilly; "and I
don't want to see him with you, for he is a villain, and he
will turn out one, if he was ten officers, ten times over."

But Natty was flying up the polished stairs with a new
happiness at her heart, singing as she went a snatch of
"Love's Young Dream."

CHAPTER VII.

TOO MANY IRONS IN THE FIRE.

R. VAL BLAKE was a young gentleman possessing a great many admirable virtues, among
others the fearful one of always saying what he
thought. Another, not quite so terrible to society, was that of early rising. The sun, whenever that luminary condescended to show its face in Speckport, which wasn't so very often, never found him in bed,
either winter or summer. Val might be up until two
o'clock in the office, as he sometimes was in busy seasons,
such as election times, but that never prevented his rising
at half-past four the next morning, as bright as a new
penny.

Val had escorted Miss Laura Blair home from his sister's little sociable—not only escorted her home, in fact,
but had gone in with her. It was past eleven then, but
Papa Blair had invited him to blow a friendly cloud, and
Val had accepted the invitation. There they sat, smoking
and talking politics until after one, and it was half-past
when he got back to No. 16 Great St. Peter's Street; but
for all that, here he was next morning at the hour of six,
coming striding along the sea-shore, a pipe in his mouth,
and a towel in his hand. Val had been taking a sea-bath,
his invariable custom every fine morning, from the first of
May to the last of October, to the alarming increase of his
appetite for breakfast. There were few to be met on the
sand, at that hour, except in the fishing seasons; and the
fishermen not being in yet from the night's work, the
shore was entirely deserted. The editor of the Speckport
Gazette had not the shore all to himself after all; for, as
he passed a jutting bowlder, he came in view of a fluttering
figure walking slowly on before. The black dress waving
in the breeze, the slender form in the long black mantle,

the little straw hat, and the brown braid were familiar by this time.

Miss Rose, the pretty little school-teacher, was taking an early constitutional as well as himself, with a book for her only companion. Val's long legs were beginning to measure off the sand in vast strides, to join her, when he was forestalled most unexpectedly. Starting up from behind a tall rock, in whose shadow on the warm sand he had been lying, his hat pulled over his eyes to protect him from the sun, a gentleman came forward, lifted his hat, and accosted her. Val knew the gentleman quite as well as he did the lady, and stopped. At the sound of his voice coming so suddenly, she had recoiled with a suppressed cry, but at sight of whom it was, she stood perfectly still, as if transfixed.

There was a path up the hillside—the very path Captain Cavendish had been shown by the young Nettlebys the day before. Val turned up this, with his hands in his pockets, and his mind in a state of soliloquy.

"I'm not wanted, I expect; so I'll keep clear! There's something queer about this—they were both taken aback last night, were they not? She's a pretty little thing, and he's been in Montreal, I know; was quartered there before he was ordered to Halifax. I suppose it's the old story—he always was a flirt, and his handsome face sets the girls loony wherever he goes. Miss Rose looks sensible, but I dare say she's as bad as the rest."

Val's suspicions might have become certainty had he been listening to the conversation of the young officer and the little school-teacher; but there was no one to listen, except the waves and the wind, and the seagulls clanging over their heads.

"Winnie!" Captain Cavendish was hurriedly saying, "I knew you would be here, and I have been waiting for the past half hour. No, do not go! Pray stay and hear me out."

"I must go!" Miss Rose said, in a violent tremor and agitation. "You have nothing to say to me, Captain Cavendish. I cannot be seen here with you."

"There is no one to see us—the shore is deserted! Winnie! you must stay."

She had turned to go; but he caught her hand, his own face pale as hers had turned.

"Let go my hand, sir!" she cried, in so peremptory a tone that he dropped it at once; "every word you speak to me is an insult! Let me go!"

"Only one moment, Winnie."

Again she interposed, her eyes quite flashing.

"Have the goodness, Captain Cavendish, to be a little less familiar; to cease calling me Winnie."

"What shall I call you, then?" he said, with a strange look, "Miss Rose?"

She turned away, and made a little passionate gesture with her hand.

"You have no right to call me anything—to speak to me at all! I do not know what evil fate has driven us together here; but if you have one feeling of honor, Captain Cavendish, you will leave me in peace—you will let me alone. My lot is not such a happy one that you should wish to destroy the little comfort I have left."

Her voice choked and something fell on her book and wet it. The face of the English officer looked strangely moved for him.

"Heaven knows, Winnie, I have no desire to disturb it; I have been a villain—we both know that—but destiny was against me. I am poor; I am in debt—I was then—what could I do?"

"Will you let me go?" was her answer, without turning her averted face to him.

"Am I, then, utterly hateful to you?" he asked, with some bitterness. "You have soon forgotten the past, but I deserve it! I do not ask what chain of circumstances brought you here; I only ask, being here, that you will not reveal the story of—of what is past and gone. Will you promise me this, Winnie?"

"What right have you to ask any promise of me?" she demanded, her gentle voice full of indignation.

"Very little, I know; but still, I want the promise, Winnie, for your own sake, as well as for me."

"I am not likely to tell; the story of one's own folly is not too pleasant to repeat. And now, in return, Captain Cavendish, I want, I demand, a promise from you! We met last night as strangers, as strangers let us meet henceforth. Go your own way. I shall not molest you, never fear; and be generous enough to grant me the same favor. My life is to be one of hard work. I do not regret that. Let me find happiness in my own way, and do not disturb me any more."

"And it has all come to this!" he said, moodily, looking out over the wide sea. "Well, Winnie, let it be as you wish, only I never thought you could be so unforgiving."

"I have forgiven long ago; I want to try and forget as well!"

She walked rapidly away. Only once had she looked at him all the time—after that first glance of recognition, her face had been averted.

Captain Cavendish watched her out of sight, took two or three turns up and down the sand, and then strolled away to his lodgings. His rooms were in the Speckport House, fronting on Queen Street; and after disposing of his beefsteak and coffee with a very good appetite, he seated himself near an open window, to smoke no end of cigars and watch the passers-by.

A great many passers-by there were, and nearly all strangers to him; but presently, two young men went strutting past, arm-in-arm, and, chancing to look at his window, lifted their hats in passing. A sudden thought seemed to flash through the officer's mind as he saw them, and, seizing his hat, he started out after them. It was young McGregor and Charley Marsh, and he speedily overtook them.

"I have been sitting there for over half an hour," he said, taking Charley's other arm, familiarly, "watching society go by, and you two were the first I knew. Being tired of my own company, I thought I would join you. Have a cigar?"

"You find Speckport rather slow, I suppose?" said

Charley, lighting his weed. "I should myself, if I had nothing to do."

"Oh, I am used to it; and," with a droll look, "I have discovered there is more than one pill to kill time, even in Speckport."

"Already! where do you mean?"

"Prince Street, for instance."

Charley laughed, and young McGregor smiled.

"You go there, do you? Well, I have lived all my life in Speckport, but I have never set foot over the threshold you mean, yet."

"Nor I," said young McGregor. "By George, wouldn't the old man look half-a-dozen ways at once if he thought I would dare look at it twice."

There was a smile on Captain Cavendish's face, half of amusement, half of contempt.

"I am going there now, and was about asking you to accompany me for an hour's amusement. Come on, better late than never."

Charley hesitated, coloring and laughing, but McGregor caught at the invitation at once.

"I say, Marsh, let us go! I've always wanted to go there, but never had a chance without the governor finding it out, and kicking up the deuce of a row!"

"I have the entree," said Captain Cavendish; "no one will be the wiser, and if they should, what matter? It is only to kill time, after all."

But still Charley hesitated, half laughing, half tempted, half reluctant. "That is all very well from Captain Cavendish, nephew of a baronet, and with more money than he knows what to do with; but it's of no use going to that place with empty pockets, and medical students, it is proverbial, never have anything to spare. No, I think you must hold me excused."

"Oh, confound it, Charley," exclaimed McGregor, impatiently, "I'll lend you whatever you want. Fetch him along, captain; what he says is only gammon."

"Perhaps," said the captain, with a cynical smile, "Mr. Marsh has conscientious scruples—some people have, I am told. If so——"

He did not finish the sentence, but the smile deepened. That mocking smile did more to overthrow Charley's resolution than any words could have done. He turned at once in the direction of Prince Street: "The only scruples I know anything about relate to weights and measures, and I believe these are in a dram. I have a couple of hours before dinner; so until then, I am at your service, captain."

The trio turned into Prince Street—a quiet street, with staid rows of white houses, and only one of any pretension, at one of its quiet corners. Captain Cavendish ran up the steps, with the air of a man perfectly at home, opened the outer door and rang the bell. There were few people passing, but Charley and McGregor glanced uneasily about them, before going in, and closed the street door after them with some precipitation.

Charley had told the captain he was at his service for two hours, but over four passed before the three issued forth again. Charley looked flushed, excited, and in high spirits, so did Alick McGregor; but Captain Cavendish, though laughing, was a trifle serious, too. "I had no idea you were such an adept, Mr. Marsh," he was saying, " but you must give me my revenge. Better luck next time."·

"All right," said Charley, in his boyish way, " whenever you like, now that the ice is broken. What do you say, Mac?"

"I'm your man. The sooner the better, as I intend keeping on until I make a fortune on my own account. Would not the governor stare if he knew the pile I made this morning."

As they passed into Queen Street, the town clock struck three. Charley looked aghast.

"Three o'clock! I had no idea it was two. Won't they be wondering what has become of me at home. I feel as though I should like my dinner."

"Dine with me," said the captain; "I ordered dinner at half-past three, and we will be in the nick of time."

The two young Speckportians accepted the invitation, and the three went up crowded Queen Street together.

Streaming down among the crowd came Miss Cherrie

Nettleby. One kid-gloved hand uplifted her silken robe, and displayed an elaborately embroidered under-skirt to the admiring beholder; the other poised a blue parasol; and, gorgeous to behold, Miss Nettleby flashed like a meteor through Speckport. All the men spoke to her— all the women turned up their fair noses and sailed by in delicate disdain. Charley blushed vividly at sight of her.

"Don't blush, Charley," drawled young McGregor, "it's too young-lady-like, but I suppose you can't help it any more than you can being in love with her. Good afternoon, Miss Cherrie."

Miss Cherrie smiled graciously, made them a bow that ballooned her silk skirt over the whole sidewalk, and sailed on. Charley looked as if he should like to follow her, but that was next to impossible, so he walked on.

"Cherrie comes out to show herself every afternoon," explained Alick; "you don't know her, Captain Cavendish, do you?"

"I have seen her before, I think. A very pretty girl."

"Charley thinks so—don't you, old fellow? Half the young men in the town are looney about her."

"I must make her acquaintance, then," said Captain Cavendish, running up the hotel steps. "The girl that all are praising is just the girl for me. This way, gentlemen."

While the triad sat over their dinner and dessert, Miss Nettleby did her shopping—that is, she chatted with the good-looking clerks over the counter, and swept past the old and ugly ones in silent contempt. Cherrie was in no hurry; she had made up her mind before starting to go through every drygoods store in Speckport, and kept her word. It was growing dusk when the dress was finally bought, cut off, and paid for—a bright pink ground, with a brighter pink sprig running through it.

"Shall we send it, Miss Nettleby?" insinuated the gentlemanly clerk, tying it up with his most fascinating smile.

"Of course," said Cherrie, shaking out her skirts with an air; "Mr. Nettleby's, Redmon Road. Good evening, Mr. Johnston."

4

Cherrie was soliloquizing as she gained the street.

"Now, I do wonder if he'll be home. They have tea at six, I know, and it's only a quarter to six, now. I can say I want a book, and he'll be sure to come home with me. I must see that new teacher."

Walking very fast Cherrie reached Cottage Street as the clocks of Speckport were chiming six, and the laborers' bells ringing their dismissal. Catty Clowrie was standing in her own doorway, but Cherrie did not stop to speak, only nodded, and knocked at Mrs. Marsh's door. Betsy Ann opened it and Cherrie walked into the sitting-room, where a fire burned, warm as the afternoon had been, and Mrs. Marsh, with a shawl about her and a novel in her hand, swayed to and fro in her rocking-chair. Miss Rose in the parlor was trying her new piano, which Natty had ordered that morning, and which had just come home.

"Dear me!" said Mrs. Marsh, looking up from the book and holding out her hand, "is it you, Cherrie? How do you do? Sit down."

Cherrie did so.

"I've been out all the afternoon shopping for Miss Natty, and I thought I would call here before I went home to ask you for another book. That last one was real nice."

"Of course. What were you buying for Natty?"

"Oh, it was only a calico dress for Midge; it's being sent up. Mrs. Marsh, who's that playing the piano?"

"That's Miss Rose, Natty's teacher. Have you seen her yet?"

"No. How nice she plays. Don't she?"

"She plays very well. And so you liked that last book—what's this it was—'Regina,' wasn't it?"

"Yes," said Cherrie; "and oh, it was lovely. That earl was so nice, and I liked Regina, too. What's that you're reading?"

"This is 'Queechy'—a very good story. Did you ever read 'The Lamplighter?' I'll lend you that."

"Thank you, ma'am," said Cherrie. "It's getting late. I suppose I must go."

"Stay for tea," said Mrs. Marsh, who liked Cherrie;

"it's all ready, and we are only waiting for Charley. I don't see where he's gone too; he wasn't home to dinner, either."

"I saw him this afternoon," said Cherrie; "him and young McGregor and Captain Cavendish were going up Queen Street."

"Was he? Perhaps they had dinner together there. How did you know Captain Cavendish, Cherrie?"

"I saw him at Redmon. He was up all yesterday forenoon. I guess he is after Miss Natty."

Mrs. Marsh smiled and settled her cap.

"Oh, I don't know. Take off your things, Cherrie, and stay for tea. It's of no use waiting for Charley. Betsy Ann, bring us the teapot, and call Miss Rose."

Cherrie laid aside her turban and lace, and was duly made acquainted with Miss Rose. Cherrie had heard the new teacher was pretty, but she had hoped she was not so very pretty as this, and a pang of jealousy went through her vain little heart. She had stayed for tea, hoping Charley would partake of that repast with them, and afterward escort her home; but it commenced and was over, but that young gentleman did not appear.

Miss Rose played after tea, and Cherrie lingered and lingered, under pretense of being charmed; but it got dark, and still that provoking Charley did not come. Cherrie could wait no longer, and a little cross and a good deal disappointed, she arose to go.

"You will perish in that lace mantle," said Miss Rose, kindly. "You had better wear my shawl; these spring nights are chilly."

Cherrie accepted the offer, rolled her lace up in a copy of the "Speckport Spouter," and started on her homeward journey. The street lamps were lit, the shop windows ablaze with illumination, and the cold, keen stars were cleaving sharp and chill through the blue concave above. A pale young crescent moon shone serene in their midst, but it might have been an old oil-lamp for all Miss Nettleby cared, in her present irate and vexed frame of mind. But there was balm in Gilead; a step was behind her, a man's step, firm and quick; a tall form was making rapid headway in her direction. Cherrie looked behind, half frightened, but there was no mistaking that commanding presence, that military stride, in the handsome face with the thick black mustache, looking down upon her. Cherrie's heart was bounding, but how was he to know that.

"I knew it was you, Cherrie," he said, familiarly. "Are you not afraid to take so long and lonely a walk at this hour ?"

"I couldn't help it," said Cherrie, all her good humor returning. "There was no one to come with me. I was down at Mrs. Marsh's, and Charley wasn't home."

"I don't want you to go to Mrs. Marsh's, and I am glad Charley wasn't home."

"I didn't go to see Charley," said Cherrie, coquettishly. "I wanted a book, and I wanted to see Miss Rose. Do you know where Charley is ?"

"He is up at Redmon."

"And you are going there, too, I suppose."

"I am going to see you home, just now. Let me carry that parcel, Cherrie, and don't walk so fast. There's no hurry, now that I am with you. Cherrie, you looked like an angel this afternoon, in Queen Street."

As we do not generally picture angelic beings in shot silks and blue parasols, not to speak of turban hats, it is to be presumed Captain Cavendish's ideas on the subject must have been somewhat vague. Cherrie obeyed his injunction not to hurry, and it was an hour before they reached the cottage.

Captain Cavendish declined going in, but stood in the shadow of the trees, opposite the house, tattling to her for another half hour, then shook hands, and went to Lady Leroy's, where he and Charley and Mr. Blake were to spend the evening.

Val and Charley were there before him, the former having but just entered. The captain had not seen Val, but Val had seen the captain, and watched him now with a comical look, playing the devoted to Nathalie.

In Mrs. Leroy's mansion there was no lack of rooms —Natty had two to herself—sleeping-room adjoining the old lady's, and a parlor adjoining that. In was in this parlor Natty received her own friends and visitors, and there the three gentlemen were now. Natty's rooms were the only light and cheerful ones in the vast, gloomy old house, and Natty had fitted them up at her own expense. Delicate paper on the walls; pretty drawings and landscapes, in water-colors, the work of her own artistic fingers, hung around; a lounge, cushioned in chintz; an arm-chair, cushioned in the same; attractive trifles of all sorts, books, a work-table, and an old piano—made the apartment quite pleasant and home-like. The only thing it wanted was a fire; for it was essentially a bleak house, full of draughts—but a fire in any room save her own was a piece of extravagance Lady Leroy would not hear of. So the gentlemen sat in their overcoats; and Lady Leroy, who had been wheeled in, in her arm-chair, looked more like an Egyptian mummy than ever.

Midge sat behind her, on her hunkers, if you know what that is; her elbows on her knees, her chin between her hands, glaring balefully on Captain Cavendish, making himself fascinating to her young mistress. If that gallant young officer had ever heard the legend of the Evil Eye, he might have thought of it then, with Midge's malignant regards upon him.

Lady Leroy, who dearly loved gossip, was chattering like a superannuated magpie to Val and Charley. Mr. Blake was giving her what he knew of the captain's history.

"His uncle," said Val, "is a baronet—a Yorkshire baronet at that—and Captain Cavendish is next heir to the title. Meantime, he has nothing but his pay, which would be enough for any reasonable man, but isn't a tithe to him."

"And he wants a rich wife," said Lady Leroy, with a spiteful glance over at him. "Ah! I see what he's coming after. Natty!"

"Ma'am!" said Natty, looking up, and still laughing at some anecdote Captain Cavendish had been relating.

"What are you laughing at?" she said, sharply.

"Only at a story I have been listening to! Do you want anything?"

"Yes. Go into my room and see what time it is."

"We bring Time with us," said Mr. Blake, producing a watch as big as a small football; "it's five minutes to nine."

"Then it's my bedtime! Natty, go and make me my punch. Midge, wheel me in, and warm the bed. Young men, it's time for you to go."

Captain Cavendish and Val exchanged an amused glance and arose. Charley stepped forward and laid his hand on the arm-chair.

"I'll wheel you in, Mrs. Leroy. Stand clear, Midge, or the train will run into you. Go ahead, fellows, I'll be after you."

"You must not mind Mrs. Leroy's eccentricities, you know," said Natty, shaking hands shyly and wistfully at the front door with the captain. "Mr. Blake is quite used to it, and thinks nothing of it."

"Think better of me, Miss Marsh. I do not mind her brusqueness any more than he does; in proof whereof I shall speedily pay my respects at Redmon again. Good night!"

"Tell Charley to overtake us. Good night, Natty!" called Val, striding down the moon-lit avenue, and out into the road.

Captain Cavendish lit a cigar, handed another to his companion, took his arm and walked along, thinking. The Nettleby cottage was in a state of illumination, as they passed it; and the shrieks of an accordion, atrociously played, and somebody singing a totally different air, and shouts of laughter, mingling together, came noisily to their listening ears. Val nodded toward it.

"Cherrie holds a levee every night—the house is full now. Will you come in? 'All the more the merrier,' is the motto there."

"No," said the captain, shrinking fastidiously; "I have no fancy for making one in Miss Cherrie's menagerie."

"Does the objection extend to Miss Cherrie herself?" asked Mr. Blake, puffing energetically.

"What do I know of Miss Cherrie?"

"Can't say, only I should suppose you found out something while seeing her home an hour ago, and standing making love to her under the trees afterward."

Captain Cavendish took out his cigar and looked at him.

"Where were you?"

"Coming through the rye—I mean the fields. The next time you try it on, take a more secluded spot, my dear fellow, than the queen's highroad!"

"Oh, hang it!" exclaimed the young officer, impatiently; "it seems to me, Blake, you see more than you have any business to do. Suppose I did talk to the little girl. I met her on the road alone. Could I do less than escort her home?"

"Look here," said Val, "there is an old saying, 'If you have too many irons in the fire, some of them must cool.' Now, that's your case exactly. You have too many irons in the fire."

"I don't understand."

"Don't you? Here it is, then! This morning, bright and early, I saw you promenading the shore with Miss Rose. This evening, I saw you making up to Cherrie Nettleby; and, ten minutes ago, you were as sweet as sugar-candy on Natty Marsh. No man can be in love with three women at once, without getting into trouble. Therefore, take a friend's advice, and drop two of them."

"Which two?"

"That's your affair. Please yourself."

"Precisely what I mean to do; and now, Val, old boy, keep your own counsel; there's no harm done, and there will be none. A man cannot help being polite to a pretty girl—it's nature, you know; and, dear old fellow, don't see so much, if you can help it. It is rather annoying, and will do neither of us any good."

Perhaps Captain Cavendish would have been still more annoyed had he known Val was not the only witness of that little flirtation with Cherrie. As that young lady, when he left her, after watching him out of sight, was about crossing the road to go into the house, a voice suddenly called, "Hallo, Cherrie! How are you?"

Cherrie looked up greatly astonished, for the voice came from above her head. Was it the voice of a spirit? —if so, the spirit must have a shocking bad cold in the head, and inclined to over-familiarity at that. The voice came again, and still from above.

"I say, Cherrie! You put in a pretty long stretch of courting that time! I like to see you cutting out the rest of the Speckport girls, and getting that military swell all to yourself."

Cherrie beheld the speaker at last; and a very substantial spirit he was, perched up on a very high branch of a tree, his legs dangling about in the atmosphere, and his hands stuck in his trowsers.

"Lor!" cried Miss Nettleby, quite startled, "if it ain't that Bill Blair! I declare I took it for a ghost!"

Bill kicked his heels about in an ecstasy.

"Oh, crickey! Wasn't it prime! I ain't heard anything like it this month of Sundays. Can't he keep company stunning, Cherrie? I say, Charley's dished, ain't he, Cherrie?"

"How long have you been up there, you young imp?" asked Cherrie, her wrath rising.

"Long enough to hear every word of it! Don't be mad, Cherrie—Oh, no, I never mentions it, its name is never heard—honor bright, you know."

"Oh, if I had you here," cried Miss Nettleby, looking viciously up at him, "wouldn't I box your ears for you!"

"Oh, no, you wouldn't!" said Bill, swinging about. "How was I to know when I roosted up here that you were going to take a whack at courting over there. I was going over to Jim Tod's, and, feeling tired, I got up here to rest. I say, Cherrie? would you like to hear a secret?"

Cherrie would like nothing better, only before he told it, she would rather he got down. It gave her the fidgets to look at him up there. Bill got lazily down accordingly.

"Now, what's the secret?" asked the young lady.

"It's this," replied the young gentleman. "Do you know who Captain Cavendish happens to be?"

"I know he's an Englishman," said Cherrie; "all the officers are that."

"Yes; but you don't know who his folks are, I bet."

"No. Who are they? Very rich, I suppose?"

"Rich!" exclaimed Mr. Blair, contemptuously. "I say, Cherrie, you won't tell, will you? It's a secret."

"Of course not, stupid. Go on."

"Say, 'pon your word and honor."

"'Pon my word! Now go on."

"Well, then," said Bill, in a mysterious whisper, "he's —Queen Victoria's—eldest—son!"

"What!"

"I told you it was a secret, and it is. I heard him telling my boss—Blake, you know, and they didn't think I was listening. Queen Victoria, when she was a young woman, was married secretly to a duke, the Duke of Cavendish, and had one son. When her folks found it out—jimminy! wasn't there a row, and the Duke was beheaded for high treason, and she was married to Prince Albert. Now, you'll never tell, will you, Cherrie?"

"Never!" answered Cherrie, breathlessly. "Well?"

"Well, Captain Cavendish was brought up private, and is the right heir to the throne; and he expects his mother to leave it to him in her will when she dies, instead of the Prince of Wales. Now, if he marries you, Cherrie, and I am pretty sure he will before long—then you are Queen of England at once."

"Now, Billy Blair," said Cherrie, puzzled whether to believe his solemn face or not, "I do believe you're telling lies."

"It's true as preaching, I tell you. Didn't I hear 'em with my own cars. That chap's sure to be King of England some day, and when you're queen, Cherrie, send for Bill Blair to be your prime-minister. And now I must go—good night."

4*

CHAPTER VIII.

VAL TURNS MENTOR

ISS NATHALIE MARSH was not the only person in existence who took a violent fancy to the pretty, pale little school-mistress, Miss Rose. Before the end of the month, Speckport pronounced her perfection; though, to do Speckport justice, it was not greatly given to overpraise. Indeed, it was a common saying with the inhabitants that Speckport would find fault with an archangel, did one of these celestial spirits think fit to alight there, and the very person most vehement in this assertion would have been the first in the backbiting. Yet Speckport praised Miss Rose, and said their Johnnys and Marys had never got on so fast in their A B abs, before, and the little ones themselves chanted her praises with all their hearts. If she appeared in the streets, they rushed headlong to meet her, sure of a smile for their pains. They brought her flowers every morning, and a reproachful look was the severest punishment known in the schoolroom. The old women dropped their courtesies; the old men pronounced her the nicest young woman they had seen for many a day, and the young men—poor things! fell in love.

There was some one else winning golden opinions, but not from all sorts of people. Only from young ladies, who were ready to tear each other's dear little eyes out, if it could have helped the matter : and the man was Captain George Cavendish. Speckport was proud to have him at its parties; for was he not to be a baronet some day? and was his family in England, their Alma Mater, not as old as the hills, and older? But he was an expensive luxury. Their daughters fell in love with him, and their sons spent their money frightfully fast with him; and all sons or daughters got in return were fascinating smiles, courtly bows, and gallant speeches. He was not a marrying man,

that was evident; and yet he did seem rather serious with
Nathalie Marsh. Miss Marsh was the handsomest girl in
Speckport; she would be the richest, and she was for
certain the only one that ever had a grandfather—that is,
to speak of: in the course of nature they all had, perhaps;
but the grandfathers were less than nobody—peddlers, rag-
men, and fish-hawkers. But her father and grandfather
had been gentlemen born; and it is well to have good
blood in one's veins, even on one side. So the young
ladies hated Miss Marsh, and were jealous of each other;
and that high-stepping young heiress laughed in their
face, and walked and talked, and rode and sailed, and
sang and danced with Captain Cavendish, and triumphed
over them like a princess born.

It was June, and very hot. Speckport was being
grilled alive, and the dust flew in choking simooms.

Cool through all the heat, Captain Cavendish walked
up Queen Street in the broiling noonday sun. Charley
Marsh and Alick McGregor walked on either side of him,
like that other day on which they had met Cherrie; and
Charley's face was flushed and clouded, and young
McGregor's drawn down to a most lugubrious length.
They had just come from Prince Street—an every-day
resort now; and Charley and McGregor seldom left it of
that late without clouded expression. Captain Cavendish
was laughing at them both.

"All in the downs!" he cried; "nonsense, Marsh.
One would think you were ruined for life."

"I soon shall be at this rate. I owe you a small
fortune now."

"Only fifty pounds," said the captain, as carelessly as
if it were fifty pence, "a mere trifle."

"And I owe you twice as much," said young Mc-
Gregor, with a sort of groan; "won't there be the dickens
to pay when it's found out at home."

"Don't let them find it out, then," said Captain Cavendish, in the same off-hand manner.

"That's easily said. How am I to help it?"

"Your father has a check-book—help yourself."

"That would be killing the goose that lays the golden

eggs," said Charley. " Let the old man find that out and good-bye to Aleck's chance of ever seeing Prince Street again. Here are my quarters—no use asking you in to hear the row old Leach will make at my delay, I suppose."

He nodded, with his own careless laugh, and entered the office of Doctor Leach. Captain Cavendish looked at his watch.

" Half-past eleven ! I believe I owe your people a call, McGregor ; so *en avant !*"

Miss Jeannette McGregor was at home, and received the captain and her brother in her boudoir, a charming little room, with velvet-pile carpet, gilding, and ormolu, and medallion pictures of celebrated beauties set in the oval paneled walls. A copy of Longfellow, all gold and azure, was in her hand ; she had once heard Captain Cavendish express his admiration of the great American poet ; and having seen her brother and he coming up the front steps, she had arranged this little tableau expressly for the occasion. If there was one young lady in all Speckport who more than another sincerely hated Nathalie Marsh, or more sincerely admired Captain Cavendish, that one was Miss McGregor. She had long been jealous of Natty's beauty, but now she detested her with an honest earnestness that, I think, only women ever feel. She kissed her whenever they met ; she invited her to every party they gave ; she made calls at Redmon : and she hated her all the time, and could have seen her laid in her coffin with the greatest pleasure. It is a very common case, my brethren ; Judas Iscariot was not a woman, but kisses after his fashion are very popular among the gentler sex.

" Evangeline," said Captain Cavendish, taking up her book ; " I always liked that, but never half so well as since I came to Speckport."

" Because you saw Miss Marsh in the character," said Jeannette, laughing, as young ladies must, in these cases.

" Miss Marsh took her character very vell, but that is not the only reason why I shall long remember that night."

A glance accompanied this speech that brought a glow

to Miss McGregor's cheek and a flutter to her heart. Captain Cavendish was a clever man. He had more irons in the fire than even Val knew of, and allowed none of them to cool; and it does take a clever man to make love discreetly to half-a-dozen women at once.

"Natty looked stunning that night," put in Aleck; "she is the handsomest girl in Speckport."

"You think so—we all know that," said Jeannette, flashing a spiteful glance at him; "you have been making a simpleton of yourself about her for the last two years. Why don't you propose at once."

"Because she wouldn't have me," blurted honest Alick; "I wish to heaven she would! I would soon do the popping."

"Faint heart never won fair lady; take courage and try," said the captain.

Jeannette looked at him with her most taking smile.

"Are you quite sincere in that, Captain Cavendish?"

"Quite! Why not?"

"Oh, nothing! Only rumor says you are going to carry a Bluenose bride back to Merrie England."

"Perhaps I may. You are a Bluenose, are you not, Miss Jeannette?"

Before Jeannette could answer, a sort of shout from Alick, who was at the window, took their attention. Miss McGregor looked languidly over.

"Oh, how noisy you are! What is it, pray?"

The door-bell rang loudly.

"It's Natty herself and Laura Blair. You ought to have seen Natty driving up, captain; she handles the ribbons in tiptop style, and that black mare of Blair's is no joke to drive."

Before he had finished speaking, the door opened, and a servant showed in the two young ladies. Miss Jeannette sprang up with the utmost effusion, and kissed each on both cheeks.

"You darling Natty! It is ages since you were here. Laura, how good it is of you to fetch her! for I know it must have been you."

"So it was," said Laura, shaking hands with Captain

Cavendish. "I haven t time, I haven't time, is always her cry. I tell her there will be time when we are all dead—won't there, captain?"

"I presume so, unless at the loss of Miss Laura Blair the whole economy of creation blows up with a crash."

"And so you see," said Laura, sitting down on a chair, and flirting out her skirts all around her, "I drove up to Redmon this morning, with a great basketful of English strawberries the size of crab-apples, as a coaxer to Lady Leroy; and through their eloquence, and the promise of another, got her to let Natty come to town with me on business."

"On business;" said Captain Cavendish; "that means shopping."

"No, sir, it doesn't; it means something serious, and that you must take share in. You, too, Jeannette, and you, Alick, if we run short."

"Thank you," said Alick, "what is it?"

"Why, you know," began Miss Blair, with the air of one about entering upon a story, "there's that Mrs. Hill—you know her, Alick?"

"What! the wife of the pilot who was drowned in the storm last week?"

"That's the one," nodded Laura. "Well, she's poor —Oh, dear me! ever so poor, and her two children down in the measles, and herself half dead with rheumatism. I shouldn't have known a thing about it only for Miss Rose. I do declare Miss Rose is next door to an angel; she found her out, and did lots of things for her, and told me at last how poor she was, and asked me to send her some things. So then I made up this plan."

"What plan?" inquired Jeannette, as Laura stopped for want of breath, and Nathalie sat listening with an amused look.

"Oh, didn't I tell you? Why, we're going to have a play, and every one of us turn into actors; admission, half a dollar. Won't it be grand?"

"And the play is Laura's own," said Nathalie; "nothing less than the adventures of Telemachus dramatized."

" That is delightful," said Jeannette, with sparkling eyes. " Have I a part, Laura ?"

" To be sure, and so has Natty, and myself, and Captain Cavendish, and Val Blake, and Charley Marsh, and as many more as we want. The new wing that pa has built to our house is just finished, and, being unfurnished, will make a lovely theater. Only a select number of tickets will be issued, and the place is sure to be crowded. The proceeds will be a little fortune to Mrs. Hill."

" You should have given Miss Rose a part, as she was the head of it," suggested Alick.

" She wouldn't have it. I tried hard enough, but she was resolute. She is such a timid little thing, you know, and she would make a lovely nymph, too."

" What part have you assigned me ?" inquired Captain Cavendish.

" Being a soldier and a hero, you are Ulysses, of course ; Charley is Telemachus ; Val is Mentor—fancy Val with flowing white hair and beard, like an old nanny-goat. Jeannette, you will be Calypso ; Natty will take Eucharis ; I, Penelope. I wanted Miss Rose to be Eucharis—the part would have suited her so well."

" I don't believe it would come natural to Charley to make love to her," said Alick ; " he'll have to, won't he, if he is Telemachus ?"

" You must change the casts, Miss Blair," said the captain, decidedly. " If Telemachus is to do the love-making, I must be Telemachus. Mr. Marsh and I must change."

" You would make such a nice Ulysses," said Laura, meditatingly, while Nathalie blushed ; " but please yourself. You must all spend the evening at our house, and when the whole *dramatis personæ* are gathered, we can discuss and settle the thing for good, fix the rehearsal and the night of the play. Don't fail to come."

" You need not be in a hurry," said Jeannette, as Laura rose and was sailing off ; " stay for luncheon."

" Couldn't possibly—promised to leave Natty back safe and sound in an hour, and it only wants ten minutes now. If we fail one second, she will never get off for rehearsals. Remember, you are all engaged for this evening."

The two long parlors of the Blairs were pretty well filled that night with young ladies and gentlemen, and a very gay party they were. There was so much laughing and chaffing over it, that it was some trouble to settle preliminaries; but Laura was intensely in earnest, and could see nothing to laugh at, and Captain Cavendish coming gallantly to her aid, matters were arranged at last. Charley Marsh, who was a Rubens on a small scale, undertook to paint the scenery, superintend the carpenters and the machinery of the stage. The young ladies arranged the costumes; everybody got their parts in MS.; rehearsals were appointed, and some time before midnight the amateurs dispersed. In the June moonlight, the English officer drove Nathalie home, and it was not all theatricals they talked by the way. There was a good deal of trouble about the thing yet, now that it was finally started. In the first place, there was that tiresome Lady Leroy, who made a row every time Natty went to rehearsal, and required lots of strawberries, and jellies, and bottles of old wine, to bring her to reason. Then they bungled so in their parts, and wanted so much prompting, and Miss Elvira Tod, sister to the Rev. Augustus, who was tall and prim, and played Minerva, objected to wearing a tin shield, and wanted to keep on her hoops.

"Now, Miss Tod," expostulated Laura, ready to cry, "you know the goddess Minerva always is painted with a breastplate, to conceal her want of a bust; and as for your skeleton, you would be a nice goddess with hoops—wouldn't you?"

On the whole, things progressed as favorably as could be expected; and the eventful night was announced, tickets were issued and eagerly bought, and Speckport was on the qui vive for the great event. When the appointed night came, the impromptu theater was crowded at an early hour, and with nothing but the upper-crust, either; the military band, which formed the orchestra, played the

"Nymph's Dance" ravishingly, and amid a breathless hush, the curtain rose.

Mrs. Hill, the destitute widow, was made happy next day by some twenty pounds, the produce of the play, and Speckport could talk of nothing else for a week. The Speckport Spouter even went into personalities. "Miss Nathalie Marsh," that journal said, "as Eucharis, astonished every one. The fire, the energy, the pathos of her acting could not be surpassed by the greatest professionals of the day. Captain Cavendish, as the hero, performed his part to the life—it seemed more like reality than mere acting; and Mr. C. Marsh as Ulysses, and Miss Laura Blair as Penelope, were also excellent."

On the morning after this laudatory notice appeared in the Spouter, a young gentleman, one of the employees of that office, walked slowly along Queen Street, his hands thrust deep in his coat-pockets, his cap very much on one side of his head, and his face lengthened to preternatural solemnity. The young gentleman was Bill Blair; and that he had something on his mind was evident, for his countenance was seriously, not to say dismally, meditative. Reaching the office, he walked deliberately up-stairs, entered the outer room, swung himself nimbly up on the handiest stool, and began flinging his legs about, without the ceremony of removing his cap. Mr. Clowrie, the only other occupant of the apartment, looked at him over his desk with a frown.

"I thought Mr. Blake told you to be here at half-past six this morning, and now it's a quarter past eight," began Mr. Clowrie; "if I was Blake, I would turn you out of the office."

"But you ain't Blake!" retorted Master Blair; "so don't ruffle your fine feathers for nothing, Jakey! If you had been up till half-past one this morning, perhaps you wouldn't be any spryer than I am.".

"What kept you up till that time? Some devilment, I'll be bound."

"No, it wasn't," said Bill; "our folks, the whole crowd but me, streaked off to the theatre; so as I couldn't see the fun of playing Robinson Crusoe at home, I just went over to Jim Tod's to have a game of all-fours, and a look at the pups, and they're growing lovely. I didn't mean to stay long, but some of the rest of the fellows were there, and Jim had a box of cigars, and a bottle of sherry he had cribbaged out of the sideboard, and it was all so jolly I'll be blowed if it didn't strike twelve before we knew where we were."

" Well, now you've come, go to work, or there will be a precious row when the boss comes."

" Blake won't row," said Bill, nodding mysteriously ; " but I know where there will be one before long. Cracky, won't there be a flare-up when it's found out !"

Mr. Clowrie laid down his pen and looked up.

" When what's found out ?"

" That's my secret," replied Bill, with a perfect shower of mysterious nods. " I saw the rummiest go last night when I was coming home ever you heard tell of."

" I don't believe it," said Jake, disdainfully ; " you're always finding mare's-nests, and a lot they come to when all's done !"

" Jake, look here ! you won't tell, will you ?"

" Bosh ! go to work. What should I tell for ?"

" Well, then," said Bill, lowering his voice, " I've found out who stole that hundred pounds from old McGregor."

" What ?"

" You remember that hundred pounds old McGregor had stole a week ago, and that went so mysteriously ? Well, I've found out who took it."

" You have !" cried Mr. Clowrie, excited ; " why, there's a reward of fifty dollars out for the thief !"

Bill nodded again.

" I know it, but I ain't going to apply. You won't tell--honor bright !"

" I won't tell ! who was it ?"

" Don't faint if you can ! It was his own son, Alick !"

" Wha-a-t !"

" I tell you it was ; I heard him say so myself, last night."

Mr. Clowrie sat thunderstruck, staring. Master Blair went on :

"Charley Marsh is in the mess too—I don't mean about the money-stealing, mind! but him and Sandy Mc-Gregor are galloping the road to ruin at a 2.40 rate!"

"What do you mean?"

Bill looked round as if fearful the very walls would hear him.

"They go to Prince Street, Jake! I met them coming out of a certain house there past twelve o'clock last night!"

"By ginger!" exclaimed Mr. Clowrie, aghast. "You never mean to say young McGregor stole the money to gam—"

"Hu-sh-sh! I wouldn't have it found out through me for the world. It's all the work of that dandified officer; he was with them in a long overcoat, but I knew him the minute I clapped eyes on him. They were talking about the bank-note, and the captain was laughing and smoking away as jolly as you please; but I saw Charley's face as they passed a gas-lamp, and I swear he was as white as a ghost!"

"I suppose he'd been losing."

"I reckon so, and Alick didn't look much better. That captain's a regular scape—he's after Cherrie Nettleby as regular as clock-work now."

Mr. Clowrie scowled suddenly, but Bill clattered on:

"I saw him twice last night; once before I met them in Prince Street. It was about nine, and Cherrie was with him. There the two of them were standing, like Paul and Virginny, at the gate, making love like sixty! That Cherrie's the preciousest fool that ever drew breath, I do think. Why don't you——"

He stopped short in consternation, for the door swung open and Val strode in, and, as he had done once before, collared him. With the other hand he turned the key in the lock to keep out intruders, and Bill fairly quaked, for Val's face looked ominous.

"Now, look you, Master Bill Blair," he began, in a tone exceedingly in earnest, "I have been listening out there for some time, and I have just got this to say to you: if ever I find you repeat it to mortal man or woman, as long as you live, I'll break every bone in your body! Do you hear that?"

Yes, Master Bill heard, and jerked himself free with a very red and sulky face.

"Don't forget, now!" reiterated Val; "I'll thrash you within an inch of your life, as sure as your name's Bill! And you, Clowrie, if you want to keep yourself out of trouble, take my advice and say nothing about it. Now get to work, you, sir, and no more gossiping."

Val strode off to his own room, and sat down to look over a file of exchanges, and read his letters. But he could neither read nor do anything else with comfort this morning. The boy's gossip had disturbed him more than he would have owned; and at last, in desperation, he pitched all from him, seized his hat, and went out.

"I played Mentor the other night on the stage. I think I'll try it in real life. Confound that Cavendish; why can't he let the boy alone? I don't mind McGregor; he's only a noodle at best, and the old man can afford to lose the money; but Charley's another story! That Cherrie, too! The fellow's a scoundrel, and she's a—! Oh, here she comes!"

Sure enough, tripping along, her blue parasol up, her turban on, a little white lace vail down, a black silk mantle flapping in the breeze, a buff calico morning-wrapper, with a perfect hailstorm of white buttons all over it, sweeping the dust, came Miss Nettleby herself, arrayed as usual for conquest. The incessant smile, ever parting her rosy lips, greeted Val. Cherrie always kept a large assortment of different quality on hand for different gentlemen. Val greeted her and turned.

"Where are you going, Cherrie?"

"Down to Mrs. Marsh's. I've got a book of hers to return. How's Miss Jo?"

"She's well. I'll walk with you, Cherrie; I have something to say to you."

His tone was so serious that Cherrie stared.

"Lord, Mr. Blake! what is it?"

"Let us go down this street—it is quiet. Cherrie,

does Captain Cavendish go to see you every evening in the week?"

"Gracious me, Mr. Blake!" giggled Cherry, "what a question!"

"Answer it, Cherrie."

"Now, Mr. Blake, I never! if you ain't the oddest man! I shan't tell you a thing about it!"

"He was with you last night, was he not?"

"It's none of your business!" said polite Cherrie; "he has as much right to be with me as any one else, I hope. You come yourself sometimes, for that matter."

"Yes; but I don't make love to you, you know."

"It wouldn't be any use for you if you did," said Miss Cherrie, bridling.

"It's a different case altogether," said Val; "you and I are old friends—he is a stranger."

"He's not! I've known him more than five weeks! If you only came to preach, Mr. Blake, I guess you had better go back, and I'll find Mrs. Marsh's alone."

"Cherrie, I want to warn you—the less you have to do with Captain Cavendish the better. People are talking about you now."

"Let 'em talk," retorted Miss Nettleby, loftily; "when Speckport stops talking the world will come to an end. I'll just do as I please, and talk to whom I like; and if everybody minded their own business, it would be better for some folks."

· With which the young lady swept away majestically, leaving Mr. Blake to turn back or follow if he pleased. He chose the former, and walked along to Dr. Leach's office. Charley was standing, looking out of the window, and whistling a tune.

"Hallo, Val!" was his greeting, "what brings you here? Want a tooth pulled, or a little bleeding, or a trifle of physic of any kind? Happy to serve you in the absence of the doctor."

"No, I don't want any physic, but I have come to give you a dose. Are you alone?"

"Quite. Leach went to visit a patient ten minutes ago. What's the matter?" —

"Everything's the matter! What's this I hear you have been about lately?"

"Turning actor—do you mean that? Much obliged to you, Val, for the puff you gave me in yesterday's Spouter."

"No, sir, I don't mean that! Isn't Alick McGregor a nice fellow to rob his own father and you his aider and abettor? Fine doings that!"

Charley fairly bounded.

"Oh, the d——! Where did you find that out?"

"Never mind, I have found it out; that is enough!"

"Is it known? Who else knows it?"

"Two that are not quite so safe to keep it as I am! No, I won't tell you who they are. Charley, what are you coming to?"

"The gallows, I suppose; but I had no hand in that. If McGregor took the money, it was his own doings, and his father could spare it."

"What did he want of it?"

"Am I his keeper? How should I know?"

"You do know! When did you turn gambler, Charley?"

Charley turned round, his face white.

"You know that, too?"

"I do! McGregor stole the hundred pounds to pay a gambling-debt to Captain Cavendish. And you—where does your money come from, Marsh?"

"I don't steal it," said Charley, turning from pale to red; "be sure of that!"

"Come, my boy, don't be angry. You know I don't deserve that speech; but surely, Charley, this sort of thing should not go on. Where will it end?"

"Where, indeed?" said Charley, gloomily. "Val, I wish you would tell me how you found this out?"

"Pshaw! do you really expect to go in and out of the most notorious gambling-house in Speckport, at all hours of the day and night, and it not be discovered? You ought to know this place better."

"That is true; but how did that infernal business of McGregor's leak out? No one knew it but ourselves."

"It has leaked out, and is known to two persons, who may blow on you all at any moment."

"And I wanted to keep it from Natty. Val, old fellow, do tell me who they are."

"You know I won't; it would do no good. Charley, I wish you would stop in time."

"Stuff! it's no hanging matter after all. Dozens go there as well as I!"

"You won't give it up, then?"

"Not until I win back what I have lost. My coffers are not so full that I can lose without trying to win it back. Don't talk to me, Blake, it's of no use; win I must, there is no alternative. Won't Alick go into white horror when he finds the murder's out?"

Val turned to leave.

"You're going, are you?" said Charley. "I need hardly tell you to keep dark about this; it will only mar, not mend matters, to let it get wind. Don't look so solemn, old boy, all's not lost that's in danger."

Val said nothing—what was the use? He passed out and went home to his domain.

"I knew how it would be," he said to himself, going along: "but I have done my duty, and that's satisfactory. I'll keep my eye on you, Captain Cavendish, and if ever I get a chance, won't I play you a good turn for this!"

CHAPTER IX.

WOOED AND WON.

"AND if ever I find her going prancing round with him any more," said Lady Leroy, clawing the air viciously with her skinny fingers, "or letting him come home with her again, I'll turn her out of doors, I will, as sure as your name's Midge."

"Which it isn't," said Midge ; "for I was christened
Prisciller. And as for turning her out, you know right
well, ma'am, you can never get along without her, so
where's the good of your gabbing."

The dialogue between mistress and maid took place,
of course, in the former's room, which she rarely left.
Midge was preparing her ladyship's dinner, all the cooking
being done in the chamber, and all the edibles being kept
under lock and key, and doled out in ounces. Midge and
Lady Leroy fought regular pitched battles every day over
the stinted allowance awarded her ; and Natty had to come
to the resue by purchasing, from her own private purse,
the wherewithal to satisfy Midge. No other servant would
have lived at Redmon on the penurious wages the old lady
grumblingly gave, probably on no wages at all, considering
the loneliness of the place, its crabbed and miserly mistress,
and hard work ; but Midge stayed through her love of
Nathalie, and contradicted and bickered with Lady Leroy
from morning till night. In the days when the Marshes
were rich and prosperous, Midge had been a hanger-on of
the household, doing pretty much as she pleased, and coming and going, and working or loafing as she liked. She
had saved Charley's life once, nearly at the risk of her
own, and loved him and Nathalie with a depth of self-
sacrificing and jealous tenderness few would have given
her credit for. Nathalie was good to her always, consid-
erate and kind, putting up with her humor and querulousness, and ready to shield her from slights at any time.
Midge scolded the young lady roundly on many an occasion, and Natty took it good-humoredly always. She was
out now, and Lady Leroy's wrath had been kindled by
something that had happened the preceding night, and
which she had found out through Cherrie Nettleby, for
Midge told no tales. Captain Cavendish, contrary to her
express orders, had seen Nathalie home from a little sociable at her mother's. Val, Miss Jo, Laura Blair, Catty
Clowrie, Jeannette and Alick McGregor, Charley, and
Captain Cavendish only had been there ; for some sick
pauper had sent for Miss Rose, and she had gone, glad to
escape. Cherrie had seen the captain and Miss Marsh

pass the cottage, and, spiteful and jealous, had tattled next morning. Lady Leroy disliked Captain Cavendish—she did most people for that matter, but she honored him with especial aversion. Nathalie had gone off after breakfast to Speckport, to attend to her music-pupils and visit the school. Cherrie had come in afterward to retail the town-gossip, and had but just departed; and now the old lady was raging to Midge.

"I tell you, Midge, I don't like him!" she shrilly cried, "I don't like him, and I don't want him coming here."

"No more don't I," retorted Midge, "I'd go to his hanging with the greatest pleasure; but where's the odds? He don't care whether we like him or not; he only laughs and jeers at both of us, so long as she does."

"It ain't her he likes," said Lady Leroy, "it's my money, my money, that I've pinched and spared to save, and that he thinks to squander. But I'll be a match for him, and for her too, the ungrateful minx, if she thinks to play upon me."

"She ain't an ungrateful minx, ma'am!" sharply contradicted Midge; "she's better nor ever you were or ever will be! She lives shut up here from one week's end to t'other, slavin' herself for you, and much she gets for it! She can do what she likes with the money when you're dead!"

Lady Leroy's face turned so horribly ghastly at this speech that it was quite dreadful to look at. The thought of death was her nightmare, her daily horror. She never thought of it at all if she could, and thus forcibly reminded, her features worked for a moment as if she had a fit. Even Midge grew a little scared at what she had done.

"There, ma'am!" she cried, "you needn't go into fits about it. My speaking of it won't make you die any sooner. I dessay you're good for twenty years yet, if your appetite holds out!"

The old woman's livid face grew a shade less deathlike.

"Do you think so, Midge? Do you think so?"

"Oh, I think so fast enough! Folks like you always is sure to spin out till everybody's tired to death of 'em.

5

Here's your dinner ready now; so swallow it, and save your breath for that!"

The sight of her meals always had an inspiring effect on the mistress of Redmon, and Natty was for the moment forgotten. Perhaps it might have spoiled her appetite a little had she seen the way that young lady was returning home, and in what company. Not walking discreetly along Redmon road, and not alone. In the pretty boat, all white and gold, with the name "Nathalie" in golden letters—the boat that had been poor Alick McGregor's gift—a merry little party were skimming over the sunlit waves, reaching Redmon by sea instead of land. The snow-white sail was set, and Nathalie Marsh was steering; the sea-wind blowing about her tangled yellow curls, fluttering the azure ribbons of her pretty hat, deepening the roses in her cheeks, and brightening the starry eyes. She sang as she steered, "Over the Sea in my Fairy Bark," and the melodious· voice rang sweetly out over the wide sea. Near her Captain Cavendish lounged over the side, watching the ripples as they flew along in the teeth of the breeze, and looking perfectly content to stay there forever. Beside him sat Laura Blair, and, near her, Miss Jo Blake. Laura was often with Miss Jo, whom she liked, partly for her own sake—for she was the best-natured old maid that ever petted a cat—and partly for her brother's, whom Miss Blair considered but one remove from an angel.

The quartet had "met by chance, the usual way," and Nathalie had invited him to have a sail. She had rowed herself to town in her batteau, but the sail back was inconceivably pleasanter. As the batteau ran up on the beach below Redmon, Natty did not ask them to the house, but no one was surprised at that. They accompanied her to the gate, Captain Cavendish slinging the light oars over his shoulder.

"And you will be at the picnic day after to-morrow, without fail," Laura was saying to Nathalie.

"Can't promise," replied Natty. "Mrs. Leroy may take it into her head to refuse permission, and I have been out a great deal lately."

"I don't care," said Laura, "you must come! If Mrs.

Leroy turns inexorable, I will go up with a basket of
oranges and let them plead in your behalf. You see,
captain, we have to 'stay that old lady with flagons and
comfort her with apples' when we want Natty very badly,
and she turns refractory."

"All the oranges in Seville would not be thrown away
in such a cause. By all means, Miss Marsh, come to the
picnic."

Speckport was famous for its picnics, and excursions
by land and water. This one was the first of the season,
and was to be held on Lady Leroy's grounds—a pretty
high price having to be paid for the privilege.

"There won't be any fun without you, Natty," said
Miss Jo; "I won't hear of your absenting yourself at all.
Is Miss Rose to have a holiday on the occasion?"

"I offered her one, but she declined; she did not care
for going, she said."

"What a singular girl she is!" said Laura, thoughtfully; "she seems to care very little for pleasure of any
kind for herself; but the poor of Speckport look upon
her as an angel sent down expressly to write their letters,
look after them in sickness, make them beef-tea, and teach
their children for nothing. I wish you would make her
go to the picnic, Natty, and not let her mope herself to
death, drudging in that horrid school-room."

Captain George Cavendish, leaning on the oars he had
been carrying, seemed not to be listening. He was looking dreamily before him, seeing neither the broad green
fields with the summer sunlight sleeping in sheets of gold
upon them, nor the white, winding, dusty highroad, nor
the ceaseless sea, spreading away and away until it kissed
the horizon-sky, nor tall Miss Blake, nor even the two
pretty girls who talked. It had all faded from before
him; and he was many a mile away in a strange, foreign-
looking city, with narrow, crooked streets, filled with
foreign-looking men and women, and priests in long black
sontanes, and queer hats, and black nuns and gray nuns,
and Notre Dame nuns and Sisters of Charity and Mercy,
all talking in French, and looking at each other with dark
Canadian eyes. He was back in Montreal, he saw the

Champ-de-Mars, the Place d'Arme, the great convents, the innumerable churches with their tall crosses pointing to the heaven we are all trying to reach, and he saw himself beside one—fairer in his eyes than all the dusky Canadian beauties in the world, with their purple-black hair and great flashing black eyes. "Winnie! Winnie! Winnie!" his false heart was passionately crying, as that old time came back, and golden-haired, violet-eyed Nathalie Marsh was no more to him than if she had been but the fantasy of a dream. He had flirted and played the lover to scores; played it so long and so often that it had become second nature, as necessary as the air he breathed; but he had only loved one, and he seemed in a fair way of going on to the end. He had been a traitor, but he could not forget. The girl he had jilted was avenged if she wished for vengeance: no pang he had ever given could be keener than what he felt himself.

A laugh aroused him, a merry, girlish laugh. He awoke from his dream with a start, and found them all looking at him.

"So you have awoke at last," laughed Laura. "Three times have I told you we were going, and there you stood, staring at empty space, and paying no more attention than if you were stone-deaf. Pray, Captain Cavendish, where were you just now?"

Before he could answer, the gate against which Nathalie leaned was pushed violently open, and the thick dwarfish figure and unlovely face of Midge was thrust out—not made more prepossessing by an ugly scowl.

"Miss Natty," she shrilly cried, "I want to know if you mean to stand here all day long? It's past two now, and when you go up to the house, perhaps the old woman won't give it you—and serve you right, too!" added Miss Midge, sotto voce.

"So late!" Nathalie cried, in alarm. "I had no idea of it! Good-bye, Miss Jo; good-bye, Laura. I must go!"

She had smiled and nodded her farewell to the captain, and was off like a dart. Midge slammed the gate in their faces, and went sulkily after.

In considerable consternation, Nathalie ran up-stairs and into the awful presence of the mistress of the house. She knew well she was in for a scolding, and was bracing herself to meet it.

Lady Leroy had never been so furiously angry since the first day the young lady had entered beneath her roof, and the storm burst before Miss Marsh was fairly in the room. Such a tempest of angry words, such a tornado of scolding, such a wrathful outbreak of old woman's fury, it has been the ill-fortune of but few to hear. Nathalie bore it like a heroine, without flinching and without retreat, though her cheeks were scarlet, and her blue eyes flashing fire. She had clinched one little hand involuntarily, and set her teeth, and compressed her lips, as if to force herself not to fling back the old woman's rage in her face; but the struggle was hard. Passionate and proud Nathalie's nature was, but the fiery steeds of pride and passion she had been taught, long ago, at her father's knee, to rein with the curb of patience. But I am afraid it was not this Christian motive that held her silent always under Lady Leroy's unreasonable abuse. Ambition was the girl's ruling passion. With her whole heart and soul she longed for wealth and power, and the first of these priceless blessings, in whose train the second followed, could only be obtained through this vituperative old beldame. If Nathalie let nature and passion have their way, and flung back fury for fury, she would find herself incontinently turned out of doors, and back again, probably, the day after, in that odious school-room, wearing out her heart, and going mad slowly with the dull drudgery of a poor teacher's life. This motive in itself was strong enough, but of late days another and a stronger had been added. If she were Miss Marsh, the schoolmistress, Captain Cavendish, the heir of a baronet, would doubtless admire, and—have nothing whatever to say to her; but Miss Marsh, the heiress of Redmon and of Lady Leroy's thousands, was quite another thing. He was poor now, comparatively speaking; she knew that—how sweet it would be to lay a fortune at the feet of the man she loved! Some day in the bright future he would lay a

title at her fair feet in return, and all her dreams of love,
and power, and greatness, would be more than realized.
Not that Nathalie for one instant fancied George Cavendish sought her for her fortune—she would have flung
back such a suspicion furiously in the face of the profferer
—but she knew enough of the fitness of things to be aware
that, however much he might secretly adore her rose-hued
cheeks, golden hair, and violet eyes, he could never marry
a portionless bride.   On this tiger-cat old Tartar, then, all
these sweet dreams depended for their fruition; and she
must pocket her pride, and eat humble pie, and make no
wry faces over that unpalatable pastry.   She must be patient and long-suffering now, that she might reign like a
princess royal hereafter; so while Lady Leroy stormed
and poured no end of vials of wrath on her ward's unfortunate head, that young person only shut her rosy lips
the harder, and bated her breath not to reply.   We are so
strong to conquer ourselves, you see, when pounds, shillings, and pence are concerned, and so weak and cowardly
to obey the commands of One who was led "as a lamb to
the slaughter, and who opened not his mouth."   So Nathalie stood, breathing quick, and only holding herself from
flying at her tormentress by main force, and Lady Leroy
stormed on until forced to stop from want of breath.

"And now, Miss," she wound up, her little eyes glaring on the young lady, "I should like to know what
you've got to say for yourself."

"I have nothing to say," replied Nathalie, speaking
for the first time.

"Oh, I dare say not!   All I say goes in one ear and
out t'other, doesn't it, now?   Ain't you ashamed of yourself, you minx?"

"No!" quietly said Nathalie.

Mrs. Leroy glared upon her with a look of fury, horribly revolting in that old and wrinkled face.

"Do you mean to say you'll ever do it again?   Do
you mean to say you'll go with that man any more?   Do
you mean to say you defy and disobey me?   Tell me!"
cried Lady Leroy, clawing the air as if she were clawing

the eyes out of Captain Cavendish's handsome head, "tell me if you mean to do this!"

"Yes!" was the fiery answer flaming in the girl's crimson cheeks and flashing eyes, "I defy you to the death!" But prudence sidled up to her and whispered, "Heiress of Redmon, remember what you risk!" and so—oh, that I should have to tell it!—Nathalie Marsh smoothed her contracted brows, vailed the angry brightness of her blue eyes under their sweeping lashes, and steadily said:

"Mrs. Leroy, you know I have no wish to willfully defy or disobey you. I should be sorry to be anything but true and dutiful to you, and I am not conscious of being anything else now."

"You are—you know you are!" the old woman passionately cried. "You know I hate this man—this spendthrift, this fortune-seeker, this smooth-spoken, false-hearted hypocrite! Give up this man—promise me never to speak to him again, and then I will believe you!"

Nathalie stood silent.

"Promise," shrilly screamed Lady Leroy, "promise or else——"

She stopped short, but the white rage in her distorted face finished the sentence with emphasis.

"I will promise you one thing," said Nathalie, turning pale and cold, "that he shall not come to Redmon any more. You accuse him unjustly, Mrs. Leroy—he is none of the things you say. Do not ask me to promise anything else—I cannot do it!"

What Lady Leroy would have said to this Nathalie never knew; for at that moment there came a loud knock at the front door, and Miss Marsh, only too glad to escape, flew down to answer it.

The alarm at the outer door proved to come from Charley Marsh; and Nathalie stared, as she saw how pale and haggard he looked—so unlike her bright-faced brother.

"What ails you, Charley?" she anxiously asked. "Are you sick?"

"Sick? No! Why should I be sick?"

"You are as pale and worn-looking as if you had been ill for a month. Something has gone wrong."

"I have been up all night," said Charley, omitting, however, to add, playing billiards. "That's why. Nathalie," hurriedly and nervously, "have you any money? I can't ask before that old virago up-stairs."

"Money! Yes, I have some. Do you want it?"

"I want you to lend me as much as you can, for a short time. There!" he said, impatiently, "don't begin asking questions, Natty. I want it particularly, and I will pay you back as soon as I can. How much have you got?"

"I have nearly twenty pounds, more or less. Will that do?"

"It will help. Don't say anything about it, Natty, like a good girl. Who's in?"

"No one but Mrs. Leroy. Won't you come up?"

"I must, I suppose. Get the money while I am talking to her, and give it to me as I go out. What a solemn face you have got, Natty!"

He laughed as he spoke—Charley's careless, boyish laugh, but Nathalie only sighed as they ascended the stairs together.

"Mrs. Leroy has been scolding ever since I came from town. If ever a fortune was dearly bought, Charley, mine will be."

"Paying too dear for your whistle—eh? Never mind, Natty! it can't last forever, and neither can Lady Leroy."

All the shadow had gone from Charley's brow, and the change was magical. Whether it was the promise of the money, or his natural elasticity of spirit rebounding, he knew best; but certainly when he shook hands with the mistress of the domain, the sunshine outside was not brighter than his handsome face. Mrs. Leroy rather liked Charley, which is saying folios in the young man's favor, considering how few that cantankerous old cat admitted to her favor—but every one liked Charley Marsh.

While Nathalie went to her own room for the money, Nathalie's brother was holding Mrs. Leroy spell-bound with his brilliant flow of conversation. All the gossip and scandal of Speckport was retailed—business, pleasure, fashion, and fights, related with appetizing gusto; and where the reality fell short, Mr. Marsh called upon his lively imagination for a few extra facts. The forthcoming picnic and its delights were discussed, and Charley advised her to strain a point and be present.

"Midge can wheel you about the field, you know, in your chair," said Charley. "You won't take cold—the day's sure to be delightful, and I know every one will enjoy themselves ten times better for having you there. You had better come. Val Blake and I will carry you down stairs!"

To the astonishment of Nathalie, Mrs. Leroy assented readily to the odd proposition; and Charley departed, having charmed the old lady into utter forgetfulness, for the time being, of her antipathy to Captain Cavendish. Speckport could talk of nothing for a week beforehand but the picnic—the first of the season. All Speckport was going, young and old, rich and poor. Admission, twenty-five cents; children, half price.

The Redmon grounds, where the picnic was to be held, were extensive and beautiful. Broad velvety fields, green lanes, among miniature forests of fragrant cedar and spruce, and all sloping down to the smooth, white sands of the beach, with the gray sea tramping dully in, and the salt spray dashing up in your face. And "I hope it won't be foggy! I do hope it won't be foggy!" was the burden of every one's cry; the fog generally choosing to step in and stay a week or two, whenever Speckport proposed a picnic. How many blinds were drawn aside in the gray and dismal dawn of that eventful morning, and how many eager pairs of eyes, shaded by night-cap borders, turned anxiously heavenward; and how delightedly they were drawn in again! for, wonderful to tell, the sky was blue and without a cloud, and the sun, rising in a canopy of rose and amber, promised all beholders a day of unremitting sunshine.

Before nine o'clock the Redmon road was alive with people—all in gorgeous array. Before ten, the droves of men, women, and children increased fourfold, and the

dust was something awful. The sun fairly blazed in the
sky; had it ever shone so dazzlingly before, or was there
ever so brilliantly blue a sky, or such heaps and heaps of
billows of snowy white, floating through it? Before eleven,
that boiling seaside sun would have grilled you alive only
for the strong sea-breeze, heaven-sent, sweeping up from
the bay. Through fiery heat, and choking dust, the cry
was "still they come," and Redmon grounds swarmed with
people, as the fields of Egypt once swarmed with locust.
A great arch of evergreens surmounted the entrance-gate,
and the Union Jack floated loyally over it in the morning
sunshine. The clanging of the band and the roll of the
drum greeted your delighted ears the moment you entered
the fairy arch, and you found yourself lost and bewildered
in a sea of people you never saw before. The swings
were flying with dizzying velocity, young belles went up
until the toes of their gaiters nearly touched the firmament,
and your head reeled to look at them. Some two or three
hundred ladies and gentlemen were tripping the light
fantastic toe to the inspiring music of a set of Irish quadrilles; and some eight hundred spectators were gathered
in tremendous circles about them, looking on, gazing as if
never in all their lives had so glorious and wonderful a
vision as their fellow-sinners jigging up and down,
dazzled their enchanted eyes. The refreshment tents were
in such a crowded and jammed and suffocating state, that
you could see the steam ascending from them as from an
escape-valve; and the fair ones behind the tables, bewildered by two dozen clamorous voices, demanding the
attention of each one at once, passed pies and tarts, and
sandwiches and soda water, and coffee and cakes frantically
and at random, and let little boys feed in corners unnoticed,
and were altogether reduced to a state of utter imbecility
by the necessity of doing half a dozen things at one and
the same time. Pink and blue, and yellow and green
ribbons fluttered, and silks and muslins and bareges trailed
the grass and got torn off the waist by masculine bootheels; and the picnic was too delightful for description,
and, over all, the fiery noonday July sun blazed like a
wheel of fire, and the sea wind swept up fresh and deli-

cious, and the waves sang their old song down on the shore, and no one listened to their mystic music or wondered, like poor little Paul Dombey, what they were saying.

No one! Yes, there was one sitting on a green bank, all alone, who had been very busy all morning until now, arranging tables and waiting on hungry pleasure-seekers, making little boys and girls behave themselves, and swinging little people who could get no one else to attend them. The breeze that set the tall reeds and fern at fandangoing waved her black barege dress, and flung back the little black lace vail falling from her hat. Tired and hot, she had wandered here to listen to the waves and to the tumult behind her.

What were the thoughts of the man who leaned against a tall tamarack tree and watched the reclining figure as a cat does a mouse? There are some souls so dark that all the beauty of earth and heaven are as blank pages to them. They see without comprehending, without one feeling of thoughtfulness for all the glory around them. Surely it were better for such to have been born blind. This man saw no wide sea spreading before him, glittering as if sown with stars. There was more to him worth watching in one flutter of that thin black dress on the bank than in all the world beside, and he stood and watched with his eyes half closed, waiting until she should see him.

He had not to wait long. Some prescience that something out of harmony with the scene was near, made her restless. She rose up on her elbow, and looked round—a second after, her face flushed, she was up off the grass and on her feet. The man lifted his hat and advanced.

"Pardon my intrusion, Winnie—Miss Rose, and—no, no—I beg you will not go!"

She had made to turn away, but he himself interposed —something of agitation in his manner, and it was but rarely, indeed, Captain George Cavendish allowed himself to be agitated. She stopped gently enough, the surprised flush faded out from her face—that pretty, pale face, tranquil as face could be, was only very grave.

"If you have anything to say to me, Captain Cavendish, please to say it quickly. I do not wish to be seen here."

"Is it such a disgrace, then, to be seen for one poor instant with me?" he said, bitterly.

She did not reply, save by an impatient tapping of one foot on the grass, and a backward glance at the crowded grounds.

"Winnie!" he broke out, passionately, as if stung by her manner, "have you turned into a flirt? Have you entirely forgotten what is past? You cannot—you cannot have ceased altogether to care for me, since I cannot, do what I will, forget you!"

Miss Rose looked at him—steadily, quietly, gravely, out of her brown eyes. If he had hoped for anything, that one look would have shivered his air-castles as a stone shivers brittle glass.

"I told you once before, Captain Cavendish, that such words from you to me were insults. The past, where you are concerned, is no more to me than if you had never existed. I have not forgotten it, but it has no more power to move me than the waves there can move those piles of rock. No! I have not forgotten it. I look back often enough now with wonder and pity at myself, that I ever should have been the idiot that I was."

His face turned crimson at the unmistakable earnestness of her words.

"Then I need scruple or hesitate no longer," he said, launching his last pitiful shaft. "I need hesitate no longer, on your score, to speak the words that will make one who is rich and beautiful, and who loves me, happy. I came here willingly to make what atonement I could for the past, by telling you beforehand, lest the shock of my marriage——"

He stopped in actual confusion, but raging inwardly at the humiliation she was making him feel—this poor little pale schoolmistress, whom he could have lifted with one hand and flung easily over the bank. She was smiling as she listened to him, a smile not of mockery or disdain, only so gallingly full of utter indifference to him.

"There is no atonement necessary," she said, with that

conscious smile still hovering on her lips; "none, I assure you. I have no hard feelings toward you, Captain Cavendish, nothing to resent or forgive. If I was an idiot, it was my own fault, I dare say, and I would not blot out one day that is gone if I could. Marry when you will, marry as soon as you please, and no one will wish you joy more sincerely on your wedding day than I."

It half-maddened him, that supreme indifference, that serene face. He knew that he loved her, herself, and her alone; and while he fancied her pining and love-lorn, he was very well satisfied and quite complacent over her case. But this turn of the story was a little too mortifying to any man's pride to stand, and the man a lady-killer by profession at that.

"I don't believe it," he said, savagely, "you have not forgotten—you cared for me too much for that. I did not think you could stoop to falsehood while playing the rôle of a saint."

Miss Rose gave him a look—a look before which, with all his fury, he shrank. She had turned to walk away, but she stopped for a moment.

"I am telling no falsehood, Captain Cavendish: before I stoop to that, I pray I may die. You know in your heart I mean what I say, and you know that you believe me. I have many things to be thankful for, but chief among them, when I kneel down to thank God for his mercies, I thank him that I am not your wife!"

She walked slowly away, and he did not follow her; he only stood there, swallowing the bitter pill, and digesting it as best he might. It was provoking, no doubt, not to be able to forget this wretched little school-ma'am, while she so coolly banished him from her memory—so utterly and entirely banished him; for Captain Cavendish knew better than to disbelieve her. He had jilted her, it is true, as he had many another; but where was his triumph now? If he could only have forgotten her himself; but when the grapes were within his reach, he had despised them, and now that they grew above his head, and he did want them, it was exasperating that he could not get them.

"Pah!" he thought bitterly, "what a fool I am! I

could not marry her were she ever so willing now, any more than I could then. This cursed debt is dragging me to—perdition—I was going to say, and I must marry a fortune, and that soon. Nathalie Marsh is the richest girl in Speckport, therefore I shall marry Nathalie Marsh. She is ten times more beautiful than that little quakeress who is just gone; but I can't love her, and I can't forget the other."

Captain Cavendish leaned against the tamarack a long time, thinking. The uproar behind him and the roar of the surf on the shore blended together in a dull, meaningless tumult in his ears. He was thinking of this marriage de convenance he must make, of this bride he must one day take home to England. He was a gambler and a spendthrift, this man, over head and ears in debt, and with no way but this one of ever getting out of it. From his friends in England? He had no friends in England on whom he could rely. His only rich relative, his uncle, the baronet, had taken it into his head, at the age of fifty-five, to get married; and what was more, there was an heir, a young gentleman of five months old, between him and the baronetcy. His commission had been purchased by his uncle, and it seemed all he need ever expect from him. He had never seen service, and had no particular desire to see any. He must marry a rich wife—there was no alternative—and he knew the power of his handsome face extremely well. He had no fear of a refusal; there was no use in delaying; he would make the heiress of Redmon happy that very day.

The sun was going down behind the waves, in an oriflamme of gold and crimson and purple and rose, flushing the whole sky with its tropical beauty, when the young officer turned away to seek for his future wife. As if his thoughts had evoked her she was coming toward him, and all alone; her white dress floating mistily about her, all her golden curls hanging damp and loose over her shoulders, and her cheeks flushed with the heat. She had taken off her hat, and was swinging it by its azure ribbons, as she came up; and she looked so beautiful that the young Engglishman thought that it would not be so very dreadful a thing to sell himself to this violet-eyed sultana after all.

"Truant!" said Nathalie, "where have you been all the afternoon? I thought you had gone away."

"And all the time I have been standing here, like Patience on a monument, wishing you would come up."

"Did you want me, then?"

"When do I not want you?"

Nathalie laughed, but she also blushed. "Then you should have gone in search of me, sir. Mrs. Leroy wants to go home now, and I must go with her."

"But not just yet. I have something to say to you, Nathalie."

And so here, in the hot warmth of the red sunset, the old, old story was told—the story that has been told over and over again since the world began, and will be told until its end, and yet is ever new. The story to which two little words, yes or no, ends so ecstatically, or gives the deathblow. It was yes this time; and when Nathalie Marsh, half an hour after, went home with Mrs. Leroy, she was wondering if there was one among all those thousands —one in all the wide world—as happy as she!

The last red glimmer of the sunset had faded out of the sky, and the summer moon was up, round and white and full, before the last of the picnickers went home. And in its pale rays, with his hands in his pockets, and a cigar between his lips, Captain Cavendish went home with Cherrie Nettleby.

CHAPTER X.

FAST AND LOOSE.

MISS NATHALIE MARSH was not the only young lady who received a proposal that memorable picnic-day. Flashing in and out among the other belles of Speckport, and eclipsing them all as she went, the belle of the bourgeois, par excellence, came Miss Cherrie Nettleby, quite dazzling to look at in a pink and white plaid silk, a white lace mantle, the blue parasol you wot of, the turban-hat, with a long white feather streaking round it, and the colored white lace vail over her blooming brunette face. Miss Nettleby had fawn-colored kid gloves, an embroidered kerchief sticking out of her pocket; and, to crown all, two or three yards of gold chain around her neck, and hanging ever so far below her waist. An overgrown locket and a carnelian cross dangled from the chain; and no giddy young peacock ever strutted about prouder of its tail than did the little black-eyed belle of these glittering fetters. She had only received the chain, and locket, and cross the night before; they had come in a box, with a huge bouquet, under the weight of which a small black boy staggered, with the compliments of Captain Cavendish, and would Miss Nettleby do him the honor of accepting them? Nettleby did him the honor, and was not able to sleep a wink all night for rapture. A gold chain had been the desire of her heart for many and many a day; and, at last, some good fairy had taken pity on her and sent it, with the handsomest man in Speckport for her ambassador. Cherrie's ecstasies are not to be described; a chain from any one would have been a delightful gift; but from Captain Cavendish, one smile from whom Cherrie would have given all the rest of her admirers for, delightedly. She had hugged Ann in her transports, until that young person, breaking indignantly from her, demanded to know if she had gone mad; and she had dressed for the picnic, expecting to have the young Englishman devotedly by her side the whole day long, before the aggravated and envious eyes of all Speckport. But Cherrie had never made a greater mistake in all her life; the blue parasol, the pink silk, the white'lace mantle, and fawn-colored kid gloves were powerless to charm—Captain Cavendish never came near her. He had not come at all until late, and then he had driven in in the McGregor barouche, with the heiress of that house by his side, resplendent to look at; and he had walked about with her, and with Miss Laura Blair, and Miss Marsh, and sundry other young ladies, a step or two higher up the ladder of life than Miss Nettleby, but he had not once walked with her. He had passed her two or three times, as he could not very well help doing, since she had put herself straight in his way; and he had nodded and smiled, and walked deliberately on. Cherrie could have cried with chagrin; but she didn't, not wishing to redden her eyes and swell her nose there, and she consoled herself by flirting outrageously with everybody who would be flirted with.

As the afternoon wore on, Cherrie began to experience that fatigue which five or six hours' dancing in a blazing July sun is apt to engender, and informed her partner in the quadrille she was roasted to death. The partner—who was Mr. Charles Marsh, and who had been her most devoted all day—was leaning against a stout elderly gentleman as against a post, fanning himself with his straw wideawake, leisurely set that headpiece sideways on his brown locks and presented his arm.

"I thought you would come to that by-and-by, Miss Nettleby, in spite of your love of dancing. Quadrilles are all very well in December, but I can't say that I fancy them in the dog-days. Suppose we go down to the shore and get a whiff of fresh air."

Miss Nettleby put her fawn-colored kid-glove inside Mr. Marsh's coat-sleeve, and poising her azure parasol in the other hand, strolled with him to the beach. On their way, Nathalie, standing with Captain Locksley, young McGregor, and a number of other gentlemen and ladies, espied them, and her color rose and her blue eyes flashed at the sight.

"Egad! I think they'll make a match of it!" laughed Locksley. "Charley seems to be completely taken in tow by that flyaway Cherrie."

Nathalie said nothing, but her brow contracted ominously as she turned impatiently away.

"Oh, that's nothing," said the Reverend Augustus Tod; "it's the fashion to go with Cherrie, and Charley is ready to follow fashion's lead. The little girl will settle down some day, I dare say, into a sensible, hard-working fisherman's wife."

Even Nathalie laughed at the idea of Miss Nettleby hard-working and sensible; and that young lady and her escort sauntered leisurely on to the breezy seashore. The sun was dipping behind the western waves, the sky all flushed and radiant with the scarlet and golden glory of its decline, the blue sea itself flooded with crimson radiance. Even Mr. Marsh was moved to admiration of its gorgeous splendor.

"Neat thing in the way of sunsets, Cherrie," he remarked, taking out a cigar, and lighting it.

"What a nice magenta color them clouds is!" said Miss Nettleby, admiringly; "they would make a lovely dress trimmed with black braid. And that mauve cloud over there with the yellow edge, I should like to have a scarf of that."

"Well," said Charley, "I can't get you the mauve cloud, but if there's a scarf at all like it in Speckport you shall have it. By the way, Cherrie, where did you get that chain?"

"You didn't give it to me, anyhow," replied Miss Nettleby, tossing her turban. "I might wait a long time for anything before I got it from you."

"I didn't know you wanted one, or I might. I wish you wouldn't take presents from anybody but me, Cherrie."

"From anybody but you!" retorted Cherrie, with scorn. "I'd like to know the time you gave me anything, Charley Marsh?"

"Come now, Cherrie, I don't want to be mean, but that's a little too bad!"

"I suppose you're hinting at that coral set you sent me last week?" said Cherrie, in a resentful tone. "But, I can tell you, there's lots of folks, not a thousand miles off, would be glad to give me ten times as much if I would take it."

"Don't take their gifts, Cherrie; there's a good girl; it's not ladylike, you know; and some day you shall have whatever you want—when I am rich and you are my wife, Cherrie."

"The idea!" giggled Cherrie, her color rising, "your wife, indeed; I think I see myself!"

"Wouldn't you have me, Cherrie?"

He was still smoking, and still looking at the sunset—not seeing it, however. Poor Charley Marsh, light as was his tone, was exceedingly in earnest. Miss Nettleby stole a glance at him from under the blue parasol, not quite certain whether he were in jest or in earnest, and her silly little heart beating a trifle faster than was its wont.

"I suppose, Mr. Marsh," said the young lady, after a moment's deliberation, thinking it best to stand on her dignity, "you think it a fine thing to make fun of me; but I can tell you I ain't going to stand it, if you are a doctor, and me only a gardener's daughter. I think you might find something else to amuse you."

"I'll take my oath, Cherrie," said Charley, throwing his cigar over the bank, "I never was so much in earnest in all my life."

"I don't believe it," said Miss Nettleby.

"What's the reason you don't? Haven't I been going with you long enough? What did you suppose I meant?"

"I didn't suppose nothing at all about it. You aren't the only one that pays attention to me."

"No; but I don't think any of the others mean anything. I intend to marry you, Cherrie, if you'll consent."

Cherrie tossed her turban disdainfully, but in her secret heart she was in raptures. Not that she meant to accept him just then, with Captain Cavendish in the background; but neither had she the slightest intention of refusing him. The handsome Englishman had given her a gold chain, to be sure, but then he had also given her the cold shoulder all that day; and if things did not turn out with him as she could wish, Charley Marsh would do as a dernier resort. Cherrie liked Charley, and he could make her a lady; and if she failed in becoming Mrs. Cavendish, it would be a very nice thing to become Mrs. Marsh, and half the young ladies in Speckport would be dying of envy. Cherrie thought all this in about two seconds and a half.

"Well, Cherrie, have you nothing to say?" inquired Charley, rather anxiously.

"Mr. Marsh," said Miss Nettleby, with dignity, remembering how the heroine of the last novel she had read had answered in a similar case, "I require time to pon—ponder over it. On some other occasion, when I have seriously reflected on it, you shall have my answer."

Mr. Marsh stood aghast for a moment, staring at the young lady, and then went off into a fit of uproarious laughter.

"Well," demanded Cherrie, facing round, rather fiercely, "and what are you laughing at, sir?"

"Oh, I beg your pardon, Cherrie," said Charley, recovering from his paroxysm; "but really you did that so well that I——"

Charley came near going off again; but, seeing the black eyes flashing, recovered himself.

"Come, Cherrie, never mind Laura-Matilda speeches, but tell me, like a sensible little girl, that you like me, and by-and-by will be my wife."

"I'll do nothing of the sort!" cried Miss Nettleby, in a state of exasperation, "either now or at any other time, if I don't choose. You'll just wait for your answer, or go without."

She sailed away as she spoke, leaving Charley too much taken aback, not to say mortified, to follow her.

"Hang it!" was Mr. Marsh's exclamation, as he turned in an opposite direction; "the idea of getting such an answer from that girl! What would Natty say? She would think it bad enough my proposing at all, but to get such a reply."

Yet, even in the midst of his chagrin, he laughed again at the recollection of Miss Nettleby's speech—careless Charley, who never let anything trouble him long.

"She'll come to it, I dare say," he reflected, as he went along, "and I can wait. I do like her, she's such a pretty little thing, and good, too, in the main, though rather frivolous on the surface. Well, Miss Rose, how are you enjoying yourself?"

Miss Rose's fair, sweet face was rather a striking contrast after Cherrie's, but Charley was not thinking of that, as he offered her his arm. Cherrie in the distance saw the act, and felt a pang of jealousy.

"He's gone off with that pale-faced school-mistress, now," she thought, resentfully. "I dare say she'd be glad to catch him, if she could. Oh!"

She stopped short with an exclamation half suppressed. She had come upon Captain Cavendish leaning against a tall tree, and talking to Nathalie Marsh. Another jealous pang pierced the frivolous heart, and—I am sorry to tell it—she crept in close under the tree, with the blue parasol furled, and—yes, she did—she listened. Listened for over twenty minutes, her color coming and going, her breath bated, her hands clenched. Then she fluttered hurriedly off, just in time to escape them, as they walked away, plighted lovers.

There was a little clump of cedar-bushes, forming a sort of dell, up the side of the bank. Cherrie Nettleby fell down here in the tall grass, dashing the blue parasol down beside her, crumpling the turban, soiling the white feather, and smearing the pink dress, tore off the gold chain, and burst into such a passion of spiteful, jealous, and enraged tears, as she had never before shed in her life. To think that all her hopes should have come to this; that the gold chain was only a glittering delusion; all his pretty speeches and lover-like attentions only hollow cheats, and Nathalie Marsh going to be his wife! Cherrie seized the chain in a paroxysm of fury, as she thought of it, and hurled it over the bank.

"The hateful, lying, deceitful scamp," she passionately cried. "I hate him, and I'll go and marry Charley Marsh, just for spite."

Charley was not hard to find. He was playing quoits with a lot of other young Speckportians; and Miss Catty Clowrie was standing gazing admiringly on, and ready to talk to him between whiles. Cherrie tapped him on the arm with her parasol, and looked shyly up in his face with a rosy blush. But the shy look and the blush were exceedingly well got up, and Charley dropped the quoits with a delighted face.

"Cherrie! what is it? Have you made up your mind, then?"

"Yes, Charley! You didn't believe I was in earnest that time, did you? I do like you, and I will be your wife as soon as ever you like."

Did Miss Catty Clowrie, standing unheeded by, with ears as sharp as lances, hear this very straightforward avowal? She had flashed a keen, quick glance from one to the other; had dropped her vail suddenly over her face, and turned away. Neither noticed her.

Charley was in raptures, and might have fallen on Miss Nettleby and embraced her there and then, only that before that maiden had quite finished speaking, Nathalie confronted them, her face haughty, her step ringing, her voice imperious.

"Charley, Mrs. Leroy is going home, and desires you to come immediately and assist Mr. Blake."

"Oh, bother!" cried Charley, politely, "let her get some of the other fellows; I can't go."

"Charley!"

"Why can't she get McGregor, or some of the rest?" said Charley, impatiently; "don't you see I'm playing quoits, Natty?"

"I see you're doing nothing of the sort, sir, and I insist on you coming this instant! Don't trouble yourself about Miss Nettleby, she has legions of adorers here, who will only be too happy to attend her home."

Miss Marsh swept away like a young queen; her violet eyes flashing, her perfect lips curling. Charley turned to follow, saying, hurriedly, as he went:

"I'll be back in half an hour, Cherrie, wait for me here."

"Proud, hateful thing!" exclaimed Cherrie, apostrophizing the receding form of Miss Marsh; "she looked at me that time as if she scorned to touch me! Wait until I am her brother's wife, we will see who will put on mistress." From where she stood, Cherrie could see the party for Redmon come. Charley and Val Blake wheeled Mrs. Leroy in her chair of state over the grass, that mummy having consented to be exhumed for the occasion, and having been the chief curiosity and attraction of the picnic. Nathalie walked on one side, and Midge on the other, but Captain Cavendish did not make one of the party now, for the moment they were out of sight, that gallant officer hurriedly walked deliberately up to her. Cherrie tossed her turban again, and curled her lip suspiciously, not deigning to notice him by so much as a glance.

"Come, Cherrie, what's the matter?" he began, in a free and easy way; "how have I got into disgrace?"

"Oh, it's you, Captain Cavendish, is it?" said Cherrie, loftily, condescending to become aware of his presence, "I don't know what you mean."

"Nonsense, Cherrie! What is the matter? Come, now, be reasonable, and tell me what I have done."

"You haven't done anything to me," quite frigidly, though; "how could you?"

"That's precisely what I want to know. Where is that chain I saw around your neck a short time ago?"

"In my pocket. You had better take it back again. I don't want it."

Captain Cavendish stared. Miss Nettleby, grasping the parasol firmly, though the sun had gone down, and the moon was rising, with a very becoming glow in her cheeks, and bright, angry light in her eyes, looked straight before her, and addressed empty space when she spoke.

"There is some mystery here, and I am going to get at the bottom of it," he said, resolutely; "Cherrie, let me go home with you, and see if we cannot clear it up by the way."

"With me?" said Cherrie, stepping back, and looking at him disdainfully; "why, what would Miss Marsh say to that?"

A light broke on the captain.

"Miss Marsh! Why, what have I to do with Miss Marsh?"

"A great deal, I should think, after what passed between you over there on the beach."

"Cherrie! where were you? Not listening?"

"I was passing," said Miss Nettleby, stiffly, "and I chanced to overhear. It wasn't my fault if you spoke out loud."

Even Captain Cavendish stood for a moment nonplussed by this turn of affairs. He had no desire his proposal to Miss Marsh should become public property, for many reasons; and he knew he might as well have published it in the Speckport Spouter, as let Cherrie find it out. Another thing he did not want—to lose Cherrie; she was a great deal too pretty, and he fancied her a great deal too much for that.

"Cherrie, that was all an—an accident! I didn't mean anything! There are too many people looking at us here, to talk; but, if you will go home, I will explain by the way."

"No," said Cherrie, standing resolutely on her dignity, but trying to keep from crying, "I can't. I promised Mr. Marsh to wait for him."

"Oh, confound Mr. Marsh! Come with me, and never mind him."

"No, Captain Cavendish; I think I'll wait. Charley thinks more of me than you do, since he asked me to marry him this afternoon, and I am going to do it."

Captain Cavendish looked at her. He knew Cherrie's regard for truth was not the most stringent; that she would invent, and tell a fib with all the composure in life, but she was palpably telling no falsehood this time. He saw it in the triumphant flash of her black eyes, in the flush of her face, and set his teeth inwardly with anger and mortification. "How blessings brighten as they take their flight!" Never had Cherrie Nettleby looked so beautiful; never had her eyes been so much like black diamonds as now, when their light seemed setting to him forever. Captain Cavendish believed her, and resolved not to lose her, in spite of all the Charley Marshes in the world.

"So Marsh has asked you to be his wife, has he? Now, Cherrie, suppose I asked you the same question, what would you say?"

"You asked Miss Marsh to-day, and I think that's enough."

"I did not mean it, Cherrie. I swear I did not! I am fifty times as much in love with you as I am with her."

And Captain Cavendish was speaking truth. Humiliating as it is to say so of one's heroine, the black-eyed grisette was a hundred times more to his taste than the blue-eyed lady. Could they have changed places, he would have married Cherrie off-hand, and never given one sigh to Nathalie. It was the prospective fortune of that young lady he was in love with.

"Cherrie, you don't believe me," he said, seeing incredulity in her face, "but I swear I am telling the truth. Let me prove it—give up Charley Marsh and marry me!"

"Captain!"

"I mean it! Which of us do you like best—Marsh or I?"

"You know well enough," said Cherrie, crying. "I like you ever so much the best; but when I heard you asking Miss Natty, I—I——" here the voice broke down in good earnest, and Cherrie's tears began to flow.

Captain Cavendish looked hurriedly about him. The last rays of the sunset had burned themselves out, and

6

the moon was making for herself a track of silver sheen
over the sea.   The crowd were flocking homeward, tired
out, and there was no one near; but in the distance his
eagle eye saw Charley Marsh striding over the dewy
evening grass. Poor Charley! The captain drew Cherrie's
arm inside his own, and walked her rapidly away.
They were out on the Redmon road before either spoke
again.

"I did not mean one word of what I said to Miss
Marsh.   But I'll tell you a secret, Cherrie, if you'll never
mention it again."

"I won't," said Cherrie.   "What is it?"

"I should like to share her fortune—that is, you and
I—and if she thinks I am in love with her, I stand a good
chance.   I should like to be richer than I am, for your
sake, you know; so you must not be jealous.   I don't
care a straw for her, but for her money."

"And you do care for me?"

"You know I do!   Are you ready to give up Charley, and marry me?"

"Oh!" said Cherrie, and it was all she replied; but it
was uttered so rapturously that it perfectly satisfied him.

"Then that is settled?   Let me see—suppose we get
married next week, or the week after?"

"Oh! Captain!" cried the enraptured Cherrie.

"Then that is settled too.   What a little darling you
are, Cherrie!   And now I have only one request to make
of you—that you will not breathe one word of this to a
living soul.   Not a syllable—do you understand?"

"Why?" said Cherrie, a little disappointed.

"My dear girl, it would ruin us both!   We will be
married privately—no one shall know it but the clergyman
and—Mr. Blake."

"Mr. Blake?   Val?"

"Yes," said Captain Cavendish, gravely, "he shall be
present at the ceremony, but not another being in Speckport must find it out.   If they do, Cherrie, I will have to
leave you forever.   There are many reasons for this that
I cannot now explain.   You will continue to live at
home, and no one but ourselves shall be the wiser.   There,

don't look so disappointed; it won't last long, my darling. Let Charley still think himself your lover; but, mind you, keep him at a respectful distance, Cherrie."

They reached the cottage at last, but it took them a very long time. Captain Cavendish walked back to Speckport in the moonlight, smoking, and with an odd little smile on his handsome face.

"I'll do it, too," he said, glancing up at the moon, as if informing that luminary in confidence. "There's a law against bigamy, I believe; but I'll marry them both, the maid first, the mistress afterward."

CHAPTER XI.

HOW CAPTAIN CAVENDISH MEANT TO MARRY CHER- RIE.

THE clerk of the weather in Speckport might have been a woman, so fickle and changeable in his mind was he. You never could put any trust in him; if you did, you were sure to be taken in. A bleak, raw, cheerless, gloomy morning, making parlor fires pleasant in spite of its being July, and hot coffee as delicious a beverage as cool soda-water had been the day before; a morning not at all suited for constitutionals; yet on this cold, wet, raw, foggy morning Charley Marsh had arisen at five o'clock, and gone off for a walk, and was only opening the front-door of the little cottage as the clock on the sitting-room mantel was chiming nine. Breakfast was over, and there was no one in the room but Mrs. Marsh, in her shawl and rocker, beside the fire which was burning in the Franklin, immersed ten fathoms deep in the adventures of a gentleman, inclosed between two yellow covers, and bearing the euphonious name of "Rinaldo Rinaldi." Miss Rose had gone to school, Betsy Ann was clattering among the pots in the kitchen; the breakfast-table looked sloppy and littered; the room, altogether dreary. Perhaps it was his walk in that cheerless fog, but Charley looked as dreary as the room; his bright face haggard and pale, his eyes heavy, and with dark circles under them, bespeaking a sleepless night. Mrs. Marsh dropped "Rinaldo Rinaldi," and looked up with a fretful air.

"Dear me, Charley, how late you are! What will Doctor Leach say? Where have you been?"

"Out for a walk."

"Such a hateful morning—it's enough to give you your death! Betsy Ann, bring in the coffee-pot!"

Betsy Ann appeared with that household god, and a face shining with smiles and yellow soap, and her mistress relapsed into "Rinaldo Rinaldi" again. Charley seemed to have lost his appetite as well as his spirits. He drank a cup of coffee, pushed the bread and butter impatiently away, donned his hat and overcoat, the former pulled very much over his eyes, and set out for the office.

Charley had enough to trouble him. It was not only Cherrie's desertion, though that was enough, for he really loved the girl with the whole fervor and strength of a fresh young heart, and meant to make her his honored wife. He was infatuated, no doubt; he knew her to be illiterate, silly, unprincipled, false and foolish, a little dressy piece of ignorance, vanity, selfishness and conceit, or might have known it if he chose; but he knew, too, she was a beautiful, brilliant, bewitching little fairy, with good-natured and generous impulses now and then, and the dearest little thing generally that ever was born. In short, he was in love with her, and love knows nothing about common sense; so when he had seen her walk off the previous evening with Captain Cavendish, and desert him, he had leaned against a tree, feeling— heaven only knows how deeply and how bitterly. Once he had started up to follow them, but had stopped—the memory of a heavy debt contracted in Prince Street, owing to this man, and hanging like an incubus about his neck, night and day, thrust him back as with a hand of iron. He was in the power of the English officer, beyond redemption ; he could not afford to make him his enemy.

How that long morning dragged on, Charley never knew ; certainly his medical studies did not progress much. Poor and in debt, in love and deserted, those were the changes on which his thoughts rang. A sulky-faced clock, striking one, made him start. It was time to go home to dinner, and he arose and went out. As he opened the shop-door, he stopped short. Tripping gayly along the foggy and sloppy streets came Cherrie herself, her dress pinned artistically up, to display a brilliant Balmoral skirt, of all the colors of a dying dolphin ; her high-heeled boots clinking briskly over the pavement. Charley's foolish heart gave a great bound, and he stepped impulsively forward, with her name on his lips.

" Cherrie ?"

Cherrie had not seen him until he spoke, and she recoiled with a scream.

" Sir ! Charley Marsh ! how you scare me ! I wish you wouldn't shout out so sudden and frighten me out of my wits !"

" You may spare your hysterics, Cherrie," said Charley, rather coldly ; " you could stand more than that if Captain Cavendish was in question."

Cherrie laughed, and tripped along beside him with dancing eyes. She liked Charley, though in a far less degree than the dashing and elegant young officer, and was in a particularly good-natured state of mind that morning. There was more than her liking for Charley to induce her to keep good friends with him—the warning of the captain and her own prudence. Cherrie, faithless herself, had no very profound trust in her fellow-creatures. Until she was actually the captain's wife, she was not sure of him ; there is many a slip, she knew ; and if he failed her, Charley was the next best in Speckport. Therefore, at his insinuation, she only tossed her turbaned head after her coquettish fashion, until all her black curls danced a fandango, and showed her brilliant white teeth in a gay little laugh.

"Oh, you're jealous, are you?" she said. "I thought you would be!"

"Cherrie!"

"There, now, Charley, don't be cross! I just did it to make you jealous, and nothing else! I was mad at you for going off the way you did!"

"You know I could not help it!"

"Oh, I dare say not. I'm nobody beside Miss Natty! So, when Captain Cavendish came up and asked leave to see me home, I just let him! I thought it wouldn't do you any harm to be a little jealous, you know, Charley."

Charley's hopes were high again; but his heart had been too deeply pained for him to forget its soreness at one encouraging word. Something wanting in Cherrie, he could not quite define what, had often struck him before, but never so palpably as now. That want was principle, of which the black-eyed young lady was totally devoid; and he was vaguely realizing that trusting to her was much like leaning on a broken reed.

Cherrie, a good deal piqued, and a little alarmed by his silence, looked at him askance.

"Oh, you're sulky, are you? Very well, sir, you can just please yourself. If you've a mind to get mad for nothing, you may."

"Cherrie," Charley said, quite gravely for him, "do you think you did right last night? After promising to be my wife, to go off and leave me as you did?"

"I didn't, either!" retorted Cherrie; "it was you went off and left me."

"That was no fault of mine, and I didn't go with another young lady. Cherrie, I want you to promise me you will let Captain Cavendish see you home no more."

"I shall promise nothing of the sort!" cried Cherrie, with shrill indignation. "Because I promised to marry you, I suppose you would like me to live like a nun for the rest of my life, and not even look at any other man. I'll just do as I did before, Mr. Charley Marsh; and if you ain't satisfied with that, you may go and marry somebody else—Miss Rose, or Miss Clowrie—she'd have you, fast enough!"

"I don't want Miss Clowrie; I only want you, Cherrie; and if you cared for me, you wouldn't act and talk as you do."

Some of poor Charley's pain was in his voice and it touched the coquette's frivolous heart. She stopped, at a dry-goods store, for an encouraging word before entering.

"You know very well, Charley, I like you ever so much—a great deal better than I do any one else; but I can't help being pretty, and having the young men after me, and I hate to be cross to them, too. Come up to Redmon this evening, I haven't time to stop to talk now."

With which the little hypocrite made a smiling obeisance, and darted into the shop, leaving her lover to pursue his homeward way, a little lighter in the region of the heart, but still dissatisfied and mistrustful.

The afternoon was as long and dreary as the morning. Charley sat in the dismal little back-office, listening listlessly to the customers coming in and out of the surgery, to buy Epsom-salts and senna, or hair-oil and bilious pills; and the shopboy droning over a song-book, which he read half aloud, in a monotonous sing-song way, when alone, staring vacantly at the rotten leaves, and bits of chips and straw and paper fluttering about the wet yard in the chill afternoon wind. And still the fog settled down thicker, and wetter, and colder than ever; and when the shopboy came in a little after six, to light the flaring gas-jet—it was already growing dark—Charley arose, drearily, to go.

"What a long day it has been!" he said, gaping in the boy's face; "it seems like a week since I got up this morning. Where's the doctor?"

"Up to Squire Todd's, sir. The old gentleman's took bad again with the gout."

The lamps were flaring through the foggy streets as he walked along, and the few people abroad flitted in and out of the wet gloom, like shadowy phantoms. Queen Street was bright enough with the illumination from shop-windows, but the less busy thoroughfares looked dismal and deserted, and the spectral passers-by more shadowy than ever. As he was turning the corner of Cottage Street, one of these phantoms, buttoned up in an overcoat, and bearing an umbrella, accosted him in a very unphantomlike voice, and with a very unphantomlike slap on the shoulder.

"How are you, Marsh? I thought I should come upon you here!"

Charley turned round, and, with no particular expression of rapture, recognized Captain Cavendish.

"Good evening," he said, coldly; "were you looking for me?"

The captain turned and linked his arm within his own.

"I was. What became of you last night? We expected you at Prince Street."

"I made another engagement."

"You will be there to-night, of course? I owe you your revenge, you know."

"Which means," said Charley, with a laugh, that sounded strange and bitter from him, "you will get me some thirty or forty dollars more in your debt!"

"Talking of debt," said Captain Cavendish, in an indifferent matter-of-fact tone, "could you oblige me with a trifle on account—say twenty pounds?"

Charley silently produced his pocketbook, and handed over the twenty he had received from Nathalie a few days before. · The nonchalant young officer pocketed it as coolly as if it had been twenty pence.

"Thanks! One often needs a trifle of this sort on an occasion. Is this your house? Who is that playing? Not your sister?"

They had halted in front of the cottage, and could hear the sound of the piano from within.

"It is Miss Rose, I presume," said Charley, in the same cold voice; "will you come in?"

"Not now. You will be up at Prince Street for certain then to-night?"

Charley nodded, and entered the house.

At her own door stood Miss Catty Clowrie. She

was often standing there; and though she returned the captain's bow, it was after Charley she looked until he disappeared. There was no one in the sitting-room when he entered; his mother's rocking-chair was vacant, and Miss Rose was playing and singing in the parlor— touching the keys so lightly and singing so sweetly that it seemed more an echo of the wind and waves than anything else. The table was set for tea, and Betsy Ann was scouring knives in the kitchen, humming some doleful ditty at her work. There was a lounge under the window overlooking the bay, sullen and stormy to-night. Charley flung himself upon it, his arm across the pillow, his face lying in it, and listened in a vague and dismal way to the music. The song was weird and mournful, truly an echo of the wailing wind and sea.

"Come to supper, ma'am!" at this juncture shrilly pealed the voice of Betsy Ann at the foot of the stairs, to some invisible person above; "Mr. Charley's here, and the biscuit is getting cold."

The song died away, as if it had drifted out on the gale surging up from the black bay, and Mrs. Marsh crept shivering down stairs.

"Come in, Miss Rose," she said, looking in at the parlor door before entering the room; "tea is ready, and Charley is here."

Charley started up; and, as he did so, the front door unceremoniously opened, and Nathalie, wrapped in a large shawl, and wearing a white cloud about her head, stepped in, to the surprise of all.

"Gracious me! Natty! is it you?" cried her mamma, in feeble consternation, "whatever has taken you out such an evening?"

"What's the matter with the evening?" said Nathalie, kissing her and Miss Rose. "A little cold sea-fog is nothing new, that it should keep me in-doors. Good evening, Charley."

"It's not a good evening," said Charley; "it's a very bad one, and you deserve to get your death of cold for venturing out in it. Did the old lady send you?"

"No, indeed! I had hard work to get off. Is tea

6*

ready, mamma? I have had no dinner, and am almost famished."

Mrs. Marsh was profuse in her sympathy. Another cup and plate were laid, and the quartet sat down to tea. It was wonderful how Nathalie's bright presence radiated the before gloomy room; the laughing light of her violet eyes made sunshine of their own, and all her luxuriant golden hair, falling loose and damp, in curls short and long around her face and shoulders, never looked so much like silky sunbeams before.

"How did you get on in school to-day?" she was asking Miss Rose; "I could not get down. The picnic must have disagreed with Mrs. Leroy; for I never saw her so cross." ·

"I should say all the cake, and pastry, and nastiness of that sort she devoured, would have disagreed with a horse," said Charley; "it was a sight only to see Laura Blair cramming her."

"I got on very well," answered Miss Rose, smiling at Charley's remark, which was perfectly true; "but the day seems long, Miss Marsh, when you do not visit us, and the children seem to think so too. I have got a new music-pupil—little Vattie Gates."

"You will make your fortune, Miss Rose, if you are not careful," said Charley; "eight dollars per quarter from each of those music-pupils, beside your school-salary. What do you mean to do with it all?"

"I should say rather she will work herself to death," said Nathalie. "Do you want to kill yourself, Miss Rose, that you take so many pupils?"

"Dear me! I think it agrees with her," remarked Mrs. Marsh, languidly, stirring her tea; "she is getting fat."

Everybody laughed. Miss Rose was not getting very fat; but she certainly had gained flesh and color since her advent in Speckport, though the small face was still rather pale, and the small brow sometimes too thoughtful and anxious. As they arose from table, Miss Clowrie came in with her crotcheting to spend the evening, Natty went to the piano, Miss Rose, with some very unfancifullooking work in a dropsical work-basket, sat down at the window to sew while the last gray ray of daylight lingered in the sky, and Charley lounged on the sofa, beside Catty.

"What are you making, Miss Rose?" inquired Miss Clowrie, looking curiously at the small black figure, drooping over the work, at the window. Miss Rose laughed, and threaded her needle.

"You needn't ask," said Nathalie; "clothes for all the poor in Speckport, of course. Why don't you become a Sister of Charity at once, Miss Winnie?"

"I came very near it one time," smiled Miss Rose; "perhaps I may yet. I wish I could."

There was no mistaking the sincerity of her tone. Nathalie shrugged her shoulders—to her it looked like wishing for something very dreary and dismal indeed. The world seemed a very bright and beautiful place to the heiress of Redmon that foggy summer night.

"Why don't you become one, then?" asked Catty, who would have been very glad of it; "I should think they would be pleased to get you."

"I am not so sure of that; I would be no great acquisition. But just at present there is a reason that renders it impossible."

Of course, no one could ask the reason, though all would have liked to know. When it grew too dark to sew or play, the lamp was lit, and they had cards, and it was nine when Nathalie arose to go.

"Couldn't you stay all night, Natty?" asked her mother; "it's dreadfully foggy to go up to Redmon to-night."

"If it were ten times as foggy, I should have to go. I don't mind it, though, in company with Charley and an umbrella."

She kissed them all good night, even Catty, in the happiness of her heart; and, wrapped in her shawl and cloud, she took her brother's arm and started. The fog was thicker, and wetter, and colder than ever; the night as wretched a one for a walk as could well be imagined, and the bleak sea wind blew raw in their faces all the way.

"How confoundedly cold it is!" exclaimed Charley, "more like January than July. You will perish, Natty, before we get to Redmon! You should not have come out this evening."

"I wanted to talk to you, Charley, on a very important matter indeed!"

Charley stared at her grave tone, but it all flashed upon him directly. Nathalie was used to talk to him more as a mother than a sister, in her superior woman's wisdom, and Charley was accustomed to take her lectures cheerfully enough; but in the damp darkness his face flushed rebelliously now.

He would not speak again, and his sister, after waiting a moment, broke the silence herself.

"It is about that girl, Charley?"

"What girl?" inquired Mr. Marsh, rather sulkily.

"You know well enough—Cherrie Nettleby."

"Well, what of Cherrie Nettleby?" this time defiantly.

"Charley, what do you mean by going with her as you do?"

"Nathalie," said Charley, mimicking her tone, "what do you mean by going with Captain Cavendish as you do?"

"My going with Captain Cavendish has nothing whatever to do with it; but if you want to know what I mean —I mean to marry him!"

"Nathalie, I don't want you to have anything to do with that man," Charley burst out passionately. "He is a villain!"

"Charley!"

"He is, I tell you! You know nothing about him—I do! I tell you he is a villain!"

"This is ungenerous of you, Charley," she calmly said; "it is cowardly. Is not Captain Cavendish your friend?"

"A friend I could throttle with the greatest pleasure in life!" exclaimed Charley, savagely.

"What has he done?"

"More than I would like to tell you—more than you would care to hear! All I have to say is, I would rather shoot you than see you his wife!"

"You are slandering him!" said Nathalie, her passion

rising in spite of herself. "You are trying to baffle me; to keep me from talking of Cherrie, but I'll not be put off. You cannot—you cannot mean to marry that girl."

"Natty look here," he said, more gently, "I don't want to be disagreeable, but I cannot be dictated to in this! I am a man, and must choose for myself. I have obeyed you all my life; but in this you must let me be my own master."

"You know what a name she has! She is the talk of all Speckport!"

"Is Speckport ever done talking? Wouldn't it slander an archangel, if it got the chance?"

"But it is true in this instance—she is all that Speckport says—an idle, silly, senseless, flirty, foolish, dressy, extravagant thing! She has nothing in the wide world to recommend her but her good locks."

"Neither has Captain Cavendish, if it comes to that!"

"Charley, it is false! He is a gentleman by birth, rank, and education!"

"Yes," said Charley, bitterly. "Nature did her best to make a gentleman of him, but I know street-sweepers in Speckport ten times more of a gentleman than he! I tell you he is corrupt to the core of his heart—a spendthrift and a fortune-hunter! If you were Miss Marsh, the school-teacher, as you were two or three years ago, he would as soon ask Miss Jo Blake to be his wife as you!"

"I don't doubt it," said Nathalie, quite calmly; "he may not be able to afford the luxury of a penniless bride, and for all that be no fortune-hunter. You can't shake my faith in him, Charley!"

"You are blind!" Charley cried, vehemently. "I am telling you Heaven's truth, Natty, with no other motive than your good!"

"We will drop the subject," said Nathalie, loftily, "and talk of you and Cherrie Nettleby!"

"We'll do nothing of the sort," replied Charley, resolutely; "go your own way, Natty, if you will, and I will go mine! The one marriage can be no madder than the other!"

"And you will really marry this girl?"

"I really will, if she will have me!'

Nathalie laughed a low and bitter laugh.

"Have you? Oh, there is little doubt of that, I fancy. Every one knows how she has been running after you this many a day!"

"But there is doubt of it. Your fine Captain Cavendish pursues her like her shadow."

"Charley, I will not listen to another word," cried Nathalie, imperiously. "Your infatuation seems to have changed your very nature. Why, oh why, has this girl crossed your path? If you wanted to marry, why could you not have chosen some one else? Why could you not have chosen Miss Rose?"

Charley smiled under cover of the darkness. The question was absurd. Why could she not have chosen any of her other suitors, all good and honorable men? Why could she not have chosen Captain Locksley, young, handsome, rich, and the soul of integrity. He did not say so, however, and neither spoke again till the gate of Redmon was reached.

"Good night," Nathalie briefly said, her voice full of inward pain.

"Good night, Natty," Charley replied, "and God bless you and," lowering his voice as he turned away "keep you from ever becoming the wife of Captain Cavendish!"

He walked on and entered the Nettleby cottage, where he found Cherrie in the parlor alone, bending over a novel. Cherrie's welcome to her lover was uncommonly cordial, for she was ennuied nearly to death. She had expected Captain Cavendish all the afternoon, and had been disappointed. Had she known that officer was making arrangements for their speedy nuptials, she might perhaps have forgiven him; and at that very moment, whilst talking to Charley of the time when she should be Mrs. Marsh, everything was arranged for her becoming, the very next week, Mrs. Captain George Cavendish.

About five o'clock of that foggy July afternoon, Mr. Val Blake sat in his private room, in the office of the Speckport Spouter, his shirt-collar limp and wilted with the heat, his hair wildly disheveled, and his expression altogether bewildered and distracted. The table at which he sat was, as usual, heaped with MS., letters, books, buff envelopes, and newspapers; and Mr. Blake was poring over some sheets of white ruled foolscap, closely written in a very cramp and spidery hand. It was a story from "the fascinating pen of our gifted and talented contributor 'Incognita,' whose previous charming productions have held spellbound hosts of readers," as the Spouter said, in announcing it the following week, and the title of the fascinating production was the "Ten Daughters of Dives." Miss Laura Blair had just finished reading the "Seven Loves of Mammon," by Mr. George Augustus Sala; hence the title and the quaint style in which the thing was written. So extremely quaint and original indeed was the style, that it soared totally beyond the comprehension of all ordinary intellects, beginning in the most disconcertingly abrupt manner, and ending with a jerk, while you were endeavoring to make out what it was all about.

"It's of no use trying," he murmured, pensively, "the thing is beyond me altogether. I'll put it in, hit or miss, or Laura will never forgive me; and I dare say the women will make out what it means, though I can't make top or tail of it."

There was a tap at the door as he arrived at this conclusion, and Master Bill Blair, in a state of ink, and with a paper cap on his head, labeled with the startling word "Devil" made his appearance, and announced that Captain Cavendish was in the office and wanted to see him.

"Tell him to come in," said Val, rather glad than otherwise of a chat by way of relaxation after his late severe mental labor."

The captain accordingly came in, smoking a cigar, and presented his cigar-case the first thing to Val. That gentleman helped himself, and the twain puffed in concert, and discussed the foggy state of the weather and the prospects of the "Spouter." As this desultory conversation began to flag, and the weed smoked out, Mr. Blake remembered he was in a hurry.

"I say, captain, you'll excuse me, won't you, if I

tell you I haven't much time to spare this evening. We go press to to-morrow, and I shall have to get to work."

Captain Cavendish came out of a brown study he had fallen into, and lit another cigar.

"I won't detain you long, Val. I know you're a good fellow, and would do me a favor if you could."

Val nodded and lit a cigar also.

"I want you to do me the greatest service, and I shall be forever your debtor."

"Right," said Val; "let us hear what it is."

"You won't faint, will you? I am going to be married."

"Are you?" said Mr. Blake, no way discomposed. "To whom?"

"To Cherrie Nettleby."

Val did start this time, and stared with all his eyes.

"To what? You're joking, ain't you? To Cherrie Nettleby!"

"Yes, to Cherrie Nettleby, but on the cross you know, not on the square. Do you comprehend?"

"Not a bit of it. I thought you were after Natty Marsh all the time."

Captain Cavendish laughed.

"You dear old daisy, you're as innocent as a new-born babe. I'm not going to marry Cherrie in earnest, only sham a marriage, and I cannot do it without your help. The girl is ready to run away with me any day; but to make matters smooth for her, I want her to think, for a while at least, she is my wife. You understand now?"

"I understand," said Val, betraying, I regret to say, not the slightest particle of emotion at this exposé of villainy; "but it's an ugly-looking job, Cavendish."

"Not as bad as if she ran away with me in cold blood —for her I mean—and she is sure to do it. You know the kind of girl pretty little Cherrie is, Blake; so you will be doing her rather a service than otherwise in helping me on. If you won't help, you know I can easily get some one who will, and I trust to your honor to keep silent. But come, like a good fellow, help me out."

"What do you want me to do? Not to play clergyman?"

"No; but to get some one—a stranger to Cherrie and I—consequently a stranger in Speckport, who will tie the knot, and on whose discretion you may depend. You shall play witness."

Val put his hands in his pockets and mused.

"Well," he said, after a pause, "it's a horrid shame, but rather than that she should run off with you, without any excuse at all, I'll do it. How soon do you want the thing to come off?"

"As early as possible next week—say Tuesday night. It will be better after night, she won't be so apt to notice deficiencies."

Val mused again.

"Cherrie's a Methodist herself; at least, she sits under the teaching of the Reverend Mr. Drone, who used to be rather an admirer of hers before he got married. The chapel is in an out-of-the-way street, and I can feign an excuse for getting the key from Drone. Suppose it takes place there?"

Captain Cavendish grasped his hand, and gave it a friendly vise-like grasp.

"Val, you're a trump! You shall have my everlasting gratitude for this."

"Next Tuesday night, then," responded Val, taking the officer's rapture stoically enough. "And now I must beg you to leave me, for I have bushels of work on hand."

Captain Cavendish, expressing his gratitude once more, lounged into the drear and foggy night. How lucky for the peace of the community at large, we cannot read each other's thoughts. The young captain's ran something after this fashion:

"I always knew Blake was a spoon, but I never thought he was such an infernal scoundrel as this. Why, he is worse than I am; for I really am in love with the girl, and he does his rascality without a single earthly motive. Well, it's all the better for me. I'll have Cherrie as sure as a gun."

Mr. Blake, in the seclusion of his room, leaned back in his chair, and indulged himself in a low and quiet laugh, before commencing work.

"I said I owed you one," he soliloquized, throwing away the stump of his second cigar, "for leading Charley . Marsh astray, and now's the time to pay you. If I don't serve you out this go, Captain Cavendish, my name's not Valentine Blake!"

CHAPTER XII.

IN WHICH THE WEDDING COMES OFF.

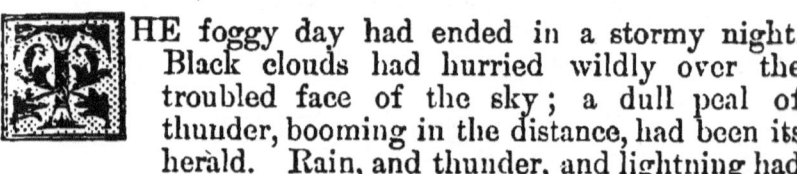

HE foggy day had ended in a stormy night. Black clouds had hurried wildly over the troubled face of the sky; a dull peal of thunder, booming in the distance, had been its herald. Rain, and thunder, and lightning had it all its own way until about midnight, when the sullen clouds had drifted slowly, and the moon showed her fair, sweet face in her place. A day of brightest sunshine, accompanied by a high wind, had been the result; and in its morning refulgence, Captain Cavendish was sauntering along the Redmon road. Not going to the big brick house, surely: Nathalie had told him the picnic day of Mrs. Leroy's growing dislike to visitors, and the hint had been taken. Perhaps it was only for a constitutional, or to kill time; but there he was, lounging in the teeth of the gale, and whistling an opera air as he went. The Nettleby cottage, fairly overrun with its luxuriance of sweetbrier, and climbing roses, and honeysuckle, was a pretty sight, and well worth looking at, and perhaps that was the reason Captain Cavendish stood still to admire it. The windows, all wreathed with crimson and pink roses, were open; and at one sat Cherrie, in all her beauty, like

a picture in a frame. The crimson July roses about her
were not brighter than her cheeks at the sight of him, and
her starry eyes flashed a welcome few men would not have
coveted. How prettily she was dressed, too—knowing
well he would come, the gypsy!—in pink muslin; her
bare neck and arms rising plump and rounded out of the
gauziness; all her shining jetty curls flashing about, and
sprays of rosebuds twisted through them. How the pale,
blue-eyed, snowy-skinned, fair-haired prettiness of Nathalie
dimmed in the young officer's ardent imagination beside
this tropical, gorgeous loveliness of the sunny South. He
opened the little gate, and was at the window before she
arose.

"My black-eyed fairy? You look perfectly dazzling
this morning. Who is in?"

"No one," said Cherrie, showing her pearl-white teeth
in her deepening smile. "The boys are off fishing;
father's up working in Lady Leroy's garden, and Ann's
gone to town for groceries."

"Allah be praised! I may come in, then, my darling,
may I not?"

Cherrie's answer was to throw the door wide open;
and the young officer entered and took a seat, screened
from the view of passers-by by the green gloom of the
vines. That green twilight of roses and honeysuckles was
just the thing for lovers to talk in; and Captain Cavendish had a great deal to say to Cherrie, and to all he said
Cherrie had nothing to give but rapturous assents, and
was altogether in the seventh heaven, not to say a few
miles beyond that lofty elysium. It was all arranged at
last as the young gentleman wished, and, lolling easily on
the sofa, he went off on another tack.

"Are you often up in Redmon House, Cherrie?" he
asked, stringing the black ringlets about his fingers.

Cherrie, seated on a low stool beside his couch, nestled
luxuriously, with her head on his knee.

"Pretty often, George." It had come to that, you
see. "Why?"

"Because—because I think you might find out some-

thing for me. I have a fancy, do you know, that the old
lady doesn't over and above like me."

"I know she don't," said Cherrie, decidedly. "She
can't bear you, nor Midge either. They scold Miss Natty
like sixty every time you go there."

"The deuce they do! Suppose she fancied—mind, I
only say fancied—I wanted to marry Miss Natty, do you
suppose she would consent?" ·

"Consent! She'd pack Miss Natty bag and baggage
out of the house, more likely. She'd die before she'd give
in, would Mrs. Leroy."

Captain Cavendish fell to musing, and mused so long
that Cherrie glanced up from under her black lashes,
wondering what made his handsome face look so grave.

"What are you thinking about?" she pouted; "Miss
Natty, I suppose."

"No, my little black-eye. I was thinking how you
could do something for me."

"What is it?"

"Couldn't you listen; couldn't you manage to hear
sometimes what Mrs. Leroy says to Natty, when they are
talking of me?"

Miss Nettleby was not at all shocked at this proposal;
but I suppose the reader is. I know very well it is dis-
graceful in one calling himself a gentleman, and altogether
dishonorable; but Captain Cavendish's ideas of honor,
and yours and mine, are rather different. Had any one
called him a liar or a swindler, or thrown a decanter at
his head, or a tumbler of wine in his face, at the mess-
table, or elsewhere, he would have considered his honor
forfeited forever, if he did not stand up to shoot and be
shot at by the offending party, as soon as possible afterward. In one word, not to mince matters, Captain Cavendish, handsome and elegant as he was, was an infidel and
a villain, and you may as well know it first as last.

"I dare say I can," was Cherrie's reply to his proposal. "I am up there often enough, and I know all the
ins and outs of the place. I'll do what I can."

Captain Cavendish rewarded her, as lovers do reward

one another, I am told, and shortly after arose to take his leave. Miss Nettleby escorted him to the gate.

"You won't forget Tuesday night, Cherrie," he said, turning to go.

"It's not very likely," said Cherrie; "but I'll see you again before that—won't I, George?"

"Of course, my darling! Take care of yourself, and good-bye."

He sauntered up the road at an easy pace; and Cherrie lingered at the gate, admiring his tall and elegant figure, and thinking, with an exultant heart beating, what a happy and lucky girl she was. Forget Tuesday night! the night that was to make her his bride. She quite laughed aloud at the thought, in the glee of her heart. He was still in sight, this Adonis of hers, and she still lingered at the gate watching him. Lingering there, she saw something not quite so pleasant as she could wish. Miss Nathalie Marsh, in a dress of blue barege, a black silk mantle, and a pretty white hat trimmed with azure ribbon, its long white plume tipped with blue, and set jauntily on her flowing sunny curls, came down the avenue from the house, opened the gate, and stepped into the road, and confronted her (Cherrie's) beloved. Cherrie saw him start eagerly forward, but could not hear what he said, and perhaps for her peace of mind it was just as well.

"My darling Nathalie! the fortunate chance I have been wishing for has come then! Are you going to town?"

Nathalie, smiling and blushing, shyly held out her hand.

"Good morning, Captain Cavendish! I——" but he interposed reproachfully.

"Captain Cavendish, from you, Nathalie; I thought you knew my name."

"Perhaps I have forgotten it," she laughed. "What are you doing up here, George," a little hesitatingly, though, and with a vivid flush, not half so glibly as Miss Nettleby had uttered it ten minutes before. "Were you going to call?"

"Hardly—remembering the hint you gave me the other day. But though I could not storm the castle of my fairy-princess, it was pleasant, at least, to reconnoiter the outside, and I hoped, too, for the lucky chance that has arrived. Am I to have the happy privilege of escorting you into town?"

Nathalie cast a half-apprehensive glance behind, but Midge was not on the watch. Had she known how dearly she was to pay for that walk—for that escort, rather—she had hardly answered with that happy, careless laugh.

"Yes, you may have that happy privilege! What did you do with yourself all day yesterday in the fog?" Cavendish thought of what he had been doing in Val's office, but he did not tell Miss Marsh. Cherrie was still standing by the cottage gate, and they were passing it now, looking like a black-eyed queen, under the arches of scarlet runners and morning-glories.

"A pretty place," said Captain Cavendish, "and that girl at the gate has a beautiful face. They tell me she has turned half the heads in Speckport."

Nathalie's fair brow contracted; not in jealousy, she never thought of that, but at the recollection of Charley. She made no answer. Her attention was attracted by a lady who was coming toward them. A young lady, nicely dressed, who stepped mincingly along, with a sweet smile on her sullen face.

"What brings Catty Clowrie up this way, I wonder?" exclaimed Nathalie, bowing as she passed, while the captain lifted his hat. "It is ever so long since I have seen her on this road before. I hope she is not going to Redmon."

But Miss Clowrie was going to Redmon. She had not started with that idea; it had never entered her head until she met the lovers; but she turned and looked after them with a smile of evil menace on her face.

"I hate her!" was her thought. "I hate her! But for her I might have had him once. Now he is that Nettleby girl's beyond hope. I wish Miss Marsh joy of her sister-in-law."

"That Nettleby girl" still stood at the gate. Miss

Clowrie bestowed the light of her smile upon her in passing, still deep in thought. "They say in Speckport Lady Leroy has forbidden Captain Cavendish the house, and threatens to disinherit Natty if she keeps his company. Perhaps she does not know of this. I think I'll go up and tell her. One good turn deserves another."

Midge answered the young lady's knock, and admitted her to the presence of Lady Leroy. That mummy she found in her usual state of wrappings, and very ready for a little gossip.

"Why don't you go out more, Mrs. Leroy," insinuated Catty; "it would do you good, I am sure."

"No, it wouldn't!" snapped the old lady. "It does me harm. I hain't got over that picnic yet."

"But I should think you would find it very lonely here, with Nathalie away so much. I hear she spends most of her time in town of late."

"So she does," Lady Leroy screamed. "She will go in spite of me. If it ain't the school, it's a party or a picnic—something or other; but she's gallivanting all the time."

"I met her just now," remarked Catty, in a careless way, "with Captain Cavendish. He had been waiting for her, I think, at the gate."

"What?" shrieked Lady Leroy, "who with, or who did you say?"

"Captain Cavendish," repeated Miss Clowrie, looking surprised. "I thought you said they were engaged! At least, every one says they are."

Lady Leroy fell back, gasping, clawing the air in her struggle with her ten talon-like fingers. Catty, quite alarmed, started up to assist her. Lady Leroy grasped her by the wrist with a fierce grip.

"You're sure of this? You're sure of this?" she huskily whispered, still gasping. "You're sure she was walking with him? You're sure she is engaged to him?"

"I am sure she was walking with him," said Catty; "and every one says she is engaged to him; and what

every one says must be true. It's very strange you did
not know it."

Lady Leroy "grinned horribly a ghastly smile." "I
do know it now! I told her not to go with him—I told
her not to go with him—and this is the way she obeys
me!"

She fell to clawing the air again, in a manner so very
uncomfortable to look at, that Miss Clowrie arose, with
some precipitation, to go.

"They say he is a fortune-hunter and very extravagant, and goes after her because she is your heiress; but
I'm sure I don't know. Good morning, Mrs. Leroy. I
am glad to see you looking so well."

With which the fair Miss Clowrie bowed herself out,
smiling more than Midge had ever seen her before,
and quite laughing, in fact, when she got out of doors.

"I think I have paid a little of my debt, Miss Natty,"
she thought. "I'll pay it all, my dear, I hope, before
either of us die."

In the silent solitude of her lonely room, Lady Leroy
had ample time to nurse her wrath before the return of
her ward. It was nearly noon before that young lady
reached home, her pretty face glowing with her rapid
walk.

"Midge," was her first breathless question, "has Catty
Clowrie been here this morning?"

Midge answered in the affirmative, and Nathalie's
heart sank. All the way up-stairs she was preparing herself for a violent outburst of wrath; but, to her astonishment, Lady Leroy was quite tranquil. She glanced
very hard at her, it is true, and her fingers were clawing
empty air very viciously, but her voice was not loud nor
angry.

"You're very late, aren't you?" she said. "What
kept you?"

"I ran down to see mamma. Miss Rose told me she
was not very well; but I hurried home as fast as I could.
I'll make out those bills now."

"Let the bills wait awhile," said the old lady. "I
have something to tell you."

This was an ominous commencement, and Nathalie looked at her in some dread.

"Who was it you walked into town with this morning?" she asked, glaring harder than ever.

Catty had told, then. All the blood in Nathalie's body seemed blazing in her face, as she answered:

"It was Captain Cavendish. I chanced to meet him near the gate, and I could not very well help his walking back to town with me."

"Didn't you promise me," said Lady Leroy, still speaking with astonishing calmness, but clawing the air fiercely with both hands, "when I forbade you going with him, that you would walk with him no more?"

"No," said Nathalie. "I said he would come here no more, and neither he shall."

"Until I am dead, I suppose," said the old woman, with a laugh that was very unpleasant to hear, "and you have all my money. Answer me one question, Natty. Are you engaged to him? Don't tell a lie."

"No," said Nathalie, proudly, "I am not in the habit of telling deliberate lies. I am!"

Lady Leroy gave a shrill gasp, her fingers working convulsively, but the spasm was over in a moment. She sat up again; and Nathalie, hurriedly and imploringly, went on:

"Dear Mrs. Leroy, don't be angry! Indeed, you misjudge Captain Cavendish; he is a good and honorable man, and respects you much. Dear Mrs. Leroy, consent to our engagement and I will be the happiest girl in the world!"

She went over and put her arms round the mummy's neck, kissing the withered face. The old woman pushed her away with another of her unpleasant laughs.

"There—there, child! do as you please. I knew you would do it anyway, only I won't have him here—mind. I won't have him here! Now, get to work at them bills. What's the matter with your mother?"

"Sick headache," said Nathalie, chilled, she scarcely knew why, by the old woman's manner. "She wanted me to stay with her this afternoon ; but I told her I was afraid you could not spare me."

Mrs. Leroy mused a few moments, while Nathalie wrote, and then looked up.

"I'll spare you this afternoon, Natty, since your mother is sick. You can take the bills in with you and collect them. If you are back by nine, it will do."

Nathalie was so amazed, she dropped her pen and sat staring, quite unable to return a word of thanks, and not quite certain she was not dreaming.

"Get on, get on !" exclaimed Lady Leroy, in her customary testy tone. "You'll never have the bills done at that rate."

Nathalie finished the bills mechanically, and with a mind far otherwise absorbed. Then she went to her room, and put on her hat and mantle for another walk to Speckport ; but all the time that uneasy feeling of doubt and uncertainty remained. Mrs. Leroy had acted so strangely, had been so ominously quiet and unlike herself, and had not consented. Nathalie came in dressed for town, and bent over her, until her long bright curls swept the yellow old face.

"Dear Mrs. Leroy !" she pleadingly said, "I cannot feel satisfied until you actually say you agree to this engagement. Do—do, if you love your Natty, for all my happiness depends upon it. Do say you consent, and I will never offend you again as long as I live ?"

Lady Leroy glared up at her with green, and glittering, and wicked old eyes.

"If I don't consent, will you break off, Natty ?"

"You know I cannot. I love him with all my heart. Oh, Mrs. Leroy ! remember you were once young yourself, and don't be hard !"

Looking at that dry and withered old antediluvian, it was hard to imagine her ever young—harder still to imagine her knowing anything about the fever called love. She pushed Nathalie impatiently away.

"Get along with you, and don't bother !" was her cry. "I told you to have your way, and you ought to be satisfied. You won't give in to me, but you'd like me to give in to you—wouldn't you ? Go along, and don't torment me !"

When Mrs. Leroy's cracked voice grew shrill and piercing, and her little eyes gleamed greenish flame, Nathalie knew better than to irritate her by disobedience. She turned to go, with a strange sinking of the heart.

"I will be back by nine," she said, simply, as she quitted the room.

Miss Nettleby, seated at her cottage door, under the roses and sweetbrier, industriously stitching on some gossamer article to be worn next Tuesday evening, looked up in some surprise at sight of Miss Marsh on her way to Speckport, for the second time that day.

"Going back to town, Miss Natty ?" she called out, familiarly.

Miss Natty's answer was a cold and formal bow, as she passed on. Cherrie dropped her work and started up.

"I'll go to the house and have a talk with Granny Grumpy herself before she comes back. Perhaps I may find out something. I wonder what sort of humor she is in."

Lady Leroy was in uncommonly serene humor for her. Before Nathalie had been ten minutes gone, she had shouted for Midge ; and that household treasure appearing, with sleeves rolled up over her elbows, and in a very soapy and steamy state, had desired her to array herself in other garments, and go right away into Speckport.

"Go into Speckport !" cried Midge, in shrill indignation. "I'll see you boiled alive first, ma'am, and that's the long and short of it. Go into town, wash-day, indeed ! What do you want in town, ma'am ?"

"I want Mr. Darcy—that's what I want !" vehemently replied her mistress. "I want Mr. Darcy, you ugly little imp ; and if you don't go straight after him, I'll heave this at your head, I will !"

"This " was a huge black case bottle, which trifle of glass the lady of Redmon brandished in a manner that made even Midge draw back a few paces in alarm.

"I want Mr. Darcy on important business, I do !" screamed Lady Leroy. "And tell him not to let the

grass grow under his feet on the way. Be off, will
you ?"

"Why didn't you tell Miss Natty ?" sulkily said Midge

"Because she isn't coming back till nine o'clock, that's
why; and I can't wait. Well, what do you want, young
woman ?"

This last polite interrogation was addressed to Miss
Nettleby, who stood smiling in the doorway, in all the
splendor of her charms.

"I just ran up to see how you were," said Cherrie.
"If you want any errand done in the town, Mrs. Leroy,
I'll go. I can walk faster than Midge, you know."

"So she can," cried Midge; "let her go, ma'am; I
won't."

With which Midge waddled off, making the hall
quake with her airy tread. Mrs. Leroy looked with unusual graciousness at the young lady.

"Will you go, Cherrie, and be quick about it. Tell
Darcy to hurry; you can drive back with him, you know."

Cherrie wanted nothing better, and was off like a
dart, scenting a secret, and determined to get at the bottom of it.

"What does she want with her lawyer, I wonder?"
soliloquized Cherrie, on the road. "I'll find out. Miss
Natty's out of the way, and Midge will be down in the
kitchen. I'll find out."

Mr. Darcy was one of the best lawyers in the town,
and was Lady Leroy's man of business ever since her
advent in Speckport. Cherrie found him in his office—a
handsome and gentlemanly old man, with gray hair,
whiskers, and mustache, and a clear, bright eye.

"What can the old lady want?" he wondered, aloud,
putting on his hat; "she didn't tell you, I suppose?
Will you drive back with me, Miss Cherrie ?"

Miss Cherrie consented, and they had a very pleasant
drive together, the old gentleman chaffing her about
her beaux, and wanting to know when she was going to
stop breaking hearts, and get married. Cherrie did not
say "next Tuesday," she only laughed, and desired to be
set down at her own gate.

There she watched the lawyer out of sight, and then went deliberately after him. Not to the front door, however, but to a back window she knew of, easily lifted, through it, up-stairs on tiptoe, and into Nathalie's room, which she locked on the inside. Nathalie's room adjoined Lady Leroy's, and the wall being thin, the conversation of the lawyer and the old woman was distinctly audible. Cherrie sat down on the floor, with her ear glued to the wall, and listened. It was a prolonged and excited talk, the lawyer angrily protesting, Mrs. Leroy angrily determined; and it ended in Mr. Darcy's yielding, but grumblingly, and still under protest. Cherrie had fairly held her breath while listening—astonishment and delight pictured on her face.

There was a long silence; Mr. Darcy was writing. In half an hour his task was completed, and he read it aloud to the mistress of Redmon. "That will do," said Lady Leroy, "I'm glad it's over."

"Do you want that paper witnessed? Call Midge."

Mr. Darcy opened the door, and shouted through the darkness for Midge, as Captain Cavendish had once done before. Midge made her appearance, as soapy and steamy as ever.

"Write your name here," said Mr. Darcy, abruptly pointing to the place.

"What is it?" inquired Midge.

"That's no affair of yours, is it? Sign it, will you?"

Midge took the pen as if it weighed half a ton or so, set her head very much on one side, thrust her tongue a little out of one corner of her mouth, and with much labor and painstaking, affixed a blotted autograph—Priscilla Short.

"That will do," said Mr. Darcy; "we want another. Call in old Nettleby—he can write."

Midge, casting a parting look of much complacence at her performance, departed on her errand, and old Nettleby coming in shortly after, affixed another blotted signature. Mr. Darcy dispatched him about his business, folded the document, put it in his pocket-book, and took his hat and cane to go. On the threshold he paused.

"This has been done under the influence of anger, Mrs. Leroy," he said; "and you will think better of it, and send me word to destroy it before long. I consider it most unjust—exceedingly unjust—altogether unjustifiable! Good afternoon, ma'am."

Cherrie waited in her hiding-place until she heard the hall door close after him, then stole noiselessly out, downstairs, through the window, and gained her own home, unobserved.

What had she heard? Her face was flushed, her eyes bright, her whole manner strangely excited. She could not keep still—she walked ceaselessly to and from the gate, straining her eyes in the direction of Speckport.

"Why don't he come! Why don't he come!" she kept repeating, hurriedly. "Oh, what will he say to this?"

CHAPTER XIII.

AFTER THE WEDDING.

ANN NETTLEBY, busy in the culinary department, never remembered seeing her restless sister so exceedingly restless as on this afternoon. When the clock struck six, and old Mr. Nettleby plodded home from his day's work, and the two young Mr. Nettleby's came whistling from town, and tea was ready, Ann came out to call her to partake. But Cherrie impatiently declined to partake; and still waited and watched, while the sunset was burning itself out of the purple sky, and the cinnamon roses drooped in the evening wind. The last amber and crimson flush was paling behind the blue western hills, when he, so long waited for, came up the dusty road, twirling a cane in his hand, and smoking a cigar. The unspeakable beauty and serenity of the summer twilight was no more

to him than to her who watched at the vine-wreathed
gate. A handsome man and a pretty girl—each was far
more to the taste of the other than all the beauty of sky
and earth.

Right opposite the cottage were the dark, silent cedar
woods. The moment he came in sight, Cherrie opened
the gate, motioning him to follow, struck into the narrow
footpath, winding among the woods. Captain Cavendish
followed, and found her sitting on a little knoll, under the
tree.

"I have been watching for you this ever so long," she
breathlessly began ; "I thought you would never come !
I have something to tell you, and I daren't tell you in the
house, for father and the boys are there."

Captain Cavendish leaned against a tree, puffed his
cigar, and looked lazily down at her.

"Well, petite, what is it ?"

"Oh, it's something dreadfully important. It's about
Miss Marsh."

The young captain threw away his cigar, and took a
seat beside Cherrie, interested at once. He put his arm
round her waist, too, but this is by-the-way.

"About Miss Marsh ? Have you been listening ?"

Cherrie gave him an account how she had gone for
Mr. Darcy, and hidden afterward in Nathalie's room.

"My clever little darling ! And what did you hear ?"

"You never could guess! O my goodness," cried
Cherrie, clasping her hands, "won't Miss Natty be in a
passion, when she finds it out."

"Will she, though ? Let us hear it, Cherrie."

"Well," said Cherrie, "you know Miss Natty was to
be heiress of Redmon, and have all Lady Leroy's money
when she dies ?"

"Yes! well ?"

"Well, she isn't to be any longer! Lady Leroy made
a new will this afternoon, and Miss Natty is disinherited !"

Captain Cavendish started with something like an oath.

"Cherrie! are you sure of this ?"

"Certain sure !" said Cherrie, with a look and tone
there was no doubting. "I heard every word of it—her

telling him so first, and him reading the will afterward and father and Midge signed it!"

"The—devil!" said Captain Cavendish between his teeth; "but what put such a freak in the old hag's head?"

"You!" said Cherrie.

"I!"

"Yes—just you! She told Mr. Darcy Natty was engaged to you, and would not give you up, all she could say; so she meant to disinherit her. She said Nathalie should never know, unless she married you before she was dead—if she didn't, she shouldn't find it out until she was in her grave, and then you would desert her when you found out she was poor, and Nathalie would be rewarded for her disobedience!"

Captain Cavendish's handsome face wore a scowl so black, and the oath he swore was so dreadful, that even Cherrie shrank away in something like terror.

"The old hag! I could throttle her if I had her here! Cherrie, who did she leave her money to?"

"To her brother—or, in case of his death, to his heirs; and five pounds to Natty to buy a mourning ring."

"Did you hear her brother's name?"

"Yes, but I forget! It was Harrington, or Harrison, or something like that. Mr. Darcy scolded like everything, and said it was unjust; but Lady Leroy didn't seem to mind him. Isn't it good I listened?"

"Cherrie! Cherrie! Cherrie!" called Ann Nettleby, "Where are you, Cherrie? There's somebody in the house wants you!"

"I must go!" said Cherrie, rising. "You stay here, so Ann won't see you. Will you be up to-morrow?"

"Yes," said Captain Cavendish; and Cherrie flitted away rapidly in the growing dusk. For once he was glad to be rid of Cherrie—glad to be calm and think, and the late-rising moon was high in the sky before he left the wood, and walked back to Speckport.

Cherrie's visitor turned out to be Charley Marsh, who received the reverse of a cordial welcome from his fickle-minded lady-love, who was more than a little provoked at his shortening her interview with one she liked better.

She seated herself by the window, with her eyes fixed on the cedar wood, rapidly blackening now, waiting for her lover to emerge; but when his tall dark figure did at length stride out through the dark path, night had fairly fallen, and it was too late to see what expression his face wore.

Whatever the young Englishman's state of mind had been on leaving the wood that night, it was serene as mood could be when, next morning, Sunday, Miss Nettleby, *en grande tenue*, gold chain and all, made her appearance in Speckport, and met him as she turned out of Redmon road. Miss Nettleby was going to patronize the cathedral this morning, confirmation was to take place, with all the magnificent and poetical ceremonies of the Catholic Church, and Cherrie would not have missed it for the world. Neither would Captain Cavendish, who went partly from curiosity, partly to kill time, partly to show himself in full uniform, and partly to hear Nathalie Marsh play and sing. Out of the great organ she was drawing such inspiring strains as Captain Cavendish thought he had never heard before; rolling out in volumes of harmony over the ears of people below, and grand and grateful were the notes the instrument gave forth to her master-hand. In front of the altar all the youthful aspirants for confirmation were seated, the girls robed in snowy white, and wearing vails and wreaths on their bowed heads, like young brides. But now the bishop, in mitre and chasuble, with a throng of attendant priests, in splendid vestments, preceded by a score of acolytes in scarlet soutanes, and white lace surplices, bearing candles and crozier, are all on the altar, and the choir have burst forth as with one voice, into the plaintive cry "Kyrie Eleison," and pontifical high massh as begun. High over all that swelling choir, high, clear and sweet, one soprano voice arises, the voice of the golden-haired organist: "Gloria in Excelsis!" Something in the deep solemnity of the scene, in the inspiring music, in the white-robed and flower-crowned girls, in the silent devotion of the thousands around him, stirred a feeling in the soul of the man, that he had never felt since, in early boyhood, before he knew

7*

Eton or Voltaire, he had knelt at his mother's knee, and
learned there his childish prayers. He forgot, for a brief
while, his wickedness and his worldliness, forgot the black-
eyed girl by his side, and the blue-eyed girl whose voice
vibrated through those lofty aisles, and, with dreamy eyes,
and a heart that went back to that old time, listened to
the sermon of the aged and white-haired priest, grown
gray in the service of that God whom he, a poor atom of
the dust, dared deride. It was one of those moments in
which the great Creator, in his infinite compassion for
his lost sheep, goes in search of us to lead us back to the
fold, in which our good angel flutters his white wings
about us, and tries to lift us out of the slime in which we
are wallowing. But the sermon was over, the benediction
given, the last voluntary was playing, and the vast crowd
were pouring out. Captain Cavendish took his hat and
went out with the rest; and before he had fairly passed
through the cathedral gates was his old, worldly, infidel
self again, and was pouring congratulations and praise into
the too-willing ears of Nathalie Marsh, on her admirable
performances, while Charley went home with Cherrie.

All that day, and the next, and the next, Captain
Cavendish never came near Re_mon, or the pretty cottage
where the roses and sweetbriers grew; but Mr. Johnston, a
pleasant-spoken and dapper young cockney, without an h
in his alphabet, and the captain's confidential valet, came
back and forth with messages, and took all trouble and
suspicion off his master. Neither had Miss Nettleby
made her appearance in Speckport; she had spent the
chief part of her time about the red-brick house, but had
learned nothing further by all her eavesdropping. In a
most restless and excited state of mind had the young lady
been ever since Monday morning, in a sort of inward fever
that grew worse and worse with every passing hour. She
got up and sat down, and wandered in and out, and tried
to read, and sew, and net, and play the accordion, and
threw down each impatiently, after a few moments' trial.
She sat down to her meals and got up without eating anything; her cheeks burned with a deep, steady fever-red,
her eyes had the unnatural brightness of the same disease,

and Ann stared at her, and opined she was losing her wits.

In rain and gloom the wedding-day dawned at last. Cherrie's fever was worse—she wandered from room to room of the cottage all day long, the fire in her eyes and the hectic on her cheek more brilliant than ever. The sky was like lead, the wind had a warning wail in its voice, and the rain fell sullenly and ceaselessly. But the rain could not keep the girl in-doors; she went out and wandered around in it all, returning dripping wet, three or four times, to change her drenched clothes. The girls had the cottage to themselves; old Nettleby was out in the shed, mending his gardening-tools, and the boys were in Speckport. The dull day was ending in a duller and rainier twilight, and Ann Nettleby was bustling about the tidy kitchen, getting tea, and wondering if Cherrie had gone to bed in her room up-stairs, she had been so quiet for the last half-hour. She did not go up to see; but set the tea to draw, laid the table, and lit the lamp. The wet twilight had now closed in, in a black and dismal night, when Ann heard a carriage stop at the gate, and, a moment after, a loud knock at the front door. Before she could open it, some person without did so, and Ann saw Mr. Val Blake, wrapped in a mackintosh, and waiting at the gate a cab, with a lighted lamp.

"How are you, Ann?" inquired Mr. Blake. "Is Cherrie in?"

"Yes, here I am!" a voice called out, and Cherrie herself came running down stairs, her heart beating so fast and thick she could hardly speak.

"I thought you would like a drive this evening, Cherrie," said Val; "it's wet, but you won't mind it in the cab, and I'll fetch you back before ten. Run and wrap up and come along."

It was not the first time Ann Nettleby had heard such impromptu invitations given and accepted, and it was none of her business to interfere. Cherrie was off like a flash, and down again directly, in out-door dress, her vail down, to hide her flushed and excited face.

Ann Nettleby, standing in the cottage-door, watched

the cab drive away through the rainy night, and then, closing the door, went back to the kitchen, to give her father his tea. She took her own with him, setting the teapot back on the stove, to keep hot for-her brothers. Old Nettleby fell asleep immediately after tea, with his pipe in his mouth, and Ann went back to her netting, wondering once more what Cherrie was about, and wishing she could have such fine times as her elder sister. Could she only have seen in some magic mirror what was at that moment going on in a humble little Wesleyan chapel in a retired street of the town! The building dimly lighted by one flickering candle; a minister, or what looked like one, in white neckcloth and clerical suit of black; the tall and distinguished man, wearing a shrouding cloak, and the little girl, who trembled and quivered so fearfully, standing before him, while he pronounced them man and wife; and that other tall young man, with his hands in his coat-pockets, listening and looking on! Could Ann Nettleby only have seen it all, and known that her pretty sister was that very night a bride!

Val Blake was certainly the soul of punctuality. As the clock on the kitchen-mantel was striking ten, the cab stopped once more at the cottage-door, and she heard his unceremonious voice bidding Cherrie good-night. Ann opened the door, and Cherrie, her vail still down, brushed past her without saying a word, and flitted up the staircase to her own room.

It was half an hour later when Ann Nettleby's two brothers came, dripping like water-dogs, home from town; and Ann having admitted them, went yawningly up-stairs to bed.

"I say, father," said Rob Nettleby, pulling off his wet jacket, "was there company up at Redmon to-day?"

"No," replied the old man. "Why?"

"Oh, because we met a carriage tearing by just now, as if Old Nick was driving. I wonder what it was about?"

CHAPTER XIV.

MINING THE GROUND.

ISS CHERRIE NETTLEBY was not a young lady of very deep feeling, or one likely to be long overcome by romantic emotion of any sort. Therefore, before a week stood between her and that rainy July night, she was all her own self again, and that night seemed to have come and gone out of her life, and left no trace behind it. She was Cherrie Nettleby still, not Mrs. Captain Cavendish; she lived in the cottage instead of the handsome suite of apartments the elegant young officer occupied in the best hotel in Speckport. She flaunted in the old gay way through her native town, and held her usual evening levee of young men in the cottage-parlor as regularly as the evening came round. It did seem a little strange to her at first that marriage, which makes such a change in the lives of other girls, should make so little in hers. She never doubted for a single second that she was really and legally his wife, and Val Blake kept his own counsel. The captain told her that he would resign his commission or exchange into the first homeward-bound regiment; and meantime she was to be a good girl and keep their secret inviolably. She was to encourage Charley Marsh still—poor Charley! while he every day played the devoted to Nathalie.

Cherrie's wedding night had been nearly the last of July. The crimson glory of an August sunset lay on the climbing roses, the sweetbrier and honeysuckle arches of the cottage, and was turning its windows into sheets of red gold. The sun, a crimson globe, was dropping in an oriflamme of indescribable gorgeousness behind the tree-tops; and at all this tropical richness of light and coloring, Cherrie, leaning over her father's garden-gate, looked.

There were not many passers-by to look at that hot

August evening; but presently up the dusty road came a young man, well-dressed and well-looking. Cherrie knew him, and greeted him with a gracious smile, for it was Mr. Johnston, Captain Cavendish's servant. Mr. Johnston, with a look of unqualified admiration at her dark, bright face, took off his hat.

"Good-evening, Miss Nettleby. Ain't it shocking 'ot? Been to the picnic to-day?"

Cherrie nodded.

"'Ad a good time, I 'ope. Weren't you nearly melted with the 'eat?"

"Yes, it was warm," said Cherrie; "got anything for me?"

"A letter," said Mr. Johnston, producing the document, "which he'd 'ave come himself honely hold Major Grove hinvited 'im to dinner."

Cherrie eagerly broke open the envelope and read:

"DEAREST:—Meet me to-night, at half-past eight, in the cedar dell, without fail. Destroy this as soon as read.   G. S."

Cherrie tore the note into atoms, and strewed them over the grass.

"There was to be a hanswer," insinuated Mr. Johnston.

"Tell him yes," said Cherrie; "that is all."

Mr. Johnston took off his hat once more, and himself immediately after. Ann Nettleby, at the same moment, came to the door to tell Cherrie tea was ready; and Cherrie went in and partook of that repast with her father, sister, and brothers.

"Did you hear, boys," said old Nettleby, "that Lady Leroy has sold Partridge Farm?"

"Sold Partridge Farm!" repeated Rob. "No! has she, though? Who to?"

"To young Mr. Oaks, so Midge tells me; and a rare penny she'll get for it, I'll warrant you."

"What does Oaks want of it, I wonder?" said his other son. "He isn't going to take to farming."

" Oaks is the richest fellow in Speckport," said Rob Nettleby; " he has more money a great deal than he knows what to do with, and he may as well lay it out in property as at the gaming-table."

" Does he gamble ?" asked Cherrie, helping herself to bread and butter.

Her brother laughed significantly.

" Doesn't he, though ? You may find him and that Captain Cavendish all hours of the day and night in Prince Street."

" Is Captain Cavendish a gambler ?" said Ann; " that's bad for Miss Natty. They say they're going to be married."

Cherrie smiled to herself, and Rob went on speaking.

" It's bad for Miss Nathalie, for that Cavendish is a villain, for all his fine airs and graces, and is leading her brother to the devil. I met him and young McGregor coming from Prince Street last night, and they hadn't a leg to put under them—either one."

" Drunk ?" said Cherrie, stirring her tea.

" Drunk as lords, the pair of 'em. I helped them both home, and found out afterward how it was. They had gone with Cavendish to the gaming-house as usual, had lost heavily also, as usual, and, excited and maddened, had drank brandy until they could hardly stand. Young Mc-Gregor will fleece his father before he stops; and where Marsh's money comes from, I can't tell."

" You ought to tell Miss Natty, Rob," said his father. " I should not like to see her throw herself away on such a man, such a handsome and pleasant-spoken young lady as she is."

." Not I," said his son, getting up; " she wouldn't thank me, and it's none of my business. Let Charley tell her, if he likes—a poor fellow like me has no call to interfere with fine ladies and gentlemen."

Cherrie, with a little disdainful toss of her black curls, but discreetly holding her tongue, went into the front room and seated herself with a novel at the window. She read until a quarter past eight, and it grew too dark to see; then, rising, she wrapped herself in a plaided shawl

and crossed the deserted road unobserved. Cedar dell,
the place of tryst, was but a few yards off—the green hollow in the woods where Cherrie had told the captain of
the result of her eavesdropping; a delightful place, shut
in by the tall, dark trees, with a carpet of velvet sward,
and a rustic bench of twisted boughs. Cherrie sat down
on the bench and listened to the twittering of the birds in
their nests, the restless murmuring and swaying of the
trees in the night-wind, and watched the blue patches of
sky and the pale rays of the new moon glancing in and
out of the black boughs. All the holy beauty of the pale
summer night could not lift her heart to the Creator who
had made it—she was only waiting for the fall of a well-
known step, for the sound of a well-known voice. Both
came presently. The branches were swept aside, a step
crashed over the dry twigs, a pale and handsome face,
with dark eyes and mustache, under a broad-brimmed hat,
looked in the white moonlight through the opening, and
the expected voice asked :-

"Are you there, Cherrie?"

"Yes, George," said Cherrie composedly. "Come
in."

Captain George Cavendish came in accordingly, embraced her in very husbandly fashion, and sat down beside
her on the bench. The gloom of the place and the hat
he wore obscured his face, but not so much but that the
girl could see how pale it was, and notice something strange
in his voice and manner.

"Is there anything the matter?" she asked. "Did
you want anything very particular, George?"

"Yes," he said, in a low, impressive voice, taking both
her hands in his, and holding them tightly. "I want you
to do me the greatest service it may ever be in your
power to render me, Cherrie."

Cherrie looked up at his white, set face, feeling
frightened.

"I will do whatever I can for you, George. What is
it?"

"You know you are my wife, Cherrie, and that my
interests are yours now. Wouldn't you like I should be-

come rich and take you away from this place, and keep you like a lady all the rest of your life?"

Yes—Cherrie would decidedly like that, and gave him to understand accordingly.

"Then you must take an oath, Cherrie—do you hear? —an oath to obey me in all things, and never reveal to living mortal what I shall tell you to-night."

Now, Cherrie, thinking very little of a falsehood on ordinary occasions, held an oath to be something solemn and sacred, and not to be broken, and hesitated a little.

"Perhaps it is something hard—something I can't do. I feel afraid to take an oath, George."

"You must take it! It is not a matter of choice, and I will ask nothing you can't do. You must only swear to keep a secret."

"Well, I'll try," said Cherrie, with a sigh, "but I hate to do it."

"I dare say you do!" he said, breaking into a slight smile; "it is not in your line, I know, to keep secrets, Cherrie; but at present there is no help for it. You know what an oath is, don't you, Cherrie?"

"Yes."

"And you swear never to reveal what I am about to say to you?"

"Yes," said Cherrie, her curiosity getting the better of her fear. "I swear! What is it?"

Was it the gloom of the place, or some inward struggle, that darkened so his handsome face. The silence lasted so long after her question, that Cherrie's heart began to beat with a cold and nameless fear. He turned to her at last, holding both her hands in his own, and so hard that she could have cried out with the pain.

"You have sworn, Cherrie, to help me. Say you hope you may die if you ever break that oath. Say it!"

The girl repeated the frightful words, with a shiver.

"Then, Cherrie, listen, and don't scream. I'm going to rob Lady Leroy to-morrow night."

Cherrie did not scream; but she gave a gasping cry, and her eyes and mouth opened to their widest extent.

"Going to rob Lady Leroy," repeated Captain Cavendish, looking at her fixedly, and magnetizing her with his powerful glance, "to-morrow night; and I want you to help me, Cherrie."

"But—but they'll put you in prison for it," gasped Cherrie, all aghast.

"No, they won't, with your help. I mean they shall put somebody else in prison for it; not through any dislike to him, poor devil, but to avert suspicion from myself. Will you help me, Cherrie? Remember, you have sworn."

"I will do what I can," shivered poor Cherrie, "but oh! I am dreadfully scared."

"There is no need—your part will be very easy, and to-morrow afternoon you shall leave Speckport forever."

Cherrie's face turned radiant.

"With you, George! Oh, I am so glad! Tell me what you want me to do, and see if I don't do it."

"That is my good little wife. Now then for explanations. Do you know that Lady Leroy has sold Partridge Farm?"

"To Mr. Tom Oaks—yes, and that he is coming up to-morrow to pay her eight thousand pounds for it."

"Who told you?"

"Father and the boys were talking about it at tea. George, is that the money you're going to steal?"

"It is. I am deucedly hard-up just at present, Cherrie, and eight thousand would be a godsend. Now, my dearest, you must be up at the house when Oaks comes, and find out where the money is put."

"I know where she always keeps the money," said Cherrie; "and she's sure to put this with the rest. It is in that black japanned tin box on the stand at the head of her bed."

"Very well. You see, I must do it to-morrow night, for she never would keep so large a sum in the house; it will go into the bank the day after. The steamer for Halifax leaves to-morrow night at eleven o'clock, and I shall go to Halifax in her."

"And take me with you?" eagerly asked Cherrie.

"No; you must go in another direction. Until our

marriage is made public, it never would do for us to go together, Cherrie. Let me see. You told me once you had a cousin up in Greentown, who wanted you to visit her, did not you?"

"Yes—Cousin Ellen."

"Well, there is a train leaving Speckport at half-past five in the afternoon. You must depart by that, and you will be in Greentown before nine. Take care to make your departure as public as possible. Go into Speckport early in the morning, and bid everybody you know good-bye. Tell them you don't know how long you may be tempted to stay."

"Yes," said Cherrie, with a submissive sigh.

"All but one. You must tell Charley Marsh a different story."

"Charley! Why, what's Charley Marsh got to do with it?"

"A good deal, since I mean he shall be arrested for the robbery. I hate to do it, but there is no help for it, Cherrie. You told me the other day that he was getting desperate, and wanted you to elope with him."

"So he did," said Cherrie. "He went on dreadfully; said he was going to perdition, and you were dragging him down, but he would take me from you if he could. He wanted me to go with him to the United States, and we would be married in Boston."

"And you—what is this you told him, Cherrie?"

"I told him I would think about it, and give him his answer in a day or two."

"Very well. Give him his answer to-morrow morning. Call at the office, and tell him you consent to run away with him, but that, to avoid suspicion for a few days, you are going to give out you are off on a visit to your cousin in Greentown. That you will actually start in the cars, but will step quietly out at the first station, which is only three miles from town, and that you will walk back and get to Speckport about dark. You understand, Cherrie? You are not really to do this, only to tell Marsh you will."

"Yes," said Cherrie, looking hopelessly bewildered.

"Tell him to come to Redmon between eight and nine, to call at your cottage first, and if you are not there, to go to Lady Leroy's and wait there as long as he can. If you are not there before the house is closed, he is to wait in the grounds for you in front of the house until you do come. I will enter by that back window you showed me, Cherrie, and the probability is Charley will wait all night, and, of course, will be seen by several people, and actually suspected of the robbery."

"It seems a pity, though, don't it?" said Cherrie, her woman's heart touched for poor Charley.

"If he is not suspected, I will be," said Captain Cavendish, sternly. "Remember your oath."

"I remember. Is there anything else?"

"Yes; you must send him a note in the afternoon. Ann will fetch it for you. To-morrow is Thursday, and at eight in the morning the steamer leaves for Boston."

"Here," said the young man, putting his hand in his pocket and producing a slip of paper, "is a draft of the note you are to send him, written in pencil. Copy it word for word, and then tear this up. Listen, and I will read it."

More from memory than the pale moon's rays glancing through the woods, Captain Cavendish read:

"DEAR CHARLEY:—I forgot to tell you this morning, when I consented to elope with you, that you had better go down to the steamboat office to-day and secure state-rooms, so that we may conceal ourselves as soon as we go on board. You can pay for this out of that money; it will do us more good than it ever would do that miser of a Lady Leroy. Ever yours,

"CHERRIE NETTLEBY."

"What money?" inquired Cherrie. "What money is he to pay for the staterooms out of?"

"Oh, I forgot. When you see him in the morning, give him this," producing a bank note. "I know he has not a stiver, and I got this from Oaks myself yesterday. It is for ten pounds, and Oaks's initials were scrawled on it, as he has a fashion of doing with all his bills. Tell him Lady Leroy gave it to your father in payment, and he presented it to you. Charley will take it; he is too hard up to be fastidious. Your note will, no doubt, be found upon him, and convict him at once."

"There's another thing," said Cherrie. "When Charley's arrested and my name found to that note, they'll think I knew about the robbery, and come up to Green-town after me. What should I do then?"

"That is true," said the captain, thoughtfully. "Per-haps, after all, then, you had better not go to your cousin's. Go on to Bridgeford; it is thirty miles further up, and a quiet out-of-the-way place, where no one ever stops, hard-ly. There is one hotel there, where you can stay quietly for a few days, and then slip off and get board in some farmer's house. Call yourself Miss Smith, and write to me when you are settled, telling all the particulars. Dis-guise your hand in writing the address, and I will run up and see you as soon as I safely can, and settle our future plans. Now, you are sure you remember and understand all I have been saying?"

"Yes," said Cherrie; "but, oh, dear me! I feel just as nervous and as scared! What will they do to Charley? Maybe they'll hang him!"

"Not the least fear of it. If they put him in prison, I'll try and get him clear off. You say they always go to bed for certain at nine o'clock at Redmon house?"

"At nine to a minute; but Lady Leroy always locks her door, nights. How will you get in?"

Captain Cavendish smiled.

"If it all was as easy as that, it would be a simple af-fair. Don't look so discouraged, my darling black eyes. With eight thousand pounds in my pocket, and the prettiest little girl in wide America as my wife, I will be off to merry England, and you and I will forget this land of fog and fish. I'm off now, Cherrie and perhaps it may be two or three weeks before I shall see you again, so take care of yourself. Here are eight sovereigns to pay your expenses; and be sure you write to me from Bridgeford."

He got up, but Cherrie clung to him, crying:

"Oh, I am afraid! O George, I am afraid I will never see you again."

"Little simpleton," he said, giving her a parting caress, "what can happen if you do your part bravely? If you fail, then, indeed, we will never meet again."

Cherrie's tears were falling fast now.

"I will not fail; but—but——"

"But what, my darling?"

"When you go to Halifax, perhaps you will never come back; perhaps you will never come to Bridgeford."

"Cherrie, you are a goose! Don't you know I am in your power, and that I must come back? Come, stop crying now, and give me a kiss, and say good-bye. It won't be long, you know."

One other parting caress, and then he was gone.

Cherrie listened until the echo of his footsteps died out in the distance, and then she threw herself on her face in the wet grass, heedless of her white dress, and cried like a spoiled child whose doll has been taken away. She was frightened, she was excited, she was grieved, but she was not remorseful. There was little compunction in her heart for the part she was to play—betraying the man who loved her and trusted her. It was the old story of Delilah and Samson over again.

The clocks of Speckport striking ten, and clearly heard this still summer night, had ceased before she came out, her cheeks pale, her eyes red with weeping. There was a dull circle round the moon, foreboding a coming storm; but what was there to give warning to poor Charley Marsh of the storm about to burst upon him?

Ann Nettleby was at the door waiting patiently for Cherrie. She turned crossly upon her when she appeared.

"I wish you would learn to come home earlier, and not keep folks out of their beds all night. What were you doing in the woods?"

"Crying," said Cherrie, quite as crossly as her sister.

"I'm tired to death of this dull place. I'll go off to Greentown to-morrow."

"I wish to mercy you would; the rest of us would have some peace then. Did you expect Charley Marsh to-night?"

"No; why?"

"He's been here, then, and only just gone. Come in, and let me lock the door."

Cherrie went up to her room, but not to sleep. She sat by the window, looking out on the quiet road, the black woods, and the moon's sickly, watery glimmer, while the long hours dragged slowly on, and her sister slept. She was thinking of the eventful to-morrow—the to-morrow that was to be the beginning of a new life to her.

CHAPTER XV.

SPRINGING THE MINE.

HEN Mr. Robert Nettleby informed his family circle that Charley Marsh was going to—well, to a certain dark spirit not to be lightly named in polite literature, he was about right. That young gentleman, mounted on the furious steed of extravagance, was galloping over the road to ruin at the rate of an express train.

Not alone, either; young McGregor, Tom Oaks, Esquire, and some dozen more young Speckportians, were keeping him company—and all ran nearly abreast in the dizzy race.

The terrible terminus—Disgrace, Misery, and Sudden Death—looked very near to some of them, very near, indeed, to the brother of Nathalie. He had taken to hard drinking of late, as a natural sequence of the other vice; gamblers must drink to drown remorse, and it was no unusual thing now for him to be helped home by pitying friends, and carried up-stairs to bed. How the mother cried and scolded; how the sister wept in passionate shame and sorrow in the silence of her own room; how he, the prodigal, suffered after, Heaven only knows, but it never came to anything.

Next day's splitting headache, and insuperable shame and remorse, must be drowned in brandy; that fatal stimulant brought the old delusive hopes—he must go back, he must win.

He was over four hundred dollars indebted to Captain Cavendish now, without possessing one dollar in the world, or the hope of one, to pay him. He had ceased to ask money from Nathalie—she had no more to give him, and Alick McGregor and Tom Oaks found enough to do to foot their own bills.

Strange to say, the primary mover of this mischief, the arch-tempter himself, George Percy Cavendish, remained unsuspected, save by a few, and went altogether unblamed. Captain Cavendish seldom lost his money, never his temper; never got excited, was ever gentlemanly and cool, though half the men about him were mad with liquor and losses, and ready to hold pistols to their heads and blow their miserable brains out.

Nathalie, humbled to the very dust with shame for Charley, never suspected her betrothed lover—never for one second; in her eyes he was the incarnation of all that was honorable and good.

It was in one of his fits of rage and remorse that Charley had asked Cherrie to fly with him. Not that he expected to atone by that; but, far from Speckport, which enchanting town was fast becoming hateful to him, and with her as his wife, he hoped to begin a new life, away from those he had disgraced. He hated Captain Cavendish with a furious and savage hatred, and it would be a demoniac satisfaction to tear Cherrie from him. For, with the eyes of jealousy, Charley saw his game, though all Speckport was blind. Miss Nettleby, at her old game of fast and loose, had put him off indefinitely. And, casting bitter reproaches to Fate, after the manner of Dick

Swiveller, Charley Marsh let himself drift with the rapid current, bearing him along to a fearful end.

The day that came after the night spent by Cherrie and Captain Cavendish in the cedar dell was one of scorching, broiling heat and sunshine. The sun was like a wheel of red flame, the sky of burnished brass, the bay a sea of amber fire.

Through all the fiery glare of this fierce August morning, went Charley Marsh to the office of Dr. Leach. No longer the Charley Marsh who had been the life of Mrs. McGregor's party, that foggy May evening when Captain Cavendish had first appeared in Speckport, but a pale, sunken-cheeked, hollow-eyed vision, with parched and feverish lip, and gaze that shrunk from meeting that of his fellow-men. His temples seemed splitting, his eyes ached with the blinding gleam, and he could have cursed the heat in his impious impatience and suffering. He glanced down toward the shining bay, and thought, if it had only looked blue and cool, instead of being a lake of fire, he could have gone and lain down in its pleasant waters, and escaped forever from the miseries of this life, at least.

"Charley!"

The voice at his elbow made him bound. He turned and saw Cherrie Nettleby, her shining ebon ringlets freshly curled, her black eyes dark and dewy, her rosy cheeks bright and unwilted, her dress airy and cool—unflushed, unheated; basking, like a little salamander, in the genial sunlight, and wearing the smile of an angel. Charley could scarce believe his eyes.

"You here, Cherrie!" he cried, "this blazing day. Have you been in Speckport all night?"

"No, I got a drive in this morning, and, Charley," dropping her wicked eyes, "I came to see you!"

They were near the office. The surgery looked cool and shady, and Charley opened the door and ushered the young lady in. The shopboy had the place to himself, and he retreated to a distant corner, with a knowing grin, at sight of the pair. Dr. Leach was rarely at home. People would persist in devouring new potatoes, and green peas,

8

and cucumbers, and string-beans, and other green stuffs, and having pains, and cramps, and cholera afterward, and the doctor was fairly run off his legs—that is to say, his horse was.

"How nice and cool it is in here," said Cherrie; "it's the hottest day came this summer, I think. What a hurry you were in leaving, last night, Charley."

"Hurry! It was past ten."

"Well, I came in a few minutes after, and was so mad when I found you were gone. I got such a jawing for being out! I won't stand it," cried Miss Cherrie, flying out in an affected temper; "I just won't!"

"Stand what?"

"Why, being scolded and put upon the way I am! It's dreadful dull, too, and I am getting tired of the place altogether; and so, I am going to leave it."

"With me, Cherrie?"

"I don't care if I do! I'm off this very day; I'll not stand it a minute longer—so, if you want me to go with you, you haven't much time to spare!"

Charley grasped both her hands, his pale face lighting with ecstasy; and the shopboy behind the pestle-and-mortar grinned delightedly at the scene, although he could not hear a word.

"My darling Cherrie!" Charley cried, "you have made me the happiest fellow alive! Wait until to-morrow, and we will be off in the boat to Boston."

Miss Nettleby fell to musing.

"Well, I don't care if I do," she said, at length. "I should like to see Boston, and the trip in the steamboat will be nice. But, look here, Charley, I've gone and told our folks and everybody else that I was going to Green-town, in this afternoon's train, and it won't do to back out."

"But you must back out, Cherrie! You cannot go to Greentown and to Boston, both."

Cherrie put on her considering-cap again, only for a moment, though, and then she looked up with a sparkling face.

"I have it, Charley! The nicest plan! This evening,

at half-past five, I'll go off in the cars, and every one will think I've gone to Greentown, so my absence to-morrow won't be noticed. I'll get out at the first station, three miles off, and walk back home, but won't go in. About eight to-night you call at our house, pretending you don't know about my being off, you know; and when our Ann tells you I have gone, you go up to Lady Leroy's and stay till bed-time. Then wait around the grounds in front of the house, and I'll come to you about ten. I can stop in one of the hotels here, where they don't know me. I'll wear a thick vail until morning, and then we will hide on board the boat. Isn't it a splendid plan, Charley? They'll think I'm in Greentown, and never suspect we have gone off together!"

No poor fly ever got entangled in a spider's web more readily than did Charley Marsh in that of Captain Cavendish. He thought the plan was capital, and he told her so.

"You must be sure to wait in front of the house until I come," said the wicked little enchantress, keeping her black eyes fixed anywhere but on his face. "And here, Charley—now don't refuse—it is only a trifle, and I won't go with you, if you don't take it. I don't suppose you have much money, and father made it a present to me after Lady Leroy paid him. I must go now, because I have ever so much to do before evening. Good-bye, Charley, you won't forget anything I've said?"

Forget! That face, fair in spite of its haggardness, was radiant. Bad as Cherrie was, she had not the heart to look at him as she hurried out of the shop and down the street. If he had only known!—if he had only known! —known of the cunning trap laid for him, into which he was falling headlong—if he had only known what was to take place that fatal night!

Charley Marsh did not go home to his dinner; he had dinner enough for that day. All that long sweltering afternoon he sat in the smothering little back-office, staring out at the baked and blistered backyard, and weaving, oh! such radiant dreams of the future. Such dreams as we all weave; as we see wither to shreds, even in the next hour.

Visions of a home, far, very far from Speckport, where the past should be atoned for and forgotten—a home of which Cherrie, his darling little Cherrie, should be the mistress and fireside fairy.

It was some time past five, when, awakening from these blissful day-dreams, Charley Marsh found that the little back office was so insufferably hot as not to be borne any longer, and that a most extraordinary change had come over the sky, or at least as much of the firmament as was visible from the dirty office-window. He took his hat and sauntered out, pausing in the shop-door to stare at the sky. It had turned livid; a sort of ghostly, greenish glare, all over with wrathful black clouds and bars of blood-red streaking the western horizon. Not a breath of air stirred ; the trees along the streets of Speckport and in its squares hung motionless in the dead calm, and feathers and bits of paper and straw lay on the sidewalk. The sea was of the same ghastly tinge as sky and air, as if some commotion in its watery bowels had turned it sick. And, worst of all, the heat was unabated, the planked sidewalks scorched your feet as you walked, and you gasped for a mouthful of air. Speckport declined taking its tea ; its butter was butter no longer, but oil ; its milk had turned sour, and the water from the street-hydrants nearly warm enough to make tea of, without boiling at all. There were very few out as Charley walked down Queen Street, but among these few he encountered Mr. Val Blake, striding in the direction of Great St. Peter Street.

Val nodded familiarly.

" Hot day, Charley. Going to be a thunder-storm, I take it. By the way, she'll have an ugly night for her journey."

" Who will ?"

" Little Cherrie, of course ; she's off to Greentown, man ! Didn't you know it ? I was down at the station ten minutes ago, and saw her off. How's the mother ?"

" Getting better. Good afternoon, Val," said Charley, passing on, and smiling at the news Mr. Blake had told him.

"What a clever head the little darling has to put them off the scent! Hallo, what do you want?"

Some one had shouted after him; and turning round, he saw Master Bill Blair, his hands in his pockets, his hat cocked on one side of his head, following at an extremely leisurely pace.

"I want you to hold on. I'll go part of the way with you, for I'm going home to tea," replied Mr. Blair, not hurrying himself. "It's hot enough to roast an ox, it is. You don't suppose the sky has got the jaundice, do you; it is turned as yellow as a kite's claw."

"You had better send up and inquire," said Charley, shortly, preferring his own thoughts to this companionship.

"I say, Marsh," said Bill, grinning from ear to ear, "Cherrie's gone, hasn't she? Good riddance, I say. What took her streaking off to Greentown, and whatever will you do without her?"

Mr. Marsh came to a sudden stand-still—they were in a quiet street—and took Mr. Blair by the collar.

"Look you here, Master Bill," said Charley, emphatically, "you see the water down there! Well, now take warning; the next time I find you making too free use of that tongue of yours, I'll duck you! Mind! I've said it!"

With which Mr. Marsh released him, and stalked on. Mr. Blair, pretty well used to being collared, took this admonition so much to heart, that he leaned against a lamp-post, and went off with a roar of laughter that awoke all the sleeping echoes of the place.

There was no one in the cottage parlor when Charley went in; and on the lounge in the sitting-room his mother lay asleep. He went softly up-stairs to his own room, so as not to awake her. That poor, pale, peevish, querulous, novel-reading, fond mother, when should he see her again?

A murmur of voices caught the young man's ear as he ascended; it came from Miss Rose's room—the door of which, that sultry evening, stood half open. Charley glanced in. Miss Rose, sitting at a little table, was writing, and an old woman on a chair near, with her shawl and

bonnet on, rocked to and fro, and dictated. Charley knew
Miss Rose was scribe to all the poor illiterate of Speckport, and knew she was at one of those sacred tasks now.
He saw the pale, sweet face in profile ; the drooping white
eyelids, hiding the hazel eyes, and the brown hair, damp
and loose, falling over her mourning-dress. He thought of
what Nathalie had said—"If you must marry any one,
why not Miss Rose?" as he closed the door without dis-
turbing them.

"No, Natty," he mentally answered. "Miss Rose is
an angel, which I am not, unless it be an angel of darkness. No ; she is too innocent and good for such a fellow
as I am. I wouldn't marry her if I could, and couldn't, I
dare say, if I would.

He changed his dress, and packed his trunk, laying out
a long waterproof coat on the bed, as a shield against the
coming rain. Before he had finished, he heard Betsy Ann
calling Miss Rose to tea. That reminded him he had had
no dinner, and was hungry ; so he went down stairs, and
Mrs. Marsh, at sight of him, broke out in petulant complainings.

Why had he not come home to dinner ? Where had
he been ? What was the reason it was so hot, and why
was he in evening dress? And Charley laughed good-humoredly as he took his place at the table.

"Be easy, mother mine ! Who could think of so preposterous a thing as dinner this sweltering day ? I have
been in the office since morning."

"Catty Clowrie was in here some time ago," pursued
Mrs. Marsh, feebly stirring her tea, "and she told me
Cherrie Nettleby had gone away up the country. What's
taken her off?"

Miss Rose was kind-hearted enough not to look at him,
and his mother was without her specs ; so neither noticed
the hot flush that arose to his face.

"How should I know ? Am I Miss Nettleby's confid-
ant ? Was Nathalie in the school-room to-day, Miss
Rose?"

"No."

" It was too hot, I suppose. This intense closeness can only end in a thunder-storm."

" I fancy we will have it shortly. The sky looks fearful; it has turned perfectly livid."

The meal ended, Charley walked to the window overlooking the wide sea, and stood blankly gazing out. It was nearly seven—time he was off to Redmon; and yet, with love and Cherrie beckoning him on, he was hesitating When should he stand here again—in this pleasant home where he had spent so many happy years? When, indeed? He was going to his fate, as we all go, blindly; and there was no foreshadowing dread to whisper to him—stand back.

The clock struck seven. It was possible to linger no longer. He went over to where his mother sat, and bent over her. Miss Rose in the next room was practicing.

" Mother!" Charley said, trying to laugh, and speaking very fast, " I have not been a very good boy lately, but I am going to turn over a new leaf from to-day. You can forgive the past, mother dear, can you not, if I promise better for the future?"

Mrs. Marsh looked up at him rather surprised, but still peevish.

" I am glad to hear it, I am sure. You have been acting disgracefully of late, just as if you wanted to break my heart."

" But I don't, mother, and I am going to amend. And when after this you hear others speaking ill of me, you will be my defender, will you not, mother?"

" Of course, Charles," his mother said, pettishly, "if you deserve it."

" Good-bye, then, mother; take care of yourself, and try and forgive me."

He kissed her, and hastily left the room. Miss Rose faintly and sweetly was playing some evening hymn. He stopped a moment to look at the slight black figure—for the last time, perhaps, he thought.

" Good-bye, Miss Rose," he called out; " I am off."

She turned round with a smile.

" Good-bye, Mr. Marsh! There is a storm coming—take care!"

How little she dreamed of the storm that was coming when she gave him that warning. He went out of the cottage, closing the hall door after him ; and the street and the figures in it looked blurred to him, seen through some foolish mist in his eyes.

With the waterproof overcoat thrown across his arm, his umbrella in his hand, and his hat pulled far over his eyes, Charley Marsh walked through the streets of Speckport steadily to his fate. There was an ominous hush in the stifling atmosphere, a voiceless but terrible menace in the sullen sky, the black and glassy bay, and the livid-hued evening. Charley's thoughts wandered to Cherrie. The storm would overtake her coming to town ; she would get drenched, and frightened half to death, for it was going to lighten. He could not walk fast, owing to the heat, and night fell before the Nettleby cottage came in sight. With it fell the storm, flash after flash of lightning cleaving black cloud and yellow air like a two-edged sword— flash after flash, blinding, intermittent, for nearly five minutes. Then a long dull roar, that seemed to shake the town, with great plashing drops of rain, as large and heavy as peas. And then the tempest burst in its might—flash, flash, flash!—the heavens seemed one sheet of flame—the earth rocking with the ceaseless roll of thunder, and the rain descending in torrents. Some low spruce-bushes, a zigzag fence, his glazed overcoat and umbrella, were shelter enough for Charley. He sat on a rock by the wayside, his hands over his eyes, feeling as though the fierce blue glare had struck him blind. The summer-hurricane was sublime in its fury, but too violent to last long. In three-quarters of an hour the lightning and thunder had ceased, but the rain still fell heavily. Charley got up, drew out his watch, struck a match—for the night had struck in pitch black—and looked at the hour. A quarter to nine, and where, oh where, in all this tempest was poor Cherrie? He hurried on at a frantic pace, fumbling in the blind blackness, until the red light of the cottage-window streamed across the inky gloom. He never stopped to imagine what they would think of his presence there at such a time ; he was too full of anxiety for Cherrie. She might have hired a cab and driven home, frightened by the storm, and he rapped loudly at the door. Ann Nettleby, lamp in hand, answered his authoritative summons.

"Is Cherrie here, Ann?"

Ann stared.

"Law, Mr. Marsh! how should she be here? Don't you know she went off to Greentown in the half-past five train?"

Charley stood looking at her, so pale and wild and wet, that Ann stared at him harder than ever.

"Is Lady Leroy worse?" she asked.

"Worse! Yes—no—I don't know. Has she been ill?"

"She's been very bad all the day. Dr. Leach has been up to see her, and our Rob's staying there all night for fear she should take another bad turn, and some one should be wanted to go for him again."

This was news to Charley.

"What is the matter with her?" he asked.

"Cramps. Did you not get Cherrie's letter?"

"What?"

"Cherrie's letter! She left a letter for you, and told me to fetch it to town to you, and I did this evening, but you weren't in, the boy said."

"Did you leave it at the office?"

"Yes."

Charley wondered what it could be about, but he did not ask Ann. He turned and walked through the darkness and the slanting rain, to Redmon House. The outer gate never was fastened, and he went under the dripping trees up to the castle of Lady Leroy. It was all in darkness, looming up a blacker spot in the blackness, but one feeble ray shone from Nathalie's room. Charley knew it was of no use entering then—past nine—when the place was closed and locked for the night, so he stood under the tall, gaunt trees, and watched that feeble, flickering ray. It seemed to connect him—to bring him in communion—with Nathalie; and when it went out, and all was dark and lonely, a light—the light of his love for her—seemed to go out of his heart with it.

8*

And now there was nothing to do but to watch for Cherrie. He seemed to have bidden farewell to all his old friends, and have only her left. His past life seemed gliding behind him, out of sight—a newer and better life opening before him, with her by his side to share it, until they should lie down at the far end, full of years and good works. He leaned against a tree, thinking of this, and waiting. The storm was abating, the rain ceasing, the clouds parting, and a pale and watery moon staring wanly across the gloom. In another hour the clouds were scudding wildly before a rising gale, and the moon had broken out, through their black bars, lighting up the grim old house with an eerie and spectral gloom. The trees looked like tall, moaning ghosts in the sickly and fitful rays, and the loneliness of the tomb reigned over all. Another weary hour of watching, and Charley was nearly mad with impatience and anxiety. Where—where—was Cherrie? The sighing night-wind, the moaning and tossing trees, the ghastly light of the fitful moon, and the ominous silence of nature, had no answer to give him.

What was that which rent the silence of the night? A shriek from the house behind him—a woman's shriek—the sound of flying feet, a key turning in a rusty lock, and the front door thrown wide open. En sac de nuit, which means, in a short night-gown and red flannel petticoat, her head tied up in a yellow silk handkerchief, Midge rushed frantically out, followed by a man. Charley had started forward, and the moon's light fell full upon his black form in the middle of the park. Quick as lightning, the iron grasp of the dwarf was upon his collar, and the shrill voice piercing wildly the night air: "I have him! I have him! Murder! Murder! Murder!"

CHAPTER XVI.

A CRIME.

HAT was done that night?

At the very hour of that fine August morning that Mr. Charles Marsh and Miss Cherrie Nettleby had the surgery of Dr. Leach so comfortably to themselves, that medical gentleman was up at Redmon, helping its mistress to fight out a battle with death. Yes, on that hot summer morning Lady Leroy was likely to die, stood even within the portal of the Valley of the Shadow, and Redmon and all earthly possessions seem about to slip from her forever. Good-natured Miss Jo, in the early morning, had sent up a present of a basket of cucumbers and lettuce, of both of which specimens of the vegetable kingdom Mrs. Leroy had partaken, well soaked in vinegar, as a sharpener to breakfast appetite. The consequence was, that before that repast was well down, she was seized with such convulsive cramps as only cholera patients ever know. Brandy applied inwardly, and hot flannel and severe rubbing applied outwardly, being without avail, Dr. Leach was sent for in hot haste. The old woman was in agonies, and Nathalie frightened nearly out of her wits. Dr. Leach looked grave, but did his best. For some hours it was quite uncertain whether he or the grim Rider of the Pale Horse would gain the battle: but victory seated herself at last on the medical banner of the Speckport physician. Mrs. Leroy, totally exhausted with her fierce sufferings, took an opiate and fell asleep, and the doctor took his hat to leave.

"She'll do well enough now, Miss Natty," he said, "only pitch the cucumbers into the fire the first thing. She'll be all right to-morrow."

Nathalie sat patiently down in the steaming and oppressive sick-room, to keep watch. The house was as still as a tomb; Midge was buried in the regions below, and the sick woman slept long and profoundly.

Nathalie took a book, and, absorbed by it, did not notice when Lady Leroy awoke. Awake she did, after some hours, and lay there quite still, looking at the young girl, and thinking. Of what? Of the long and weary months that young girl had in a manner buried herself alive in this living tomb of a house, to minister to her, to arrange all her business, to read to her, to talk to her, to do her all manner of good service, and to bear patiently her querulousness and caprice. It had been a lonely and eerie life for her, but when had she ever complained? and now what was she to gain by it all! For one act of disobedience she was disinherited—all these months and years wasted for nothing. She had come there in the belief—implanted by Mrs. Leroy herself—that she was to be the heiress of Redmon. Had she any right to go back from her word—to make her memory accursed—to go into that shadowy and unknown world opening before her with a lie on her soul? Dared she do it? She had an awful fear of death, this miserly old woman—an awful fear of what lay beyond death; and yet, with strange inconsistency, she felt herself on the verge of the grave—a long life of sin lying behind her, and making no effort to atone—only letting herself drift on. Yet is the inconsistency strange? Are we not, every one of us, doing the same? We are younger, perhaps, and fuller of life; yet do we not know the terrible truth, that death and ourselves are divided but by a single step?

Nathalie, bending over her book, all her fair hair dropping loose about her, saw not the eyes so closely watching her. How pale she looked. Perhaps it was the fright, not yet over; perhaps the heat; but her face was like a lily-leaf. While she watched her, Midge came softly in, and Mrs. Leroy closed her eyes again.

"Is she sleeping still?" Midge asked, looking toward the bed.

"Yes," said Nathalie, glancing up.

Midge bustled out, and presently returned with a cup of tea.

" Who do you think was here this morning to say good-bye?" she asked, while Nathalie was drinking it. -

" I don't know. Who?"

" Cherrie Nettleby, no less. She wanted to come up here whether or no, to see you and the missis, but I sent her to the right about quicker. The flyaway good-for-nothing's off to Greentown in the cars this afternoon."

" Indeed. And how long is she going to stay?"

" I told her I was glad to hear it," said Midge, " and that I hoped she wouldn't come bothering back in a hurry; and she laughed and shook back them black curls of hers, and said perhaps she would stay all summer. The place is well rid of her, and I told her so."

Nathalie, reverting to Charley, perhaps, thought the same, but she did not say so. Midge departed, refreshed by her bit of gossip, and Nathalie resumed her book. The steaming sick-room was irksome enough to her, but she would not leave Mrs. Leroy even for a moment in her present state. That old lady opened her eyes again; and as she did so, Midge came bolting back.

" Miss Natty, here's Mr. Tom Oaks come to pay that there money, I expect. Shall I send him off again?"

-Before Nathalie could reply, Lady Leroy half sat up in bed, feeble as she was, the ruling passion strong in death.

" No, no, no!" she shrilly cried, " don't send him away. Fetch him up here—fetch him up!"

Nathalie dropped her book and was bending over her directly.

" Dear Mrs. Leroy, are you awake? How do you feel now?"

" Better, Natty, better. Fetch him up, Midge—fetch him up."

Midge trotted off, soliloquizing as she went:

" Well, I never! I do think if she was dead and buried, the sound of money jingling atop of her grave would bring her out of it. You're to come up, Mr. Oaks. Missis is sick abed, but she'll see you."

Mr. Tom Oaks, a dashing young fellow, well-looking

of face, and free and easy of manner, strolled in, hat in hand. Nathalie rose to receive him.

"Good day to you, Miss Nathalie. How are you, Mrs. Leroy? Nothing the matter, I hope."

"She is better, now," said Nathalie, placing a chair for him by the bedside.

"I suppose you've come up to pay the money?" Mrs. Leroy inquired, her fingers beginning to work, as they always did when she was excited.

Yes, Mr. Oaks had come to pay the money and obtain possession of the documents that made him master of Partridge Farm. Sundry papers were signed and handed over—a long roll of bank-bills, each for fifty pounds, were presented to Lady Leroy and greedily counted by her, over and over again. Then Nathalie had to go through the performance, and the roll was found to be correct. Mr. Oaks, master of a magnificent farm, bowed himself out, the perspiration streaming from every pore.

When he was gone, the old woman counted the bills over again—once, twice, three times; her eyes glittering with the true miser's delight. It was not to make sure of their accuracy, but for the pure and unalloyed pleasure it gave her to handle so much money and feel that it was hers.

A knock at the front door. Mrs. Leroy rolled the bills hastily up.

"Give me the box, Natty; some one's coming, and it's not safe to let any one know there's so much money in the house, and only three poor lone women of us here."

Nathalie handed her the large japanned tin box Cherrie had spoken of, which always stood at the head of the bed, and the bills were placed in it, the tin box relocked and replaced, before the visitor entered. It proved to be Lawyer Darcy; and Nathalie, availing herself of his presence, left the room for a few moments to breathe purer air.

"I was very sorry to hear of your illness," the lawyer said, "and ran in as I was going by, although I am in rather a hurry. By the way, I am expecting every day to be summoned back here to alter that last unjust will of yours. I hope you have begun to see its cruel injustice yourself."

"Yes," Lady Leroy gravely replied, "I have. There is no one living has so good a right to whatever I possess as Nathalie Marsh. I did wrong to take it from her, but it is not too late yet. Come up here to-morrow morning and draw out another—my last will—she shall have everything I own."

The old lawyer grasped the sick woman's hand delightedly.

"Thank heaven, my dear Mrs. Leroy, that you have been brought to see matters in their true light. Natty's the best girl alive—ain't you, Natty?"

"What, sir?" Nathalie asked, as she re-entered the room.

"The best and prettiest girl alive! There, don't blush. Good afternoon to you both. I'll be up to-morrow morning without fail, Mrs. Leroy, and I trust I shall find you quite restored."

He went out. How little did he think that never again, this side of eternity, should he meet that woman; how little did he think that with those words he had bidden her an eternal farewell.

Midge brought up some tea and toast to her mistress after the lawyer's departure; and feeling more comfortable after it, the old woman lay back among her pillows, and requested her ward to "read a piece for her."

The book Nathalie was reading had been one of her father's, and she loved it for his sake and for its own. It was not a novel, it was "At the Foot of the Cross," by Faber; and seating herself by the bedside, she read aloud in her sweet, grave voice. The touching story of Calvary was most touchingly retold there; more than once the letters swam on the page through a thick mist of tears, and more than once bright drops fell on the page and blistered it.

The long, sultry afternoon hours wore over, and in that shuttered room it had grown too dark to see the words, before the girl ceased. There was a silence;

Nathalie's heart was full, and Mrs. Leroy was quiet, looking unwontedly thoughtful.

"It's a beautiful book," she said, at last, "a beautiful book, Natty; and it does me good to hear it. I wish you had read to me out of that book before !"

"I will read it all through to you," Nathalie said; "but you are tired now, and it is past seven. You had better have some tea, and take this opiate and go to sleep. You will be quite well again to-morrow."

Nathalie got the old woman's tea herself, and made the toast with her own white hands. Mrs. Leroy wished her to share the meal, but Nathalie could not eat there; the steaming and fetid atmosphere of that close chamber made her sick and faint. She was longing for the old woman to go to rest for the night, so that she might get out. She removed the tea-tray, and turned to leave the room.

"I am going out for a walk in the grounds," she said, "but I will be back by eight to give you the sleeping draught; and, for fear you might be taken ill again in the night, I will ask one of the Nettlebys to sleep here."

Without hat or mantle, she ran down-stairs and out into the hot twilight. The brassy hue of the sky, and the greenish-yellow haze filling the air, the ominous silence of nature, and the scudding black clouds, gave her warning for the first time of the coming storm.

She went down the avenue, through the gate, and along the dusty road to the cottage. The roses about it were hanging their heavy heads, the morning-glories and the scarlet-runners looked limp and wilted. She found Ann washing the dishes, and the two young Nettleby's lying lazily on the grass behind the cottage, smoking pipes. Nathalie preferred her request, and Rob Nettleby at once volunteered.

"I'll go up in half an hour, Miss Natty," he said, "and, if I'm wanted, I can gallop into town in ten minutes."

"Thank you, Rob !"

She went back to the kitchen, lounging a minute before she left.

"And so Cherrie's gone, Ann?"

"Yes," said Ann; "and I'm glad of it. We will have some peace for a while, which we don't have when she's here, with her gadding."

Nathalie walked slowly back to the house, wondering and awed by the weird and ghostly look of the sky. The evening was so close and oppressive that no breath of air was to be had; yet still it was better than the house, and she lingered in the grounds until the lightning shot out like tongues of blue flame, and the first heavy raindrops began to fall.

Hurrying in out of the coming storm, followed by Bob Nettleby, who opined it was going to be a "blazer of a night," she saw that all the doors and windows were secured, and then returned to Mrs. Leroy's room to administer the opiate. She found the old woman in a doze, from which her entrance aroused her, and raised her with her right arm in bed, while she held the glass to her lips with her left hand.

"It will make you sleep, dear Mrs. Leroy," the girl said, "and you will be as well as ever to-morrow."

"I hope so, Natty.—Is that thunder?"

"Yes; it is going to be a stormy night. Is there anything else I can do for you before I go?"

"Yes; turn down that lamp; I don't like so much light."

A little kerosene lamp burned on the table. Nathalie lowered the light, and turned to go.

"Good-night," she said, "I will come in once or twice through the night to see how you are. You are sure you do not want anything more?"

The sleeping-potion was already taking effect. The old woman drowsily opened her eyes:

"No," she said; nothing else. You're a good girl, Natty, and it was wrong to do it; but I'll make it all right, Natty; I'll make it all right!"

They were the last words she ever spoke! Nathalie wondered what she meant, as she went into her own room, and lit her lamp.

The storm without was raging fast and furious; the

blaze of the lightning filled the room with a lurid blue glare, the dull and ceaseless roll of the thunder was appalling, and the rain lashed the windows in torrents.

"Heaven help any poor wanderer exposed to such a tempest!" Nathalie thought.

If she had only known of him who cowered under the spruce bushes on Redmon road, waiting for it to subside.

Nathalie brushed out her long, shining, showering curls, bathed her face, and said her prayers. The furious and short-lived tempest had raged itself out by that time, and she blew out the lamp and sat down by the window—it was too hot to go to bed. She made a pile of the pillows, and leaned her head against them where she sat; and, with the rushing rain for her lullaby, fell asleep.

What was that? She awoke with a start. She knew she had not slept long, but out of a disturbed dream some noise awoke her—a sharp metallic sound. Her room was weirdly lighted by the faint rays of the wan and spectral moon, and with her heart beating thick and fast she listened. The old house was full of rats—she could hear them scampering over her head, under her feet, and between the partitions. It was this noise that had awoke her; the trees were writhing and groaning in the heavy wind, and tossing their green arms wildly, as if in some dryad agony—perhaps it was that. She listened, but save these noises all was still. Yes, it was the rats, Nathalie thought, and settling back among the pillows once more, she fell into another light slumber.

No, Nathalie. Neither the wailing wind, nor the surging trees, nor the scurrying rats made the noise you heard. In the corridor outside your room a tall, dark figure, with a black crape mask on its face, is standing. The figure wears a long overcoat and a slouched hat, and it is fitting a skeleton key in the lock of Mrs. Leroy's door; for Nathalie has locked that door. Like some dark and evil spirit of the night, it glides into the chamber; the lamp on the table burns low, and the old woman sleeps heavily. Softly it steals across the room, lays hold of the japanned tin box, tries key after key from a bunch it carries, and at last succeeds. The box is open—the

treasure is found. Fifty—fifty—fifty! they are all fifties
—fifty-pound notes on good and sound Speckport banks.
The eyes behind the mask glitter—the eager hands are
thrusting the huge rolls into the deep pockets of the overcoat. But he drops the last roll and stops in his work
aghast, for there is an awful sound from the bed. It is
not a scream, it is not a cry; but something more awful
than ever came from the throat of woman in all the history of woman's agony. It is like the death-rattle—
hoarse and horrible. He turns and sees the old woman
sitting up in bed, one flickering finger pointing at him,
the face convulsed and livid, the lips purple and foaming,
the eyes starting. One cry, and all for which he has
risked so much will be lost! He is by the bedside like a
flash; he has seized one of the pillows, and hurled her back;
he has grasped her by the throat with one powerful hand,
while with the other he holds the pillow over her face. Fear
and fury distort his own—could you see it behind the
mask—and his teeth are set, and his eyeballs strained.
There is a struggle, a convulsive throe, another awful
rattle in the throat, and then he sees the limbs relax, and
the palpitating throat grow still. He need fear no cry
now; no sound will ever again come from those aged
lips; the loss or gain of all the treasures in the wide earth
will never disturb her more. He loosens his grasp, removes the pillow, and the lamplight falls on a horrible
sight. He turns away with a shudder from that blackened and convulsed visage, from the starting eyes forced
out of their sockets, and from the blood which trickles
in a slow, dreadful stream between purple lips. He dare
not stop to look or think what he has done; he thrusts the
last roll into his pocket and flies from the room. He is
so furiously impatient now to get away from that horrible
thing on the bed, that he forgets caution. He flies down
the stairs, scarcely knowing that the noise he makes
echoes from cellar to attic of the silent old house. He
takes the wrong turning, and swears a furious oath, to
find himself at a door instead of the window by which he
had entered. He hears a shriek, too; and, mad with terror, tears off his mask and turns down another passage.

Right at last! this is the window! He leaps through it —he is out in the pale moonlight, tearing through the trees like a madman. He has gained the road—a horse stands tied to a tree, and he leaps on his back, drives his spurs furiously into the beast's side, and is off like the wind. In ten minutes, at this rate, he will be in Speckport, and safe.

———

The apartment in which Midge sought sleep after the fatigues of the day, was the kitchen, and was on the first floor, directly under Lady Leroy's room. She had quartered Rob Nettleby in the adjoining apartment—a big, draughty place, where the rats held grand carnival all the year round. Midge, like all honest folks in her station, who have plenty of hard work, and employ their hands more than their heads, was a good sleeper. But on this stormy August night Midge was destined to realize some of the miseries of wakefulness. She had not dared to go to bed during the first fury of the storm; for *Midge was scared beyond everything by lightning and thunder; but after that had subsided, she had ventured to unrobe and retire. But Midge could not sleep. Whether it was the heat, or that the tempest had made her nervous, or why or wherefore, Midge could never afterward tell; but she tossed from side to side, and listened to the didoes of the rats, and the whistling of the wind about the old house, and the ghostly moonlight shimmering down through the fluttering leaves of the trees, and groaned and fidgeted, and felt just as miserable as lying awake when one wants to go asleep, can make any one feel. There were all sorts of strange and weird noises and echoes in the lonely old house; so when Midge fancied she heard one of the back windows softly opened, and something on the stairs, she set it down to the wind and the rats, as Nathalie had done. She heard the clock overhead in Lady Leroy's room—the only timepiece in the house—strike eleven, and thought it had come very soon; for it hardly seemed fifteen minutes since it had struck ten. But she set this down to her fidgetiness, too; for, how was she to know that the black shadow in the

room above had moved the hands on the dial-plate before
quitting? But that other noise! this is no imagination,
surely. Midge starts up with a gasping cry of affright.
A man's step is on the stairs—a man's hurried tread is in
the hall—she hears a smothered oath—hears him turn and
rush past her door—hears a leap—and then all is still.
The momentary spell that has made Midge speechless is
broken. She springs to her feet—yes, springs, for Midge
forgets she is short and fat and given to waddling, in her
terror, throws on the red flannel undergarment you wot
of, and rushes out of her room and up-stairs, shrieking
like mad. She cannot conceive what is the matter, or
where the danger lies, but she bursts into Nathalie's room
first. Nathalie, aroused by the wild screams from a deep
sleep, starts up with a bewildered face. Midge sees she
is safe, and still uttering the most appalling yells, flies to
the next, to Lady Leroy's room, Nathalie after her; and
Mr. Rob Nettleby, with an alarmed countenance and in a
state of easy undress, making his toilet as he comes, brings
up the rear.

"What is it? Is Mrs. Leroy worse?" he asked, staring
at the shrieking Midge.

"There's been somebody here—robbing and murdering the house! Ah—h—h——!"

The shriek with which Midge recoiled was echoed
this time by Nathalie. They had entered the fatal room;
the lamp still burned on the table, and its light fell full
on the livid and purple face of the dead woman. Dead!
Yes, there could be no doubt. Murdered! Yes, for
there stood the open and rifled box which had held the
money.

"She's killed, Rob Nettleby! She's murdered!"
Midge cried, rushing headlong from the room; "but
he can't have got far. I heard him going out. Come!"

She was down the stairs with wonderful speed, followed by the horrified Nettleby. Midge unlocked and
flung open the hall-door, and rushed in the same headlong
way out. There was a man under the trees, and he was
running. With the spring of a tigress Midge was upon
him, her hands clutching his collar, and her dreadful yell

of "Murder!" piercing the stillness of the night. The
grasp of those powerful hands was not to be easily shaken
off, and Rob Nettleby laid hold of him on the other side.
Their prisoner made no resistance; he was too utterly
taken by surprise to do other than stand and stare at them
both.

"You villain! you robber! you murderer!" screamed
Midge, giving him a furious shake. "You'll hang for
this night's work, if anybody hung yet! Hold him fast,
Rob, while I go and send your brother to Speckport after
the p'lice."

The address broke the spell that held their captive
quiet. Indignantly endeavoring to shake off the
hands that held him, he angrily demanded what they
meant.

Rob Nettleby, with a shout of astonishment, released
his hold—he had recognized the voice. Midge, too, loosed
her grasp, and backed a step or two, and Charley Marsh,
stepping from under the shadow of the trees into the
moonlight, repeated his question with some asperity.

"Charley!" Midge gasped, more horror-stricken by
the recognition than she had been by the murder.

"What the deuce is the matter, Nettleby?" Charley
demanded, impatiently. "What is all this row about?"

"There has been a murder done," said the young
man, so confounded by the discovery as to be scarcely
able to speak.

"Mrs. Leroy has been murdered!"

Charley recoiled with a white face.

"Murdered! Good heavens! When? By whom?"

"To-night—just now."

He did not answer the last query—he thought it super
fluous. To his mind, Charley Marsh was as good as caught
in the act.

"And Nathalie! Where is she? Is she safe?"

"She is in Lady Leroy's room."

Charley only waited for the answer, and made a precipitate rush for the house. The other two followed,
neither daring to look at the other or speak—followed him
up-stairs and into the chamber of the tragedy. All was

as it had been. The ghastly and discolored face of the
murdered woman was there, even the pillow, horrible to
look at. But going partly across a chair as she had fallen,
all her golden hair tossed about in loose disorder, and her
face white, and fixed, and cold as marble, Nathalie lay
near the center of the room. There, by herself, where
the dreadful sight had first struck her, she had fainted
entirely away.

CHAPTER XVII.

FOUND GUILTY.

R. VAL BLAKE sat in his office, in that inner
room sacred to his privacy. He sat at that
littered table, writing and scissoring, for they
went to press that day, and the editor of the
Speckport Spouter was over head-and-ears in
work. He had just completed an item and was slowly re-
perusing it. It begins in a startling manner enough:

"Mysterious murder! The night before last a most
shocking tragedy occurred at Redmon House, being no less
than the robbery and murder of a lady well known in our
town, Mrs. Leroy. The deceased owned and occupied
the house, together with her ward, Miss Nathalie Marsh,
and one female servant. About eleven o'clock on the
night of the 15th, this servant was alarmed by the sound
of footsteps on the stairs, and aroused a young man,
Robert Nettleby, who chanced to be staying in the house,
and they proceeded together to discover the cause. On
entering the chamber occupied by Mrs. Leroy, they found
her dead; the protruding tongue and eyeballs, and purple
visage, telling plainly her death had been caused by stran-
gulation. A box, containing a large sum of money, eight
thousand pounds, we believe, was found broken open and

rifled. The assassin escaped, and no clue to him has as yet been discovered, but we trust the inquest which is to be held on the premises this morning will throw some light on the subject. It is a most inhuman affair, and, we are sure, no effort will be wanting on the part of the officials concerned to root out the heart of the matter, and punish the barbarous perpetrator as he deserves!"

Mr. Blake read this last neatly-rounded period with a complacent face, and then pulled out his watch.

"Ten o'clock!" he muttered, "and the inquest commences in half an hour. Busy or not busy, I must be present."

Speckport was in a state of unprecedented excitement. A murder—and people did murder one another sometimes, even in Speckport—always set the town wild for a week. Even the civic elections were nothing to it; and there having been a dearth of bloodshed lately, the tragedy at Redmon was greedily devoured in all its details. Like a rolling snowball, small enough at first, but increasing as it goes along, the story of the robbery and murder had grown, until, had Midge heard the recital, as correctly received in the town, she would have stared aghast. Crowds had flocked up Redmon Road the whole of that livelong day following the murder, and gazed with open-mouthed awe on the gloomy and lonely old house—gloomier and lonelier than ever now. Crowds were pouring up still. One would think from their morbid curiosity they expected the old house to have undergone some wonderful transformation. The Speckport picnics were nothing to it.

Mr. Blake, going along at his customary swinging pace, speedily reached No. 14 Great St. Peter Street, and letting himself in with his latch-key, went up-stairs to his sleeping-apartment, to make some alteration in his toilet before proceeding to Redmon. There was no one in the house; for Miss Blake had been absent on a visit to some friend out of town for the past few days, and Val took his meals at a restaurant. Thinking himself alone, therefore, Mr. Blake, standing before the glass, adjusting an

obstinate and painfully stiff collar, was not a little surprised to hear the street-door open and shut with a slam,
then a rapid rush up-stairs, a strong rustling of silk in the
passage, and his own door flung violently open. Mr. Blake
turned round and beheld his sister, in a state of perspiration, her face red with heat and haste, anger in her eyes
and in every rustle of her silk gown.

"It's not true, Val!" she burst out, before that gentleman could speak; "it can't be true! They never can
have been such a pack of fools!"

"What can't be true? Who's a pack of fools?"

"All Speckport! Do you mean to say they've really
gone and taken up Charley Marsh?"

"Oh, is that it?" said Mr. Blake, returning to his
toilet. "They haven't taken him up that I know of.
What brings you home? I thought you weren't coming
until Saturday."

"And do you mean to say you thought I could stop
one moment after I heard that poor old thing was dead,
and Charley Marsh taken up for it. If you can be un-
feeling and cold-blooded," said Miss Jo, turning from deep
pink to brightest scarlet, "I can't."

"My dear Jo, don't make such a howling! Charley
Marsh isn't taken up, I tell you."

"But he's suspected, isn't he? Doesn't all Speckport
point at him as the murderer? Isn't he held to appear
at the inquest? Tell me that."

"Yes," said Mr. Blake, looking critically at his cravat,
"he is. Is that collar straight, Jo?"

Miss Jo's only answer was a withering look.

"And he can talk of collars at such a time! And he
pretended he used to be a friend of that poor boy!"

"Don't be a fool, Jo," said Val, testily. "What can
I do? I don't accuse him!"

"You don't accuse him!" retorted Miss Jo, with
sneering emphasis. "That's very good of you, indeed,
Mr. Blake! Oh no, you don't accuse, but you stand up
there, like—like a cold-blooded kangaroo" (Miss Blake
could think of no better simile in the heat of the moment)
"fixing your collar, while all Speckport's down on him,

9

and no one to take his part! You won't accuse him,
indeed! Hadn't you better run up and do it now?
Where's Natty? Answer me that."

Miss Jo turned so fiercely upon her brother with
this query that Mr. Blake wilted at once.

"At home with her mother!"

"Poor dear girl!" and here Miss Jo softened into
tears; "poor dear child! What a shock for her! How
does she bear it?"

"She has been ill and hysterical ever since. They
don't suppose she will be able to give evidence at the
inquest."

"Poor dear Natty! And how does Mrs. Marsh
take it?"

"Very hard. Betsy Ann had to run to the nearest
druggist's for fourpence-worth of smelling-salts, and she
has been rocking, and reading, and smelling at it ever
since."

"Ah, poor dear!" said sympathetic Miss Jo, whose
first fury had subsided. "Does she know they suspect
Charley?"

"Of course not. Who would tell her that? Oh,
I say, Joanna, you haven't heard that about Miss Rose,
have you?"

"What about Miss Rose? Nobody suspects her of
the murder, do they?"

"Not exactly! She is going away."

"Going where?"

"To England!—hand me that vest, Jo—with Mrs.
Major Wheatley."

Miss Jo sat agape at the tidings.

"It is very sudden," said Val, getting into his Sunday
waistcoat. "Miss Rose had notice of it day before
yesterday—it was that night, the night of that terrible
affair at Redmon, you know, that it was proposed to her.
She declined then, although the terms were double what
she gets now, and the work very much less; but yesterday afternoon she accepted."

"She did! What made her change her mind?"

" Well, Mrs. Marsh told her, I believe, that now Lady
Leroy was gone, and Nathalie come into her fortune,
there would no longer be any need to keep the school,
and that, in point of fact, it would break up. Of course,
Miss Rose at once accepted the other offer, and leaves in
a very few days."

" Direct for England ?"

" Yes, that is to say, by way of Quebec. Mrs. Major
Wheatley is a very great lady, and must have a companion for herself, and a governess for her little girl, and
Miss Rose suits to a T. It's a very good thing for the
little school-mistress, but she will be missed here. The
poor looked upon her as an angel sent direct from heaven,
to make their clothes and buy their blankets, and look
after them when sick, and teach their young ones for
nothing."

" Well, I am sure! I declare, Val, I'm sorry! She
was the nicest little thing!"

" So she was," said Val, " and now I'm off! Don't
you go howling about the town, Jo, and making a fuss
about Marsh; if he is innocent, he will come out all
square—don't you be afraid."

" If!" screamed Miss Blake; but her brother was
clattering down-stairs half a dozen steps at a time, and
already out of hearing.

Droves of people were still flocking out the Redmon road, raising blinding clouds of dust, and discussing
the only subject proper to be discussed then in Speckport.
Val's long strides outstripped all competitors; and arriving
at the red brick house, presently ran the blockade of a
group of some two hundred idlers, and strode into the
house as one having authority. As Mr. Blake entered,
Dr. Leach stepped forward and joined him, with a very
grave face.

" How are they getting on ?" Val asked.

" They are getting on fast enough," the doctor
answered, in a dissatisfied tone. " They've been examin-
ing me. I had to describe that last interview with her,"
jerking his thumb toward the ceiling, " and prove to their

satisfaction she came to her death by strangling, and in no other way. They had Natty up there, too."

"Oh, she is better, then."

"Not much! but she had very little to tell, and Laura Blair has driven her off again. They have detained Mrs. Marsh—she does not know for what, though —and will examine her presently."

"To find out the cause of Charley's absence from home that night! Do you know, doctor, I begin to think things look black for Charley."

"Ah! you might say so?" said Dr. Leach, with a significant nod, "if you knew what I do."

Val looked at him.

"What you do! Do you mean or pretend to say——"

"There! there! there! Don't speak so loud. I may tell you, Blake—you're a friend of his and would do nothing against him. Read that."

He handed him a note. Val read it with a blank face. It was the note sent by Cherrie to Charley, which Ann had told him of, and a verbatim copy of that given Cherrie by Captain Cavendish.

"How did you get this?" Val asked, with a still whiter face.

"It was sent by that gadfly, Cherrie, to the shop, the evening of the murder. Her sister brought it, and, Marsh being out, gave it to the boy. Now, what do you think the young rascal did? Why, sir, broke it open the minute the girl's back was turned, and read it. As luck would have it, I pounced in and caught him in the act. You ought to have seen his face, Blake! I took the note from him and read it myself, not knowing it was for Marsh, and I have it ever since. I meant to give it to him next day, and tell him what I have told you; but next day came the news of the murder, and underhand whispers of his guilt. Now, Val, what do you think of it? Isn't the allusion to Lady Leroy's money plain enough?"

"That bit of paper might hang him," Val emphatically said, handing it back. "What do you mean to do with it?"

" There is only one thing I can do with it, as a conscientious man—and that is, hand it over to the coroner. I like the boy, but I like justice more, and will do my duty. If we only had that Cherrie here, she might throw some light on the business."

" What can she mean by that allusion to state-rooms ?" said Val. " Can they have meant to run off together in the steamer, and was Greentown only a ruse ? I know Charley has been spooney about her this long time, and would be capable of marrying her at a moment's notice."

" Blake, do you know I have been thinking she is hiding somewhere not far off, and has the money. The police should be set on her track at once."

" They will, when that note is produced. But, doctor, you seem to take it for granted that Charley is guilty."

" How can I help it ? Isn't the evidence strong enough ?"

" Circumstantial, doctor, circumstantial. It seems hard to believe Charley Marsh a murderer."

" So it does, but Scripture and history, ever since the times of King David, are full of parallel cases. Think of the proof—think of this note, and tell me what you infer candidly yourself."

" The note is a staggerer, but still— Oh, hang it !" cried Mr. Blake, impatiently, " I won't believe him guilty as long as I can help it. Does he say nothing in his own defense ?"

" Not a syllable, and the coroner and jury are all in his favor, too. He stands there like a sulky lion, and says nothing. They'll bring him in guilty without a doubt."

" Who have been examined ?"

" All who saw Lady Leroy that day—Miss Marsh, Midge, myself, Lawyer Darcy, and Tom Oaks, who swore roundly when asked that Marsh knew of his paying the money that day, for he had told him himself. He also swore that he knew Charley to be over head and ears in debt—debts of honor, he called them. Debts of dishonor, I should say."

"I think I'll go in! Can we speak to Charley, I wonder?"

"Of course. He is not held precisely as a prisoner, as yet. They have Midge up again. I never knew her name was Priscilla Short, until to-day."

"What do they want with her a second time?"

"She was the first to discover the murder. Her evidence goes clear against Marsh, though she gives it with the greatest reluctance. Come, I'll go in with you."

The two gentlemen went in together, and found the assemblage smiling at some rebut of Midge's. That witness, with a very red and defiant face, was glaring at the coroner, who, in rather a subdued tone, told her that would do, and proceeded to call the next witness, Robert Nettleby.

Robert Nettleby took his place, and was sworn. In reply to the questions put to him, he informed his hearers that he had heard nothing until the yells of Midge aroused him from sleep, and, following her up-stairs, he found her in Miss Marsh's room.

"Had Miss Marsh retired?" the coroner wanted to know.

Mr. Nettleby was not sure. If, by retiring, the coroner meant going to bed, no; but if he meant going asleep, yes. She was sitting by the window, dressed, but asleep, until Midge aroused her by her screams. Then she started up, and followed them into the room of Mrs. Leroy, whom they found dead, and black in the face, as if she had been choked. Midge had run down stairs, and he had run after her, and they saw some one running under the trees, when they got out. Midge had flown out and collared him, and it proved to be Mr. Charley Marsh.

Here the coroner struck in.

"He was running, you say: in what direction?"

Mr. Nettleby couldn't say positively—was inclined to think he was running toward, not from them. Couldn't swear either way, for it was a queer, shadowy kind of a night, half moonlight, half darkness. They had all three gone back to the house, Mr. Marsh appearing very much shocked at hearing of the murder; and on returning to the room of the deceased, had found Miss Marsh in a fainting-fit. They brought her to with water, and then her brother had taken her to her mother's house in Speckport, in a gig. He and Midge had gone to his father's cottage, where they had remained all night. Further than that Mr. Nettleby knew nothing, except—and here he hesitated.

"Except what, sir?" the coroner sharply inquired. "Remember you are upon oath."

"Well, sir," said Bob, "it isn't much, except that when we came back to the room, I picked this up close to the bed. It looked as if it belonged to a man, and I put it in my pocket. Here it is."

He produced from his coat-pocket, as he spoke, a glove. A gentleman's kid glove, pale-brown in color, and considerably soiled with wear. Val started as he saw it, for those were the kind of gloves Charley Marsh always wore —he had them made to order in one of the stores of the town. The coroner examined it with a very grave face— there were two letters inside, "C. M."

"Do you know to whom this glove belongs?" the coroner asked.

"I know I found it," said Nettleby, not looking at it, and speaking sulkily, "that's all I know about it."

"Does any one you know wear such gloves?"

"Plenty of gentlemen I've seen wear brown kid gloves."

"Have you seen the initials, 'C. M.,' inside this glove?"

"I have."

"And—on your oath, recollect—are you not morally certain you know its owner?"

Nettleby was silent.

"Speak, witness," the coroner cried; "answer the question put to you. Who do you suspect is the owner of this glove?"

"Mr. Marsh! Them letters stands for his name, and he always wears them kind of gloves."

" Had Mr. Marsh been near the bed, after your return to the room together, before you found this glove ?"

" No; I found it lying close by the bedside, and he had never been nearer than the middle of the room, where he was trying to fetch his sister to."

Robert Nettleby was told he might stand down, and Mr. Marsh was called upon to identify his property. Charley, who had been standing at one of the windows listening, in gloomy silence, and closely watched by two policemen, stepped forward, took the glove, examined it, handed it back, and coldly owned it was his.

How was he going to account for its being found by the bedside of the murdered woman ?

Mr. Marsh was not going to account for it at all—he knew nothing about it. He always had two or three such pairs of gloves at once, and had never missed this. Amid an ominous silence, he resumed his place at the window, staring out at the broad green fields and waving trees, bathed in the golden August sunshine, and seeing them no more than if he had been stone-blind.

Mrs. Marsh was the next witness called, and came from an adjoining room, dressed in black, and simpering at finding herself the cynosure of so many eyes. Mrs. Marsh folded one black-kid-gloved hand over the other after being sworn, with a mild sigh, and prepared to answer the catechism about to be propounded. The coroner began wide of the mark, and asked her a good many questions, that seemed to have little bearing on the matter in hand, all of which the lady answered very minutely, and at length. Presently, in a somewhat roundabout fashion, he inquired if her son had been at home on the night of the murder.

" No; he not been at home, at least not until he had come driving home with Natty, both of them as pale as ghosts, and no wonder, though they quite made her scream to look at them; but when she had heard the news, she had such a turn, it was a mercy she hadn't fainted herself, and she hadn't half got over it yet."

Here Mrs. Marsh took a sniff at a smelling-bottle she carried, and the ammonia being strong, brought a tear

into each eye, which she wiped away with a great show
of pocket-handkerchief.

"What time had her son left the house before returning with his sister?"

"After tea. He had been home to tea, which in itself
was so unusual a circumstance, that she, Mrs. Marsh, felt
sure something was going to happen. She had had a feeling on her all day, and Charley's conduct had increased
that feeling until she was perfectly convinced something
dreadful was going to happen."

"In what manner had her son's conduct augmented
her presentiments?"

"Well, she did not know exactly, but Charley had behaved odd. He had come over and talked to her before
going out, telling her he had been bad, but meant to be
good, and turn over a new leaf for the future; and, bidding her take his part if ever she heard him run down,
which she meant to do, for Charley was a good boy as
ever lived, in the main, only he had been foolish lately;
but mothers, it is well known, can forgive anything, and
she meant to do it; and if he, the coroner, was a mother,
she would do it herself."

"Was her son in the habit of stopping out nights?"

"Not until lately; that is, within the last two weeks,
since when he used to come home in a dreadful state of
drink, worrying her nearly to death, and letting all her
advice go in one ear and out of the other."

Mrs. Marsh was shown the glove, and asked if she
knew it. Yes, of course she did; it was one of Charley's;
he always wore those kind, and his initials were inside.
The coroner examined her further, but only got wordy
repetitions of what she had already said. Everything was
telling terribly against Charley, who stood, like a dark
ghost, still moodily staring out of the window. Val Blake
crossed over and laid his hand heavily on his shoulder as
Mrs. Marsh left the room.

"Charley, old boy! have you nothing at all to say for
yourself?"

Charley lifted his gloomy eyes, but turned away again
in sullen silence.

9*

"You know they will charge you with this crime, and you know you are not guilty. Can you not prove yourself innocent?"

"How? Will they take my word for it?"

"Explain why you were found in the grounds at that hour of the night."

"They have already asked me to do so, and I have already declined."

"But this is folly—this is madness! What motive could you possibly have for being there at such an hour?"

Charley was silent. Val laid his hand on his shoulder with a kindly look.

"Charley, will you not tell me?"

"No."

"You know I am your friend."

"You will not be so long. Those fellows over there will settle the matter shortly to their own satisfaction, and I am not going to spoil their sport."

"Charley," said Val, looking him steadily in the face, "where is Cherrie?"

Charley Marsh's face, white and haggard an instant previously, turned scarlet, and from scarlet whiter than before. But he lifted his eyes fearlessly to Val's face, roused to eagerness at last.

"Where is she?" he repeated. "Do you know?"

"No; but I think you do."

"Why do you think so?"

"That's not the question! Where is she?"

"I don't know."

"What!"

"I don't know. I tell you I don't! She is a false-hearted, lying, treacherous——"

His face was white with fury. His name, called by the coroner, restored him to himself. Turning round, he saw that gentleman holding out to him a letter. It was Charley's fatal note, given to him by Dr. Leach, while Val and Charley had been speaking.

"Do you know this, Mr. Marsh?" the coroner asked.

Charley glanced over the note, the coroner still holding it. It was all written on the first page, in a pothook-

and-hanger fist; an l Charley turned crimson for the second time, as he finished it and read the name at the bottom.

"Do you know anything of this, Mr. Marsh?" the coroner repeated.

"No," Charley coldly and briefly said.

"You recognize the writing and the name?"

"Yes."

"The writer of this, Cherrie Nettleby, alludes to money which she says will do you and her more good than it ever did Lady Leroy. To what money does she refer?"

Charley thought of the bank-note he had taken from her through sheer necessity, and once more the blood rushed in a scarlet tide to his face, ebbing again, and leaving him white as ashes.

Coroner, jury, and spectators saw his changing face, and set it down to conscious guilt.

"To what money does she refer?" reiterated the coroner.

"Sir, I decline answering that question."

"Indeed! Are you aware, Mr. Marsh, such a refusal tells very much against you?"

Charley smiled coldly, contemptuously.

"I am quite aware, sir, every circumstance tells very much against me. Nevertheless, I refuse to answer that and any other question 1 choose."

"The boy is either mad," thought Val Blake, "or else guilty. In either case, his doom is sealed!"

The coroner now explained to his court how the letter came into the hands of Doctor Leach, and read it aloud, handing it over to the jury for their inspection when he had finished. The allusion to his taking state-rooms for them both puzzled all who knew of the girl's departure for Greentown; but was set down by them, as it had been by Val, as a blind to deceive her friends.

Ann Nettleby was next called, and, in a state of great trepidation, related Charley's call at the cottage and inquiry for Cherrie. Informed the coroner, in reply to his question, that Mr. Marsh was "after" Cherrie, a constant visitor at their house, and had asked Cherrie not long before to run away with him to the States. Had not heard from her sister since her departure, but supposed she was up in Greentown.

One or two other witnesses were called, who had nothing to relate concerning the murder, but a good deal about Mr. Marsh's late dissipated habits and gambling-debts. When these witnesses were gone, Mr. Marsh was called upon, and requested, if he had anything to say in his own behalf, to say it.

Mr. Marsh had but little to say, and said that little with a recklessness that quite shocked the assemblage. The secret of his bitter tone and fiercely-scornful indifference they had no clue to, and they set it down to the desperation of discovered guilt. He informed them, in that reckless manner, flinging his words at them like a defiance, that Ann Nettleby's testimony was correct, that he had called at the cottage between eight and nine on the night of the murder, and on leaving her had gone straight to the old house, and remained in the grounds until discovered by Midge and Rob Nettleby. What had taken him there, what his motive in lingering, was what Cherrie meant in her note, and all else concerning his motives and actions he refused to answer. He was a drunkard, he was a gambler, he was in debt—"his friends" with sneering emphasis, "have given his character with perfect correctness. But for all that, strange as it might seem, incredible as he knew they would think it, he had neither robbed nor murdered his sister's benefactress. Further than that he had nothing to say."

He returned to the window again, flashing fierce defiance on every hand, and the coroner summed up the evidence. He was an old man, and had known Charley Marsh since he was a pretty little fair-haired, frolicsome boy, and he would have given a good round sum in hard cash to be able to find him innocent. But he could not, and justice must be done. He recapitulated his irregular conduct on the evening of the murder, as related by his own mother, his lingering in the grounds from dark until discovered by Priscilla Short and Robert Nettleby, confessed by himself; his glove found at the bedside, as if dropped in his haste and alarm; his knowledge of the large sum of money paid the deceased that afternoon by Mr. Oaks; his knowledge, also, of the house, as proved by his entering the back-window, found open, and of its lonely and unprotected state; and lastly, this note of Cherrie Nettleby's, with its distinct allusion to the money of Mrs. Leroy, to benefit him. It was a pity this girl was not here—but she soon would be found; meantime, the case was perfectly clear without her. It was evident robbery, not murder, had been the primary instigation; but the unfortunate woman awakening, probably, had frightened him, and in the impulse of the moment he had endeavored to stifle her cries, and so—strangled her. Perhaps, too, his sister being her heiress, and inheritrix of all she possessed, he had persuaded himself, with the sophistry of guilt, that he had some right to this money, and that he was only defrauding his own sister, after all. His debts were heavy and pressing, no way of paying them open, and desperation had goaded him on. He (the coroner) trusted that the sad case of this young man, once so promising, until he had fallen into evil habits, would be a warning to others, and an inducement not to stray away from the path of rectitude into that broad road whose end was disgrace and ruin. The money stolen had not been found, but there had been ample time given him to conceal it. He begged the jury to reflect on the evidence they had heard, consult together, and return a verdict according to their conscience.

The jury retired from the room, and in the awful silence which followed, you might have heard a pin drop. Charles Marsh, in this supreme crisis of his life, still stood looking out of the window. He neither moved nor spoke, nor looked at any one, nor betrayed the slightest sign of agitation; but his teeth were rigidly locked, and the palm of his strong right hand was bleeding where he had clenched it, in that silent agony, until the nails had sunk deep into the flesh. He had been reckless and defiant, and braved it out with a high hand; but Charles Marsh had had the misfortune to be born with a keenly sensitive heart, and a pride that had lain latent under all his careless life; and what he felt in that hour of disgrace and degradation, branded as a thief and a murderer before the friends who knew him all his life, was known only to Heaven and himself.

The jury were not long away. Evidently, his case had been settled in their minds before they had left their seats. And in that dread silence the foreman, Mr. Blair, with a grave, sad face, stood up to announce their verdict. It was only one word—the terrible word, "Guilty."

There was a swaying sound among the crowd, as if they had drawn breath for the first time. That dismal vord fled from lip to lip like wildfire, until it passed from the room to the crowd in the hall, and from them to the swaying mob without. It was quite a lively scene, in fact, out there, where that big crowd of men stood broiling under the meridian sun, when the verdict was announced, and the inquiries as to how "young Marsh" behaved and looked were many and eager. The question was not very easily answered. Young Marsh, standing by that sunny window, was so screened by the towering figure of Mr. Valentine Blake, that the gaping and exasperated throng craned their throats and stood on tip-toe for nothing. They would see him, however, when he came out to enter the cab, already in waiting, that was to convey him in the custody of the constables into town, and it was worth while waiting even for that fleeting glimpse.

Five, ten, fifteen, twenty minutes passed. The expectant crowd were getting angry and impatient; it was shameful, this dallying. But two or three policemen are out now with their red batons and brass buttons of authority, clearing a way for the gentlemen who are coming out, and for the cab which is to draw up close to the front door. · Still, the mob press forward, the coroner and jury are departing; and now the prisoner's coming. But a new disappointment is in store for them; for when he comes, he has his hat pulled so far over his eyes, and springs in so quickly, that they don't even get that fleeting glimpse of him they are crushing each other to death to obtain. The constables follow; it is pleasant even to see them; the blinds are pulled down; the cab drives off rap-

idly, and the crowd go home, ravenous for their dinner.
And Charles Marsh is on his way to Speckport jail, to
await his trial for the willful murder of Jane Leroy!

CHAPTER XVIII.

THE DARKENING SKY.

HE day after the inquest, the funeral took place.
As the clock of Speckport cathedral chimed
in sonorous sweetness the hour of ten, all that
was earthly of Mrs. Leroy was placed in the
hearse, and the gloomy cortege started. A
great many carriages followed the mistress of Redmon to
her last long home; and, in the foremost, two ladies, robed
in sable, and vailed in crape, rode. The outward mourning
was for the dead, the deeper *devil* of the heart for the living—for him who, on this wretched August day, was a
prisoner in Speckport jail, awaiting his trial for the greatest crime man can commit, doomed to suffer, perhaps, the
greatest penalty man can inflict.

Nobody in all the long line of carriages talked; they
crouched into corners, and shivered, and were silent, and
sulky, and cross, and uncomfortable, and gaped, and
wished the thing was well over, or that they had never
come.

They got their wish after a while. The last sod was
beaten down, and the carriages rattled back into the foggy
town—all but three or four; and they drove back to the
eerie old house, never so lonely and desolate as now. One
ceremony was yet to be gone through—that ceremony
the reading of the last will and testament of Mrs. Leroy.
Here, where it had been written, in the ghostly reception-
room, where the inquest had taken place, and where the
rats and black beetles had it all their own way, it was **to**

be read. It was this that brought Mrs. Marsh, who had been ill and hysterical ever since she had heard the result of the inquest, to the funeral at all. To her it was a great and joyful thing this wealth that after to-day was to be theirs, and not even in her grief could she forego the pleasure of being present. Heaven knows, it was nothing of the sort brought her daughter—the silent agony she had endured since yesterday can never be told; but she had hope yet. She had hope in this very wealth that was to be hers to help him. Young as she was, she knew enough of the power of money to be aware it can do almost anything in this world, and smooth the road to the next; and she trusted in its magic power to free her imprisoned brother. They all went into the silent and forlorn house together; Mr. Darcy, who was to read the will, and whose face was distressed and troubled to the last degree; Mr. Blair, as an intimate friend of the family; Mr. McGregor, Senior, and Dr. Leach; Mrs. McGregor and Mrs. Blair were with Mrs. Marsh, and Miss McGregor and Miss Blair were deeply sympathetic with Miss Marsh—the heiress!—and Mr. Val Blake, with his sister on his arm; and Midge, who had been at the signing of the will, brought up the rear.

The shutters of the closed rooms had all been opened, and the casements raised, for the first time in many a day, and the pale light of the foggy morning poured in. Lawyer Darcy took his seat at a table, and laid out on it a legal-looking document tied with red tape. The others seated themselves around the apartment; and Nathalie Marsh, in her deep mourning-robes, and her thick black crape vail down over her face, took her seat beside one of the open windows, and leaned her forehead on her hand, as if it ached.

Long afterward, when she was gone from them forever, they remembered that drooping black figure and bowed young head, with one or two bright curls, like lost sunbeams, shimmering out from under her crape bonnet. Long afterward, they thought of how she had sat that dull and miserable day, suffering as these patient womanly martyrs only suffer, and making no sign.

Lawyer Darcy seemed strangely reluctant to commence his task. He lingered and lingered, his face pale and agitated, his lips twitching nervously, and the fingers that untied the document before him, trembling. His voice, too, when he spoke, was not quite steady.

"I am afraid," said the lawyer, in that unsteady voice, "that the reading of this will will be a shock—a disappointment! I know it must astonish all, as it did me, and I should like to prepare you for it, before it is read."

There was a surprised and alarmed murmur, but no one spoke.

"You are all aware," the lawyer went on, keeping his eyes resolutely from that drooping figure at the window, "that when Mrs. Leroy made her will after coming to Speckport she bequeathed all she possessed to her ward, Miss Marsh. I drew up the will, and she made no secret of her intentions."

There was another painful pause. Val Blake broke it.

"Of course," he said, impatiently, "we all know Mrs. Leroy left Miss Marsh heiress of Redmon."

"But you do not know," said Mr. Darcy, "that a short time ago—in fact, a few days before her tragical death, she revoked that first will and made a new one."

"What?" the cry was from Val Blake, but no one heeded him; every eye was strained upon the lawyer.

"Made a new one," the lawyer repeated, still averting his eyes from the black form at the window; "a new one, entirely different; leaving, I am sorry to say, Redmon away from Miss Marsh—in point of fact, disinheriting her."

There were two little feminine shrieks from the Misses Blair and McGregor, a hysterical cry from Mrs. Marsh, but the bowed figure at the window never stirred. In the unnatural stillness of her attitude, her face hidden behind her crape mask, there was something more fearful than any outbursts of wild womanly distress.

"The new will was made, as I told you," continued Mr. Darcy, "but a few days before her death; made whilst smarting under a sense of anger, and what she called ingratitude. Miss Marsh had offended her, disobeyed her in a matter on which she had set her heart, and for this she was going to disinherit her. I expostulated, entreated, did all I could, but in vain. She was obstinate, and this new will was made, which I now hold in my hand."

Mrs. Marsh's face had turned as white as that of a dead woman, and great beads of cold sweat stood on her forehead. But she sat rigidly still, listening, and feeling as though she were in some dreadful dream.

"I drew up the will," pursued Mr. Darcy, "and Midge yonder and old Nettleby signed it. I fancied when her first resentment cooled, she would see the injustice of her act, and retract it. I was right; the day preceding the night of her death, hearing she was ill, I called to see her, and she told me to come the next morning, and a third will should be made, leaving all to Nathalie as at first. Next morning she was dead."

To the dark form, whose drooping face was pitifully hidden by the black vail, did any memory come of the words spoken to her by the dead woman that fatal night, and which had then been so mysterious:

"I'll make it all right, Natty! I'll make it all right!" Did she know what was meant now?

"And do you mean to say, Mr. Darcy," Val Blake cried, astonished and indignant, "that Nathalie Marsh is not the heiress of Redmon?"

"I do! this will disinherits her! It is a crying wrong, but no fault of mine."

"And who, then, is the heir?" asked Mr. McGregor.

"She bequeaths all she possesses, unconditionally, to her brother, Philip Henderson, or, in case of his death, to his children. I will read the will."

Amid that profound and impressive stillness, the lawyer read the last will and testament of Jane Leroy. It was concise enough, and left the whole of her property, real and personal, without conditions, to her brother, Philip Henderson, and his heirs, with the exception of five pounds to Miss Nathalie Marsh, to buy a mourning-ring.

Mr. Darcy hesitated over this last cruel passage, and felt inclined to leave it out; but he did not, and there was a suppressed murmur of indignation from every lip on hearing it.

Poor Mrs. Marsh was catching her breath in hysterical gasps, and being fanned and sprinkled with cold water, and the palms of her hands slapped by Miss Jo and the two married ladies. And still the vailed figure at the window sat rigidly there, uttering no cry, shedding no tears.

There are griefs too deep for words, too intense for tears, when we can only sit in mute and stony despair, while the world reels under our feet, and the light of the sun is blackness. To Nathalie Marsh, the loss of fortune was the loss of everything—brother, lover, home, happiness—the loss of all to which she had looked forward so long, for which she had endured so much. And now, she sat there, like a figure carved in ebony; and only for the ghastly pallor of her face in the indistinct glimpses of it they could catch through the vail, could they tell that she even heard.

It was Val Blake who again broke the silence that followed the reading of the will.

"I protest against this will!" he indignantly cried. "It is unjust and ungrateful! You should never have produced it, Mr. Darcy. You should have read the former will."

"You are jesting, Mr. Blake! While regretting as much as you can possibly do this unfortunate change, my duty is sacred, and by this will we must abide. Mrs. Marsh seems very ill; I think she had better be conveyed home."

No one ventured to speak to Nathalie, her unnatural manner awed them; but when her mother was supported from the room, and she arose to follow, good natured Miss Jo was beginning a homily on resignation, and on its being all for the best, perhaps, in the end. Her brother, however, cut her short with very little ceremony, and handed Miss Marsh in after her mother, and seating himself by the coachman, they started off rapidly. He might have spared himself the trouble; good Miss Jo might have preached for an hour, and Nathalie would not have heard one word of it. She sat looking straight before her, seeing nothing, hearing nothing, conscious of nothing, save only that dull and dark despair at her heart. Midge, who had come with them in the carriage, waited on Mrs. Marsh, and cried quietly all the way, bestowing anything but blessings on the memory of her late mistress.

Mr. Blake assisted both ladies into the house when they reached Cottage Street. Mrs. Marsh, who was very ill and in a state of hysterics, he carried in his arms and laid on the sofa. Nathalie entered the parlor, closed the door, and, still wearing her bonnet and mantle, sat down by the window that looked out on the blurred and misty street. She had flung back her vail, and in her white and ghastly face and dilated violet eyes you could read a waiting look. Nathalie was waiting for one, who, by some secret prescience, she knew would soon come.

Doctor Leach entered the cottage soon after their return, prescribed for Mrs. Marsh, and departed again. Had he been able to minister to a mind diseased, he might have prescribed for Nathalie, too; but that not coming within his pharmacopœia, he left without seeing her.

It was dusk when he for whom she waited came. The dull wet day was ending in a duller and wetter evening, and the tramp, tramp of the long-roaring waves on the shore made a dull bass for the high, shrill soprano shrieks of the wind. The lamps were flaring through the foggy twilight in the bleak streets, when Captain Cavendish, in a loose overcoat, and bearing an umbrella, wended his way to that house of mourning. He had not been two hours in Speckport, but he had heard all that had transpired. Was there one in the town, from the aristocratic denizens of Golden Row and Park Lane to the miserable dwellers in filthy back-alleys and noisome water-side streets, that did not know, and were not discussing these unhappy events with equal gusto? The robbery and murder of Mrs. Leroy, the inquest, the sentence and imprisonment of Charley Marsh, the will, and the disinheriting of Nathalie, all were as well known in the obscurest corner of Speckport as in that unhappy home to which he was going.

In the course of that long afternoon Midge had only once ventured into the parlor, and that was in fear and trembling, to ask her young mistress to take a cup of tea and some toast which she brought.

Nathalie had tasted nothing since the day before; and poor Midge, with tears in her fretful eyes, urged it upon her now. The girl looked at her out of a pair of hollow eyes, unnaturally large and bright, in a vague way, as if trying to comprehend what she said; and when she did comprehend, refusing. Midge ventured to urge; and then Nathalie broke out of her rigid, despairing stillness, into passionate impatience.

"Take it away!" she cried, "and leave me alone! Leave me alone, I tell you!"

Midge could do nothing but obey. As she quitted the room with the tray, there came a knock at the front door. She set down the tray and opened it, and the tall form of the young English officer confronted her. Midge had no especial love for Captain Cavendish, as we know; but she was aware her young lady had, and was, for the first time in her life, glad to see him. It was good of him to come, she thought, knowing what had happened; and perhaps his presence might comfort her poor Miss Natty, and restore her to herself.

"Yes," Midge said, in answer to his inquiry; "Miss Marsh was at home, and would see him, she thought. If he would wait one minute she would ascertain."

She returned to the parlor to ask. But Nathalie had already heard his voice, and was sitting up, with a strained white face, and her poor wasted hands pressed hard over her heart. She only made an assenting motion to Midge's question, should she show him in, and a negative one when she spoke of bringing a lamp. Through all her torpor of utter misery, she was dimly conscious of a change in herself; that she was haggard and ghastly, and the beauty which had won him first to her side, utterly gone. That gloomy twilight hour was best befitting the scene so soon to take place; for her prophetic heart told her, as surely as if she had read it in the Book of Fate, that this meeting was to be their last.

Midge admitted him, and closing the door behind him, retired into a distant corner of the hall, and throwing her apron over her head, cried quietly, as she had done all day. She would have given a good deal if the white painted panels of the parlor door had been clear glass, and that she could have seen this man comforting her beloved young lady. Much as she had disliked him, she could have knelt down in her gratitude, and kissed the dust off his feet.

Even in the pale, sickly half-twilight of the dark evening, Captain Cavendish could see the haggard cheeks, the sunken eyes, and the death-like livid pallor of the girl's face, and was shocked to see it. He had expected to find her changed, but not like this; and there was real pity for the moment in his eyes as he bent over her and took her hand. He started to find it cold as ice, and it lay in his passive, and like a bit of marble.

"Nathalie," he said, "my darling! I am sorry; I cannot tell you how sorry I am for you. You have suffered indeed since I saw you last."

She did not speak. She had not looked at him once. Her dilated eyes were fixed on the blackening night-sky.

"I only reached Speckport an hour ago," he went on, "and I can never tell you how deeply shocked I was to hear of the dreadful events that have taken place since my departure. Is it all true?"

"Yes—all!" she said. Her voice sounded strange and far-off, even to herself, and she was aware it must sound hollow and unnatural to him.

"All is true! My brother is in prison, accused of murder, and I am a beggar!"

Her hand felt so icily deathlike in his, that he dropped it with a shiver. She still sat looking out into the deepening gloom, her white, set face gleaming marble-white against her black dress and the darkening room.

Captain Cavendish rose up from the seat he had taken, and began pacing rapidly up and down, heartily wishing the scene was over.

"I know," said the hollow voice, so unlike—so unlike

the melodious voice of Nathalie, "that all between us must end now. Disgrace and poverty must be my portion from henceforth, and you will hardly care to marry so fallen and degraded a creature as I am. From all that binds you to me, Captain Cavendish, I free you now!"

In the depths of her heart, unseen in the darkness of despair even by herself, did any feeble ray of hope—that great gift of a merciful God—still linger? If so, the deep and prolonged silence that followed her words must have extinguished the feeble glimmer forever. When Captain Cavendish spoke, and it was some time before he did so, there was a quiver of shame in his tones, all unusual there. Very few ever had a better opinion of their own merits, or were less inclined to judge hardly of themselves, than George Percy Cavendish, but she made him despise himself now, and he almost hated her for it.

"You are generous, Miss Marsh," he said—cold and cruel words, and even he felt them so to be, "and I thank you for that generosity. Loss of fortune would be nothing to me—that is to say, I could overlook it—though I am not rich myself, but this other matter is different. As you say, I could hardly marry into a family stained with— unjustly let us hope—the brand of murder. I shall ever esteem and respect you, Miss Marsh, as the best and bravest of women, and I trust that you will yet make happy some one worthier of you than I am."

Is murder, the murder of the body, when a man plunges a knife into his fellow-man's breast, and leaves him stark and dead, the greatest of all earthly crimes? Earthly tribunals consider it so, and inflict death on the perpetrator. But is there not another murder—a murder of the heart— committed every day, of which we hear nothing, and which man has never made a law to punish. There are wounds which leave little outward trace; but the patient bleeds inwardly, yet bleeds to death for all that, and it is the same ultimatum, death, by a different means. But there is a higher tribunal; and perhaps before that, the sins overlooked by man shall be judged and condemned.

Captain Cavendish took his hat and turned to depart. He felt exceedingly uncomfortable, to say the least of it.

He wished that black figure would not sit so petrified and stone-like, he wished that white face gazing out into the night would look a little less like the face of a corpse. He wished she would flame up in some wrathful outburst of womanly fury and insulted pride, and order him to depart, and never show her his false face again. He wished she would do anything but sit there, in that frozen rigidity, as if slowly turning to stone.

"Nathalie!" he said, venturing to take her icy fingers again, "will you not speak one word to me before I go?"

She withdrew her fingers, not hastily or in anger, but never looked at him.

"I have nothing to say," her unnatural voice replied.

"Then good-bye, Nathalie!"

"Good-bye!"

He opened and closed the parlor door, opened and closed the front door, and was gone. He looked at the window of that dark room as he strode by, and fancied he saw the white face gleaming on him menacingly through the gloom. The white face was there, but not menacing. Whatever she might feel in the time to come, when the first terrible shock of all this was over, she could feel nothing so petty as resentment now. Her anguish was too supreme in this first dreadful hour. The world to her stood still, and the blackness of desolation filled the earth. "All for love, and the world well lost!" had been her motto. It was for his sake she had risked everything, and verily, she had her reward!

CHAPTER XIX.

THE FLIGHT.

RS. MAJOR WHEATLY was a very fine lady, and lived in a very fine house two or three miles out of town. Having secured a traveling companion and a governess for her daughter, in the person of Miss Rose, the little Speckport school-mistress, she had desired that young person to come out to their place immediately, and assist in the packing and other arrangements, preparatory to starting. Miss Rose had obeyed, and being out of town had heard nothing of the inquest and the verdict until that night, when the major drove in, after dusk, with the news. Mrs. Major Wheatly, like any other fine lady, was greatly addicted to news, and received a severe shock in her nervous system by the manner in which her paid companion received the intelligence. They were all sitting at tea when the major blurted out the story, and his conviction that "the young scamp would be hung, and serve him right," and Miss Rose had fallen suddenly back in her chair in a violent tremor and faintness. All the next day she had gone about so pale and subdued that it gave Mrs. Wheatly the fidgets to look at her; but whatever she felt, she had wisely kept to herself, and made her moan inwardly, as dependents who know their places always should. "Sufficient unto the day is the evil thereof"—that day brought its own evil tidings. The major returning at his usual hour of the evening from town, announced the astounding intelligence that Miss Nathalie Marsh was disinherited, and the broad lands of Redmon given to another. Mrs. Major Wheatly sipped her tea and ate her buttered toast, and was deeply sympathetic. She had met the pretty, golden-haired, violet-eyed heiress often in society, and had admired and liked her, as most people did, and

10

was as sorry for her as was consistent with the dignity of so great a lady.

"Of course Captain Cavendish must recede now," she said : "he paid her very marked attentions, but of course he will not marry a penniless bride. Were they engaged, I wonder ?"

"Cavendish is a fortune-hunter," said the major. "Miss Marsh is a very nice girl, and a very pretty one, and altogether too good for him. No fear of his marrying her, my dear; he wouldn't marry the Venus Celestis herself, without a handsome dowry."

"Mrs. Wheatly," Miss Rose said, "I must go into town to-morrow morning, to see my friends and say good-bye."

She was so pale and tremulous saying this, that the lady hastened to assent, nervously, lest she should make another scene.

"I am going in about nine o'clock," the major said, "and will drive you. Harris will take you back."

"And you must not stay long, Miss Rose," his lady languidly said; "remember we start at half-past two, and there is so much to be done."

The clock on the sitting-room mantel of that silent house on Cottage Street was pointing to half-past nine, when Betsy Ann, with fuzzy hair and sleepy face, hastened to answer a knock at the front door. She stared sleepily at her visitor, who came hurriedly in.

"Is she here, Betsy Ann?—Miss Marsh?"

"Yes'm," Betsy Ann said, "she's up in your room, and Miss Laura Blair and Midge, they've been and sot up with her all night, and me and Miss Jo Blake we've been sitting up with Mrs. Marsh. Midge, she's gone to bed now, and you'd better go up-stairs."

Miss Rose ascended the stairs, and tapped at the door that had been her own. It was opened by Laura Blair, looking pale and fagged.

"Is it you, Miss Rose?" she said, in a low voice, kissing her. "I was afraid you were not coming to say good-bye."

"I could not come sooner, and can stay only an hour now. How is she?"

"There is no change. She has lain all night as she is lying now."

Miss Rose looked at the bed, tears slowly swelling up and filling her soft brown eyes. Nathalie lay among the white pillows, her amber tresses trailing and falling loose all about, her hands clasped over her head, her haggard face turned to the window overlooking the bay, her wide-open blue eyes staring blankly at the dim gray sea melting away into the low gray sky.

"She lies like that," Laura softly said, "all the time. We sat up with her all night, but she never slept, she hardly moved; whenever we went near the bed, we found her eyes wide open and vacant, as they are now. If she could only talk or cry, she would be better, but it makes one's heart ache to look at her."

"Does she not talk?"

"She will answer you if you speak to her, but that is all. She is quite conscious, but she seems to be in a sort of torpor. I will leave you with her, and lie down for half an hour. She was very fond of you, and perhaps you can do more with her than I could."

Laura departed; and Miss Rose, going over to the bed, stooped down and kissed the cold, white face, leaving two bright tears upon it.

"Nathalie, dearest," she said, "do you know me?"

Her large, melancholy eyes turned upon her sweet, tender face.

"Yes," she said, in that voice so unlike her own, that it startled her hearer. She seemed so unlike herself every way, that Miss Rose's tears rained down far faster than they would have done at any outbreak of grief.

"You are ill, my darling," Miss Rose faltered through her tears. "I wish I could stay and nurse you back to health, but I am going away to-day—going, perhaps, never to come back."

"Going away? Oh, yes. I remember!"

She turned wearily on the pillow, still gazing out over the wide sea, as if her thoughts were far away.

"I am very sorry for you, dear, dear Nathalie! Very, very sorry for you! It seems to me, sometimes, there is nothing in all this world but suffering, and sorrow, and death."

"Death!" Nathalie echoed, catching with sudden and startling vehemence at the word. "Miss Rose, are you afraid to die?"

The question was so sudden and so strange, that Miss Rose could not for a moment answer. A wild gleam of light had leaped into the sick girl's eyes, and irradiated her face so unnaturally, that it struck her companion with terror.

"Afraid to die?" she faltered. "To die, Nathalie?"

"Yes," Nathalie repeated, that abrupt energy yet in her voice; "you are good and charitable, better than any other girl I know, and you ought not to be afraid to die. Tell me, are you?"

She laid hold of Miss Rose's wrist, and looked wildly into her frightened face. The girl tried to still her beating heart and answer.

"I am not good, Nathalie. I am an erring and sinful creature; but, trusting in the great mercy of God, I think I shall not be afraid to die when it shall please him to call me. We must rely on his mercy, Nathalie, on that infinite compassion for our misery that made him die for us. If we thought of his justice, we might all despair."

Nathalie turned away, and looked out again over the dark, tossing bay. The sweet voice of Miss Rose broke the stillness.

"To the just, Nathalie, there is no such word as death! To quit this world, to them, is only passing from earth to Heaven in the arms of angels. Why should we ever grow to love this world, when day after day it is only passing from one new trouble and sorrow to another?"

"Sorrow!" Nathalie repeated, in a voice sadder than any tears. "Yes, sorrow, sorrow, sorrow! There is nothing left now but that."

"Heaven is left, my darling," Miss Rose whispered, her fair face radiant. "Oh, look up, Nathalie! When all the world deserts us, there is One left who will never turn away when we cry out to him. We may turn our backs upon him and forget him in the hour of our happiness and prosperity, but when the world darkens around us, and all earthly love fails, he will never leave us or forsake us, but will lead us lovingly back to a better and purer bliss. Remember, Nathalie, the way to heaven is the way of the Cross. It is a hard and thorny one, perhaps; but think of the divine feet that have trodden it before us."

"Stop, stop, stop!" Nathalie impatiently cried out, "why do you talk to me like this! I am not good—I am only miserable and despairing, and I want to die, only I am afraid!"

She moved away her face; but Miss Rose, bending over her still, kissed once more the averted face.

"There was a time, Nathalie," she said softly, "when I was almost as miserable as you are now, when, God forgive me, I prayed in my passionate and wicked rebellion to die too. There was a time, Nathalie, when I was rich and flattered, and beloved and happy—as happy as we can ever be with the blind happiness of a lotus-eater when we never think or thank the good God from whom that happiness comes. I thought myself an heiress as you did, Nathalie; my father was looked upon as a rich and honorable man, and his only daughter the most enviable girl in all the city of Montreal. It was balls and parties, and the theater and the opera, every night; and riding and driving, and dressing and shopping all day long. I had my carriage to ride in, a fine house to live in, servants to wait on me, and rich dresses and jewels to wear; and I thought life was one long holiday, made for dancing and music, and sunshine and joy. I had a lover, too, whom I thought loved me, and to whom I had given my whole heart, and we were on the verge of being married. Are you listening to me, Nathalie?"

"Yes," Nathalie said. She had been listening intently, forgetting for the first time her own sorrows, to hearken to the story, so like her own.

"Well, Nathalie, in one day, almost as you have done,

I lost all—father, lover, fortune, honor. My father went out from breakfast, hale and well, and was carried home two hours afterward, struck dead. Congestion of the brain they said it was. I was so frantic at first, I could realize nothing but his death, but I was soon sternly compelled to listen to other bitter facts. Instead of being an heiress, I was a beggar. I was far poorer than you, for I was motherless and without a home to shelter me. The creditors seized everything—house, furniture, carriages, horses, plate, pictures—and turned me, in point of fact, into the street. I had been educated in a convent, and the good nuns gave me a home; but for that, I might have gone to the almshouse, for the friends of prosperity are but frail reeds to lean upon in adversity. He whom I was to have wedded, Nathalie, cast me off; he could never disgrace his English friends by bringing to them as his wife the daughter of a wretched defaulter. Dearest Nathalie, I need not tell you what I suffered—you are feeling the the same anguish now—and I was rebellious and despairing, and wished impiously for nothing but death. The nuns, with the sweetness and patience of angels, as they are, used to sit by me for hours, telling me that blessed are they who mourn and are chastened; but I could not listen. Oh! it was a miserable, miserable time! and there seemed no light for me either in earth or heaven. If I had been 'cursed with the curse of an accomplished evil prayer,' and died then in my wicked despair, I shudder to think of what would have been my fate. But that merciful and loving Father had pity on me in spite of myself, and it is all over now, and I am happy. Yes, Nathalie, happy, with a far better and more rational happiness than I ever felt in the most joyous days of my prosperity; and I have learned to thank God daily, now, for what I then thought the greatest misery that could ever befall me. I wished to take the vail; but the nuns knew the wish proceeded from no real vocation, but from that weary heart-sickness that made me so disgusted with the world, and would not consent, at least not then. I was to go out into the world again, and mingle in its ceaseless strife once more; and if at the end of a year the desire

was as strong as ever, I was to go back to that peaceful
haven, like the dove to the ark, and be sheltered from the
storms of life forever. So I came here, Nathalie; and I
am happy, as I say—happy, as with Heaven's help you
will one day be. I labor for a sacred cause, and until that
is accomplished, I shall enter no convent—it is to pay my
father's debts. They are not so very large now; and in
three or four years, if life and health be granted me, I
hope to accomplish my task.

"And now, Nathalie, you have heard my story; it is
not a very romantic one, but in many ways it is similar
to your own. This fever of wretchedness will pass, as
mine has done, if you only pray. All the secret lies
there, pray; and he who has said 'Seek and ye shall
find,' will not refuse you peace."

Her face was like the face of an angel. Nathalie
looked into the inspired eyes, and felt how sinful and lost
she was beside this heroic girl—this simple, womanly
martyr, kissing meekly the rod which struck her—this
patient, humble soul, rebelling not, but thanking God
alike for the joy and suffering it pleased him to send.
She felt, through all the dull torpor of suffering, how un-
worthy she was beside her; but she could not, in that
first bitter hour, imitate her. She could not; she only
turned away again in gloomy silence.

"You will think of all this, dearest Nathalie," the
soft, tender voice went on; "for all this pain, like every
other earthly pain, must pass away. The great lesson of
life is endurance; and all, from the king to the beggar,
must learn it."

She rose, as she spoke, to go, for more than an hour
had passed, and kissed the cold and averted face again.

"I must leave you, Nathalie," she said, her tears falling on that colorless face. "Good-bye, and God bless
and comfort you."

"Good-bye," was the only response; and Miss Rose
left the room. Laura Blair met her in the lower hall.

"Are you going?" she asked; "the gig is waiting for
you."

" Yes ; but I think I should like to see Mrs. Marsh, to say good-bye."

" She is asleep, and so is Miss Blake. I will say it to both of them for you. I am very sorry you are going, Miss Rose. Do you think you will ever come back ?"

" Oh, yes, I hope so ! If I send you my address, Miss Blair, will you write and tell me how—how all my friends get on ?"

" Yes, with pleasure."

Betsy Ann came out to bid farewell, and Laura kissed her, and watched her as she entered her gig and was driven away. Miss Rose had no time to bid good-bye to any one else ; but when she reached the station early in the afternoon, in the carriage, with Major and Mrs. and Miss Wheatly, she found all her pupils assembled, in Sunday attire, waiting to say farewell. Mrs. Wheatly shrugged her shoulders at the scene, and stared through her eye-glass, and was relieved when they were all seated in the car and the scene was over. As they took their place, a gentleman on the platform leaned his elbow on the window, and lifted his hat in salutation to the ladies.

" Hallo, Blake !" said the major, nodding familiarly, " come to see us off ?"

" No," said Val ; " I've come to see myself off. I'm going to take a couple of holidays and look at the country. Keep a place for me, Miss Rose ; I want to talk to you. I'll be in in a brace of shakes."

It is probable a brace of shakes meant fifteen minutes, for at the expiration of that period of time, and just as the train was in motion, Mr. Blake lounged in, laden with oranges, peaches, and newspapers, which he distributed promiscuously, and then took a seat beside Miss Rose. It was pleasant to have Val for a traveling companion, for he knew every inch of the country, and was so full of stories and anecdotes as to be perfectly fascinating. He talked of the murder, asserted his belief in Charley's innocence, in spite of any amount of circumstantial evidence, and his firm conviction that the mystery would be speedily cleared up ; his present journey, he hinted, being taken to bring about that desirable result.

The fact was, Mr. Blake had of his own choice turned amateur detective, and was on the track of Miss Cherrie Nettleby, and positively resolved never to stop until he had hunted that young lady down. A telegram had been dispatched to Greentown the day before, and the answer Val had expected returned; Cherrie had never been near her relations in Greentown at all. The reply threw the family at the cottage into consternation, but Val reassured them by expressing his resolution to find her, if she was above ground. From his inquiries at the station, he had found out from the clerk, who knew her (who did not know Cherrie?) that she had taken a through ticket to the terminus, thirty miles beyond Greentown. The conductor remembered very well the pretty girl with the dark eyes and curls, and rosy cheeks; had found her dozing every time through the night he had passed in that car; remembered her ticket was for S——, the terminus, but was positive she had got out before they reached the final station. Where or when she had left, he could not say; it was after night, and passengers were getting out and coming in at every station, and she could easily depart among them unnoticed. He did not know whether she had gone as far as Greentown; but he did not remember seeing her after they passed that place. Val got out at nearly every station where they made any stop, and inquired for the pretty girl with the dark eyes and curls, but without success. At Greentown, he bade Miss Rose farewell; told her to take care of herself and not be sea-sick, and not to go and marry an Englishman before she returned to them; and, carpet-bag in hand, and the address of Cousin Ellen in his pocket, strolled along through the gray twilight to pursue his inquiries. He found the farmhouse easily enough, but not Cherrie. She had never been seen there, and no one who had been at the station that night had seen any young lady whatever alight.

Val remained in Greentown that night, and went on pursuing his inquiries next day, but with the like result. He went on to S——; it was just possible she had gone on there, and taken the steamer for Quebec. He inquired at all the hotels, but no one answering to her description had stopped at any of them, and her name was not on the list of passengers by the last steamer.

Mr. Blake spent three days in the search, and was then compelled by business to return to town. Short as had been his absence, Speckport had received a new shock—no less than the escape of the prisoner from jail. Charley Marsh had broken prison and fled! How, could not very clearly be ascertained, though the bars had been wrenched from his window and the casement found wide open, his quilts torn into strips, and dangling from it. But the window was high, and there was a wall to be got over afterward, and how he had accomplished that last feat, puzzled Speckport. He had accomplished it, however, and was flown; and the police were after him, scouring the woods. Rewards were offered for his capture. Mr. Blake put his hands in his pockets and whistled, when he heard it. The recollection of a certain fact, not known to all Speckport as it was to him, rushed upon his memory. In the days gone by, when the late Mr. Marsh had been a wealthy man, and the jailer of the prison (not jailer then) sued for a debt he could not pay, Mr. Marsh had come to his relief, paid the debt, and freed him. It was hardly probable the man had forgotten this obligation, and the bread cast then upon the waters had returned after many days. But the jailer was not suspected, and he and Val kept their own counsel.

"I hope he'll get clear off," thought Val; "for if ever he's caught now, unless the real criminal turns up, there will be nothing to save him. This flight of his is enough to hang him, in itself."

CHAPTER XX.

"ONE MORE UNFORTUNATE."

HE first person to tell Val Blake of Charley's flight was Captain Cavendish. He found that officer killing time by lounging on the platform, and staring at the passengers, as he alighted. Speckport, from time immemorial, had had a great fancy for crowding steamboat wharves and railway-platforms, to look at new arrivals; and strangers in the place fell into the habits of the natives, unconsciously.

"Poor devil!" said the captain, swinging his cane airily about, and linking his arm in Val's; "I hope he'll dodge them, and escape Jack Ketch. I never like to see any one I've been on friendly terms with once, coming to that."

"Are your friends in the habit of coming to it?" Mr. Blake asked, innocently.

"Bah! How did you enjoy your trip up the country?"

"As well as I expected."

"And did you find Cherrie?"

"What?"

"Did you find Cherrie?" serenely repeated Captain Cavendish.

"No," said Val. "Do you know where she is!"

The question might have disconcerted any other man, but it only made the young officer stare.

"I! My dear fellow. I don't understand you!"

"Oh, yes, you do," said Mr. Blake. "I think you are about as apt to know the hiding-place of little ·Cherrie as any other man in this province. That she is in hiding I am positive; and I'll ferret her out yet, as sure as my name's Blake."

There was a certain determination in Mr. Blake's voice

that the captain by no means liked, but he only laughed indifferently.

"Success to you! No one will be more rejoiced to see the little dear back in Speckport than I! The place is a desert without her; but I give you my word of honor, Blake, she might be in the moon for all I know to the contrary."

And in saying this, Captain Cavendish spoke the truth, for Cherrie had not yet written.

The notion had been vaguely floating through Val's mind, ever since the robbery and murder and Cherrie's flight, that the English officer was in some way connected with the affair. He might even have mentally suspected him of the crime, but for one circumstance. It was at precisely eleven o'clock Midge had first been alarmed by the flying footsteps of the assassin; and at precisely eleven the Princess Royal had left Speckport, with the captain on board. It was clear he could not be in two places at once; so Val had acquitted him of the murder, but not of knowing Cherrie's whereabouts. Even now, he was anything but ready to take him at his word, but it was useless to press the question.

"How do they get on in Cottage Street?" he asked. "I presume you are there every day."

"I call every day, of course," replied Captain Cavendish, a slight flush coloring his nonchalant face; "but I never see any one except Midge, or that other girl."

"Betsy Ann?"

"I suppose so. No one is permitted to enter, it appears, except your sister and Miss Blair."

"Indeed," said Val; "I should think you would have the entry above all others. Have you not seen Nathalie since those melancholy changes have occurred?"

"Yes. Once."

"Ah! At Cottage Street?"

"Yes."

"Well," said Val, who was never restrained by sentimental delicacy, "what did she say?"

"Not much, but what she did say was exceedingly to the point. She gave me my *coup de congé*."

" You don't say so ! Did you take it ?"

" What could I do ? She was inexorable ! Of course, as a man of honor, I should have made her my wife, in spite of all, but she was determined."

A queer smile went wandering for a second or two round Mr. Blake's mouth, but he instantly called his risible faculties to order, and became grave again.

" How are they ? How do they take Charley's escape ?"

" Mrs. Marsh is poorly—confined to her bed, I believe, but Nathalie, they tell me, appears better, and takes care of her mother. Your sister, however, will be able to tell you all particulars."

" I say, Cavendish," exclaimed Val, " you could go in for Jane McGregor, now. She is nearly as rich as poor Natty was to be."

"Bah ! What do I care for her riches ?"

" Oh, yes, I understand ; but just reflect that her papa will give her ten thousand pounds on her wedding-day, and three times that much at his death ; and I am sure you will be brought to take pity on her."

" Take pity on her ?"

" Tah ! Tah ! Tah !" cried Val ; " don't play innocent. You know as well as I do, she is dying for you."

" But, my dear Blake," expostulated the captain, " she has red hair and freckles."

" Auburn hair—auburn ! As for the freckles, her guineas will cover them. Will you come in ?" They were at the office door, but Captain Cavendish declined.

" I have to go to barracks," he said. " Good morning."

Mr. Blake spent some two hours in his office, attending to business, and then sallied forth again. His steps were bent in the direction of Cottage Street, where he expected to find his sister. The house looked as if some one were dead within—the blinds all down, the doors all closed—and no one visible within or without. It was Midge who opened the door, in answer to his loud knock. " How are you, Midge ?" inquired Mr. Blake, striding in, " and how are Mrs. and Miss Marsh ?"

Midge's reply was a prolonged and dismal narrative of the sufferings of both. The elder lady was unable to leave her bed—she had fretted herself into a low, nervous fever, and was so cross, and captious, and quarrelsome, and peevish, that she made the lives of every one in the house a misery to them. She did nothing but sigh, and cry, and moan, and complain from morning till night, and from night till morning. Nothing they did pleased her.

Of Nathalie, Midge had the reverse of this story to tell—she never complained at all. No, Midge wished she would; her mute despair was far harder to bear than the weary complainings of her mother. She sat by that petulant invalid mother's side the livelong day, holding cooling drinks to her poor parched lips, bathing the hot brow and hands, and smoothing the tossed pillow; rarely speaking, save to ask or answer some question; never replying to the endless reproaches of the sick woman; never uttering one complaint or shedding one tear.

Mr. Val Blake was ushered by Midge into the darkened chamber of Mrs. Marsh, and looked at Nathalie sitting by her bedside. In spite of what he had heard, he was shocked at the change which the past week had made in her—shocked at the wasted and shadowy form, the wan, transparent hands, the hollow eyes and haggard cheeks. She was dressed in mourning, and the crape and bombazine made her look quite ghastly by contrast.

Mr. Blake's visit was not a long one. Nathalie scarcely spoke at all, and his sister was not there. Mrs. Marsh, who had been asleep when he entered, awoke presently, and poured her dreary wailings into his ear. Val consoled her as well as he could; but there was no balm in Gilead for her, and he was glad when he could with decency get out of the reach of her querulous voice. Her time, of late, seemed pretty equally divided between dozing and bewailings; and she fretted herself into another slumber shortly after.

Left alone, Nathalie Marsh sat by the window, while the dull afternoon wore away, looking out over the gloomy bay, with a darkly brooding face. Her desolation had never seemed so present to her as on this eerie evening. She had been stunned and stupefied by the rapidly-falling blows, but the after-pain was far more acute and keen than that first dull sense of suffering. "Ruined and disgraced!" they were the two ugly words on which all the changes of her thoughts rang. Ruined and disgraced! Yes, she was that; and she who had once been the belle and boast of the town could never hold up her head there any more. How those who had envied and hated her for her beauty and her prosperity, would exult over her now! What had she done that such misery should fall upon her? What had she done?

The little house in Cottage Street was very still. Mrs. Marsh yet dozed fitfully; Midge had gone out to give herself an airing, and Betsy Ann was standing in the open front door, looking drearily out at the rain, which was beginning to fall with the night. Like Mariana, she was "a-weary,"—though, not being quite so far gone in the blues as that forlorn lady, she did not wish she was dead—and was staring dismally at the slanting rain, when the rustle of a dress on the stairs made her turn round, and become transfixed with amazement at beholding Miss Marsh, in bonnet and shawl, arrayed to go out. Betsy Ann recoiled as if she had seen a ghost, for the white face of the young lady looked awfully corpse-like, in contrast with her sable wrappings.

"Good gracious me! Miss Natty!" she gasped, "you're never going out in this here rain! Ye'll get your death!"

If Nathalie heard her, she did not heed, for she walked steadily out and on through the wet evening, until she was lost to Betsy Ann's shivered view. There were very few abroad that rainy evening, and those few hurried along with bent heads and uplifted umbrellas, and saw not the black figure flitting by them in the gloom. On she steadfastly went, through the soaking rain, heeding it no more than if it were rays of sunshine; on, with one purpose in her face, with her eyes ever turned in one direction—toward the sea.

Cottage Street wound away with a path that led directly to the shore. It had been familiar to her all her

life, and there was an old disused wharf at the end, where
she and Charley had used to play in the sunny summer
days long ago—a hundred years ago, it seemed, at the
least.   It was a useless old wharf, rotten, and slippery,
and dangerous, to which boats were made fast, and where
fishermen mended their nets.   To this wharf Nathalie
made her way in the thickening darkness, the piteous
rain beating in her face, the sea-wind fluttering her black
vail and soaking dress.   Heaven knows what purpose the
poor half-delirious girl had in her mind! Perhaps only to
stand on the familiar spot, and listen to the familiar
voices of the wind and waves dashing against the rotten
logs and slimy planks of the old wharf, on which she had
spent so many happy hours.   No one ever knew how it
was; and we must only pity her in her dumb agony of
despair, and think as mercifully of the dark and distracted soul as we can.   The night was dark, the wharf
dangerous and slippery with the rain, and one might easily
miss their footing and fall.   Who can say how it was?
but there was a suppressed cry—the last wail of that
despairing soul—a sullen plunge, a struggle in the black
and dreadful waters, another smothered cry, and then the
wharf was empty, and the devouring waves had closed
over the golden head of Nathalie Marsh!

In the roar of the surf on the shore, and the wailing
cry of the night wind, there was no voice to tell what had
happened in the lonely gloom of the rainy night.   No,
surely, or the faithful servant, who entered the cottage
dripping, after her constitutional, would have fled wildly
to the scene of the tragedy, instead of standing there in
the kitchen, talking to Betsy Ann, as she placed her wet
umbrella in a corner to drip.

"I went up to Miss Jo's," said Midge, shaking herself,
and giving Betsy Ann an impromptu shower-bath, "and
she made me stay for tea, and fetch this umberel home.
How's the Missis—asleep?"

"Yes," said Betsy Ann, looking nervous and scared,
for she was mortally afraid of the dwarf; "but you didn't
—I mean to say, was not Miss Natty to Blake's?"

" Miss—What !" screamed Midge; " how should Miss Natty get there, stupid ! Isn't she in her own room ?"

" No, she ain't," said Betsy Ann, looking still more scared ; " and I don't know where she is, neither ! She came down stairs just afore dark, with her things on, and went out in all the rain. She wouldn't tell me where 'she was going, and she wouldn't stay in for me ; and you needn't look so mad about it, for I couldn't help it ! There !"

Midge's florid face turned ashen gray with terror ; a vague, nameless, dreadful fear, that brought cold beads of sweat out on her brow. Betsy Ann had no need to back in alarm ; it was not anger that blanched the homely face, and her ears were in no danger of being boxed.

" Which way did she take ?" she asked, her very voice husky with that creeping fear.

" She went straight along," Betsy Ann replied, " as if a going to the shore."

It was the answer Midge had expected, but the hands fastening her shawl shook so, as she heard it, that she could hardly finish that operation.

" Go to Mr. Blake !" she said ; " run for your life, and tell Mr. Val to hurry to the beach, and fetch a lantern. Tell him I am afraid something dreadful has happened."

She hurried off herself, as she spoke, heedless of the invalid up-stairs, of lashing rain, and driving wind, and black night. Heedless of all but that terrible fear, Midge hurried through the storm to the shore.

In the next day's issue of the Speckport Spouter, the following item appeared :

" MYSTERIOUS DISAPPEARANCE !—Yesterday evening, about seven o'clock, Miss Nathalie Marsh quitted her residence in Cottage Street, without informing her friends where she was going, and has not since been heard of. Upon the discovery of her absence, search was made along the shore, in which direction she was seen to go, and a crape vail, recognized as belonging to Miss Marsh, found on the old wharf at the end of Cottage Street. The vail had been caught by a spike projecting from the wharf,

immediately above the water. It is feared that a dread
ful accident has happened, and the young lady has been
drowned. She had been ill and a little delirious some time
before, and we presume wandered down to the old wharf, a
most dangerous place at all times, and particularly so on a
dark and stormy night, such as last night was, and fell
in. Any intelligence of her will be thankfully received,
and liberally rewarded, by her afflicted friends. The
young lady was dressed in deep mourning, and might
easily be recognized by the luxuriant abundance of her
golden hair."

Speckport read this paragraph over its breakfast
coffee and toast, and was profoundly shocked thereby.
And so poor Miss Marsh had drowned herself! They
had expected as much all along—she was not the girl to
survive such disgrace! But it was very dreadful; and
they wouldn't wonder to hear next that the poor
bereaved mother had died of a broken heart. They
hoped the body would be recovered—it would be a
melancholy consolation to her friends, not to say to her
enemies, who would then be out of doubt as to her fate.
People went past the house in Cottage Street with the
same morbid curiosity that had driven them to Redmon
after the murder, and stared at the closed blinds and
muffled knocker, and thought of the wretched mother
lying within, whose footsteps were even then crossing the
Valley of the Shadow of Death.

Two weeks passed, and these charitable wishes were
not fulfilled. The mother of Nathalie still lay ill unto
death, and still faithfully waited on by Midge and Miss
Jo. It was toward the close of the second week that Val
received a note from the coroner of a fishing-village, some
ten miles up the coast, informing him that, the day previously, the body of a woman answering the description
of Miss Marsh had been washed ashore, that an inquest
had been held, and a verdict of "Found drowned" returned. If the missing girl's friends would come immediately they might be able to identify the corpse.

Before noon, after the receipt of this missive, Mr. Va.

Blake was bending over the corpse of the drowned woman, as it lay in its rough deal coffin in the village dead-house. Before sunset he was back in Speckport, and bore the deal coffin and its quiet contents to No. 16 Great St. Peter Street. The slender girlish form, the mourning dress, the long fair hair, were not to be mistaken, though what had been the face was too horrible to look upon. Val turned away from what had once been so beautiful, with a shudder; and thought of the Duke of Gandia, made a saint by a similar sight. Before morning, the deal coffin was inclosed in another of rosewood, and a grave dug in Speckport Cemetery. The funeral was an unusually quiet and solemn one, though there was no requiem mass for the soul of the departed offered up in the cathedral—why should there for a wretched suicide, forever lost?

Mr. Val Blake, with no sentimentality about him, and not over straight-laced either, in some things, was yet a generous, good-hearted fellow in the main, and placed a white marble cross over the dead girl's grave. Some very good people were rather scandalized by the act. A cross over the grave of a suicide!—it was sacrilege. But Mr. Blake did not care much what good people or bad people thought or said of his actions; and did just as he pleased, in spite of their teeth. So the white cross remained gleaming palely in the spectral moonlight, and casting its solemn shadow over the grave in the sunshine. It bore no inscription—what inscription could be placed over such a grave?—only the name "Nathalie." Her story was told, her life ended, the world went on, and she was forgotten! O sublime lesson of life! told in three words: Dead and forgotten!

So, while Charley skulked in dark places, a hunted criminal, with a price on his head, and his mother lay still hovering on that narrow boundary that divides life and death, morning sunlight and noonday shadows brightened and darkened around that pale cross in the cemetery, and the night winds sighed over Nathalie's grave.

CHAPTER XXI.

MRS. BUTTERBY'S LODGINGS.

HE bleak blasts of a raw March afternoon swept through the city streets, cold and piercing, driving the dust in whirlwinds blindingly into the eyes of all it encountered.

In spite of the cold and the piercing wind, Broadway was not empty—Is Broadway ever empty, I wonder?—and business-men, buttoned up to the chin in overcoats, and with caps drawn over their frosty noses, tore along like comets, to home and dinner; ladies in silks, and velvets, and furs, swarm down the pave to meet them, and young and old, rich and poor, jostled and elbowed, and pushed and trod on one another's heels and toes, as usual in that thronged thoroughfare.

Moving among the ceaseless sea of human life, continually ebbing and flowing in Broadway, came a young woman, walking rapidly. I say "young woman" advisedly, for she was not a lady. Her black dress was gray and dingy, and frayed round the bottom; her black cloth mantle was of the poorest texture and simplest make, and her black straw bonnet was as plain and untrimmed as bonnet could be, and who could be a lady in such array as that? To a good many of the Broadway loungers, who devote their manly intellect to picking their teeth in front of first-class hotels, and stare at society going by for a living, her face was well known. It was a face not likely to pass unnoticed—not at all to be passed in a crowd; and more than once some of these expensively-got-up loafers had condescended to follow the young woman with the "deuced fine eyes;" but the black figure flitted along as if shod with the shoes of swiftness, and these languid admirers soon gave up the chase in despair.

I don't think she ever was conscious of this attention; she walked steadfastly on, looking straight before her,

never to the right or left, her shawl drawn closely around
her tall, slight figure, as much alone as if she had been on
Peter Wilkins's desert island. To a home-sick stranger in
New York, I wonder if Broadway, at the fashionable
hour, is not the loneliest and dreariest of places? Hundreds of faces, and not one familiar or friendly countenance among them; not one smile or glance of recognition to the lonely and heart-weary brother or sister jostled
about in their midst. The men and women who passed
might have been a set of automatons, for all the interest
the young person dressed in shabby mourning appeared
to take in them, as she hurried on with that rapid step
and that darkly-sullen face. For I am sorry to say this
heroine of mine (and she is that) wore a look of habitual
sullenness that was almost a scowl, and something fierce
lay latent behind the flashing of those brilliant eyes, and
bitter and harsh in the compressed lips. A passing phy-
siognomist, not over-choice in his phrases, meeting her
once in the street, had carelessly observed to a friend
walking with him, that "there was a spice of the devil
in that girl;" and perhaps the girl herself might have
agreed with him, had she heard it.

Down town and west of Broadway, there is a certain
unfashionable locality, known as Minetta Street. The
houses are tall and dingy, and swarm with dirty children
and noisy mothers; and it is dark and narrow, and utterly
unknown on Fifth Avenue and Madison Square. Among
the tall and dingy houses—all so much alike that they
might have been cast in a mold—there is one with a white
board in the front window of the ground-floor, bearing,
in black letters, the name "Mrs. Butterby," and beneath
this legend, "Lodgings." And in this bleak, windy twilight of this cold March day, the young woman dressed
in black turns into Minetta Street, and walks into Mrs.
Butterby's with the air of one having the right; for she
is one of Mrs. Butterby's lodgers, this young person, and
a lodger of some consequence, not only to the house, but
to the whole street. And for this reason—she has a piano
in her room! An old and battered piano, it is true, for
which she only pays four dollars per month; but still it is

a piano, and the wonderful harmonies her fingers evoke from its yellow keys, transfix Minetta Street with amazement and delight. She has the best room in Mrs. Butterby's house, the first floor parlor, front, and there is the faded remains of a Brussels carpet on the floor: and a yellow-painted washstand in the corner, two cane-seated chairs, with three legs between them, a little table, with an oilcloth cover, and a sheet-iron stove; and these elegant luxuries all of which she has for the stipend of three dollars per week. There is a bed, too, and a small trunk, and the battered little high-backed piano, and there is almost room to turn round in the space which they leave. There is nothing like this elegant apartment in all Mrs. Butterby's house, and the other lodgers look into it with envious and admiring eyes. They are all young ladies, these lodgers—young factory-ladies, and young ladies in the dressmaking, and pantmaking, and vestmaking, and capmaking, and bookbinding lines of business, not to speak of an actress, a real actress, who performed in a Broadway theater, and whom they look upon with mingled awe and envy. But they like her better than they do the first-floor lodger, whom they unite in hating with a cordial hatred that would have delighted Dr. Johnson. They are all young ladies, but they stigmatize her as "that young woman," "that stuck-up thing," and would like to scratch those bright eyes of hers out of her head, though she never did anything to them in her life.

They knew very little about her, either Mrs. Butterby or her fair lodgers, although she had been two months in the house, except that her name was Miss Wade, that she earned her living as an embroideress, and that she put on a great many unnecessary airs for a New York seamstress. She embroidered slippers, that were pictures in themselves, on rich velvets and silks, with floss and Berlin wool, and spangles, and beads; and cobweb handkerchiefs, that might have been the wonder of a Brussels lace-maker. She worked for a fashionable Broadway establishment, who asked fabulous prices for these gems of needlework, and who doled out a miserable pittance to the pale worker, whose light glimmered far into the night, and who bent

over the glistening fabric in the gray and dismal dawn.
They heard all this in the house, and nothing more; for,
except to the landlady, she had never, scarcely, exchanged
a word with a soul in it—with one exception—she had
spoken to the actress, who occupied the room above her
own, and who was nearly as cold and unsociable as herself.
"Birds of a feather," the young ladies said, when Mrs.
Butterby told how Miss Wade had been in Miss Johnston's room (the actress was Miss Johnston, in every-day
life, and Miss St. John on the bills), sewing spangles and
gold braid on Miss Johnston's theatrical robes, and how
Miss Johnston had taken Miss Wade to the theater, and
had made her stay and take tea with her in her own room.
No human being of the "earth earthy," can quite live
without any one to speak to; the heart must turn to some
one, let it be ever so proud and self-sustained, and the
actress was made of less coarse and rough clay than the
young factory-ladies, who went dirty and hoopless all the
week, and flaunted in gaudy silks on Sunday.

Up in her own room, Miss Wade took off her bonnet,
and sat down to work with her mantle still on, for the
fireless apartment was perishingly cold. She had sat there
for nearly an hour, and the cheerless March gloaming was
falling drearily on Minetta Street, when there was a sham-
bling footstep on the stairs, a shuffling, slip-shod, down-at-
the-heel tread in the hall, and a rap at her door. Miss
Wade, work in hand, opened it, and saw her portly landlady smiling in the doorway.

"Miss Johnston's compliments, Miss, and would you
please to step up to her room, she says. Bless my heart!
ain't you got no fire on, this perishing evening?"

"It was too much trouble to light it," Miss Wade said,
shutting and locking her room-door, and going along the
dark and dirty hall, up a dark and dirty staircase, into
another hall, darker and dirtier still, and tapping at the
first door she met.

"Come in!" a feminine voice said, and Miss Wade
went in accordingly. It was a smaller chamber than her
own, and far less sumptuously furnished, with no fine frag-
ments of Brussels on the bare floor, no piano in the corner,

no yellow washstand, or oilclothed table. Its one dim window looked out on that melancholy sight, a New York backyard, and the gray and eerie dusk stole palely in, and the wild spring wind rattled the rickety casement. But it had a fire, this poor little room, in a little ugly black stove, and, sitting in the one chair the apartment boasted of, crouching over the heat, in a strange and wretched position, was the room's mistress. A poor, faded, pallid creature, young, but not youthful, with sharp cheekbones, and sunken eyes. She was wrapped in a plaid shawl, but she looked miserable and shivery, and crouched so low over the stove, that she nearly touched it. Sundry gaudy garments, all tinsel and spangles and glitter, lay on the bed, with two or three wigs keeping them company, a rouge-pot, and a powder-box. These were her stage-dresses; but, looking at her, as she sat there, you would as soon think of seeing a corpse tricked out in that ghostly grandeur as she.

She rose up as her visitor entered, with a pale smile of welcome, and placed the chair for her. There was a certain quiet grace about her that stamped her, like Miss Wade herself, God help her! as "one who had seen better days." But she was far more fragile than the seamstress. Whatever she had once been, she was nothing but a poor, wasted shadow now.

"Mrs. Butterby said you sent for me," Miss Wade remarked, taking the chair, and looking with a certain eagerness in her great eyes. "You spoke to the manager, I suppose?"

Miss Johnston, who had seated herself on a wooden footstool, did not look up to meet that eager, anxious gaze.

"Yes," she said, "but, I am sorry to say, I have been disappointed. The company was full, he said, and he wanted no more novices. He would not have taken me, had it not been at the earnest solicitation of a friend, and there was no room or need for any more."

The sullen look that had left Miss Wade's face for a moment returned, and a dark gloom with it. She did not speak; she sat with her brows drawn into a moody form, staring at the ugly little black stove.

"A friend of mine, though," the actress went on, "who has considerable influence, has promised to try and get you a situation in some other theater. I told him you would certainly be successful, and rise rapidly in the profession. I know you possess all the elements of a splendid tragic actress."

If we might judge by the darkly-passionate face and fiercely-smoldering eyes, the young woman who sat so gloomily staring straight before her, was capable of acting a tragedy in real life, quite as fast as on the stage. There was a certain recklessness about her, that might break out at any moment, and which told fate and poverty had goaded her on to desperation. When she spoke, her words showed she had neither heard nor heeded the actress's last remark.

"And so goes my last hope," she said, with slow, desperate bitterness; "the last hope of being anything but a poor, starved, beggarly drudge all the days of my life! I am a fool to feel disappointed. I might know well enough by this time, that there is nothing but disappointment for such a wretch as I!"

The reckless bitterness of this speech jarred painfully on the hearer's nerves. Miss Johnston looked at her half-pityingly.

"There is no need to despair," she quietly said; "the friend of whom I have spoken will be successful, and I am certain you will be a great actress yet. With me it is different. I will never rise above mediocrity."

"You don't seem to care much," said Miss Wade, looking at her pale, still face.

"I don't," said the actress, in the same quiet way.

"Have you no ambition at all, then?"

"No!"

She did not say it indifferently, but in a tone of hard endurance. Miss Wade's large eyes were fixed curiously on her face.

"I think," she said, "you have seen a great deal of trouble, and that it has crushed the ambition out of you. You were never born to be one of Mrs. Butterby's lodgers! Pardon me if I am impertinent."

11

"You are not," the actress said, neither denying nor acknowledging the charge. "Whatever I once was, I am Mrs. Butterby's lodger now, and a poor actress, who must sew the spangles on her own dress."

She took off the bed a short pink gauze skirt, and a bunch of tinsel braid, and began the womanly work of sewing, with her swift fingers.

"Are you to wear that to-night?" asked Miss Wade.

"Yes; it is the dress of a flower-girl."

"What is the play?"

"I forget the name," said the actress, indifferently; "it is a French vaudeville, written expressly for us. I am Ninon, a flower-girl, with two or three songs to sing. Will you come?"

"Thank you, I should like to go. It keeps me from thinking for a few hours, and that in itself is a blessing. What a miserable, worthless piece of business life is! I think I shall buy twenty cents worth of landanum, some of these days, in some apothecary-shop, and put an end to it altogether."

The jarring, reckless tone had returned, and was painful to hear. The actress sewed steadily on, replying not.

"It is well enough for those girls," Miss Wade said; "those rough, noisy, factory girls, brawny arms, and souls that never rise above a bean or silk dresses; but for me and for you, who were born ladies—it is enough to drive us mad! Look at me!" she cried, rising to her feet; "look at me, Miss Johnston! Do I look like one born for a drudge? Do I look like the women who fill this house?"

Miss Johnston looked up at the speaker, doing a little private theatrical tragedy, with her pale, quiet face, unmoved. Perhaps she had grown so used to tragedy that it had become stale and wearisome to her; and the regal figure drawn up to its full height, the white face, and flaring eyes, disturb her no more in her poor room, than Lady Macbeth, in black velvet, with blood on her hands, did on the theatrical boards.

"No," she said, "you are not at all like the factory-hands, Miss Wade. I never doubted you were born a lady."

"And a lady, rich and happy, flattered and courted, I should have been yet, but for the villainy of a man. My curse upon him, whether he be living or dead."

She began pacing up and down the floor, like any other tragedy-queen. Miss Johnston, finding it too dark to sew, arose, lit a candle, stood it on a wooden box that did service for a table, and composedly pursued her work.

"How was it?" she asked; "is it long ago?"

"Long!" exclaimed Miss Wade; "it seems hundreds of years ago; though I suppose scarcely seven have really passed since he fled, taking all he possessed with him, and leaving my mother and I to beg, or starve, or die, if we pleased. Of all the villains Heaven ever suffered to pollute this earth, I think Philip Henderson was the worst!"

"Philip Henderson!".Miss Johnston repeated, looking up from her work; "was that the name of the man who defrauded you?"

"He was my step-father—the villain! My own father I do not recollect—he died in my infancy, leaving my mother wealthy—the possessor of half a million nearly. She had married this man Henderson before I was three years old; and I remember how pleased I was when he first came, with the little baby-sister he brought me—for he was a widower with a child not two years old. Shortly after my mother's second marriage, we left Rochester, where I was born. Mr. Henderson purchased, with my mother's money, of course, for he had none of his own, a magnificent place up at Yonkers—a house like a castle, and magnificent grounds. Everything was in keeping; the furniture, pictures, and plate superb; a whole retinue of servants; the fastest horses and finest carriages in the country. It is like a dream of fairy-land to me now to . look back upon. Olly and I (his daughter's name was Olive), as we grew up, had a governess, and masters in the house, and played in bright silk dresses among the pastures, and fountains, and graperies of our palace-like home. The place was filled with company all the summer through —nothing but balls and soirees, and dressing and dancing, and fetes champetre; and in the winter, Mr. and Mrs. Henderson came down to the city, leaving us in charge of the housekeeper and governess. It is a very pleasant thing, no doubt, spending money as freely as if it were water; but, unfortunately, even half a million of dollars will not last forever. Mr. and Mrs. Henderson, and their two daughters—for I passed as his child, too, and scarcely knew the difference myself—were all the fashion for nearly ten years, and then the change began to come. I was only thirteen, and not old enough to understand the stormy scenes between Henderson and my mother—her passionate reproaches of his folly and extravagance, his angry recrimination, and the ominous whisperings of the servants. Suddenly the crash came—Henderson had fled, taking Olly with him, and the few thousands that yet remained of our princely fortune. He was over head and ears in debt; the creditors seized everything—house, furniture, plate, and all—and my mother and I were penniless. Miss Johnston, the shock killed her. She had always been frail and delicate, and she never held up her head after. She was buried before a month passed; and I, at the age of thirteen, was alone in the world, and a pauper. But a child of that age cannot realize misery as we can in after-years. I was fully conscious of present discomfort, but of the future I never thought. My mother had left Yonkers immediately after the creditors' seizure, too keenly sensitive to remain a beggar where she had once reigned a queen, and came here to the city. She came here to an old servant of hers, to whom she had been a kind friend in other days, and the woman did not forget it. She was comfortable enough with her husband and two children, and she kept me and sent me to learn the business I now work at. I remained with her nearly six years, realizing more and more every day what I had lost in losing wealth. She is dead now. Her husband is married again and gone to California, and I am here, the most miserable creature, I believe, in all this great desert of a city."

She had been walking up and down all the time, this

impetuous Miss Wade, with rapid, excited steps, speaking
in a rapid, excited voice, a fierce light flaring in her large
angry eyes. The actress had finished her work; it lay on
her lap now, her quiet hands folded over it, her quiet eyes
following the passionate speaker.

"Wade, I suppose," was her first remark, "was your
own father's name. When did you adopt it?"

"Only when I came here. The name of Henderson
had long been odious to me, but the family I lived with
was too accustomed to it to change."

"And have you never heard from this man Henderson or his daughter since?"

"I have heard of them, which is as good; and, thank
God! retribution has found them out! They are both
dead—he committed a forgery, and shot himself to escape
the consequences; and Olly—she was always a miserable,
puling, sickly thing—died in a hospital. They have been
made an example of, thank Heaven! as they deserved
to be."

She uttered the impious thanksgiving with a fierce joy
that made the actress recoil. But her mood changed a
second after; she stopped in her walk, the darkly-sullen
look settling on her face again, and stared blankly at the
flaring candle, dripping tears of fat over the candlestick.
So long she stood that the actress rose and began folding
up the flower-girl's dresses, preparatory to starting for the
theater.

"Are you going?" Miss Wade asked, coming out of
her moody reverie.

"Yes, when I have had a cup of tea—it is drawing
down stairs at Mrs. Butterby's fire. Will you not take
another?"

"No, thank you; I can't eat. I will wait here while
you take it."

There was a newspaper on the bed. Miss Wade took
it, and sat down to read whilst she waited. The actress
left the room, returning a moment or two after, with a
small snub-nosed teapot and a plate of buttered toast. She
was standing at a little open pantry pouring out the tea,
when she suddenly laid down the teapot, and turned round

to look at her companion. It was not an exclamation
Miss Wade had uttered, it was a sort of cry; and she
was holding the paper before her, staring at it in blank
amaze.

"What is the matter?" Miss Johnston inquired, in her
calm voice.

Miss Wade looked up, a sudden and strange flush passing over her colorless face.

"Nothing," she said, slowly. "That is—I mean I saw
the—the death of a person I knew, in this paper."

She held it up before her face, and sat there while the
actress drank her tea and ate her toast, never moving or
stirring. Miss Johnston left the pantry, put on her bonnet and shawl, and took up her bundle as if to go.

"I beg your pardon, Miss Wade," she said, "but it is
time for us to go."

Miss Wade arose, with the paper still in her hand.
Two bright spots, all unusual there, and which strong excitement alone could bring, burned on either cheek, and a
strange dusky fire shone in her eyes.

"I do not think I will go to the theater to-night, Miss
Johnston," she said. "My head aches. I will take this
paper, if you will let me, and read it in my room for a
little while, and then go to bed."

The actress assented, looking at her curiously, and Miss
Wade passed down the dark stairs to her own room.
There was a lamp on the table, which she lit, then she
locked the door; and with that same red spot on each
cheek, and that same bright light in each eye, sat down
with the paper to read. But she only read one little paragraph among the advertisements, and that she read over
and over, and over again. The paper was the Montreal
True Witness, some two or three weeks old, and the paragraph ran thus:

"INFORMATION WANTED.—Of Philip Henderson or his
heirs. When last heard from he was in New York, but
is supposed to have gone to Canada. He or his descend-
ants will hear of something to their great advantage by
applying to John Darcy, Barrister-at-Law, Speckport."

CHAPTER XXII.

THE HEIRESS OF REDMON.

T is three days by steamer and rail-cars from New York to Speckport; but as steam never traveled half as fast as story-tellers, we are back there in three seconds. Dear, foggy Speckport, I salute thee!

In a grimy office, its floor freshly sprinkled, its windows open to admit the March-morning sunshine, in a leathern-covered armchair, before a littered table, Mr. Darcy, barrister-at-law, sits reading the morning paper. It is the "Daily Snorter," and pitches savagely into the "Weekly Spouter," whose editor and proprietor, under the sarcastic title of "Mickey," it mildly insinuates is an ignorant, blundering, bog-trotting ignoramus, who ought still to be in the wilds of Connemara planting potatoes, instead of undermining the liberty of this beloved province, and trampling the laws of society under his ruthless feet, by asserting, as he did yesterday, that a distinguished member of the Smasher party had been found lying drunk in Golden Row, and conveyed in that unhappy state to his residence in that aristocratic street, instead of to the watch-house, as he should. Much more than this the "Daily Snorter," the pet organ of the Smasher party, had to say, and the anathemas it fulminated against "that filthy sheet," the "Spouter," and its vulgar, blockheaded, addle-pated editor, was blood-curdling to peruse. Mr. Darcy was deep in it when the office door opened, and Mr. Val Blake lounged carelessly in. Mr. Darcy looked up with a nod and a laugh.

"Good morning, Blake! Fine day, isn't it? I am just reading this eulogy the 'Snorter' gives you."

"Yes," said Mr. Blake, mounting the back of a chair as if it were the back of a horse, and looking the picture of calm serenity. "Severe, is it? Who do you suppose I had a letter from last night?"

"How should I know?"

"You won't faint, will you? It was from Charley Marsh!"

Mr. Darcy dropped the "Snorter," and stared.

"Char—ley Marsh! It's not possible, Blake?"

"Yes, it is. I am on my way to Cottage Street at this present writing, to tell his mother."

"Well, this is an astonisher! And where is the boy?"

"You'd never guess. A captain in the Southern army."

"You don't say so! How did he ever get there?"

"You see," said Val, "it's a long letter, and he explains everything. After he broke jail that time (of course, Turnbull helped him off), he skulked in the woods for two or three weeks, visited occasionally by a friend (Turnbull again), and through him heard of Nathalie's death. At last, he got the chance of a blockade-runner. The 'Stonewall Jackson' was leaving here, and he got on board, ran the blockade, and found himself in Dixie. There he was offered a captainship, if he would stay and fight a little. He accepted, and that's the whole story. I must tell the mother. It will do her more good than fifty novels and fifty thousand blue pills. Jo went into hysterics of delight when she heard it at breakfast, and I left her kicking when I came away."

"Does he say anything at all about the murder?"

"Oh, yes. I forgot that. He wants to know if Cherrie has turned up yet, and says he may thank her for all his trouble. He was up at Redmon that night to meet her. She had promised to elope with him, but she never came. He protests his innocence of the deed, and I believe him."

"Humph!" said Mr. Darcy, reflectingly. "It is most singular Cherrie does not turn up. I dare say she could throw light on the subject, if she chose."

"I don't despair, yet," said Val. "I'll find her before I stop, if she's above ground. No news yet, I suppose, from the heirs of Redmon?"

"None; and I am sick and tired of advertising. Not

a New York or Canadian paper I have not tried, and all alike unsuccessfully. I believe the man's dead, and it's of no use."

"Well," said Mr. Blake, dismounting from the chair, "I'm off. I must get back to the office after I've seen Mrs. Marsh, and give the 'Snorter' such a flailing as it won't get over for a month of Sundays."

Off went Mr. Blake like a long-legged steam-engine; and Mr. Darcy's office boy entered with a handful of letters from the post-office. The lawyer, laying down his paper, began to break the envelopes and read. The first three were business communications, brief and legal, in big buff envelopes. The fourth bore a different aspect. It was considerably stouter. The envelope was white; the writing, a lady's delicate spidery tracery; the post-mark New York. The lawyer surveyed it for a moment in grave surprise, then broke it open and began to read. The letter was a long one—three sheets of note-paper closely written; and before he had got to the end of the first, Mr. Darcy, with a sort of shout of astonishment, began at the beginning again. Once, twice, three times, and Mr. Darcy perused the letter; and then rising, with the rest unopened, began pacing up and down the floor. The windows of the office faced the street, and, glancing out, he saw Mr. Blake striding past presently, as if shod with seven-league boots. Mr. Darcy put his head out of the window and hailed him.

"Hallo, Blake! Come up here a moment, will you?"

Mr. Blake looked up, ran up-stairs, and entered the office."

"You'll have to be quick, Mr. Darcy," he said. "Time's precious this morning, and my conscience is uneasy until I give the 'Snorter' fits. Anything up?"

"Yes. The heir of Redmon has turned up at last!"

"By Jove!" cried Val, "you don't say so? Where is he?"

"It's not a he. I should have said the heiress of Redmon has come to light. I have had a letter from Philip Henderson's daughter this morning."

"And where's Philip himself?"

11*

" Where Heaven pleases. The man's dead, and has
been these three years. No wonder he never answered
our advertisements."

" But it is a wonder this daughter of his did not ?"

" She never heard it until the day before she wrote,
and then by the merest chance, she says. She is very
poor, I fancy, though she does not exactly say so, and
without the means to come on here."

" Where is she ?"

" In New York. Mrs. Leroy told me her brother
resided in Yonkers, with his wife and two daughters, she
believed, and the writer of this letter corroborates that
statement. They did live in Yonkers, she says, and were
in affluent circumstances for a number of years, until she,
the writer, was thirteen years old, when they became involved in debt, and everything was seized by the creditors.
Henderson, the father, went to Canada. Mrs. Leroy told
me she heard he had gone there, but they never held any
correspondence. He went to Canada and died there about
three years ago. The youngest daughter died about the
same time, and the mother shortly after their loss of fortune. The writer of this letter, then, is the only survivor
of the family, and the rightful heiress of Mrs. Leroy's
fortune. She speaks of Mrs. Leroy, too ; says her father
had an only sister, who married a New York Jew of that
name, for which low alliance, her father ever afterwards
refused to have anything to do with her. She refers me
to several persons in Yonkers, who can confirm her story,
if necessary ; though, as she has not been there since she
was a child of thirteen, and is now a young lady of twenty,
they would hardly be able to identify her. She works for
her living, she says—as a teacher, I presume—and tells
me to address my reply to 'Station G, Broadway.' Her
story bears truth on the face of it, I think. Here is the
letter—read it."

Mr. Blake took the lady-like epistle, and, apparently
forgetful of his late haste, sat down and perused it from
the date " New York, March 7th, 1862," to the signature,
" Yours respectfully, Olive W. Henderson." He laid
it down with a thoughtful face.

"Her statement is frank and clear, and coincides in every particular with what Mrs. Leroy told you. I don't think there is any deception, but you had better write to Yonkers and ascertain."

"I shall do so: and if all is right, I will forward money to Miss Henderson to come here at once. I am heartily glad to be rid of the bother at last. What will Speckport say ?"

"Ah, what won't it say ! It's an ill wind that blows nobody good ; and what killed poor Natty Marsh is the making of this girl. I wonder if she's good-looking. I shouldn't mind making up to her myself, if she is."

"You might make down again, then. She wouldn't touch you with a pair of tongs. How did Mrs. Marsh take the news ?"

"She cried a little," said Val, turning to go, "and then went back to 'Florinda the Forsaken,' I having disturbed her in the middle of the ninety-eighth chapter."

Nodding familiarly, Mr. Blake took his departure, and Mr. Darcy sat down to write to Station G, Broadway, and to Yonkers.

The very winds of heaven seemed to carry news in Speckport, and before night everybody at all concerned knew that the heiress of Redmon had turned up.

Before the expiration of a fortnight, Mr. Darcy received an answer from Yonkers. Mr. and Mrs. Philip Henderson had resided there with their two daughters some years before, but he had absconded in debt, and his wife had left the place, and died shortly after. Harriet and Olive, they believed, were the names of the children ; but they knew nothing whatever of them, whether they were living or dead. Mr. Henderson, they had read in the papers, had died very suddenly in Canada—committed suicide, they believed, but they were not certain.

Mr. Darcy, upon receipt of these letters, forwarded a hundred dollars to Miss Henderson, desiring her to come on without delay to Speckport, and take possession of her property. The hunt for the heirs had given Mr. Darcy considerable trouble, and he was very glad to be rid of the bore. He directed the young lady to come to his house immediately upon landing, instead of a hotel ; if she sent him word what day she would come, he would be at the boat to meet her.

Mr. Val Blake, among less noted people, went down to the wharf one Tuesday afternoon, nearly a fortnight after Mr. Darcy had dispatched that last letter containing the hundred dollars, to New York. It was late in March now, a lovely, balmy, June-like day ; for March, having come in like a lion, was going peacefully out like a lamb. There was not a shadow of fog in Speckport. The sky was as blue as your eyes, my dear reader—unless your eyes happen to be black—with billowy white clouds sailing like fairy ships through a fairy sea. The soft breezes and warm sunshine rendered fans unnecessary, and the bay was a sheet of sapphire and gold. The wharf, a superb wharf, by the way, and a delightful promenade, was thronged. All the pretty girls in Speckport—and, oh ! what a lot of pretty girls there are in Speckport—were there ; so were the homely ones, and all the nice young men, and the officers with canes under their arms, staring at the fair Speckportians. Young and old, rich and poor, lined the wharf, sitting down, standing up, and walking about, attracted by the beauty of the evening, and the report that the new heiress was coming in that day's boat.

Mr. Val Blake, with his hands in his trowsers' pockets as usual, and his black Kossuth hat pushed far back on his forehead, not to obstruct his view, also as usual, lounged down through the crowd, nodding right and left, and joined a group near the end of the wharf, of whom Miss Jeannette McGregor, Miss Laura Blair, Miss Catty Clowrie, and Captain Cavendish formed prominent features. Two or three more officers and civilians hovered around, and way was made for Mr. Blake.

"Oh, Mr. Blake, do you suppose we'll know her when she lands?" eagerly inquired Miss McGregor. "I am dying to see what she is like !"

"Darcy's going on board after her," said Val, "you'll see him linking her up the wharf. I say, Laura, Bill told me you had a letter from Miss Rose." •

"Why, yes, didn't you know? And she is coming back with Mrs. Wheatly, and I am so glad!"

"Have you been corresponding with Miss Rose all this time, Laura?" inquired Miss Clowrie.

"No; this is the first letter I have received. I sent her the 'Spouter,' containing Nathalie Marsh's death, to Quebec, and she wrote back in reply. This is all I have heard of her until now. She says she has had scarcely a moment to herself."

"Do you know, Laura," said Miss McGregor, "I used to think she was half in love with Charley Marsh before that terrible affair of his. He was a handsome fellow, and she must have seen a great deal of him, living in the same house."

"One might fall in love with Charley without living in the same house with him, mightn't they, Catty?" asked Mr. Blake, with a grin; "but it's all nonsense in saying the little school-mistress cared about him. She was too much of a saint to fall in love with any one."

"There's the boat!" cried Captain Cavendish; "coming round Paradise Island!"

"And there goes Darcy down the floats," echoed Val. "Watch well, ladies, and you will behold the heiress of Redmon in a jiffy."

The steamer swept around the island and floated gracefully up the harbor. In twenty minutes she was at the wharf; a little army of cabmen, armed with whips, stood ready, as if to thrash the passengers as they came up. A couple of M. P.'s, brass-buttoned, blue-coated, and red-batoned, stood keeping order among the rabble of boys, ready to tear each other's eyes out for the privilege of carrying somebody's luggage. Our party flocked to the edge of the high wharf overlooking the floats, up which the travelers must come, and strained their necks and eyes to catch sight of the heiress. Mr. Darcy had gone on board the first moment he could, and the passengers were flocking out and up the floats. Some of them, who had been to Speckport before, or had heard from others that it was one of the institutions of the place for the population of the town to flock down on such occasions, passed on indifferently; but others, more ignorant, looked up in amazement, and wondered if all those people expected friends. Most of the passengers had gone, when there was an exclamation from more than one mouth of "Here she is!" "There's the heiress with Mr. Darcy!" "Look, she's coming!" and all bent forward more eagerly than before. Yes, Mr. Darcy was slowly ascending the floats with a lady on his arm, a tall lady, very slender and graceful of figure, wearing a black silk dress, a black cloth mantle trimmed with purple, a plain dark traveling bonnet, and a thick brown vail. The vail defied penetration—the eyes of Argus himself could not have discovered the face behind it.

"Oh, hang the vail!" cried Captain Cavendish; "they ought to be indicted as public nuisances. The face belonging to such a figure should be pretty!"

"How tall she is!" exclaimed Miss McGregor, who was rather dumpy than otherwise. "She is a perfect giantess!"

"Five feet six, I should say, was mademoiselle's height," remarked Val, with mathematical precision. "I like tall women. How stately she walks!"

"I suppose she'll be putting on airs now," remarked Miss McGregor, with true feminine dislike to hear another woman praised; "and forget she ever had to work for her living in New York. Or perhaps she'll go back there and take her fortune with her."

"You wouldn't be sorry, Jeannette, would you?" said Laura. "She's a terrible rival, I know, with her thirty thousand pounds, and her stately stature. Val, I wish you would find out what she is like before you come to our house this evening. You can do anything you please, and I am dying to know."

"All right," said Val; "shall I drop into Darcy's, and ask Miss Henderson to stand up for inspection, in order that I may report to Miss Blair?"

"Oh, nonsense! you can go into Mr. Darcy's if you like, and see her, without making a goose of yourself."

"And I'll go with him, Miss Laura," said Mr. Tom Oaks, sauntering up. "Blake has no more eye for beauty than a cow, or he would not have lived in Speckport all

these years, and be a single man to-day. We'll both drop
in to Darcy's on our way to you, Miss Blair, with a full,
true, and particular account of Miss Henderson's charms."

"Oh, her charms are beyond dispute, already," said
Captain Cavendish; "she has thirty thousand, to our certain knowledge."

"And of all charms," drawled Lieutenant the Honorable Blank, "we know that golden ones are the most to
your taste, Cavendish. You'd better be careful and not
put your foot in it with this heiress, as they tell me you
did with the last."

Very few ever had the pleasure of seeing Captain
Cavendish disconcerted. He only stared icily at his
brother-officer, and offered his arm to Miss McGregor to
lead her to her carriage, which was in waiting, while Mr.
Oaks did the same duty for Laura. Mr. Blake saw her
led off under his very nose, with sublimest unconcern,
and lounged along the wharf, watching the deck-hands
getting out freight, with far more interest than he could
ever have felt in Laura's pretty tittle-tattle. If that lady
felt disappointed, she knew the proprieties a great deal
too well to betray it, and held a laughing flirtation all the
way up the wharf with Mr. Tom Oaks.

"You will be sure to find out what the heiress is
like," she said, bounding into the carriage. "I shall
never know a moment's peace until I ascertain."

"I will go to Darcy's with Blake," answered Tom;
"that's all I can do. If she shows it is all right; if she
don't, a fellow can't very well send word to her to come
and exhibit herself. Adieu, mesdemoiselles!"

The two gentlemen tipped their chapeaux gallantly as
the carriage rattled off up the hilly streets of Speckport;
for every street in Speckport is decidedly "the rocky road
to Dublin." Mr. Oaks hunted up Mr. Blake, and led him
off from the fascinating spot, where the men were noisily
getting out barrels, and bales and boxes.

"I'll call round for you, Blake," he said; "and we'll
drop into Darcy's, promiscuous, as it were, before going to
Laura's. I want to see the heiress myself, as much as the
girls do."

Mr. Blake was of much too easy a nature to refuse any common request; and when, about seven o'clock, Mr. Oaks, magnificently got up in full evening costume, partly concealed by a loose and stylish overcoat, called at Great St. Peter's Street, he found the master of No. 16 putting the finishing touches to a characteristically loose and careless toilet.

The two young men sallied forth into the brightly starlit March night, lighting their cigars as they went, and conjecturing what Miss Henderson might be like. At least Mr. Oaks was, Mr. Blake being constitutionally indifferent on the subject.

"What's the odds?" said Val; "let her be as pretty as Venus, or as ugly as a blooming Hottentot, it makes no difference to you or I, does it?"

"Perhaps not to you, you dry old Diogenes," said Tom; "but to me it's of the utmost consequence, as I mean to marry her, should she turn out to be handsome."

Mr. Blake stared, for Mr. Oaks had delivered himself of this speech with profoundest gravity; but as they were at the lawyer's door, there was no time for friendly remonstrance on such' precipitate rashness. Val rang, and was shown by the young lady who answered the bell, and did general housework for Mrs. Darcy, into the parlor. Mr. and Mrs. Darcy were there, and so was the new heiress, to whom they were presented in form. She still wore her black silk dress, and lay back in a cushioned rocker, looking at the bright coal-fire, and talking very little. It was very easy to look at her; had she been a tall statue, draped in black, it could scarcely have been easier; and the two gentlemen took a mental photograph of her, for Miss Blair's benefit and their own, before they had been two minutes in the room.

"We were on our way to Miss Blair's tea-splash," Mr. Blake explained, "and dropped in. You're not coming, I suppose?"

No, a note-apology had been sent. They were not going. Mrs. Darcy was saying this when the young lady looked suddenly up.

"I beg you will not stay on my account," she said. "I am rather fatigued, and will retire. I shall be sorry if my arrival deprives you of any pleasure."

She had a most melodious voice, deep, but musical, and her smile lit up her whole dark face with a luminous brightness, most fascinating, but not easily described. You know the magnetic power some of these dark faces have, of kindling into sudden light, and how bewitching it is. Mr. Oaks seemed to find it so; for she was gazing with an entranced absorption that rendered him utterly oblivious of all the rules of polite breeding.

Mr. and Mrs. Darcy hastened to disclaim the idea of her presence depriving them of any pleasure whatever, as people always do on these occasions, and repeated their intention of not going. Messrs. Blake and Oaks accordingly took their leave, and sallied forth again under the quiet stars for the residence of Miss Laura Blair.

The pretty drawing-room of Laura's home was bright with gaslight and flowers, and fine faces and charming toilets, and red coats, for the officers were there when they entered. What Mr. Blake had denominated a "tea-splash" was a grand birth-day ball. Miss Laura was just twenty-one that night. She danced up to them as they entered, looking wonderfully pretty in rose-silk, and floating white lace, white roses in her hair and looping up her rich skirt. "So you have come at last!" was her cry, addressing Tom Oaks, and quite ignoring Mr. Blake—the little hypocrite! "Have you seen Miss Henderson?"

"Yes," said Val, taking it upon himself to reply, "and she's homely. Her nose turns up."

There was a cry of consternation from a group of ladies, who came fluttering around them, Miss Jo, tall and gaunt, and grand, in their midst.

"Homely!" shouted Mr. Oaks, glaring upon Val. "You lying villain, I'll knock you down if you repeat such a slander. She is beautiful as an angel! the loveliest girl I ever looked upon."

Everybody stared, and there was a giggle and a flutter among the pretty ones at this refreshingly frank confession.

"Nonsense!" said Val. "You can't deny, Oaks, but her nose turns up!"

"I don't care whether it turns up or down!" yelled Mr. Oaks, "or whether she's got any nose at all! I know it's perfect, and her eyes are like the stars of heaven, and her complexion the loveliest olive I ever looked at!"

"Olive!" said Mr. Blake. "I'll take my oath it's yellow, and she's as skinny as our Jo there."

"I'm obliged to you, Mr. Blake, for the compliment, I'm sure!" exclaimed Miss Jo, flashing fire at the speaker; "and I think you might have a little more politeness than running down the poor young lady, if her nose does turn up. Sure, she is not to blame, poor creature! if she is ugly!"

"But, I tell you, ma'am," roared Mr. Oaks, growing scarlet in the face, "she is not ugly! She's beautiful! She's divine! She's an angel!—that's what she is!"

"Well," said Mr. Blake, resignedly, "if she's an angel, all I've got to say is, that angels ain't much to my taste. She is not half as pretty as yourself, Laura; and now I want you to dance with me, after that."

Miss Blair, with a radiant face, put her pretty white hand on Val's coat-sleeve, and marched him off. A quadrille was just forming, and they took their places.

"So she's really not handsome, Val? What is she like?"

"Oh, she's tall and thin, and straight as a poplar, and she has big, flashing black eyes, and tar-black hair, all braided round her head, and a haggard sort of look that I don't admire. I dare say, Lady Macbeth looked something like her; but she is not the least like poor Nathalie Marsh."

"Ah! poor Nathalie! dear Nathalie!" Laura sighed. "It seems like yesterday since that night last May, at Jeannette McGregor's, when she was the belle and the heiress of Redmon, we all thought, and Captain Cavendish came for the first time. I remember, too, Miss Rose arrived that night, and we were asking Charley—poor Charley!—what she looked like. And now to think of all the changes that have taken place! I declare, it seems heartless of us to be dancing and enjoying ourselves here, after all!"

"So it is," said Val, "and we are a heartless lot, I expect; but, meantime, the quadrille is commencing, and as you have not taken the vail yet, Miss Blair, suppose you make me a bow, and let us have a whack at it with the rest!"

CHAPTER XXIII.

THE HEIRESS OF REDMON ENTERS SOCIETY.

 PRETTY room—Brussels carpet on the floor, marble-topped table strewn with gayly-bound books and photograph-albums, chairs and sofas cushioned in green billiard-cloth, hangings of lace and damask on the windows, a tall Psyche mirror, a dressing-table, strewn with ivory-backed brushes, perfume bottles, kid gloves, and cambric handkerchiefs; and marble mantel, adorned with delicate vases filled with flowers. You might have thought it a lady's boudoir but for the pictures on the papered walls—pictures of ballet-dancers and racehorses, with one or two Indian scenes of pig-sticking, tiger and jackal hunts, and massacres of Sepoys, and the pistols and riding-whips over the mantel, and the gentleman standing at the window, looking out. He wore a captain's uniform, and nothing could have set off his fine figure so well; and this lady-like apartment was his, and told folios about the man's tastes and character. He stood looking out on the lamp-lit street, with people passing carelessly up and down, not looking at them, but thinking deeply—thinking how the best-laid plans of his life had been defeated by that invincible Fate, which was the only deity he believed in, and laying fresh plans, so skillfully to be carried out as to baffle grim Madam

Fate herself. He was going to a party to-night—a party given by Mrs. Darcy, to introduce the new heiress of Redmon to Speckportian society.

Captain George Percy Cavendish, standing at the window, looking abstractedly out at the starlit and gaslit street, was thinking. No one had wished more to see the heiress than he. 'She was the fashion, the sensation, the notoriety of the day. What eclat for him, not to speak of the solid advantages in the way of dollars and cents, to carry off this heiress, in fair and open combat, from all competitors. Tom Oaks, the most insensible of mankind, had seen her but once, and had gone raving about her ever since. Then, she was the heiress of Redmon, and Captain Cavendish had vowed a vow long ago, that Redmon and its thousands should be his, in spite of the very old Diable himself. Did he think remorsefully of that other heiress who had staked all for him, and lost the game? I doubt it.

A little toy of a clock on a Grecian bracket struck ten. There had been a noisy mess-dinner to detain him, and he was late; but he did not mind that. Mr. Johnson, his man, appeared, to assist him on with his greatcoat, and Captain Cavendish started to behold his fate!

The drawing-room of the lawyer's house was filled when he entered—he being himself the latest arrival. He stood near the door for some time, watching the figures passing and re-passing, gliding in and out of the dance— for they were dancing—glancing from one to the other of those pretty mantraps, baited in rainbow-silk, jewelry, and artificial flowers, for the capture of such as he. He was looking for the heiress, but all of those faces were familiar, and almost all deigned him their sweetest smiles in passing —for was there another marriageable man in all Speckport as handsome as he? While he waited, Lieutenant the Honorable L. H. Blank, in a brilliant scarlet uniform, approached with a lady on his arm, and Captain Cavendish knew that he was face to face with the heiress of Redmon! She had been dancing, and the lieutenant led her to a seat, and left her to fulfill some request of hers. Captain Cavendish looked at her, with an electric thrill flashing through every nerve. Tom Oaks was right when he had called this woman glorious. It was the only word that seemed to fit her, with her dark Assyrian beauty, her flaming black eye, and superb wealth of dead-black hair. Yes, she was glorious, this black-eyed divinity, who was dressed like the heroine of a novel, in spotless white, floating like a pale cloud of mist all about her, and emblematic of virgin innocence, perhaps; only this dark daughter of the earth would hardly do to sit to an artist for an ideal Innocence.

She was dressed with wonderful simplicity, with a coronal of vivid scarlet berries and dark-green leaves in the shining braids of her black hair, and a little diamond star, shining and scintillating on her breast. Her nose might turn up, her forehead might be too broad and high, her face too long and thin for classic beauty, but with all that she was magnificent. There was a streaming light in her great black eyes, a crimson glow on her thin cheeks, and a sort of. subtle brilliant electricity about her, not to be described, and not to be resisted. This flashing-eyed girl was one of those women for whom worlds have been lost—dark enchantresses not to be resisted by mortal man.

While Captain Cavendish stood there, magnetized and fascinated, a ringing laugh at his elbow made him look round. It was Miss Laura Blair, of course; no one ever laughed like that, but herself.

"Love at first sight, is it?" she asked, with a wicked look; "come along, and I'll introduce you."

A moment after he was bowing to the dark divinity, and asking her to dance. Miss Henderson assented, with a bewitching smile, and turned that dark entrancing face of hers to Laura.

"Do you know I wanted you, and have sent my late partner off in search of you. I suppose the poor fellow is scouring the house in vain. They are going to take me to Redmon and around the town to-morrow, it seems, and I want to know if you will come?"

Come! Laura's sparkling face answered before her words. The enchantress had fascinated her as well as the rest; and, in a superb and gracious sort of way, she seemed

to have taken a fancy in turn to the laughter-loving Bluenose damsel.

While Laura was speaking, Lieutenant Blank came up,
looking dazed and helpless after his search ; and directly
after him, Mr. Tom Oaks, who had been hovering around
Miss Henderson all the evening, like a moth round a
candle. Mr. Oaks wanted her to dance, and glared vindictively upon Captain Cavendish on hearing she was engaged
to that gentleman, who led her off with a calm air of
superiority, very galling to a jealous lover.

The dance turned out to be a waltz, and Miss Henderson waltzed as if she had indeed been the ballet-dancer
envious people said she was. She floated—it was not motion—and the young officer, who was an excellent waltzer
himself, thought he never had such a partner before in
his life. Long after the rest had ceased, they floated round
and round, the cynosure of all eyes, and the handsomest
pair in the room. Tom Oaks, looking on, ground his
teeth, and could have strangled the handsome Englishman
without remorse.

As he stood there glowering upon them, Mr. Darcy
came along and slapped him on the back.

"It's no use, Oaks. You can't compete with Cavendish ! Handsome couple, are they not ?"

Mr. Oaks ground out something between his teeth, by
way of reply, that was very like an oath, and Mr. Darcy
went on his way, laughing. Standing there, scowling
darkly, Mr. Oaks saw Captain Cavendish lead Miss Henderson to the piano.

Miss Henderson was a most brilliant pianiste, and quite
electrified Speckport that night. Her white hands swept
over the ivory keys, and a storm of music surged through
the room, and held them spell-bound.

Those who had stigmatized her as a ballet-dancer and
a dress-maker were staggered. Ballet-dancers and dressmakers, poor things ! don't often play the piano like that,
or have Mendelssohn's and Beethoven's superbest compo-
sitions at their finger-ends. In short, Miss Henderson
bewitched Speckport that night, even as she had bewitched
poor Tom Oaks. Never had a debut on the great stage of

life been so successful. Where the witchery lay, none could tell; she was not beautiful of feature or complexion, yet half the people there thought her dazzlingly beautiful.

In short, Olive Henderson was not the sort of woman fire-side fairies and household angels and perfect wives are made of, but the kind men go mad for, and rarely marry. She was so brightly beautiful that she defied criticism; and she moved in their midst a young empress, crowned with the scarlet coronal and jetty braids, her diamond-star scintillating rays of rainbow fire, and that smiling face of hers alluring all. Even that slow Val Blake felt the spell of the sorceress, recanted his former heresy, and protested he was as near being in love with her as he had ever been with any one in his life.

The confession was made to Laura Blair, of all people in the world; but the glamour was over her eyes, too, and she heard it without surprise, almost without jealousy.

"Oh, she's splendid, Val," the young lady enthusiastically cried. "I never loved any one so much in my life as I do her! How could you say she was ugly?"

"Upon my word, I don't know," responded Mr. Blake helplessly; "I thought she was at the time, but she don't seem like the same person. How that Cavendish does stick to her, to be sure."

The cold pale dawn of the April day was lifting a leaden eye over the bay and the distant hill-top, when the assembly broke up. It was four o'clock of a cold and winter morning before the lights were fled, the garlands dead, and the banquet-halls deserted. Speckport was very quiet as the tired pleasure-seekers went wearily home, the chill sweeping wind penetrating to the bone.

Leaning against a lamp-post, opposite Mr. Darcy's house, and gazing with ludicrous earnestness at one particular window of that mansion, was a gentleman, whom the cold and uncomfortable dawn appeared to affect but very little. The gentleman was Mr. Tom Oaks, his face flushed, his hair tumbled, and his shirt-bosom in a limp and wine-splashed state, and the window was that of Miss Henderson's room. Heaven only knows how these mad lovers find out things; perhaps the passion gives them some mysterious indication; but he knew the window of her room, and stood there watching her morning-lamp burn, with an absorption that rendered him unconscious of cold and sleet and fatigue. While he was gazing at the light, with his foolish heart in his eyes, a hand was laid on his shoulder, and a familiar voice sounded in his ear:

"I say, Oaks, old fellow! What are you doing here? You'll be laid up with rheumatic fever, if you stand in this blast much longer."

Tom turned round, and saw Captain Cavendish's laughing face. The young officer was buttoned up to the chin, and was smoking a cigar.

"It's no affair of yours, sir," cried Mr. Oaks, rather more fiercely than the occasion seemed to warrant. "The street's free, I suppose!"

"Oh, certainly," said the captain, turning carelessly away; "only Miss Henderson might consider it rather impertinent if she knew her window was watched, and there is a policeman coming this way who may possibly take you up on suspicion of burglary."

It is not improbable, if Captain Cavendish had not already been some paces off, Tom's fist would have been in his face, and his manly length measured on the pavement. Tom never knew afterward what it was kept him from knocking the Englishman down, whom he already hated with the cordial and savage hatred of a true lover. But the captain was not knocked down, and walked home to his elegant rooms, a contemptuous smile on his lips, but an annoyed feeling within. He was so confoundedly good-looking, he thought, this big, blustering, noisy Tom Oaks, and so immensely rich, and women had such remarkably bad taste sometimes that—

"Oh, pshaw!" he impatiently cried to himself, "what am I thinking of to fear a rival in Tom Oaks—that overgrown, blundering idiot. What a glorious creature she is! By Jove! If she were a beggar, those eyes of hers might make her fortune!"

Early in the afternoon of the next day, the plain dark carryall of the lawyer, containing himself and Miss Henderson, drove up to Mr. Blair's for Laura.

Laura did not keep them long waiting; she ran down the steps, her pretty face all smiles, and was helped in and driven off. Miss Henderson lay back like a princess among the cushions, a black velvet mantle folded around her, and looked languidly at the beauties of Speckport as Laura pointed them out. Queen Street stared with all its eyes after the heiress, and the young ladies envied Miss Blair her position, the cynosure of all. The windows of Golden Row were luminous with eyes. If the heiress of Redmon had been the pig-faced lady, she could hardly have attracted more attention. But she might have been a duchess, instead of an ex-seamstress, she was so unaffectedly and radically indifferent; she looked at banks, and custom-houses, and churches, and squares, and men, and women, with listless eyes, but never once kindled into interest. Yes, once they did. It was when they reached the lower part of the town, Cottage Street, in fact, and the bay, all alive with boats, and schooners, and steamers, and ships, came in sight, its saline breath sweeping up in their faces, and its deep, solemn, ceaseless roar sounding in their ears. The heiress sat erect, and a vivid light kindled in her wonderful eyes.

"Oh, the sea!" she cried; "the great, grand, beautiful sea! Oh, Laura! I should like to live where its voice would sound always, night and day, in my ears!"

She had grown so accustomed to hear every one the night before call Miss Blair Laura, that the name came involuntarily, and Laura liked it best.

"It is down here Nathalie Marsh used to live," Laura said; "there is the house. Poor Nathalie!"

"Mrs. Darcy was telling me of her. She was very pretty, was she not?"

"She was beautiful! Not like you," said Laura, paying a compliment with the utmost simplicity; "but fair, with dark blue eyes, and long golden curls, and the loveliest singer you ever heard. Every one loved her. Poor Natty!"

Tears came into Laura's eyes as she spoke of the friend she had loved, and through their mist she did not see how Olive Henderson's face was darkening.

12

" I never received such a shock as when I heard she was missing. I had been with her a little before, and she had been talking so strangely and wildly, asking me if I thought drowning was an easy death. It frightened me; but I never thought she would do so dreadful a deed."

" There can be no doubt, I suppose, but that it was suicide?"

" Oh no! but she was delirious; she was not herself—my poor, poor Natty! They talk of broken hearts—if ever any one's heart broke, it was hers!"

The strange, dark gloom falling like a pall on the face of the heiress, darkened, but Laura did not notice.

" Was it," she hesitated, and averted her face; " was it the loss of this fortune?"

" That, among other things; but I think she felt most of all about poor Charley. Ah! what a handsome fellow he was, and so fond of fun and frolic—every one loved Charley! I suppose Mrs. Darcy told you all the story?"

" Yes. You are quite sure it wasn't he, after all, who committed the murder?"

" Sure!" Laura cried, indignantly. " I am certain! If everybody hadn't been a pack of geese, they would never have suspected Charley Marsh, who wouldn't hurt a fly! No, it was some one else, and Val—I mean Mr. Blake—says if ever Cherrie Nettleby is found, it will be sure to come out!"

" And Mr. Blake supports Mrs. Marsh, Mrs. Darcy says. That is very good of him."

Laura's eyes sparkled.

" Good! Val Blake's the best, the kindest-hearted, and most generous fellow that ever lived. He has that offhand, unpolished way, you know; but at heart, he is as good, and kind, and tender as a woman!"

She spoke with an eagerness—this impulsive Laura—that told her secret plainly enough; but the heiress was thinking of other things.

" She was engaged to Captain Cavendish—this Miss Marsh—was she not?" she asked.

" Yes, I believe so; but it never was so publicly given out. He was her shadow; and every one said it would be

a match after Mrs. Leroy's death, for she detested
him."

"How did he act after she lost her fortune?"

"Well, the time was so short between that and her
dreadful death, that he had very little opportunity of doing anything; but the general opinion was, the engagement would be broken off. In fact, he told Val himself
that she broke off, immediately after—for Natty was proud.
He went to the house every day, I know, until—Oh!
quand on parle de diable—there he is himself!"

Laura did not mean by this abrupt change that his Sa-
tanic Majesty was coming, though it sounded like it. It
was only one of his earthly emissaries—Captain Cavendish,
on horseback. Captain Cavendish looked handsomer on
horseback than anywhere else, a fact of which he was fully
convinced, and he rode up and lifted his hat to the ladies
with gallant grace.

"Good day to you, mesdemoiselles! I called at your
house, Mr. Darcy, but found Miss Henderson out! I trust
I find you well, ladies, after last night's fatigue?"

He addressed both, but he spoke only to one. That
one lifted her dark eyes and bowed distantly, almost coldly,
and it was Laura who answered.

"Seven or eight hours' incessant dancing have no
effect on such constitutions as ours, Captain Cavendish!
We have been showing Miss Henderson the lions of Speckport!"

"And what does Miss Henderson think of those animals?"

"I like Speckport," she said, scarcely taking the trouble
to lift her proud eyes; "this part of it particularly."

She was in no mood for conversation, and took little
pains to conceal it. "Not at home to suitors," was printed plainly on those contracted black brows, and in the
somber depths of those gloomy eyes. Captain Cavendish
lifted his hat and rode on, and the distrait beauty just
deigned a formal bend of her regal head, and no more.

Laura smiled a little maliciously to herself, not at all
sorry to see the irresistible Captain Cavendish rather
snubbed than otherwise. There was nowhere to go now

but to Redmon, and they drove along the quiet road, in the gathering twilight of the short March afternoon. A gray and eerie twilight, too, the low flat sky, of uniform leaden tint, hanging dark over the black fields and moaning sea. The trees, all along the road, stretched out gaunt, bare arms, and the cries of the whirling sea-gulls came up in the cold evening blasts. They had fallen into silence, involuntarily—the gloom of the hour and the dreary scene weighing down the spirits of all. Something of the gloominess of the flat dull landscape lay shadowed on the face of the heiress, as she shivered behind her wraps in the raw sea-gusts.

Ann Nettleby stood at her own door as the party drove by. The cottage looked forlorn and stripped, too, with only bare poles where the scarlet-runners used to climb, and a dismal entanglement of broom-stalks, where the roses and sweetbrier used to flourish. Mr. Darcy drew rein for a moment to nod to the girl.

"How d'ye do, Ann! Any news from that runaway Cherrie yet?"

"No, sir," said Ann, her eyes fixed curiously on the heiress.

"Is this Redmon?" asked Miss Henderson, looking over the cottage at the red brick house. "What a dismal place!"

Dismal, surely, if house ever was! All the shutters were closed, all the doors fastened, no smoke ascending from the broken chimneys, no sound of life within or without; not even a dog, to humanize the ghostly solitude of the place. Black, and grim, and ghostly, it reared its gloomy front to the gloomy sky; the stripped and skeleton trees moaning weirdly about it, an air of decay and desolation over all. Forlorn and deserted, it looked like a haunted house, and such Speckport believed it to be. The two young ladies leaning on Mr. Darcy's arms as they walked up the bleak, bare avenue, between the leafless trees, drew closer to his side, in voiceless awe. The rattling branches seemed to catch at the heiress as she passed them, to catch savagely at this new mistress, out of whose face every trace of color had slowly died away.

"It's a dismal old barrack," Mr. Darcy said, trying to laugh; "but you two girls needn't look like ghosts about it. If the sun was shining now, I dare say you would be laughing at its grimness, both of you."

"I don't know," said the heiress, "I cannot conceive this place anything but ghostly and gloomy. I should be afraid of that murdered woman or that drowned girl coming out from under those black trees in the dead of night. I shall never like Redmon."

"Oh, pooh!" said Mr. Darcy, "yes, you will. When the sun is shining and the grass is green, and the birds singing in these old trees, you'll sing a different tune, Miss Olive. We'll have a villa here, and this old rookery out of the way, and fine doings up here, and, after a while, a wedding, with Laura here, for bridesmaid, and myself to give you away. Won't we, Laura?"

"I'm sure I don't know, sir. Who do you want to give her away to?"

"Well, I'm not certain. There's Tom Oaks looney about her; and there's that good-looking Englishman, all you girls are dying for. You like soldiers, don't you, Miss Olive?"

"Not particularly. Especially soldiers who never smell powder except on parade-day, and whose only battles are sham ones. I like those poor fellows who are fighting and dying down South, but carpet-knights I don't greatly affect."

"That's a rap over the head, Mr. Darcy," cried Laura, with sparkling eyes. "I wish he heard you, Miss Henderson."

"He might if he liked," said the heiress, scornfully.

"Well," said the lawyer, taking the "rap" good-humoredly, "he can make whom he marries, 'my lady,' some day. Is not that an inducement, my dear?"

"Is he of the nobility, then?" asked Olive Henderson, indifferently, and not replying to the question.

"He is next heir to a baronetcy. Lady Olive Cavendish does not sound badly, does it?"

"He used to come here often enough in the old days,"

Laura said, looking at the gloomy old mansion; "he was all devotion to poor Nathalie."

Miss Henderson's beautiful short upper-lip curled.

"He seems to have got wonderfully well over it in so brief a time, for a love so devoted."

"It is man's nature, my dear," said Mr. Darcy; "here's the house, will you go through?"

Laura absolutely screamed at the idea.

"Good gracious, Mr. Darcy! I would not go in for all the world. Don't go, Olive—I mean Miss Henderson."

"Oh, call me Olive! I hate Miss Henderson. No, I don't care for going in—the place has given me the horrors already."

As they walked back to the carriage, Laura asked her what she thought of Mr. Darcy's plan of the villa.

"I shall think about it," was the reply. "Meantime, Mr. Darcy, I wish you would look out for a nice house for me, one with a garden attached, and a stable, and in some nice street, with a view of the water."

"But, dear me!" said Laura, "I should think it would be ever so much nicer and handier to board. It will be such a bother, housekeeping and looking after servants, and all that kind of thing. If I were you I would board."

She turned upon Laura Blair, her eyes, her face, her voice, so passionate, that that young lady quite recoiled.

"Laura!" she cried out, in that passionate voice, "I must have a home. A home, do you hear, not a boarding-house. Heaven knows I have had enough of them to last me my life, and the sound of the word is hateful to me. I must have a home where I will be the mistress, free to do as I please, to come and go as I like, to receive my friends and go to them as it suits me, unasked and unquestioned. I must have a home of my own, or I shall die."

Mr. Darcy looked out a house for the heiress; and after a fortnight's search, found one to suit. It belonged to a certain major, who was going with his bride, a fair Speckportian, home to old England, on a prolonged leave of absence. It was to be let, all ready furnished; it was situated around the corner from Golden Row, commanding a fine view of the harbor, and with two most essential requisites, a garden and a stable. It was a pretty little cottage house, with a tiny drawing-room opening into a library, and a parlor opening into a dining-room. There was a wide hall between, with a delightful glass porch in front, a garden fronting the street, and the door at the other end of the hall opening into a grass-grown back-yard. Altogether it was a pleasant little house, and Miss Henderson took it at once, as it stood, on the major's own terms, and made arrangements for removing there at once

"I must have a horse, Laura, you know," she said to Miss Blair, as they inspected the cottage together, for the two girls had grown more and more intimate, with every passing day. "I must have a horse, and a man to take care of him; and besides, I shall feel safer with a man in the house. Then I must have a housekeeper, some nice motherly old lady, who will take all that trouble off my hands; and a chambermaid, who must be pretty, for one likes to have pretty things about one; and I shall get new curtains and pictures, and send to Boston for a piano and lots of music, and oh, Laura! I shall be just as happy as a queen here all day long."

She waltzed round the room where they were alone, in her new glee, for she was as fitful of temper as an April day—all things by turns, and nothing long. Laura, who was lolling back in a stuffed rocker, looked at her lazily. "A housekeeper, Olly! There's Mrs. Hill, that widow you told me once you thought had such a pleasant face. She is the widow of a pilot, and has no children. She lives with her brother-in-law, Mr. Clowrie, and would be glad of the place."

Miss Henderson gave a last whirl and wheeled breezily down upon a lounge.

"Would she? But perhaps she wouldn't suit. I want some one that can get up dinners, and oversee everything when I have a party. I must have a cook, too—I forgot that."

Laura laughed.

"If you went dinnerless one day, you would be apt to remember it afterward. Mrs. Hill is quite competent to a dinner, or any other emergency, for she was housekeeper in some very respectable English family, before she married that pilot. I am sure she would suit, and I know she would like to come."

"And I know I would like to have her. I'll go down to Mr. Clowrie's to-morrow, and make her hunt me up a cook and housemaid, and stableman. I shall want a gardener, too—that's another thing I forgot."

"Old Nettleby will do that. I say, Olly, you ought to give us a house-warming."

"I mean to ; but they never can dance in these little rooms. Oh, how nice it is to have a house of one's own!"

Laura wondered at the morbid earnestness of Miss Henderson on this subject. She knew very little of the prior history of the heiress, beyond that from great wealth she had fallen to great poverty, and had had unpleasant experience in New York boarding-houses ; the probable origin of this desperate heart-sick longing for a house of her own—a home where she would be the mistress, the sovereign queen.

Mrs. Hill, the pilot's widow, was very glad of Miss Henderson's offer, and gratefully closed with it at once. Perhaps the bread of dependence, never very sweet, was unusually bitter, when sliced by the fair hand of Miss Catty. She was a tall, portly old lady, with a fair, pleasing, unwrinkled face, and kindly blue eyes, that had a motherly tenderness in them for the rich young orphan girl.

"And I want you to find me a cook, and a groom, and a housemaid, Mrs. Hill," Olive said ; "and the girl must be pretty. I mean to have nothing but pretty things about me. I am going to the cottage on Monday, and you must have them all before then."

Mrs. Hill was a treasure of a housekeeper. Before Saturday night she had engaged a competent cook, whose husband knew all about horses, and took the place of groom and coachman. She got, too, a chambermaid, with a charmingly pretty face and form ; and the new window-draperies of snowy lace and purple satin were festooned from their gilded cornices ; and the new fur-

niture was arranged; and the new pictures, louely little
landscape-scenes, hung around the walls. It was a perfect little bijou of a cottage, and the heiress danced from
room to room on Monday morning with the glee of a
happy child delighted with its new toy, and hugged
Laura at least a dozen times over.

"Oh, Laura, Laura, how happy I am! and how happy
I am going to be here! I feel as if this great big world
were all sunshine and beauty, and I were the happiest
mortal in it!"

"Yes, dear," said Laura, "but don't strangle me, if
you can help it. The rooms are beautiful, and your dear
five hundred are dying to behold them. When does
that house-warming come off?"

Miss Henderson was whirling round and round like a
crazy teetotum, and now stopped before Miss Blair with
a sweeping courtesy that ballooned her dress all out around
her.

"On Thursday night, mademoiselle, Miss Henderson
is 'At Home'. The cards will be issued to day. Come
and practice 'Come Where my Love Lies Dreaming.'
Captain Cavendish takes the tenor, and Lieutenant Blank
the bass. We must charm our friends with it that
night."

Miss Henderson did not invite all her dear five hundred friends that Thursday night—the cottage-rooms
would not have held them. As it was, the pretty dining-
room and parlor were well filled, and the heiress stood receiving her guests with the air of a royal princess holding
a drawing-room. She looked brilliantly beautiful, in her
dress of rich mauve silk sweeping the carpet with its
trailing folds, its flounces of filmy black lace, a circlet of
red gold in her dead black hair, twisted in broad shining
plaits around her graceful head, a diamond necklace and
cross blazing like a river of light around her swanlike
throat, and a diamond bracelet flashing on one rounded arm
Speckport, ah! ever-envious Speckport, said these were
but Australian brilliants, and that the whole set had not
cost three hundred dollars in New York; but Speckport
had nothing like them, and Speckport never looked on

12*

anything so beautiful as Olive Henderson that night. She was no longer wan and haggard; her dark cheeks had a scarlet suffusion under the brown skin, and the majestic eye a radiance that seemed more and more glorious every time you saw her.

No one could complain that night of caprice or coquetry, or partiality; all were treated alike; Tom Oaks, Lieutenant Blank, Mr. Val Blake, and Captain Cavendish; she had enchanting smiles, and genial hostess-like courtesies for all, love for none. Whatever beat in the heart throbbing against the amber silk, the lace and the diamonds of her bodice, she only knew—the beautiful dark face was a mask you could not read.

Miss Henderson's reception was a grand success; Mrs. Hill's supper something that immortalized her forever after in Speckport. The guests went home in the gray morning light with a dazed feeling that they had been under a spell all night, and were awakening uncomfortably from it now. They were under the spell of those magical smiles, of that entrancing face and voice—a spell they were powerless to withstand, which fascinated all against their better judgment, which made poor Tom Oaks wander up and down in the cold, before the cottage, until sunrise, to the imminent risk of catching his death; which made half a score of his young townsmen lose their sleep and their appetite, and which made Captain George Percy Cavendish pace up and down his room in a sort of fever for two mortal hours, thrilling with the remembrance of the flashing light in those black eyes, in the bewildering touch of those hands. For you see, Captain Cavendish, having set a net to entrap an heiress, was getting hopelessly entangled in its meshes himself, and was drunk with the draught he would have held to her lips.

And so the reeling world went round, and she who wove the spell, who turned the heads, and dazed the hot brains of these young men, lay tossing on a sleepless pillow, sleepless with the excitement of the dead hours, sleepless with something far worse than excitement—remorse!

CHAPTER XXIV.

THE SPELL OF THE ENCHANTRESS.

THE changes which Mr. Darcy had prophesied were going on at Redmon. Before the middle of May, the transformation had begun. The weird old red-brick house, haunted by so many dismal associations, lay on the ground a great heap of broken bricks and mortar, and the villa was going up with a rapidity only surpassed by Aladdin's palace. Miss Henderson had drawn out the plans herself, and superintended the works, with a clear head and a bright eye for all shortcomings and deficiencies. She rode over every day from the cottage, mounted on her black steed Lightning, her black-velvet cap with its long scarlet-tipped plume flashing in among the workmen, as, with gathered-up skirt, she inspected the progress of the building.

She entered with a true womanly interest into the erection and beautifying of this new home, and had quite got over her superstitious awe of the place. Perhaps this was owing to an artfully-laid plan of that scheming lawyer, Mr. Darcy, who, being absurdly fond of the dark-eyed heiress, and fearful of her depriving Speckport of the light of her beautiful countenance, by flying off somewhere, resolved she should like Redmon, and reside there. Accordingly, about a week after Miss Henderson had gone to the cottage, he had gotten-up a picnic to Redmon—a select picnic, with the military band and a platform for dancing.

The picnic day had dawned in cloudless splendor. Coquettish April, finding she must yield in spite of all her tears and smiles to her fairer sister, May, seemed resolved to put up with the inevitable with a good grace; and the day was more like sunny June than early spring. Before ten in the morning the party were on the grounds, swinging among the trees, dancing on the

shaded platform, wandering among the grand old woods,
or fishing in the clear streams running through them.
The string band, perched up in a gallery, played away
merrily; and what with sunshine and music, and gay
laughter and bright faces, Redmon was a very different-
looking place from the Redmon of a few weeks before.
Miss Henderson had driven Laura Blair up in a little
pony-carriage she had purchased, and owned that Redmon was not so lifeless after all. But she did not enter
into the spirit of the thing with any great zest. Laura
whispered it was one of her "dark days" to those who noticed the silent, abstracted, almost gloomy manner of the
heiress. She danced very little, and had walked moodily
through the quadrille, chafing at its length, and then had
broken from her partner, and gone wandering off among
the trees. Laura Blair made up in herself for all that
was wanting in her friend. She was everywhere at once;
now flying through a crazy cotillon; now on the swings,
flashing in and out among the trees; now superintending
the unpacking, and assisting Mrs. Hill and Catty Clowrie
to set the table. The cloth was laid on the grass; the
cold hams and fowls; the hot tea and coffee; the pies,
and cakes, and sandwiches; the hungry picnickers called,
and great and mighty was the eating thereof.

After dinner, the house was to be explored, the sight
of ghosts, Mr. Darcy considered, being unfavorable to digestion. Some weak-minded persons declined with a
shiver; they had no desire for cold horrors then, or the
nightmare when they went to bed; and among the number was Captain Cavendish. He had no fancy for explor-
ing ratty old buildings, he said; he would lie on the grass,
and smoke his cigar while they were doing the house.
Did any thought of unfortunate Nathalie Marsh obtrude
itself upon the selfish Sybarite as he lay there, smoking
his cigar, on the fresh spring grass, and looking up through
the leafy arcades at the serene April sky? Did any
thought of the old days, and she who had loved him so
true and so well, darken for one moment that hard, handsome mask—his face? Did any more terrible recollection
of a ghostly midnight scene that old house had witnessed,

come back, terribly menacing? Who can tell? The past is haunted for the whole of us; but we banish the specter as speedily as possible, and no doubt Captain Cavendish did the same.

Miss Henderson, of course, was one of the party, leaning on Mr. Darcy's arm; but her face was very pale, and her great eyes filled with a sort of nameless fear, as she crossed its gloomy portal. Laura Blair clung tightly, with little delightful shudders of apprehension, to the arm of Mr. Val Blake, who took it all unconcernedly, as usual, and didn't put himself out any to reassure Miss Blair. The house had a damp and earthy odor, as of the grave; and their footsteps echoed with a dull, dismal sound, as footsteps always do in a deserted house. Dark, dreary, and forlorn, it looked, indeed, a haunted house, and every voice was silent in awe; the gayest laugh hushed; the most fearless feeling a cold chill creeping over him. Rats ran across their path; black beetles swarmed everywhere; the walls were slimy, and fat bloated spiders swung from vast cobwebs wherever they went. It was all dismal, but in the chamber of the tragedy most dismal of all. They hurried out of it almost before they had entered it, and went into the next room, the room that had been Nathalie's. In the darkness, something caught Val Blake's eye in one corner. He picked it up. It was "Paul and Virginia," bound in blue and gold; and on the title-page was written, in a man's hand: "To Nathalie, from hers in life and death—G. P. C." The book passed from hand to hand. No one spoke, but all knew those initials, and all wondered what the heiress thought of it. That young lady had not spoken one word since they had entered the house, and her face was as white as the dress she wore. But they had seen enough now, and they hurried out, heartily thankful when the front door boomed slowly behind them, and they were in the sunshine and fresh air once more. Every tongue was at once unloosed, and ran with a vengeance, as if to make up for lost time. Captain Cavendish started from the grass, flung away his cigar, and approached.

"Well, ladies—well, Miss Laura," he asked, "have you seen the ghost?"

"Yes," said Laura, gravely. "Here is a ghost we found in Nathalie's room. I presume you have the best right to it!"

She handed him the book before them all, and every eye was turned upon him as he glanced at the title-page. His face changed, in spite of all his self-control, turning nearly as colorless as Miss Henderson's.

"I believe I did give Miss Marsh this once," he said, trying to be at his ease. "I suppose you gave the rats a rare fright! There's the music. Miss McGregor, I believe I have this dance?"

The band was playing the "Aline Polka," and no mortal feet could resist that. All the girls were soon whirling about like teetotums, and the elderly folks sat down for a game of euchre on the grass. Olive Henderson, declining, coldly, a dozen eager aspirants for the honor of her hand in the polka, strolled off unsociably herself, as she had done before. They were too busy enjoying themselves to notice her absence at first, and only one followed her. That one was poor Tom Oaks; and to him, in her absence, the sun was without light, the world empty, since the universe held but her. She did not hear him—she was leaning against a tree, looking out with that darkly-brooding face of hers, over the spreading fields and wood, sloping down to the sea, and all her own. Looking out over that wide sea, with a dreary stare, that told plainly all the wealth she had inherited, all the love and admiration she had won, had not the power to make her happy. Her white dress fluttered in the spring breeze; her shawl, of rich gold-colored crape, fell in loose, graceful folds, like sunlight-drapery, around her, held together with one little brown hand. Her head was bare, and the shining profusion of thick black hair was twisted in great serpent-like coils around her head. She looked more sultana-like than ever, holding that mass of glowing golden drapery around her, a woman to command a kingdom, not to be wooed for a household-angel; but that poor Tom Oaks was down on the grass at her feet, before she

knew he was near, imploring her to take pity upon him.
Heaven only knows what he said—Tom never did; but
he was pouring out his whole heart in a vehement outburst of passionate pleading. The man had chosen ar
unpropitious moment.

"Get up, Mr. Oaks," the cold sweet voice said;
"don't make such a scene! Hush! some one will hear
you."

She might as well have told a rushing waterfall to hush.
Tom got up, pleading vehemently, passionately, wildly,
for what seemed to him—poor, foolish fellow!—more
than life.

"No, no, no!" she said, impatiently; "go away, Mr.
Oaks. It is of no use."

It seemed like the old parable of asking for bread and
receiving a stone. Tom Oaks turned away, but something in his despairing face touched her woman's heart.
She laid her hand lightly on his arm, and looked compassionately into his white face.

"I am sorry," she said, in a voice that faltered a little,
"I am sorry! I did not think you cared for me like
this, but I cannot help you! You must forget me, Mr.
Oaks!"

There was one other witness to this little love-passage
besides the birds, singing their songs, in the green
branches. Captain Cavendish had seen Tom Oaks follow
Olive Henderson off the grounds, and knew, by the prescience of jealousy, as well what was going to happen, as
he did after the scene was over. He had followed the
young man, and, in the tangled green heart of the wood,
had heard every word, and watched the white and amber
figure flit out of sight. He leaned against a tree now, almost as pale as Tom Oaks had been. But if she should
refuse him, too! It was the first time in his life he had
ever asked himself that question; and he had made love,
and offered marriage even, to more than Winnifred Rose
and Nathalie Marsh. What if she should refuse him like
this? Pride, love, ambition, all were at stake with Captain Cavendish now, and what if he should lose her?
He set his breath and clenched his hand at the thought.

"I will not lose her!" he said to himself. "I will not! I should go as mad as that idiot on the grass there is, if I lost that glorious girl!"

He might have gone after her, and proposed on the spot, had he not possessed so fully that sixth sense, tact. Like the lady immortalized in the Irish poem of "Paddy, Would You Now," she must be taken when she was "in the humor," and that most decidedly was not to-day. So he strolled back to the rest, and had the satisfaction of seeing her waltzing with his superior officer, Major Marwood, who was unmarried, and rich, and one of her most obedient very humble servants.

The picnic was to wind up with what Mr. Blake called a "danceable tea," at Mr. Darcy's, whither they all drove, in the pleasant April twilight, and the handsome captain enjoyed the privilege of sitting beside the heiress in the pony carriage, to the great envy of every one else. They drove very slowly, watching the moon rise in a long glory of silvery radiance over the sleeping sea, while he told her of Italian moon-rises, and Alpine sunsets, he had gazed upon; and she listened, lying back with half-vailed eyes, and a longing sensation of pleasure in it all at her heart. Was she in love with Captain Cavendish? No; but she liked him best of all her admirers; and there were few women who would not have listened with pleased interest to those vivid word-pictures of far-off lands, and looked with admiration, at least, into that pale, high-bred, classically handsome face.

Captain Cavendish retained his advantage all that evening, and left competitors far behind. He sang duets with Miss Henderson, danced with her, took her in to supper, and folded the shawl around her when they were going home. She might be the veriest iceberg to-morrow, the haughtiest and most imperious Cleopatra; but she was gentle, and graceful, and all feminine sweetness to-night. His hopes were high, his heart all in a glow of thrilling ecstasy, as he went home, under the serene stars. The cup of bliss was almost at his lips, and the many slips were quite forgotten.

The afternoon following the picnic, Olive sat in her

cottage drawing-room entertaining some callers. The callers were Major Marwood, Lieutenant Blank, and Captain Cavendish. Mrs. Darcy, who was spending the day with her, sat at a window crotcheting, and playing propriety, with Mrs. Hill and Mrs. Hill's niece, Miss Clowrie. Somehow this young lady was very fond of dropping in to see her aunt, and staying for dinner, and often all night. The heiress sat at the piano, playing some exquisite "song without words," when a servant entered and ushered in Miss Blair. The officers, who had been there some time, took their departure, and Laura burst out into thanksgiving.

"Now, thank goodness! they're gone. Run up and get your hat, Olly, and come down to see the boat come in."

"I don't care about seeing the boat come in," said the heiress, lazily, lying back in a fauteuil. "I feel comfortable where I am."

"But you must come, I tell you!" cried Laura, "there's a lot of delegates coming from somewhere, about something, and everybody will be there, and I want to see them."

Miss Henderson laughed at this lucid explanation.

"I shan't go," she said.

Miss Blair changed from the imperative mood to the potential, exhorting, entreating..

"Now, Olly, don't be hateful, but go and put your things on, like a darling. I am just dying to go, and I can't go without you, so do come, there's a dear!"

"But don't you see I have company," laughed Olive; "I can't be rude; I can't leave them."

"Nonsense, Olive, my love," cut in Mrs. Darcy; "you don't call Catty and I strangers, I hope. Go down to the wharf; the sea-breeze will sharpen your appetite for dinner."

"A very romantic reason, certainly," said Olive, sauntering out of the room, however. "You had better come too, Miss Clowrie."

This was said for politeness' sake, for the attorney's daughter was no favorite with the heiress. Catty, only

too glad to be seen in public with Miss Henderson, accepted at once, and went up to dress.

"Is it true, Laura," asked Mrs. Darcy, "that Miss Rose
came back last night?"

"Yes," said Laura, "she called this morning, and I
was so glad to see her. She looks extremely well. England must have agreed with her."

"Where is she stopping? I should like to see her."

"At —— House, with Mrs. and Major Wheatly. She
told me she would be at the boat this afternoon, when she
would see all the old faces, if Speckport had not changed
greatly in her absence."

"Tell her to call and see me," said Mrs. Darcy; "I
always liked Miss Rose. I think she has the sweetest face
I ever saw."

"Now, then, Laura," exclaimed Olive, appearing at
the door with Catty, "I am ready, and I hear the steamer
blowing."

The three young ladies walked down to the wharf,
which, as usual, was crowded. One of the first persons
they met was Val Blake, watching the passengers, who
were beginning to come up the floats, running the gauntlet
of all eyes. He was telling them something about Tom
Oaks, who had started off up the country, when he
stopped in the middle of what he was saying with a sort
of shout of astonishment, and stared at a gentleman coming up the floats, with a valise in one hand, and an overcoat across his arm.

"Now, of all the people coming and going on the face
of the earth," cried out Mr. Blake, in his amazement,
"whatever has sent Paul Wyndham to Speckport?"

The next instant he was off, flinging the crowd right
and left out of his way, and arresting the traveler with a
sledge-hammer tap on the shoulder. The girls laughingly
watched him, as he shook the stranger's hand as vigorous-
ly as if he meant to wrench it off, crying out in a voice
that everybody heard: "Why, Wyndham, old fellow!
what the deuce drove you here?"

Mr. Wyndham smiled quietly at his impetuous friend,
and walked away with him to a cab, which they both en-

tered, and Olive Henderson, still laughing at Mr. Blake, looked carelessly after them, and never dreamed that she had met her fate. No; who ever does dream it, when they meet that fate first!

So Paul Wyndham passed Olive Henderson, and the curtain of the future shrouded the web of life destiny was weaving. She forgot him as soon as seen, and turned to Laura, who was speaking animatedly.

"Look, Olly! there's the Miss Rose you have heard me speaking of so often—that little girl with the black silk dress and mantle, and black straw hat, talking to Miss Blake. Look! hasn't she the sweetest face! I'll call her over."

The crowd of men, women and children, thronging the wharf and floats, were strangely startled a moment after, and every eye turned in one direction. There had been a long, wild, woman's shriek, and some one had reeled and fallen to the ground like a log. There was a rushing and swaying, and startled talking among the people; and Dr. Leach, coming along, took the Rev. Augustus Tod by the button, and wanted to know what was the matter.

"Miss Olive Henderson had fainted," the Rev. Augustus said, with a startled face. "She had been standing on the wharf, apparently quite well, only a second before, when she had suddenly screamed out and fallen down in a fainting-fit. It was really quite shocking."

CHAPTER XXV.

THE DOUBLE COMPACT.

LIVE HENDERSON lay on a sofa in her bedroom, her face half buried among the pillows, her cloud of tar-black hair all loose and disordered, falling about her, and still wearing the out-door dress of yesterday. Bright streaks of crimson glory, in the dull dawn sky, heralded the rising

of another sun, of another day to the restless, feverish
little planet below. Dressed in that uncomfortable attire
for repose, Olive Henderson, while the red morning broke,
lay there and slept. Stuff! It was more stupor than
sleep, and she had only sank into it half an hour before,
from sheer physical exhaustion. Those in the cottage had
been disturbed all night long, by the sound of restless
footsteps pacing up and down the chamber where she now
lay, up and down, up and down, ceaselessly, the live-long
night. When they had lifted her up, and carried her
home in that death-faint, and Dr. Leach had brought her
to, her first act had been to turn every soul of them out
of her room, Laura Blair included, to lock the door, and
remain there alone by herself, ever since. Everybody
wondered ; Catty Clowrie, most of all, and tender-hearted
Laura cried. That sympathizing confidante had gone to
the locked door, and humbly and lovingly entreated "Olly"
to let her in ; but Olly turned a deaf ear to all her entreaties, and never even condescended to reply. Mrs.
Hill felt deeply on the subject of refreshments—if her
young lady would but partake of some weak tea and dry
toast, or even water-gruel, and go to bed comfortable, and
sleep it off, she would be all right to-morrow ; but to shut
herself up, and her friends out, was enough to give her
her death. Catty Clowrie said very little, but she thought
a good deal. She had remained all night at the cottage,
and had listened to that troubled footstep, and had mused
darkly, instead of sleeping. At day-dawn the restless
pacing had ceased, and Olive Henderson lay sleeping, a
deep, stupor-like sleep. Her face, lying among the pillows, contrasting with her black hair, looked ghastly
white in the pale dawn, and her brows were drawn, and
her position strangely wretched and unnatural.

Mrs. Hill came to the door several times and tried to
get in, but in vain. Her feeble knocks failed to awake
her young mistress from that deep sleep, and the sun was
high in the purple arch outside, before the dark eyes slowly opened to this mortal life again. She sat up feeling
stiff, and cold, and cramped, and unrefreshed, and put the
black cloud of hair away from her face, while memory

stepped back to its post. With something like a groan she dropped her face once more among the pillows, but this time not to sleep. She lay so still for nearly half an hour, that not a hair of her head moved, thinking, thinking, thinking. A terrible fear came upon her, a horrible danger threatened her, but she was not one easily to yield to despair. She would battle with the rising tide, battle fiercely to the last, and if the black waves engulfed her at the end, she would die waging war against relentless doom, to the close.

Olive Henderson rose up, twisted her disordered tresses away from her face, searched for her ink and paper, and sat down to a little rosewood desk, to write. It was very short, the note she rapidly scrawled, but the whole passionate heart of the girl was in it.

"For God's sake come to me!" (this abrupt note began) "every second is an age of agony till I see you. I thought you were dead—as Heaven is my witness, I did, or I should never have come here! By the memory of all the happy days we have spent together, by the memory of your dead father, I conjure you be silent, and come to me at once!   H."

The note had neither date, address, nor signature, save that one capital letter, but when it was folded and in the envelope, she wrote the address:—"Miss W. Rose, —— House, Queen Street, Speckport."

Then, rising, she exchanged the crumpled robe in which she had slept for one of plain black silk, hastily thrust her hair loose into a chenille net, put on a long black silk mantle, a bonnet and thick brown vail, placed the letter in her pocket, and went down stairs. There was no possibility of leaving the house unseen; Mrs. Hill heard her opening the front door and came out of the dining-room. Her eyes opened like full moons at the sight of the street costume, and the young lady's white, resolute face.

"My patience, Miss Olive, you're never going out?"

"Yes," Miss Henderson said, constraining herself to

speak quietly. "My head aches, and I think a walk in the air will do it good. I will be back d'rectly."

"But, do take something before you go. Some tea, now, and a little bit of toast."

"No, no! not any, thank you, until I come back."

She was gone even while she spoke; the thick vail drawn over her face, her parasol up, screening her effectually. Catty Clowrie, watching her from the window, would have given considerable to follow her, and see where she went. She had little faith in that walk being taken for the sake of walking; some covert meaning lay hidden beneath.

"I declare to you, Catty," exclaimed Mrs. Hill, coming back, "she gave me quite a turn! She was as white as a ghost, and those big black eyes of hers looked bigger and blacker than ever. She is turning bilious, that's what she's doing."

Miss Henderson walked to Queen Street by the most retired streets, and passed before the hotel, where Major and Mrs. Wheatly boarded. She had some idea of putting the letter in the post-office when she started, but in that case Miss Rose would not receive it until evening, and how could she wait all that time, eating out her heart with mad impatience? There was a man standing in the doorway of the ladies' entrance, a waiter, and quite alone. With her vail closely drawn over her face, Miss Henderson approached him, speaking in a low voice:

"There is a young lady—a governess, called Miss Rose, stopping here—is there not?"

"Yes, ma'am."

"Is she in now?"

"Yes'm."

"Will you please give her this letter! give it into her own hand, and at once!"

She gave him the letter, and a fee that made him stare, and was gone. The man did not know her, and Olive reached home without once meeting any one who recognized her.

Miss Catty Clowrie did not leave the cottage all that day. She was sewing for Mrs. Hill; and, seated at the

dining-room window, she watched Miss Henderson furtively, but incessantly, under her white eyelashes. That
young lady seemed possessed of the very spirit of restlessness, since her return from her walk. It had not done
her much good, apparently, for it had neither brought
back color nor appetite; and she wandered from room to
room, and up-stairs and down-stairs, with a miserable feverish restlessness, that made one fidgety to look at her.
And all the time in her dark colorless face there was only
one expression, one of passionate, impatient waiting. Waiting, waiting, waiting! For what? Catty Clowrie's greenish-gray eyes read the look aright, but for what was she
waiting?

"I'll find it out, yet," Miss Clowrie said, inwardly.
"She is a very fine lady, this Miss Olive Henderson, but
there is an old adage about 'All that glitters is not gold.'
I'll wait and see."

There were a great many callers in the course of the
morning, but Miss Henderson was too indisposed to see
any of them. Even Miss Blair was sent away with this
answer, when she came; but Miss Henderson had left
word, Mrs. Hill said, that she would be glad to see Miss
Laura to-morrow. Miss Henderson herself, walking up
and down the drawing-room, heard the message given,
and the door closed on her friend, and then turned to go
up-stairs. She stopped to say a word to her housekeeper
as she did so.

"There is a person to call to-day, Mrs. Hill," she said,
not looking at the pilot's widow, "and you may send her
up to my room when she comes. It is Miss Rose, Mrs.
Major Wheatly's governess!"

Her foot was on the carpeted stair as she said this, and
she ran up without giving her housekeeper time to reply.
Catty Clowrie, industriously sewing away, listened, and
compressed her thin lips.

"Miss Rose coming to see her, and admitted to a private interview, when every one else is excluded! Um—
m—m! That is rather odd; and Miss Rose is a stranger
to her—or is supposed to be! I wonder why she fainted
at sight of Miss Rose, on the wharf, yesterday, and why

Miss Rose's face turned to pale amazement at sight of her. She did not ask any questions, I noticed; but Miss Rose was always discreet; and no one observed her but myself, in the hubbub. There is something odd about all this!"

She threaded her needle afresh, and went on with her sewing, with the patient perseverance of all such phlegmatic mortals. Mrs. Hill came in, wondering what Miss Henderson could possibly want of Miss Rose, but her niece could throw no light on the subject.

"Perhaps she wants a companion," Miss Clowrie remarked; "fine ladies like Miss Henderson are full of freaks, and perhaps she wants some one to play and sing and read to her, when she feels too lazy to do it herself."

Catty Clowrie had read a good many novels in her life, full of all sorts of mysteries, and secret crimes, and wicked concealments, and conspiracies—very romantic and unlike every day-life—but still liable to happen. She had never had the faintest shadow of romance, to cover rosily her own drab-hued life—no secret or mystery of any sort to happen to herself, or any of the people among whom she mingled. The most romantic thing that had ever occurred within her personal knowledge was the fact of this new heiress, this Olive Henderson, rising from the offal of New York, from the most abject poverty, to sudden and great wealth.

Miss Clowrie sat until three o'clock, sewing at the dining-room window. Luncheon-hour was two, but Miss Henderson would not descend, and asked to have a cup of strong tea sent up, so Mrs. Hill and her niece partook of that repast alone. As the clock was striking three, a young lady, dressed in half-mourning, came down the street and rang the door-bell; and Catty, dropping her work, ran to open it, and embrace with effusion the visitor. She had not spoken to Miss Rose before since her return, and kissed her now, as though she were really glad to see her.

"I am so glad you are back again, dear Miss Rose!" the young lady cried, holding both Miss Rose's hands in hers; "you cannot think how much we have all missed you since you went away!"

Now, it was rather unfortunate for Miss Clowrie, but

nature, who will always persist in being absurdly true to
herself, had given an insincere look to the thin, wide
mouth, and a false glimmer to the greenish-gray eyes, and
a clammy, limp moistness to the cold hand, that made you
feel as if you had got hold of a dead fish, and wished to
drop it again as soon as possible. Miss Rose had taken an
instinctive aversion to Miss Clowrie the first time she had
seen her, and had never been quite able to get over it
since, though she had conscientiously tried; but she never
betrayed it, and smiled now in her own gentle smile, and
thanked Miss Clowrie in her own sweet voice. She turned
to Mrs. Hill, though, when that lady appeared, with a far
different feeling, and returned the kiss that motherly old
creature bestowed upon her.

"It does my heart good to see you again, Miss Rose,"
the housekeeper said. "I haven't forgotten all you did
for me last year when poor, dear Hill was lost, going after
that horrid ship. You can't think how glad I was when
I heard you were come back."

"Thank you, Mrs. Hill," the governess said. "It is
worth while going away for the sake of such a welcome
back. Is Miss—" she hesitated a moment, and then went
on, with a sudden flush lighting her face; "is Miss Henderson in?"

"Yes, my dear; I will go and tell her you are here."

The housekeeper went up-stairs, but reappeared almost
immediately.

"You are to go up-stairs, my dear," she said; "Miss
Henderson is not very well, and will see you in her own
room."

Miss Rose ascended the stairs, entered the chamber of
the heiress, and Catty heard the door closed and locked
after her. As Mrs. Hill re-entered the dining-room, she
found her gathering up her work.

"I left the yokes and wristbands in your room, aunt,"
she explained. "I must go after them, and I'll just go
up and finish this nightgown there."

There were four rooms up-stairs, with a hall running
between each two. The two on the left were occupied
by Miss Henderson, one being her bedroom, the other a

13

bath-room. Mrs. Hill had the room opposite the heiress, the other being used by Rosie, the chambermaid.

Miss Clowrie (one hates to tell it, but what is to be done?) went deliberately to Miss Henderson's door, and applied first her eye, then her ear, to the key-hole. Applying her eye, she distinctly beheld Miss Olive Henderson, the heiress of Redmon, the proudest woman she had ever known, down upon her knees, before Miss Rose, the governess—the ex-school-mistress; holding up her closed hands, in wild supplication, her face like the face of a corpse, and all her black hair tumbled and falling about her.

To say that Miss Catty Clowrie was satisfied by this sight, would be doing no sort of justice to the subject. The first words she caught were not likely to lessen her astonishment—wild, strange words.

"I thought you were dead! I thought you were dead!" in a passion of consternation, that seemed to blot out every thought of prudence. "I thought you were dead! As Heaven hears me, I thought you were dead, or I never would have done it."

Miss Rose was standing with her back to the door, and the eavesdropper saw her trying to raise the heiress up.

"Get up, Harriet," she distinctly heard her say, though she spoke in a low voice; "I cannot bear to see you like this; and do not speak so loud—some one may hear you."

If they had only known of the pale listener at the door, hushing her very heart-beating to hear the better. But Miss Henderson would not rise; she only knelt there, white and wild, and holding up her clasped hands.

"I will never get up," she passionately cried. "I will never rise out of this until you promise to keep my secret. It is not as a favor, it is as a right I demand it! Your father robbed my mother and me. But for him I would have never known poverty and misery—and God only knows the misery that has been mine. But for him, I should never have known what it is to suffer from cold and hunger, and misery and insult; but for him I would have been rich to-day; but for him my mother might still be alive and happy. He ruined us, and broke her heart, and I tell you it is only justice I ask! I should never have come here had I not thought you dead; but now that I have come, that wealth and comfort have been mine once more, I will not go. I will not, I tell you! I will die before I yield, and go back to that horrible 'ife, and may my death rest forever on your soul!"

Catty Clowrie, crouching at the door, turned as cold as death, listening to these dreadful words. Was she awake—was she dreaming? Was this Olive Henderson —the proud, the beautiful, the queenly heiress—this mad creature, uttering those passionate, despairing words. She could not see into the room, her ear was at the keyhole—strained to a tension that was painful, so absorbed was she in 'listening. But at this very instant her strained hearing caught another sound—Rosie, the chambermaid, coming along the lower hall, and up-stairs. Swift as a flash, Catty Clowrie sprang up, and darted into her aunt's room. She did not dare to close the door, lest the girl should hear her, and she set her teeth with anger and suppressed fury at the disappointment.

Rosie had come up to make her bed, and set her room to rights, and was in no wise disposed to hurry over it. She sang at her work; but the pale-faced attorney's daughter in the next room, furious with disappointment, could have seen her choked at the moment with the greatest pleasure. Half an hour passed—would the girl never go? Yes—yes, there was Mrs. Hill, at the foot of the stairs, calling her, and Rosie ran down. Quick as she had left it, Catty was back at her post, airing her eye at the keyhole once more.

The scene she beheld was not quite so tragic this time. The heiress and the governess were seated opposite one another, an inlaid table between them. There was paper and ink on the table; Miss Henderson held a pen in her hand, as if about to write, and Miss Rose was speaking. Her voice was sweet and low, as usual; but it had a firm cadence, that showed she was gravely in earnest now.

"You must write down these conditions, Harriet," she was saying, "to make matters sure; but no one shall ever see the papers, and I pledge you my solemn word, your secret shall be kept inviolable. Heaven knows I have done all I could to atone for my dead father's acts, and I will continue to do it to the end. He wronged your mother and you, I know, and I am thankful it is in my power to do reparation. I ask nothing for myself—but others have rights as well as you, Harriet, and as sacred. Two hundred pounds will pay all the remaining debts of my father now. You must give me that. And you must write down there a promise to pay Mrs. Marsh one hundred pounds a year annuity, as long as she lives. Her daughter should have had it all, Harriet, and neither you nor I; and the least you can do, in justice, is to provide for her. You will do this?"

"Yes—yes," Miss Henderson cried; "that is not much to do! I want to do more. I want you to share with me, Olly."

"No," said Miss Rose, "you may keep it all. I have as much as I want, and I am very well contented. I have no desire for wealth. I should hardly know what to do with it if I had possessed it."

"But you will come and live with me," Miss Henderson said, in a voice strangely subdued; "come and live with me, and let us share it together, as sisters should."

That detestable housemaid again! If Catty Clowrie had been a man, she might have indulged in the manly relief of swearing, as she sprang up a second time, and fled into Mrs. Hill's room. This time, Rosie was not called away, and she sat for nearly an hour, singing, at her chamber window, and mending her stockings. Catty Clowrie, on fire with impotent fury, had to stay where she was.

Staying there, she saw Miss Henderson's door opened at last; and, peeping cautiously out, saw the two go down-stairs together. Miss Rose looked as if she had been crying, and her face was very pale, but the fierce crimson of excitement burned on the dark cheeks and flamed in the black eyes of Miss Henderson. It was the heiress who let Miss Rose out, and then she came back to her room, and resumed the old trick of walking up and down, up and down, as on the preceding night.

Catty wondered if she would never be tired. It was all true, then; and there was a dark secret and mystery in Olive Henderson's life. "Olive!" Was that her name, and if so, why had Miss Rose called her "Harriet." And if the governess's name was Winnie, why did the heiress call her "Olly?"

Catty Clowrie sat thinking while the April day faded into misty twilight, and the cold evening star glimmered down on the sea. She sat there thinking while the sun went low, and dipped into the bay, and out of sight. She sat thinking while the last little pink cloud of the sunset paled to dull gray, and the round white moon came up, like a shining shield. She sat there thinking till the dinner-bell rang, and she remembered she was cold and hungry, and went slowly down-stairs—still thinking.

To her surprise, for she had been too absorbed to hear her come out of her room, Miss Henderson was there, beautifully dressed, and in high spirits. She had such a passion for luxury and costly dress, this young lady, that she would array herself in velvets and brocades, even though there were none to admire her but her own servants.

On this evening, she had dressed herself in white, with ornaments of gold and coral in her black braids, broad gold bracelets on her superb arms, and a cluster of scarlet flowers on her breast. She looked so beautiful with that fire in her eyes, that flush on her cheek, that brilliant smile lighting up her gypsy face, that Mrs. Hill and Catty were absolutely dazzled. She laughed—a clear, ringing laugh—at Mrs. Hill's profuse congratulations on her magical recovery.

"You dear old Mrs. Hill!" she said, "when you are better used to me, you will cease to wonder at my eccentricities! It is a woman's privilege to change her mind sixty times an hour, if she chooses—and I choose to assert all the privileges of my sex!"

She rose from the table as she spoke, still laughing, and went into the drawing-room. The gas burned low, but she turned it up to its full flare, and, opening the piano, rattled off a stormy polka. She twirled round presently, and called out:

"Mrs. Hill!"

Mrs. Hill came in.

"Tell Sam to go up to Miss Blair's, and fetch her here. Let him tell her I feel quite well again, and want her to spend the evening, if she is not engaged. He can take the gig, and tell him to make haste, Mrs. Hill."

Mrs. Hill departed on her errand, and Miss Henderson's jeweled fingers were flying over the polished keys once more. Presently she twirled around again, and called out: "Miss Clowrie."

"I wish Laura would come!" Miss Henderson said, pulling out her watch, "and I wish she would fetch a dozen people with her. I feel just in the humor for a ball to-night."

She talked to Catty Clowrie vivaciously, and to Mrs. Hill, because she was just in the mood for talking, and rattled off brilliant sonatas between whiles. But she was impatient for Laura's coming, and kept jerking out her watch every five minutes, to look at the hour.

Miss Blair made her appearance at last, and not alone. There was a gentleman in the background, but Miss B. rushed with such a frantic little scream of delight into the arms of her "dear, darling Olly," and so hugged and kissed her, that, for the first moment or two, it was not very easy to see who it was. Extricating herself, laughing and breathless, from the gushing Miss Blair, Olive looked at her companion, and saw the amused and handsome face of Captain Cavendish.

"I hope I am not an intruder," that young officer said, coming forward, "but being at Mr. Blair's when your message arrived, and hearing you were well again, I could not forbear the pleasure of congratulating you. The Princess of Speckport can be ill dispensed with by her adoring subjects."

Some one of Miss Henderson's innumerable admirers had dubbed her "Princess of Speckport," and the title was not out of place. She laughed at his gallant speech, and held out her hand with frank grace.

"My friends are always welcome," she said, and here she was interrupted by a postman's knock at the door.

"Dear me! who can this be?" said Mrs. Hill, looking up over her spectacles, as Rosie opened the door.

It proved to be Mr. Val Blake. That gentleman being very busy all day, had found no time to inquire for Miss Henderson, until after tea, when, strolling out, with his pipe in his mouth, for his evening constitutional, he had stepped around to ask Mrs. Hill. Miss Henderson appeared in person to answer his friendly inquiries, and Mr. Blake came in, nothing loth, and joined the party.

Some one proposed cards, after a while; and Mr. Blake, and Miss Blair, and Mrs. Hill, and Miss Clowrie, gathered round a pretty little card-table, but Miss Henderson retained her seat at the piano, singing, and playing operatic overtures. Captain Cavendish stood beside her, turning over her music, and looking down into the sparkling, beautiful face, with passionately loving eyes. For the spell of the sorceress burdened him more this night than ever before, and the man's heart was going in great plunges against his side. He almost fancied she must hear its tumultuous beating, as she sat there in her beauty and her pride, the red gold gleaming in her black braids and on her brown arms. It had always been so easy before for him to say what was choking him now, and he had said it often enough, goodness knows, for the lesson to be easy. But there was this difference—he loved this black-eyed sultana; and the fever called love makes a coward of the bravest of men. He feared what he had never feared before—a rejection; and a rejection from her, even the thought of one, nearly sent him mad.

And all this while Miss Olive Henderson sat on her piano-stool, and sang "Hear me, Norma," serenely unconscious of the storm going on in the English officer's breast. He had heard that very song a thousand times better sung, by Nathalie Marsh. Ah! poor forgotten Nathalie!—but he was not listening to the singing. For him, the circling sphere seemed momentarily standing still, and the business of life suspended. He was perfectly white in his agitation, and the hand that turned the leaves shook. His time had come. The card-party were too much absorbed in scoring their points to heed them, and now, or never, he must know his fate. What he said he never afterward knew—but Miss Henderson looked strangely startled by his white face and half incoherent sentences. The magical words were spoken; but as the self-possessed George Cavendish had never spoken thus before, and the supreme question on which his life's destiny hung, asked.

The piano stood in a sort of recess, with a lace-draped window to the right, looking out upon Golden Row. Miss Henderson sat, all the time he was speaking, looking straight before her, out into the coldly moonlit street. Not once did her color change—no tremor made the scarlet flowers on her breast rise and fall—no flutter made the misty lace about her tremble. She was only very grave, ominously grave, and the man's heart turned sick with fear, as he watched her unchanging face and the dark gravity of her eyes. She was a long time in replying—all the while sitting there so very still, and looking steadfastly out at the quiet street; not once at him. When she did reply, it was the strangest answer he had ever received to such a declaration. The reply was another question.

"Captain Cavendish," she said, "I am an heiress, and you—pardon me—have the name of a fortune-hunter. If I were penniless, as I was before this wealth became mine —if by some accident I were to lose it again—would you say to me what you have said now?"

Would he? The answer was so vehement, so passionate, that the veriest skeptic must have believed. His desperate earnestness was written in every line of his agitated face.

"I believe you," she said; "I believe you, Captain Cavendish. I think you do-love me; but I—I do not love you in return."

He gave a sort of cry of despair, but she put up one hand to check him.

"I do not love you," she steadily repeated, "and I have never loved any one in this way. Perhaps it is not in me, and I do not care that it should be: there is misery enough in the world, Heaven knows, without that! I do not love you, Captain Cavendish, but I do not love any one else. I esteem and respect you; more, I like you: and if you can be content with this, I will be your wife. If you cannot, why, we will be friends as before, and——"

But he would not let her finish. He had caught her hand in his, and broke out into a rhapsody of incoherent thanks and delight.

"There, there!" she smilingly interposed, "that will do! Our friends at the card-table will hear you. Of one thing you may be certain: I shall be true to you until death. Your honor will be safe in my hands; and this friendly liking may grow into a warmer feeling by-and-by. I am not very romantic, Captain Cavendish, and you must not ask me for more than I can give."

But Captain Cavendish wanted no more. He was supremely blessed in what he had received, and his handsome face was radiant.

"My darling," he said, "I ask for no more! I shall think the devotion of a whole life too little to repay you for this."

"Very well," said Miss Henderson, rising; "and now, after that pretty speech, I think we had better join our friends, or my duty as hostess will be sadly neglected."

She stood behind Miss Laura Blair for the rest of the evening, watching the fluctuations of the game, and with no shadow of change in her laughing face. She stood there until the little party broke up, which was some time after ten, when Mr. Blair called around for Laura himself. Miss Laura was not to say over and above obliged to her pa for this act of paternal affection—since she would have infinitely preferred the escort of Mr. Blake. That gentleman hooked his arm within that of Captain Cavendish, and bade Miss Blair good-night, with seraphic indifference.

Miss Henderson's bedroom windows commanded an eastward view of the bay, and when she went up to her room that night, she sat for a long time gazing out over the shining track the full moon made for herself on the tranquil sea. "Gaspereaux month" had come around again, and the whole bay was dotted over with busy boats.

She could see the fishermen casting their nets, now in the shadow, now in the glittering moonlight, and the peaceful beauty of the April night filled her heart with a deep, sweet sense of happiness. Perhaps it was the first time since her arrival in Speckport she had been really happy —a vague dread and uncertainty had hung over her, like that fabled sword, suspended by a single hair, and ready to fall at any moment. But the fear was gone, she was safe now—her inheritance was secure, and she was the promised wife of an honorable gentleman. Some day, perhaps, he might be a baronet, and she "my lady," and her ambitious heart throbbed faster at the thought. She sat there, dreaming and feeling very happy, thinking of the double compact ratified that most eventful day, but she never once thanked God—never gave one thought to him to whom she owed it all. She sat there far into the night, thinking, and when she laid her head on the pillow and fell asleep, it was to act it all over in dreamland again.

Some one else lay awake a long time that night, thinking, too. Miss Clowrie, in the opposite chamber, did not sit up by the window; Mrs. Hill would, no doubt, not have permitted it, and Miss Clowrie was a great deal too sensible a person to run the risk of catching cold. But, though she lay with her eyes shut she was not asleep, and Olive Henderson might not have dreamed quite such happy dreams had she known how dark and ominous were the thoughts the attorney's pale daughter was thinking.

CHAPTER XXVI.

MR. PAUL WYNDHAM.

N the morning after the day fraught with so many events to the heiress of Redmon, the mother of the late heiress sat in the sitting-room of her pleasant seaside home, reading a novel. The firelight shone on her mourning-dress, but the inward mourning was not very profound. She had cried a good deal at first for the loss of her son and daughter; she cried sometimes still when people talked to her about them; but she cried quite as much over the woes of her pet heroes and heroines, bound in paper and cloth, and slept just as soundly, and took her meals with as good a relish as ever she had done in her life. Mrs. Marsh was not greatly given to borrowed trouble; she took the goods the gods provided, and let to-morrow take care of itself, so long as she had enough for to-day. Mr. Val Blake paid the butcher's, and baker's, and grocer's bills quarterly; settled with Betsy Ann, and Miss Jo saw that she was well dressed; and Mrs. Marsh took all as a matter of course, and I don't think even once thanked Mr. Blake for his kindness.

On this sunny spring morning Mrs. Marsh sat comfortably reading, so absorbed in her book as to be out of the reach of all mundane affairs. The book had a bright yellow cover, with a striking engraving of one man grasping another by the throat, and presenting a pistol at his head, and was called the "Red Robber of the Rocky Mountains"—a sequel to the "Black Brigand,"—when, just in the middle of a most thrilling chapter, Mrs. Marsh was disturbed by a knock at the front door. Betsy Ann answered the summons, and stood transfixed at the shining apparition she beheld. A beautiful young lady, with big black eyes, that shone on Betsy Ann like two black diamonds, arrayed in rustling silk, and a rich creamy crape shawl, with a bonnet fine enough for the queen of England, stood before her, asking, in a silvery voice, if Mrs. Marsh were at home. Standing before the door was a small open carriage, drawn by two milk-white ponies; and Miss Laura Blair sat within, nodding pleasantly to her, Betsy Ann, and holding the reins. The girl, quite dazzled by the splendor of this early visitor, ushered the radiant vision into the room where her mistress sat, and Mrs. Marsh arose with an exclamation of surprise she could not repress. They had met a few times before at the houses of mutual friends, but this was the young lady's first call.

"Miss Henderson," Mrs. Marsh stammered, utterly at a loss what to say—"I am sure I am very glad to see you; I have not had many visitors of late."

Tears rose to her eyes as she spoke, with the thoughts of the pleasant days gone by, when the friends of Nathalie and Charley, the friends of their prosperity, had made the cottage more gay with laughter and music. Miss Henderson was not looking at her, but into the red coal-fire.

"I have come on a little matter of business, Mrs. Marsh," she said. "I have come to fulfill a duty I owe to you. I know the story of the past, and, I am afraid, you must feel in some degree as if I had taken from you what should have been yours. Your—your daughter had no doubt a prior claim to what I now possess, and common justice requires you should not be defrauded. I am aware of Mr. Blake's great generosity, but the duty —and, I assure you, it is a pleasure to me—lies with me, not with him. I have, therefore, settled upon you, for life, an annuity of one hundred pounds per annum, which will be paid to you at my banker's, monthly or quarterly, as you may prefer. It was to say this I came so early this morning, but, if you will permit me, this visit shall be but the forerunner of many others."

She was standing up as she finished, with a look of intense relief at having accomplished her task, and

Mrs. Marsh altogether too dazed and bewildered to utter
a word.

"And I shall be very, very happy, my dear Mrs.
Marsh," the heiress said, bending over her, and taking
her hand, "if you will sometimes come up and see me.
I have no mother, and I will look upon you as such, if
you will let me."

Mrs. Marsh saw her go, feeling as though she were
in a dream, or acting a chapter out of one of her own
romances.

Miss Henderson took her place beside Laura in the
pony carriage, and they drove slowly along Cottage Street,
looking at the broad blue bay, sparkling in the sunshine,
as if sown with stars. The beach, with its warm, white
sands, edged the sea like a silver streak; and the waves
sang their old music, as they crept up on its breast.

"How beautiful it all is!" the heiress cried, her dark
face lighting up as it always did at sight of the ocean.
"Let us get out, Laura; I could-stay here listening to
those sailors singing forever."

There were some idle boys at play on an old wharf,
overgrown with moss and slimy seaweed, its tarry planks
rotting in the sun.

Miss Henderson dropped a bright silver shilling into
the dirty palm of one, and asked him to hold the ponies
for ten minutes; and the two girls walked along the de-
caying and deserted old wharf together.

"My solemn Laura!" the heiress said, looking at her
friend's grave face; "what a doleful countenance you
wear! Of what are you thinking?"

"I am thinking of poor Nathalie Marsh," Laura answered; "it was on this very wharf she met her death,
that wild, windy night. I have never been near the place
since."

It is a remarkable trait of these swarthy faces that
emotion does not pale them as it does their blonde neighbors—they darken. Miss Henderson's face darkened
now—it always seemed to do so when the name of the
dead girl was mentioned. She turned away from her
friend, and stood staring moodily out to sea, until an ex-

clamation from that young lady caused her to turn round
and perceive that either the sea-wind or some other
cause had very perceptibly heightened Miss Blair's
color.

"I declare if that's not Val," Laura cried, "and that
strange gentleman with him that came from New York
the other day. There! they see us, and are coming
here."

Miss Henderson looked indifferently as Mr. Blake and
his friend approached. Val introduced his companion to
the ladies as Mr. Paul Wyndham, of New York, and
that gentleman was received graciously by Miss Blair,
and coldly, not to say haughtily, by Miss Henderson.

The heiress did not like people from New York. She
never talked about that city, if she could help it, and
rather avoided all persons coming from it. She stood,
looking vacantly out at the wide sea, and listening to the
sailors' song, taking very little part in the conversation.
She turned round, when the singing ceased, in the direction of her carriage, with a listless yawn she was at little
trouble to suppress, and a bored look she took no pains to
conceal. The gentlemen saw them safely off, and then
loitered back to the old wharf.

"Well, Wyndham," Val asked, "and what do you
think of the Princess of Speckport?"

Mr. Paul Wyndham did not immediately reply. He
was leaning lazily against a rotten beam, lighting a cigar,
for he was an inveterate smoker.

Mr. Wyndham was not handsome, he was not dashing
—he had neither mustache nor whisker, nor an aquiline
nose; and he could not dance or sing, or do anything else
like any other young Christian gentleman. He was very
slight and boyish of figure, with a pale, student-like face,
a high forehead, deep-set eyes, a characteristic nose, and a
thin and somewhat cynical mouth. There was character
in everything about him, even in the mathematical precision of his dress, faultlessly neat in the smallest particular, and scrupulously simple. He looked like a gentleman
and a student, and he was both. More, he was an author,
a Bohemian, with a well-earned literary fame, at the age

of seven-and-twenty. When he was a lad of seventeen
he had started with his "knapsack on his back," containing a clean shirt, and a quire of foolscap, and had traveled
through Europe and Asia, and had written two charming
books of travel, that filled his pockets with dollars, and
established his fame as an author. Since then he had
written some half-dozen delightful novels, over which
Laura Blair herself had cried and laughed alternately, although she did not know now that Mr. Wyndham and
—————— were one and the same. He had written plays
that had run fifty nights at a time, and his sketches were
the chief charm of one or two of the best American
magazines. He was a poet, an author, a dramatist, sometimes an actor, when he took the notion, and a successful
man in all. He looked as those inspired men who chain
us with their wonderful word-painting should look, albeit
I reiterate he was not handsome. He stood now leaning
against the rotten beam, smoking his cigar, and looking
dreamily over the shining sea, while Mr. Blake repeated
his question.

"I say, Wyndham, how do you like her—the beauty,
the belle, the Princess of Speckport?"

"She is a fine-looking girl," Mr. Wyndham quietly replied. "And those big black eyes of hers are very handsome, indeed. It strikes me I should like to marry that
girl!"

"Yes," said Mr. Blake, composedly, "I dare say. I
know several other gentlemen in Speckport who would
like to do the same thing, only they can't, unfortunately."

"Can't they? Why?"

"Because there is an absurd law against bigamy in this
province, and the young lady has promised to marry one
man already."

"Ah! who is he?"

"Captain Cavendish. You met him yesterday, you
remember. He proposed the other night at the house, and
told me about it coming home. She accepted him; but
the affair has not yet been made public, by the lady's express desire."

Mr. Wyndham took out his cigar, knocked off the ashes with the end of his little finger, and replaced it.

"Captain Cavendish is a lucky fellow," he said. "But yet I don't despair. Until the wedding-ring actually slips over the lady's finger, there is room for hope."

"But, my dear fellow, she is engaged."

"*C'est bien!* There is many a slip. I don't believe she will ever be Mrs. Cavendish."

Mr. Blake stared at his friend; but that gentleman looked the very picture of calm composure.

"My dear Wyndham," Mr. Blake remarked, compassionately, "you are simply talking nonsense. I know you are very clever, and famous, and all that sort of thing, and brain is excellent in its way; but I tell you it has no chance against beauty."

"By which you would imply, I stand no chance against Captain Cavendish. Now, if you'll believe me, I am not so sure of that. I generally manage to accomplish whatever I set my heart upon; and I don't think—I really don't, old boy—that I shall fail in this. Besides, if it does come to beauty, I am not such a bad-looking fellow, in the main."

To say that Mr. Blake stared after hearing this speech would be but a feeble description of the open-mouthed-and-eyed gape with which he favored its deliverer. To do Mr. Wyndham justice, he was that phenomenon not often seen—a modest author. He never bored his enemy about "My last book, sir!" he never alluded to his literary labors at all, unless directly spoken to on the subject; and certainly had never before displayed any vanity. Therefore, Mr. Blake stared, not quite decided whether he had heard aright; and Mr. Wyndham, seeing the look, did what he did not often do, burst out laughing.

"My dear old Val," he cried, slapping him on the shoulder, "I have not lost my senses; so there is no need of that look. I should like to have a tall wife—small men always do, you know—with black eyes and two hundred thousand dollars; and I shall enter the lists with this fascinating Captain Cavendish, and bear off the prize if I can, in spite of his sword, and uniform, and handsome face.

I think, on the whole, I shall make the young lady quite as good a husband as he."

"Well," said Mr. Blake, drawing a long breath, and appealing to the deep, "for cool impudence and self-conceit, Paul Wyndham hasn't his match in broad America. Here he comes from New York; and before he is a week in the place he talks of marrying the richest and handsomest girl it contains, as coolly as if he were Sultan of all Turkey, and she a Circassian slave. Yes, Mr. Wyndham, ask her, by all means, and when you get your *conge*, let me know—it will be one of the happiest days of my life."

"But I don't think I shall get my *conge*," persisted Paul Wyndham. "Do you know if she is in love with this Captain Cavendish?"

"I never asked her," responded Mr. Blake. "I leave that for Mr. Wyndham to ascertain."

"Because I don't think she is," went on his friend. "When she stood here a few minutes ago, you and the other young lady, Miss—what's her name?—were talking of the gallant captain, and she listened with a face of perfect indifference. I was watching her, and I don't think she cares about him."

"I saw you watching her," said Val, "and so did she, and I don't think she liked it. I saw those black brows of hers contract once or twice, and that is an ominous sign with Miss Henderson."

"Miss Henderson could fly into a dickens of a passion, too, if she liked. Your black-eyed, black-haired, brown-skinned women raise the very old diable herself, if you stroke them the wrong way. They are something like big black cats. I tell you, Blake, I don't believe she cares about that military popinjay, Cavendish."

"Don't you," said Mr. Blake, with his hands in his pockets. "Of course, if you say so it must be so."

"No; but I really think so. Are his family anything in England?"

"It is currently believed he is next heir to a baronetcy. But the baronet got married in his old days, and there is a little shaver in petticoats to cut Master George out. Still, he lives in hope. The new baronet has the measles and the mumps, and the whooping-cough, and the scarlatina, and the chicken-pox, and a tribe of other diseases, his teeth included, to struggle through, before he reaches man's estate. There is no telling but Cavendish may be a baronet yet."

"That is it, then!" said Wyndham. "It is for his prospective baronetcy the girl has promised to marry him. Pride and ambition, the two sins that hurled Lucifer from heaven to hell, are strong in that woman."

"Oh, come now," said Val, starting up, "I think we had better get out of this, and drop the subject. It strikes me your language is rather forcible, Mr. Wyndham; and there is no telling what you may work yourself up to, if you keep on. It wouldn't be healthy for you, I'm thinking, if Miss Henderson heard you."

"Nevertheless," Paul Wyndham persisted, flinging away his smoked-out weed, "I shall marry Miss Henderson."

The two friends walked away together to the office in Queen Street—Mr. Blake disdaining all reply to the last remark.

On their way they met Captain Cavendish, mounted on his favorite bay, and looking the very beau ideal of a military rider, slowly cantering beside the pretty pony-carriage where the Princess of Speckport sat in state. The contrast between the handsome officer on horseback and the young author on foot was great; but Mr. Wyndham bowed to the soldier and his fair friends with undisturbed placidity.

"You see!" said Mr. Blake, significantly.

"I see," serenely answered Mr. Wyndham; "and I repeat, I shall marry Miss Olive Henderson!"

There was nothing at all of boasting in the tone of Mr. Paul Wyndham in saying this—simply one of deep, quiet determination. You had only to look at his face—that pale, steadfast face—if you were any judge of physiognomy, to perceive that his assurance to Mr. Blake, of seldom failing in any undertaking, was no idle bravado. He was one of those men of iron inflexibility, of invincible daring, of overmastering strength of will, bending all other wills to their own. Men of the Napoleon Bonaparte stamp, made to sway empires, and move about other men, kings and knights, queens and bishops, as they please, on the great chessboard of life. Mr. Val Blake, knowing Paul Wyndham, had some dim perception of this; but he knew, too, that Olive Henderson was no ordinary woman. He had a strong will, and so had she; but it was only a woman's will after all, and with it went womanly weakness, passion, and impulse, and the calm, passionless man was the master-mind.

"But I think she will baffle him here, after all," Mr. Blake said to himself, as he ceased thinking about the matter. "I don't believe Olive Henderson will ever marry Paul Wyndham, not but what he's a great deal better fellow than Cavendish, after all!"

It seemed as though he was right, for a whole week passed before Mr. Wyndham and Miss Henderson met again. The engagement of the heiress with Captain Cavendish, though not formally announced, was pretty generally known; and it was rumored that the wedding was to take place early in June. May had come in, draped in a sodden sheet of gray wet fog; but the villa at Redmon went steadily up, despite of wind and weather. Landscape-gardeners were turning the potato-patches and broad meadows and turnip-fields into a little heaven below, and the place was to be completed in July, when Mrs. Grundy said the happy pair would be returning from their bridal-tour, and take up their abode therein.

Mr. Paul Wyndham heard all this as he smoked his cigars and wrote away placidly at his new novel, and was in nowise disturbed. Mr. Val Blake heard it, and grinned as he thought of the egotistical young author getting baffled for once. Miss Henderson's innumerable admirers heard it, and gnashed their teeth with impotent, jealous fury, and, lastly, Miss Henderson herself heard it, and frowned and laughed alternately.

"This horrid gossiping town of yours, Laura!" she said impatiently; "how do they find out everything as soon as one knows it one's self, I wonder! I wish people would mind their own business and let me alone!"

"Great people must pay the penalty of greatness, my dear," Miss Blair answered, philosophically; "and, besides, it is only a question of time, so don't get into a gale about it! It doesn't matter much whether it is known this minute or the next."

The conversation between the young ladies took place in Miss Henderson's room, and while dressing for a ball. It was to be a very grand ball indeed, given by the officers, and to which only the tiptop cream of the cream of Speckport society was to be invited. Of course Miss Henderson was the first lady thought of, and of course her friend Miss Blair came next; but Mr. Val Blake, who didn't belong to the crême at all, was to be there too. But Mr. Blake was such a good fellow, and hand and glove with the whole barracks, and was so useful to puff their concerts and theatricals in the "Spouter," and praise the bass of Lieutenant the Honorable L. H. Blank, and the tenor-solo of Captain G. P. Cavendish, etc., etc., that it would have been an unpardonable breach to have omitted him. Mr. Paul Wyndham, whose fame as an author had by this time reached Speckport, was also to be there; and the ball was expected to be the most brilliant thing of the season.

As far as weather went, it was rather a failure already. The dismal, clammy fog had subsided at last into rain, and the rain lashed the windows of Miss Henderson's room, and the wind shrieked about the cottage, and roared out at sea as if bent on making a night of it. The heiress, with Rosie, the maid, putting the finishing touches to her toilette, stood listening to the storm, and drearily watching the reflection of her own face and figure in the tall glass. She had taken a fancy to be grandly somber to-night, and wore black velvet and the diamonds Speckport talked so much of, ablaze on throat and arms. There were blood-red flowers in her tar-black hair, and in her bouquet which lay on the dressing table, but she looked more superb in her sable splendor than ever.

Was Miss Laura Blair, with her commonplace prettiness of fair skin, pink cheeks, and waving brown hair, laying herself out as a foil to the black-eyed siren? She was dressed in white moire antique, gemmed with seed-pearls, and with a train of richness that swept half way across the room. She had white roses in her hair, on her breast, and in her bouquet. She wore pearl bracelets and necklace, and looked fair as a lily—a vivid contrast to her black and crimson neighbor.

Miss Henderson sent Rosie out of the room, and stood listening in silence for a while to the raging of the storm. Presently she turned to Laura, who was all absorbed settling her laces and jewels, with a rather singular inquiry on her lips.

"Laura," she said, abruptly, "what is the matter with me to-night? Why am I afraid to go to the ball?" Miss Blair turned round and gazed aghast at this question. The shadow that sometimes lay on her friend's face was there now, like a dark vail.

"Dear me, Olly! I'm sure I don't know what you mean! Afraid to go to the ball?"

"Yes," repeated Olive, "afraid! I feel as though something were going to happen! I have a presentiment that some misfortune is before me! I have had it all day!"

"It's the weather, dear," said Laura, retiring to the toilet, "or else it's indigestion. Don't be foolish!"

Olive Henderson was in no laughing humor, but she did laugh, half fretfully, though, at this reply. "It's not the weather, and it's not the indigestion, Miss Blair," she said, "it is the moral barometer giving warning of a coming storm—it is coming events casting their shadows before. I have half a mind not to go to the ball to-night."

"Nonsense, Olly!" exclaimed Laura, in some alarm, knowing very well Olive was just the girl not to go if she took it in her head, "how absurd you are. Presentiments! pooh! You've been reading some German trash—that's what you've been doing, and you have caught some absurd German silliness! I should like to see you try to stay away from the ball, the last, the best, the brightest of the season, and you looking divine, too, in that black velvet! What could possibly happen you at the ball, I should like to know?"

Miss Henderson and Miss Blair were rather late in arriving—nearly every one was there before them. There were two gentlemen who came considerably late, but no one noticed them much, being only Mr. Val Blake and his New York friend, Mr. Paul Wyndham. Mr. Blake was fond of dancing, and was captured by Miss Blair almost as soon as he entered, and led off; for Miss Laura did make love to this big stupid Val in pretty roundabout feminine fashion, as women have a way of doing all the world over. Mr. Wyndham did not dance, and as he was not at liberty to smoke, the ball was rather a bore than otherwise. He stood leaning against a pillar, watching the dancers; his pale, grave, quiet face and thoughtful gray eyes ever turned in one direction. A great many more gentlemen's faces turned presently in the same quarter, for the loadstone of the ball shone there, magnificent, in black velvet, and with eyes that outshone her diamonds. Was there rapport between them? Was it some inward magnetism that made the belle of the ball, in the height of her triumph and power, aware of this fixed, steadfast gaze, and uneasy under it? Flatterers and sycophants surrounded her on every hand, but she had to turn restlessly away from them and look over every now and then to that pale, watchful face, and those fixed, grave gray eyes.

Paul Wyndham still watched her. She grew nervously miserable at last, and enraged with herself for becoming so. If this strange man stared rudely, what was it to her? She would take no further notice of him, she would not look at him; and saying this to herself, she floated away in the waltz, with her eyes persistently fixed on her partner or on the floor.

The waltz concluded, and Miss Henderson, being tired and hot, her partner led her to a seat, and left her to get an ice. It was the first time all that evening she had been for a moment alone, and she lay back among the cushions of her chair and listened to the raging of the storm without.

The seat was in the recess of a bay window, partly shut out from the room by scarlet drapery, and she was glad to think she was alone. Alone! No, for there opposite to her stood Paul Wyndham, his magnetic eyes fixed with powerful intensity on her face. A cold thrill of fear, vague and chilling, crept through every vein—she would have risen, in undefined panic, but he was by her side directly, speaking quietly the commonest of commonplace words.

"Good evening, Miss Henderson. I trust I see you well and enjoying yourself. It is the first time I have had the pleasure of approaching you, you have been so surrounded all the evening."

She did not speak; a cold bend of the head answered him, and she rose up, haughty and pale. But he would not let her go; the power of his fixed gaze held her there as surely as if she had been chained.

"I fear," he said, in that quiet voice of his, "I fear you thought me rude in watching you, as I must own to having done. But I assure you, Miss Henderson, it was no intentional rudeness; neither was it my admiration, which, pardon me, is great! I watched, Miss Henderson, because I find you bear a most startling, a most wonderful resemblance to a person—a young girl—I once knew in New York."

She caught her breath, feeling the blood leaving her face, and herself growing cold. Paul Wyndham never took his pitiless eyes off her charming face.

"In saying I knew this young girl," he slowly went on, "I am wrong; I only saw her in the city streets. You came from New York, but you could not have known her, Miss Henderson, for she was abjectly poor. She lived in a mean and dirty thoroughfare called Minetta Street; she lodged in a house filled with rough factory-women, and kept by one Mrs. Butterby; and the young woman's name was Harriet Wade."

A moment after Mr. Wyndham said this, he came out of the curtained recess, and crossed the ballroom rapidly. On his way he met Laura Blair, and paused to speak.

"I am going for a glass of water," he said, "for Miss

Henderson. I was talking to her at that window when
she was taken suddenly ill. You had better go to her,
Miss Blair I am afraid she is going to faint."

CHAPTER XXVII.

MR. WYNDHAM'S WOOING.

 BLEAK and rainy morning in Speckport—a
raw and windy morning, with a sky all lead-
color, except where it was inky black. A
wild, wet, rainy day, on which nobody wanted
to stir out if they could help it. An utterly
black and miserable day, that which followed the officers'
ball.

On this wretchedly wet and windy day Olive Henderson sat at her chamber window, and looked out over the
black and foam-crested bay. The room looked very cozy
and pleasant, with its soft, warm, bright-hued Brussels
carpet, its cushioned easy-chairs and lounges, its white-
draped bed, its pretty pictures and tables, and bright coal
fire burning in the glittering steel grate, its costly window-
draperies of lace and damask, looking all the more pleasant
and luxurious by contrast with the black, bleak day outside.

A delightful room this bad May morning, a room to
bask and luxuriate in, this chamber of Olive Henderson.
But Olive Henderson herself, sitting by the window,
staring blankly out, seemed to take very little enjoyment
in its comfort and beauty. She wore a white loose muslin
wrapper, tied carelessly round the slender waist with a
crimson cord, its every fold, as it hung straight about her,
telling how indifferently the simple toilette had been
made. All her profuse black hair was drawn away from
her face, haggard and worn in the gray morning light, and

fastened in a great careless knot behind. But, somehow, the stateliness that was a part of herself characterized her as strikingly in this primitive simplicity as when robed in velvet and diamonds last night. Perhaps Semiramis, Queen of Assyria, when in trouble with foreign parts, wore white muslin wrappers, and her black hair dishevel-ed, before her subjects, and managed to look Queen Semi-ramis withal. It isn't likely, you know, but she may.

Rain, rain, rain! How ceaselessly it lashed the win-dows, and how piteously it beat on the heads of the poor little newsboys, passing up and down Golden Row, and chanting, disconsolately, "Morning Snorter," the "Sn-o-o-or-ter!" Perhaps, looking up at the curtained-window, where the young lady sat, these newsboys thought it was a fine thing to be Miss Olive Henderson, the heiress of Redmon, and live in a handsome house, with servants to wait on her, and nothing to do but play the piano, and drive about in her carriage all day long. But, I am pretty sure, there was not a pug-nosed urchin coming there that particular morning, who was not a thousand times happier than the heiress of Redmon.

Discovered—disgraced—in the power of this man—this stranger! Liable to be exposed as a liar and a cheat to the world at any hour! Liable to have all this wealth and luxury, for which she had done so much—for which she had risked her very soul—torn from her at any instant, and she herself thrust out to fight the battle of life, with poverty and labor and misery once more. She seemed to have grown old in four-and-twenty hours, with her hag-gard cheeks and great hollow eyes. She had sat as she was sitting now for hours, her hands clasped loosely in her lap, her vacant gaze fixed on the wretched day, but seeing nothing. Only yesterday, and she had been so sure, so secure, so happy, and now—and now!

She had not fainted the night before. Laura Blair found her lying back ghastly and white in her chair, but not insensible. The ballroom had been filled with con-sternation. and she was so surrounded immediately that Mr. Wyndham, returning with his glass of water, could find no possibility of approaching her. They had led her

14

into the ladies' dressing-room, and Captain Cavendish had gone for a cab; and when she was a little better, they took her home, and the rest went back to the ballroom. People began to think that in spite of Miss Henderson's apparent physical perfection, she was subject to fainting-fits, and pitied her very much, as they resumed their dancing. But the eclipsed belles of Speckport rejoiced, I am afraid, in their wicked little hearts, that the conqueress was gone, and held up their pretty heads, which had drooped in the sunlight of her shining presence before.

Once at home, Miss Henderson professed herself perfectly restored, and insisted on Laura and her mamma, who had been their chaperone, and Captain Cavendish, going back to the ball once more.

"I shall do well enough now," she said, wearily. "I am very foolish, but——"

Her voice died away, and her head drooped forward on her arm. Captain Cavendish bent tenderly over her, as she lay on a sofa, with a pale and anxious face.

"My darling," he said, "I am afraid you are very ill. Let me go for Dr. Leach—this may be something serious."

But Miss Henderson positively refused, and insisted on their returning to the ball.

"I shall lie down and go asleep," she said, "and I will be quite restored to-morrow. Go at once."

"I shall go," the captain said, holding her hands, "but not back to the ball. Do you think there could be any pleasure for me there, and you absent, Olive? Good night, my love—get rid of this white face before I see you to-morrow."

Olive Henderson slept that night, but it was more like stupor than healthful sleep, and she awoke with a dully throbbing headache, and a numbing sense of misery at her heart. She had arisen in the black and wretched dawn of that miserable May morning, and had sat staring vacantly out at the ceaseless rain, and dark and turbid sea. She was not thinking—she was sitting there in a dull torpor of despair, waiting for the end.

There was a knock at the door. It had to be repeated

two or three times before she comprehended what it meant, and then she arose and opened the door. It was Rosie, the housemaid; and the girl recoiled at sight of her, as if she had seen a ghost.

"My patience, Miss! how bad you do look! I am afraid you are worse than you was last night."

"No. What is it you want?"

"It's a gentleman, Miss, that has called, and is in the drawing-room, although it is raining cats and dogs."

She presented a card to her mistress, and Olive read the name of "Paul Wyndham." She turned sick at sight of that name—that name so lately heard for the first time, but so terribly familiar now; and looked at the girl with a sort of terror in her great black eyes.

"Is this man—is this Mr. Wyndham here?"

"Down in the drawing-room, Miss, and his overcoat and umbrella making little streams of rain-water all along the hall. Will you go down, Miss?"

Olive Henderson's hand had closed on the pasteboard with so convulsive a pressure, that the card was crushed into a shapeless mass. Her stupor was ending in a sort of sullen desperation. Let the worst come, it was Fate; and she was powerless to battle with so formidable a foe. Whatever brought this man now, his coming was merciful; the most dreadful certainty was better than this horrible suspense, which had made the past night a century of misery.

Rosie, the pretty housemaid, watched her young lady's changing face, as she walked rapidly up and down, her eyes staring straight before her with a fierce and feverish luster, and her lips so rigidly set. Rosie saw all this, and greatly marveled thereat. A gentleman had called very early on a very wet morning; but that was no reason why Miss Henderson should be prancing up and down her room, with the look of an inmate of a lunatic asylum.

"Will I tell him you'll come down, Miss?" Rosie ventured to ask, when she thought the silence had lasted long enough.

The voice of the girl drew Olive out of her darkly-brooding fit, and she turned to close her door.

"Yes," she said. "Tell him I will be down in five minutes."

She walked to the glass, and looked at herself. I dare say Lady Jane Grey and Mary Queen of Scots did the same before they were led to the block; and I doubt if either wore a more ghostly face at that horrible moment than the girl standing there did now. She smiled in bitter scorn of herself, as she saw the haggard face and the hollow, burning eyes.

"I look as if I had grown old in a night," she said. "Where is the beauty now that so many have praised since I came here?"

She made no attempt to change her dress, but with the loose white muslin wrapper trailing in long folds around her, and girdled with scarlet, she descended the stairs, and entered the drawing-room.

Mr. Paul Wyndham was sitting at a window, watching the ceaseless rain beating against the glass. At that very window, looking out at the silvery moonlight, she herself had sat a few nights before, while she promised Captain Cavendish she would be his wife. Perhaps she thought of this as she swept past, à la princesse, just deigning to acknowledge her visitor's presence by her haughtiest bow. She could not have acted otherwise, had a hundred fortunes depended on it, and she did not sit down.

She stood beside the mantel, her arm, from which the flowing white sleeves dropped away, leaning on it, her eyes fixed steadily upon the man before her, waiting in proud silence for what he had to say. Any one else might have been disconcerted; but Mr. Wyndham did not look as if he was. He looked pale and quiet and gentlemanly, and entirely self-possessed.

"You do not ask the object of my visit, Miss Henderson," he said, "although the hour is unfashionably early, and the day not such as callers usually select. But I presume you have been expecting me, and are not surprised."

"I am not surprised," she said, coldly.

"I thought that at this hour I should be most certain of finding you at home and alone. Therefore, I have

come, knowing that after what passed last night, the
sooner we come to an understanding the better."

"How have you found out my secret?" she abruptly
demanded. "You never knew me in New York?"

"That is my secret, Miss Henderson—I presume you
prefer being called by that name—that is my secret, and
you will pardon me if I do not reveal it. I do know your
secret, and it is that knowledge which has brought me to
this place."

"And knowing it, what use do you intend to make
of it?"

He smiled slightly.

"You are very straightforward, Miss Henderson. It
is almost as easy getting on with you as if you were a
man. I foresee that we shall settle this little matter pleasantly, after all."

Olive Henderson contracted her black brows, and
reiterated her question.

"Knowing this secret, sir, what use do you intend
making of it?"

"That depends upon yourself, madam."

"How?"

"I shall keep your secret, Miss Henderson," Paul
Wyndham said, "I shall keep it inviolably; you shall
still be Olive Henderson, heiress of Redmon, the lady
paramount of Speckport, on one condition."

Her heart beat so fast and thick that she had to press
her hands over it to still its tumultuous throbbing. Her
hollow, burning black eyes never left his face, they were
strained there in suspense too intense for words.

"You are aware, Miss Henderson," the cold, clear,
yet melodious voice of Paul Wyndham went on, "of the
position in which you stand. You have usurped the place
of another—your stepsister—you have assumed a name
which does not belong to you, and you have come here to
dupe the people of this place, to pass yourself off for what
you are not, and possess yourself of wealth to which you
have no shadow of claim. In doing this, Miss Henderson, you must be aware you are guilty of a felony, punishable by law, punishable by trial, imprisonment, and

life-long disgrace. All this you know, and knowing it, must be aware how entirely and irrevocably you are in my power!"

"Irrevocably and completely in my power," the pitiless voice went on, "you see it yourself as well as I. You know also much better than I do, the misery, the shame, the degradation exposure must bring. Your name published, your crime published far and wide, yourself the scoff and jeer of every boor in the town, the horrors of a jail, of a criminal cell, of a public trial before gaping thousands, of——"

Paul Wyndham stopped. It was not a cry she had uttered, but a gasping sob, telling more of the unutterable agony, the intense misery she was suffering, than any wild outbreak of womanly shrieks. She put out her hands with a passionate cry.

Paul Wyndham looked at the disturbed, crouching form, convulsed with despairing agony, with Heaven only knows how much of pity in his face.

"Miss Henderson! Miss Henderson!" he cried, "I did not mean—I did not think what I said would affect you like this. I only told you what might be, but it never will be, for you will listen to what I have yet to say, and I never will reveal your secret to a living soul!"

She lifted her head, and looked at him as a hunted stag might, with the knife at its throat.

"Mr. Wyndham," she said, with that dignity which is born of extreme misery, "what have I ever done to you that you should come here and torment me like this?"

Paul Wyndham turned away from that reproachful face, with a dark shadow on his own.

"Heaven knows, Miss Henderson, I hate the necessity which compels me to cause you this pain, but it is a necessity, and I must do it; you never have wronged me —I have no wish to give you a moment's suffering, but a fatality against which I am powerless, urges me on. I hate myself for what I am doing—but what can I do— what can I do?"

He seemed to ask himself the question, as he sprang

up and took, like herself, to walking excidedly up and down. His face was so darkly troubled that Olive Henderson looked at him with searching, wondering eyes.

"I do not understand you," she said, chilled with a new fear, "does any one but yourself know my secret?"

She was still sitting, and never ceasing to watch him. Paul Wyndham leaned against the mantel, as she had done a moment before, and looked down at her.

"Miss Henderson, I can tell you nothing but that your secret is safe with me if you will comply with the condition I have to name. You may trust me; I shall never reveal it!"

"And that condition is——"

There was a pause, during which Olive could have counted the raindrops on the window or the loud beating of her heart.

Paul Wyndham's large, clear, bright gray eyes steadily met her own.

"The condition is, that you become my wife."

She gave a cry, she was so utterly astonished, and sat staring at him, speechless.

"Your—wife!" she slowly said, when her returned senses enabled her to speak.

"Yes, Miss Henderson, my wife! I am no more insensible to the power of wealth than you are. You have risked everything for the future; you can only hold it now, on condition of becoming my wife!"

Olive Henderson rose up, white and defiant. "I never will!" she said, "I never will! I will lose every shilling of it, I will die before I consent!"

"Oh, no!" Mr. Wyndham said, quietly, "I do not think you will, when you come to reflect. It is not pleasant to die when one is young and handsome and prosperous, particularly if one has not been very good, and not at all sure of going to Heaven. You will not die, Miss Henderson; you will keep the fortune and marry me."

"I never will!" she vehemently cried; "what if I told you my stepsister, the real Olive Henderson, were alive, that I have seen her lately, and that she has made over everything to me. What if I told you this?"

He smiled incredulously.

"You do not believe me, but I swear to you I state the truth. Olive Henderson lives, though I thought her dead; and I have seen her, I tell you, and she has consented to my keeping all."

"Well," said Mr. Wyndham quietly, "supposing, for argument's sake, what you say to be true, it does not alter your position in the least. Should I go to a lawyer and tell him your story, the arrest, the exposure, the disgrace all follow as inevitably as ever. The rightful heiress may, as you say, be alive, and willing you should usurp her birthright, though it does not sound very likely; but even if so, Harriet Wade is too proud a woman to incur life-long disgrace and humiliation, when she can avert it so easily."

She turned away from him, dropped into her seat, and laid her hand on a table near. The action, the attitude, told far more than words, of the cold, dark despair thickening around her.

She never lifted her head. She was suffering, as other women have suffered, dumbly.

"In asking you to be my wife, Miss Henderson," Mr. Wyndham still continued, "I make no pretense of being in love with you myself. I am not—I may as well tell you plainly—and I shall never ask love from you. In becoming my wife, you will go through a legal ceremony that will mean nothing. I shall never intrude upon you one single moment out of all the twenty-four hours, unless you desire it, or when the presence of others makes our being together unavoidable. We may dwell under the same roof, and yet live as far apart as if hemispheres divided us. Believe me, I shall not force myself upon you against your will; but for your own sake, Miss Henderson, and to still the whispers of busy tongues, it would be as well to keep your sentiments regarding me to yourself, as well we should be apparently on cordial terms. Are you listening, Miss Henderson?"

He really thought she was not. She was lying so still, so rigid, with her poor white face on the table, and the thick coils of her dead-black hair unloosing themselves, and trailing and twining about her like black snakes. She was not hysterical now; she was lying there in a sort of dumb anguish, that none but very proud and sensitive hearts, crushed to the very dust in shame and humiliation, can ever feel.

"Miss Henderson," Mr. Wyndham repeated, looking at the drooping, girlish figure, its very attitude speaking so much of supreme misery, "I am waiting for my answer."

She lifted her head and looked at him, with something the look of a deer at bay.

"Have you no pity?" she said. "Will you not spare me? I am only a girl, alone in the world, and you might pity me and be merciful. I have done wrong, I know, but Heaven alone knows what I have suffered from poverty, and the degradation it inevitably entails. I was tempted, and I yielded; but I think I never was so miserable in the worst days of my suffering as I have been at times since I came here. I am not good, I know, but I am not used to wickedness and plotting like this, and I think I am the most miserable creature on the face of this wide earth. But I never wronged you, sir; and you might pity me and spare me."

Her head dropped down again with a sort of sob, and the pitiful pleading was touching to hear from those proud lips. If Paul Wyndham had possessed the hardest heart that ever beat in a man's breast since the days of Nero, I think it must have been touched by the sight of that haughty spirit so bowed and crushed before him. His face showed no sign of whatever he might feel, but his clear voice shook a little as he replied.

"It is of little use, Miss Henderson, for me to say how deeply I do pity you—how sorely against my will I wage this unequal warfare, since the battle must go on all the same. It would only sound like mockery were I to say how grieved I am to give you this pain, since I should still remain inexorable."

"Will nothing bribe you?" she asked. "Half the wealth I possess shall be yours if——"

14*

She had lifted her face again in eager hopefulness, but he interrupted with a gesture.

"I said I was inexorable, Miss Henderson, and I must repeat it. Besides," he added, with a slight smile, that showed how credulous he was about the story, "the real heiress, though she might make over the fortune to you, might object to your handing the half of it over to a stranger. No, Miss Henderson, there is only the one alternative—be my wife, or else——"

"Or else you will tell all?"

He did not speak. He stood, quietly waiting his answer—quiet, but very inflexible.

Olive rose up and stood before him.

"Must you have your answer now?" she asked, "or will you not even give me a few hours respite to think it over?"

"As many as you please, Miss Henderson."

"Then you shall have it to-night," she said, with strange, cold calmness. "I promised Miss Blair to go to the theater—you will see me there, and shall have your answer."

Mr. Wyndham bowed, and with a simple "Good morning," walked out of the room. As he shut the door behind him, he felt as though he were shutting Olive Henderson in a living tomb, and he her jailer.

"Poor girl! poor girl!" he was thinking, as he put on his overcoat; "what a villain I must seem in her eyes, and what a villain I am, ever to have consented to this. But it is only retribution after all—one ill turn deserves another."

Paul Wyndham walked to his hotel through the drenching rain and cold sea-wind, and Olive Henderson listened to the tumult of the storm, with another storm quite as tumultuous in her own breast.

The play that night was the "Lady of Lyons." There is only one theater in Speckport, so Mr. Wyndham was not likely to get bewildered in his search. The first act was half over when he came in, and looked round the dress circle, and down in the orchestra stalls. In the glare of the gas-light Olive Henderson looked superb. Never had her magnificent black eyes shone with such streaming luster as to-night, and a crimson glow, quite foreign to her usual complexion, beamed on either cheek—the crimson glow, rouge, worn for the first time in her life; and though she was a New York lady, she had the grace to be ashamed of the paint, and wear a thin black vail over her face. She took her eyes off Mademoiselle Pauline for a moment, to fix them on Mr. Wyndham, who came along to pay his respects, and to find a seat directly behind that of the heiress, but she only bent her head in very distant acknowledgment of his presence, and looked at Pauline again.

The curtain fell on the first act. Miss Henderson was very thirsty—that feverish thirst had not left her yet, and Captain Cavendish went out for a glass of ice-water. Laura was busy chattering to Mr. Blake, and Paul Wyndham bent forward and spoke to the heiress, who never turned her head.

"I have come for my answer, Miss Henderson," he said; "it is 'Yes,' I know."

"It is 'Yes,' Mr. Wyndham, and, with my consent, take the knowledge that I hate and despise you more than any other creature on the face of the earth."

She never turned while saying this. She stared straight before her at the row of gleaming footlights. The music was croaking out, every one was talking busily, and not one of the young ladies who looked enviously at the beautiful and brilliant heiress, nor the men who worshiped her at a distance, and who hated the young New Yorker for the privilege he enjoyed of talking to her—not one of them all dreamed ever so faintly of that other play being enacted off the stage.

Captain Cavendish came back with the water, the play went on, but I doubt if Olive Henderson heard a word, or knew whether they were playing "Othello" or the "Lady of Lyons," but none of the others knew that; that serviceable mask, the human face, is a very good screen for the heart.

The play was over, and they were all going out. Mr. Wyndham had not addressed her since, but she knew he was behind her all the time, and she knew nothing else.

He was by her side as they descended the stairs, and the cold night-wind struck them on the face. She was leaning on the arm of Captain Cavendish, but how was that conquering hero to know it was for the last time?

"I will have the pleasure of calling on you to-morrow, Miss Henderson," he distinctly said, as he bowed an adieu and was lost in the crowd.

CHAPTER XXVIII.

MR. WYNDHAM'S WEDDING.

APTAIN CAVENDISH, sitting at the window of his room in the hotel, stared at the red sunset with a clouded face and a gloomy abstraction of manner, that told how utterly its lurid glory was lost upon him.

Captain Cavendish had been sitting there since four in the afternoon, thinking this over and over again, and never able to get beyond it. His day of retribution had come. He was feeling the torture he had so often and so heartlessly made others feel; he was learning what it meant to be jilted in cold blood. Olive Henderson had turned out the veriest, the most capricious, the most heartless of flirts, and Captain Cavendish found himself incontinently snubbed! He had asked for no explanation yet, but the climax had come to-day. He had ridden over to escort the heiress on her breezy morning gallop, and had found Mr. Wyndham just assisting her into the saddle. She had bowed distantly to him, cut her horse a stinging blow across the neck, and had galloped off, with Paul Wyndham close beside her. Catty Clowrie looked out of the cottage window, and laughed a voiceless laugh, to see the captain's blank consternation.

"Tit for tat!" Catty said; "you are getting paid back in your own coin, Captain George Cavendish!"

So, while the fierce red sun blazed itself out in the purple arch, and the big round yellow moon rose up, like another Venus, out of the bluish-black bay, Captain Cavendish sat at his window, telling the same refrain over and over in his mind, as perseveringly as ever any holy monk told the Ave Maria on his rosary:—"What has changed her? what has changed her? what has changed her?"

The moon was high in the sky before he roused himself from his long and somber musing-fit, and, pulling out his watch, looked at the hour.

"Half-past seven," he said; "they were to start at eight, and she promised to go. I shall ask for an explanation to-night."

He rang for his servant, and desired that young man, when he appeared, to fetch him his overcoat. Mr. Johnston brought that garment, and assisted his master into it, and the captain put on his hat and gloves, and with his cane under his arm (for, of course, as an officer of the British army, it was his duty at all times to carry a cane under his arm), he set off for the cottage of my Lady Caprice.

The whole front of the pretty cottage was in a state of illumination, as he opened the little gate and walked up the gravel path, and men's shadows moved on the curtained windows as he rang the bell. Rosie, with pink ribbons in her hair, and her Sunday dress on, opened the door and showed him into the drawing-room.

"I'll tell Miss Olive you're here," she said; "she is engaged with company just now."

Captain Cavendish said nothing. He walked over to the low chimney-piece, and leaned moodily against it, as Paul Wyndham had done that rainy morning, little better than a week before. He had seen something as he came in that had not tended to raise his spirits. The dining-room door stood half-open, and glancing in as he passed, he perceived that Miss Henderson had given a dinner-party, and that the company was still lingering around the table. He saw the Rev. Augustus Tod and his sister—and the Tods were the very cream of Speckport society—Major and Mrs. Wheatly, and Mr. Paul Wyndham. That was all; but he, her betrothed husband, her accepted suitor, had known nothing of it—had never been invited!

Captain Cavendish, leaning against the mantel, listened to the laughter, and pleasant mingling of voices, and the jingling of glasses in the dining-room, and he could plainly distinguish the musical laughter of Olive, and her clear voice as she talked to her guests. He stood there for upward of half an hour, raging with inward fury, all the more fierce for having to be suppressed. Then he heard the dining-room door open, a rustle of silk in the passage, an odor of delicate perfume in the air, and then the drawing-room door opened.

Miss Henderson swept into the room, bowing and smiling as she passed him, and sinking gracefully into a low violet-velvet chair, her rosy skirts and misty white lace floating all about her like pink and white clouds, and she looked up at him with the same glance of inquiry she might have given any lout of a fisherman in Speckport, had such a person presumed to call.

"I fear I intrude, Miss Henderson," he said, suppressing, as a gentleman must, his rage. "I did not know there was a dinner-party at the cottage."

"Oh, it is of no consequence," Miss Henderson said, carelessly, toying with her watch and chain; "my guests are all friends, who will readily excuse me. Will you not take a seat, Captain Cavendish?"

"No, Miss Henderson! in a house where I am made to feel I am an intruder I must decline being seated. I believe you promised to join the sailing-party on the bay to night, but I suppose it is useless to ask you if you are going now."

"Why, yes," in the same careless way, "it is hardly probable I should leave my friends, even for the moonlight excursion. Are you going? I am sure you will have a very pleasant time; the night is lovely."

"Yes," said Captain Cavendish, "I am likely to have a pleasant time, as I have had, you must be aware, all through the past week. If you can spare a few minutes from these very dear friends of yours, Miss Henderson, I should be glad to have an explanation of your conduct."

"Of my conduct?" still in that careless way. "How?"

Captain Cavendish choked down an oath, but there was a subdued fierceness in his voice when he spoke.

"Miss Olive Henderson, has it quite escaped your memory that you are my promised wife? It strikes me your conduct of late has not been altogether in keeping with this fact. Will you have the goodness to explain the contempt, the slights, the strangeness of your conduct?"

"It is very easily explained," Miss Henderson answered, with supreme indifference, which, whether real or assumed, was very natural. "I have repented that rash promise, and now retract it. I have changed my mind; it is a woman's privilege, Captain Cavendish, and here is your engagement ring."

She drew the little golden circlet off her finger and held it out to him, as she might have returned it to some jeweler who had asked her to purchase it. He did not take it—he only stood looking at her, stunned!

"Olive!"

"I am sorry to give you pain, Captain Cavendish," Miss Henderson replied to that cry, still toying with her chain; "but you know I told you that night I did not love you, so you ought not to be surprised. I suppose it seems heartless, but then I am heartless; so what can you expect."

She laughed to herself a little hard laugh, and looked up at him with coldly-shining eyes. He was white, white even to his lips; for, remember, he loved this woman—this cold-blooded and capricious coquette.

"Olive! Olive!" was all he could cry, and there was nothing but wild astonishment and passionate reproach in his voice. There was no room for anger now. He loved her, and it made him a coward, and he faltered and broke down.

Olive Henderson rose up as if to end the interview.

"Better we should understand one another now, Captain Cavendish, than later. Perhaps the day may come

and sooner than you expect, when you will thank me for
this. I am not good, and I should not have made you a
good wife, and you have more cause for thankfulness
than regret. Here is your ring, and with it I renounce
all claim to you! We are from henceforth what we were
before you spoke—friends! In that character I shall at
all times be happy to see you. Good evening, Captain
Cavendish!"

Captain Cavendish walked back to his hotel in a
stunned and stupefied sort of way, much as a man might
who had received a heavy blow on the head, and was
completely benumbed. He had received a blow, a most
unexpected and terrible blow; a blow so inconceivable,
he could hardly realize it had really fallen. His worst
enemy could scarcely have wished him a more miserable
night than that which he spent, ceaselessly walking his
room, and acting over and over again the scene that had
so lately passed. O Nathalie Marsh! could you have
risen up in spirit before him then, surely you would have
thought yourself completely avenged.

Was Miss Olive Henderson, lying in luxurious ease
among the satin pillows of a lounge in the dining-room,
next morning, wearing a most becoming matin negligee,
and listlessly turning over the leaves of a novel, thinking
of her rejected lover, I wonder? Catty Clowrie, sitting
sewing industriously at the window—for Catty was not
above doing plain sewing for the heiress—and watching
her stealthily between the stitches, wondered if she were
really reading, or only thinking, as she lay there, turning
over the leaves with restless fingers, and jerking out her
pretty little watch perpetually to look at the hour. It
was very early, only nine o'clock, too soon for her to expect visitors—even that indefatigable Mr. Wyndham,
who came like clockwork every day, could hardly have
made his appearance so early. Catty, thinking this,
stopped suddenly, for a gentleman was ringing the door-
bell—a gentleman with a white, fierce face, and a look
about him, altogether, Miss Clowrie had never seen him
wear before. Olive sat up and looked at Catty.

"Who is it?" she asked.

"Captain Cavendish."

The black brow contracted suddenly, and Catty saw it. She, as well as all Speckport, knew there was a breach between the two, and she and all Speckport set Mr Wyndham down as the cause.

Olive Henderson rose up, with her brows still contracted, and walked into the drawing-room. She shut the door behind her; and oh! what would not Catty Clowrie have given had the painted panels of that door been clear glass, that she might see what was going on. She could hear, not their words, but the voice of the captain, passionate and then reproachful, then pleading, then passionately angry again. Once she crept to the door; it was after an unusually vehement outburst on his part; and when her curiosity was excited beyond all bounds, she affixed her ear to the keyhole.

"It hardly becomes you, Captain Cavendish," she heard the voice say, in a tone of cold disdain; "it does not become you to talk like this of infidelity. If all tales be true, you have been rather faithless yourself in your time. People who live in glass houses are always the readiest to throw stones, I think!"

Catty dared not stay, lest they should suddenly open the door, and went back to her work.

"She has refused him!" she thought. "What new mystery is this?"

Had Miss Clowrie been able to look into the room, she would have seen Captain Cavendish pacing it like a caged tiger, and Miss Henderson standing up and leaning against the mantel, and looking icily at him out of her great black eyes. He stopped abruptly before her, controlling his passion, and steadfastly returned her gaze.

"And is it for Mr. Paul Wyndham," he asked, with sneering emphasis, "the little pitiful quill-driver, that I am rejected?"

The black eyes of Olive Henderson flashed flame at the gibing tone.

"Yes!" she flashed, impetuously, "it is for Mr. Paul Wyndham, whose name is a household word in lands

where he has never been—who will be remembered by
thousands when you are dead and forgotten!"

If Captain Cavendish could, with any propriety, have
knocked the defiant young lady down at that moment, I
think he would have done it. He set his strong white
teeth, and clenched his hands, in the impotence of his
fury.

"And this insult, am I to understand, is your final
answer?"

"The answer is final," Olive said, frigidly. "The insult, if such it be, you provoked yourself, by first insult-
ing me. I wished to part friends with you; if you prefer
we should part enemies, it is immaterial to me. I do not
know why you have come to make this scene this morning, when you received your answer last night."

The morning sunshine was streaming brightly into the
room; but, as she spoke, it was suddenly darkened, and
Paul Wyndham, riding past, strung his horse at the door.
An instant after, Catty Clowrie saw Captain Cavendish
leave the house, his hat slouched over his eyes, and stride
away as if shod with seven-league boots. Mr. Wyndham
had come to escort Miss Henderson on her customary
morning-ride to Redmon, and Olive ran up-stairs to put
on her riding-habit. But not until Catty had seen how
haughtily cold her reception of Mr. Wyndham was, and
how ghostly pale she looked as she ran up-stairs.

Catty Clowrie was not the only young lady in Speckport puzzled by Miss Henderson's remarkable conduct.
Laura Blair was bothering her poor little brain with
the enigma, and could not solve it, though she tried ever
so.

"Olly, dear," she said, in a perplexed tone, when she
came to the cottage next day, and up in Olive's room
seated herself for a confidential chat, "have you quarreled
with Captain Cavendish?"

Olive was reclining in a vast Sleepy Hollow of an arm-
chair, looking pale and fagged; for she had been at a ball
the previous night, and lay with her hands folded listlessly in her lap, and the lazy lids hiding the splendor of her

eyes. She hardly took the trouble to lift these heavy eye-lids, as she replied:

"No—yes. Why?"

"Because, he's gone away, dear! I thought you knew it. He has gone off on leave of absence to Canada, I believe."

"Indeed!" Miss Henderson said, indifferently. "When did he go?"

"He left in the steamer for Portland, Maine, this morning. Olly, dearest, will you not tell me what it is all about?"

"All what is about?" asked Olive, impatiently.

Laura looked frightened; she always got scared when Miss Henderson's big black eyes flashed.

"You won't be angry, my darling Olly? but I thought —every one thought—you were going to marry Captain Cavendish."

"Did they? Then it's a pity 'every one' must be disappointed, for I am not going to marry Captain Cavendish."

Laura sat silent after this quencher. She was seated on a low stool at her friend's feet, with her brown head lying on her lap. The heiress bent down and kissed the pretty face.

"My poor, silly, inquisitive little Laura!" she said, "you would like a wedding, I know. You have a feminine love of bridal-vails and orange-wreaths, and you would like to look pretty in white silk and Honiton lace, as my bridemaid—wouldn't you, now?"

"Yes," said Miss Blair.

"Well, then, Laura, you shall!"

Laura started up, and stared.

"What?"

"I say," repeated Olive, quietly, "you shall be gratified. You shall wear the white silk and the Honiton lace, my dear. and be first bridemaid, for I am going to be married!"

Laura Blair clasped her hands.

"Oh, Olly! and to Mr. Wyndham!"

"Yes; to Mr. Wyndham."

Laura sat like one transfixed, digesting the news. Somehow, she was not so much surprised, but the suddenness of the intelligence stunned her.

Olive Henderson laughed outright as she looked at her.

"Well, Miss Blair," she said, "if I had told you I had committed a murder, and was going to be hanged for it, you could hardly look more aghast! Pray, is there anything so very terrible in my marrying Mr. Wyndham?"

"It's not that," said Laura, recovering herself slowly, "but the news came so suddenly, so unexpectedly, that——"

"Unexpectedly! Is it possible, Laura, Speckport has not decided before now I should marry Mr. Wyndham?"

"Speckport doesn't know what to think," said Laura; "it decided upon your marriage with Captain Cavendish; it said that you were engaged, and that all was settled, when, lo! this Mr. Wyndham appears, and presto! all is changed. Captain Cavendish flies out of the country, and Mr. Wyndham becomes the hero of the story. Speckport never was so pleased before; you are as erratic as a comet, Miss Henderson, and it is as useless trying to account for your vagaries."

"I am glad Speckport has found that out. Well, Laura, you will be bridemaid?"

"Of course. Oh, how strange it all seems! When is it to come off?"

"What, the wedding? Oh, near the end of next month, I believe. Mr. Wyndham, like any other ardent lover, objects to long engagements."

She laughed, as she spoke, a little disdainful laugh, that made Laura fix her brown eyes thoughtfully on her face.

"Olly—don't be angry, please—do you love Mr. Wyndham?"

"Of course, you silly child," the heiress laughed, carelessly, "if not, should I marry him? You have read a great many novels, my Laura, of the high-pressure school,

and have formed your own ideas of lovers from the rapturous proceedings therein recorded. But Mr. Wyndham
and I are not romantic; it is not in my nature to be, and
all the romance in his he reserves as his stock-in-trade for
his books, and has none left for this prosy every-day life.
He is sufficiently well-looking, he is gentlemanly and attentive, and he is famous, and he has asked me to marry
him, and I have said yes; and I will do it, too, if I don't
change my mind before the day comes."

"Does Mr. Wyndham love you, Olly?" she asked,
after a long, grave pause, during which Olive had been
humming an opera air.

"Of course, my love! How can he help it?"

"And you are really going to be married so soon, and
to this stranger? Oh, Olly! take care!"

"You absurd Laura! Take care of what? Are you
afraid Mr. Wyndham will beat me after the magic words
are spoken?"

"I suppose it is the suddenness of it all that makes me
feel so strange about it. I like Mr. Wyndham very much,
and I think his books are lovely! I dare say you will be
very happy with him, after all. How many bridemaids
are you going to have, and what are we to wear?"

After this truly feminine turn to the conversation, love
and happiness were forgotten in the discussion of silks
and moire antiques, and the rival merits of pink or white
for the bridemaids' bonnets. They were a very long time
deciding; for somehow Olive Henderson, with all her
inborn love of dress, did not seem to take much interest
in the matter.

"We'll settle it all again, Laura," she said, impatiently,
"there's no hurry—six weeks is a long time. Come, and
let us have a drive."

As the young ladies entered the little pony-carriage,
Mr. Wyndham rode up on his bay, looking his best, as
good riders always do on horseback. Laura, who was on
very friendly, not to say familiar, terms with the young
author, held out her hand.

"Accept my congratulations," she said, "I am to be
bridemaid-in-chief on the happy occasion; and, next to

being married myself, there is nothing we girls like better than that!"

Mr. Wyndham smiled, lifted her hand to his lips gallantly, and made some complimentary reply; but there was no rapture in his face, Laura noticed, even although his bride-elect, in the dark splendor of her beauty, sat before him among the rich cushions, like an Egyptian queen.

"He does not love her," thought Laura; "he is like all the rest; he wants to marry her because she is handsome, and the fashion, and the heiress of Redmon. I wonder, if I were in her place, if that stupid Val would ever come to the point. I know he likes me, but the tiresome creature won't say so."

Mr. Wyndham had but just left Mr. Blake's office, after having bewildered that gentleman with the same news Olive had imparted to her friend.

Mr. Blake's hands were very deep in his pockets, and he was whistling a dismally perplexed whistle, as the young author left his sanctum.

"It's very odd!" Mr. Blake was thinking, "it's very odd, indeed! He said he would do it, and I didn't believe him, and now it's done. It's very odd! I know she doesn't care about him, rather the reverse; and then, she was promised to Cavendish. What can she be marrying him for? Wyndham, too, he isn't in love with her; it's not in him to be in love with any one. What can he want marrying her? It can't be her money—at least, it's not like Paul Wyndham, if it is. And then he's a sort of novel-writing hermit, who would live on bread and water as fast as turtle-soup, and doesn't care a button for society. It's odd—it's uncommonly odd!"

Speckport found it odd, too, and said so, which Mr. Blake did not, except to himself. But then the heiress with the imperious beauty and flashing eyes was a singular being, anyhow, and they put it down as the last coquetry of my Lady Caprice. And while they talked of it, and conjectured about it, and wondered if she would not jilt him for somebody else before the day came round—while Speckport gossiped ravenously, Mr. Wyndham was a daily visitor at the cottage, and Speckport beheld the betrothed

pair galloping together out along the lovely country-roads
and over the distant tree-clad hills, and saw the new villa
at Redmon going up with magical rapidity, and the once
bleak and dreary grounds being transformed into a fairy-
land of beauty. All the head dressmakers and milliners of
the town were up to their eyes in the wedding-splendors,
and such a lot of Miss Henderson's dear five hundred had
been invited to the wedding that the miracle was how the
cottage was going to hold them all. Speckport knew all
about the arrangements beforehand; how they were to be
married in Trinity Church, being both High-Church people; how they were going on a bridal-tour through the
Canadas, and would return toward the close of August,
when the villa would be ready to receive them.

Speckport talked of all this incessantly, and of the five
bridemaids; of whom Laura Blair, Jeannette McGregor
and Miss Tod, were the chief; and while they talked, the
day came round. A dull and depressing day, with a clammy yellow fog that stuck to everything, and a bleak wind
that reddened the pretty noses of the bridemaids, and
made them shiver in their white satin shoes. The old
church was crowded. Young and old, gentle and simple,
all flocked to see the beautiful black-eyed heiress who had
set so many unhappy young men crazy, married at last to
the man of her choice. The dismal weather had no effect
on her, it seemed; for she swept up the aisle, leaning on
the arm of Mr. Darcy, who was to play papa, in a dress
whose splendor electrified Speckport, and which had been
imported direct from Paris; all in white, an immense vail
floating all around her like a silvery mist, she didn't, as
scandalized Speckport said, for all, look a bit like a bride.
Where was the drooping of the long eye-lashes; where
the paling and flushing cheek; where the shy and timid
graces of virginhood? Was it not the height of impropriety to walk up the aisle with her head erect, her black
eyes bright and defiant, her lips compressed, and her color
never varying? It was the vulgarity and brazenness of
the New York grisette breaking out, or the spangles and
sawdust of the circus-rider. But Speckport said all this
under their breath; and when it was all over, and the

names down in the register, kissed the bride, at least female Speckport did, the beings in broadcloth and white vests only looking as if they would like to. And then they drove back to the cottage; and Miss Henderson—no, it, was Mrs. Wyndham now—went to her room at once to put on her traveling-dress, for the steamer started in half an hour. There was a great crowd on the wharf to see them off; and the bride and bridegroom stood to be looked at—he, pale, quiet, and calm; she, haughty and handsome, and uplifted to the end.

So it was all over, and the heiress of Redmon was safely married at last! The news came out in next day's "Spouter," with a string of good wishes from the editorial chair for the happy pair. Two young men—Captain George P. Cavendish, in the reading-room of a Montreal hotel, and Mr. Tom Oaks, in an Indian's tent up the country, where he shot and fished—read it, and digested the bitter pill as best they might. Some one else read it, too; Mr. Wyndham, with his own hands, posted the first copy of that particular "Spouter" he received to a young lady, who read it with strange eagerness in her own room in a quaint New York hotel. A lady who read it over and over and over again, as often and as eagerly as Miss Wade had read that advertisement long before in the Canadian paper shown her in Mrs. Butterby's lodgings, by the pale actress.

CHAPTER XXIX.

MR. WYNDHAM'S MOTHER.

R. WYNDHAM and Miss Henderson had had but one confidential interview after that first one, during the length of their brief engagement. It was the day after the evening at the theater. Mr. Wyndham had called early and found the heiress waiting for him in the drawing-room.

There was no terror, no humiliation in her manner now, nothing but reckless, scornful defiance, and fierce pride, with which she seemed to dare him and Fate to do their worst.

"I was afraid of you yesterday, Mr. Paul Wyndham," she said, with an unpleasant laugh. "I shall never be afraid of you again. I see that it is of no use to struggle against Destiny—Providence, good people would say, but I make no pretense of goodness. The French have a saying that embodies the character of the nation : ' *Cour-onnons nous des roses avant qu'elles ne se fleurissent.*' I take that for my motto from henceforth, and crown myself with roses before they fade. I shall dress and spend money and enjoy this fortune while I may—when it goes, why, let it go,—I, shall know what to do when that time comes !"

Mr. Wyndham bowed in grave silence, and waited to hear all she might have to say. "To retain this wealth," she went on in the same reckless tone, and with her black deriding eyes seeming to mock him, "I consent to marry you ; that is, I consent to go through a civil and religious ceremony which the world will call a marriage, and which to us will simply mean nothing but an empty form. It will give you a right to my money, which is all you want ; it will give you a right to dwell under the same roof, but no right ever to intrude yourself upon me for one second, except when others are present and it is necessary to avoid suspicion. The world will call me by your name ; but I shall still remain Olive Henderson, free and unfettered— free to come and go and do as I please, without interfer- ence or hindrance from you. Do I make myself under- stood ?"

"Perfectly," Mr. Wyndham said, coolly, "and ex- press my views entirely. I am delighted with your good sense, Miss Henderson, and I foresee we shall make a model couple, and get on together famously. Now, as to our wedding arrangements. When is it to be ?"

"Whenever you please," she said, scornfully ; "it is a matter of perfect indifference to me."

15

"I do not like to hurry you too much, but if the end of June——"

Olive made a careless gesture with her ringed hand:

"That will do! One time is as good as another."

"And our bridal tour? There must be a bridal tour, you know, or people will talk."

"I told you," she said, impatiently, "it was of no consequence to me! Arrange it as you please—I shall make no objection."

"Then suppose we go to Canada for a couple of months? The villa at Redmon can be ready upon our return."

And this tender tête-à-tête between the plighted pair settled the matter. And in due time the solemn mockery was performed by the Rev. Augustus Tod, and Mr. and Mrs. Wyndham departed on their wedding tour. The upholsterer had received his orders, and the villa would be in readiness upon their return, and there would be a famous house-warming, to which half Speckport was to be invited. About three weeks after the amicable adjustment of affairs between the author and the heiress, Mr. Wyndham made a little investment in landed property on his own account. There was a delightful little dwelling, known as "Rosebush Cottage," for sale. A real bijou of a cottage, painted cream color, with vivid green window-shutters and door, and with a garden in front that was a perfect sea of roses—crimson roses, and monthly roses, and damask roses, and bridal roses, all kinds bloomed here, until the air became faint with perfume; and behind there was a gnarled old orchard, where apple-trees and plum-trees nearly covered the creamy cottage with their long green arms. This delicious Rosebush Cottage was for sale; and Mr. Wyndham, who had for some time been quietly on the look-out for just such a place, became its purchaser. When asked what he could possibly want of it, Mr. Wyndham answered it was for his mother.

"For your mother!" exclaimed Mr. Blake, when Mr. Wyndham first told him. "You never mean to say, Wyndham, your mother is going to exchange the genial and spicy breezes of Westchester County for our bleak province—hey?"

"Westchester County is a delightful place, no doubt," responded Mr. Wyndham; "but in my absence, it is only vanity and vexation of spirit to my poor mother. What are all the Westchester Counties in America to her without her Paul, her only one! I shall send for her as soon as I return from Canada, to come here."

"Perhaps she won't come," said Val; "perhaps she will think of the old adage, 'My son's my son till he gets him a wife,' and prefer remaining where she is."

"No," said Mr. Wyndham, "my mother knows her son will be her son all the days of his life. She is very much changed, Blake, since you knew her; she never was very fond of society, as you are aware; but of late she has become a perfect recluse, shutting herself in and shutting the world out. Rosebush Cottage will make her a very nice hermitage, I think, and it is conveniently near Redmon. The next thing is to look out for a competent and trustworthy servant—not a young girl, you know, giddy and frivolous, but a quiet and sensible woman, who would not object to the loneliness."

Mr. Blake put on his considering-cap.

"There's Midge," he said, "she's out of place, and stopping with us—you saw her at our house last night, you remember; but I'm afraid she mightn't suit."

"That little dwarf, do you mean? She would do well enough, as far as looks are concerned, if that is the only objection."

"But that isn't the only objection," said Val; "more's the pity, for she is perfectly trustworthy, and can work like a horse. As for the loneliness, she would rather prefer it on that very account."

"Then what is the objection?"

"Why, you see," said Mr. Blake, "we're none of us perfect in this lower world, and Midge, though but one remove from an angel in a general point of view, has yet her failings. For instance, there's her temper."

"Bad?" inquired Mr. Wyndham.

Mr. Blake nodded intelligently.

"It never was of the best, you know; but after she lost Nathalie Marsh, it became—well, she is never kept in any place over a week, and then she comes to us and makes a purgatory of No. 16 Great St. Peter Street, until she finds another situation. I'm afraid she wouldn't. do."

Mr. Blake, smelling audibly at the roses as he said this, did not see the sudden change that had come over Mr. Wyndham's face, nor the eagerness hardly repressed in his voice when he spoke.

"She was formerly a servant, then, of this Miss Nathalie Marsh, of whom I have heard so many speak since I came here?"

"Yes, for years, and devotedly attached to her. Poor Natty! I think Midge felt her loss ten degrees more than her own mother; but grief, I regret to say, hasn't a sweetening effect on Midge's temper."

"Still I think I shall try her," said Paul Wyndham, carelessly. "My mother is very quiet and easy, and I don't believe they will quarrel. I will see Midge about it this very day."

Which he did accordingly, sending her off at once to keep the cottage until his mother's arrival. The upholsterer furnishing Redmon Villa had his orders for Rosebush Cottage also, and both were to be in readiness when September came round.

Olive Henderson heard with extreme indifference of the expected arrival of Mr. Wyndham's mother, from the lips of Miss Jo Blake, next day.

"Ah! is she?" the heiress said, suppressing a yawn; "well, as she is to reside a mile and a half from Redmon, I don't suppose she will be much trouble to me. If the mistress be like the maid, Laura," said the heiress, turning with a scornful laugh to her friend, "I am likely to have a charming mamma-in-law."

Good Miss Jo, who thought the motherless heiress would rejoice at the tidings she brought her, was scandalized at the speech. Indeed, Miss Jo—the best of women and old maids—did not approve of Miss Henderson's capers at all. She had always thought her too proud;

for Miss Jo's simple Irish belief was, that we earthly worms have no business at all with that sin which drove Lucifer, Star of the Morning, from Paradise, and was sorry to see her favorite Laura so much taken up with the queenly coquette.

"Laura was such a nice little girl, Val," Miss Jo said, to the editor of the "Speckport Spouter," across the tea-table that evening; "and now, I am afraid, she will fall into the ways of that young girl, whom everybody is running crazy after. If Miss Henderson was like poor Natty, or that little angel, Miss Rose, now!"

"How is Miss Rose, Jo?" asked Val; "I haven't seen her this month of Sundays?"

"She isn't out much," said Miss Blake; "Mrs. Wheatly keeps her busy; and when she does come out, it's to Mrs. Marsh's she goes, or to see her poor pensioners. Miss Henderson asked her to be one of her bridemaids, I hear, but she refused."

"Stuff!" said Val, politely. "Miss Henderson isn't the woman to ask a governess to be her bridemaid. Not but that Miss Rose is as good as she is!"

"As good!" cried Miss Jo, in shrill indignation, "she's fifty thousand times better. Miss Rose is a little pale-faced angel on the face of the earth; and that rich young woman with the big black eyes is no more an angel than I am!"

Miss Jo manifested her disapprobation of the heiress by not going to see her married, and by declining an invitation to the wedding-breakfast; neither of which slights, had she known of them, which she didn't, would have troubled the high-stepping young lady in the least.

But Miss Jo was destined to become an heiress herself; for, a fortnight after the great wedding, and just as Speckport was getting nicely round after the shock, it received another staggerer in the news that a great fortune had been left to Miss Jo Blake. Thirty thousand pounds, the first startling announcement had it; thirteen, the second; and three, the final and correct one.

Yes; Miss Jo had been left the neat little sum of three thousand pounds sterling, and was going home to take possession of the fortune. An old maiden aunt, after whom Miss Joanna had been named, and from whom she had long had expectations—as all Speckport had heard a million times, more or less—had died at last, and left Miss Jo the three thousand and her blessing.

Upon receiving the tidings, Miss Blake was seized with a violent desire to revisit the scenes of her infantile sports, and gave warning of her intention of starting in the first vessel bound for Liverpool.

"And it's not in one of them dirty steamboats I'll go," said Miss Jo, decisively, "that's liable to blow up any minute; but I'll go in a ship that's slow and sure, and not put a hand in my own life by trusting to one of them new-fangled inventions!"

Mr. Blake expostulated with his sister on the impropriety of leaving him alone and unprotected to the mercies of heartless servant-girls. Miss Jo was inexorable.

"If you don't like keeping house and fighting with the servants," said Miss Blake, "go and board. If you don't like boarding, why, go and get married! it won't hurt your growth any, I'm sure!"

As Mr. Blake was on the wrong side of thirty, and had probably done growing, there was a great deal of sound truth in Miss Jo's remark. Mr. Blake, however, only stood aghast at the proposal.

"It's time you were getting married, Val," pursued Miss Jo, busily packing; particularly now, that I'm going to leave you. You're well enough off, and there's lots of nice girls in Speckport who would be glad to snap at you. Not that I should like to see you marry a Bluenose—Lord forbid! if it could be helped; but there's Miss Rose, or there's Laura Blair, both of them as nice girls as you will find. Now, why can't you take and marry one of them?"

Mr. Blake was beyond the power of replying. He could only stare in blank and helpless consternation at his brisk, match-making sister.

"I would rather you took Miss Rose," pursued Miss Blake, "she's the best of the two, and a rock of sense ; but Laura's very fond of you, and—where are you going now?"

For Mr. Blake had snatched up his hat and started out, banging the door after him. The first person he met, turning the corner, was Mr. Blair.

"So you're going to lose Jo, Blake," he said, taking his arm. "Laura tells me she is off next week in the Ocean Star. What are you going to do with yourself when you lose her?"

"Become a monk, I think," said Mr. Blake, helplessly. "I don't know anything else for it! Jo talks of boarding, but I hate boarding-houses, and where else can I go?"

"Come to us," cried Mr. Blair, heartily. "Mrs. B. thinks there's nobody like you, and you and I will have a fine chance to talk things over together. Come to us, old boy, and make our house your home!"

Mr. Blake closed with this friendly offer at once, on condition that the ladies of the house were satisfied.

"No danger of that," said Laura's father; "they will be in transports. Come up this evening and have a smoke with me, and see if they don't."

Laura Blair's eyes danced in her head when her father told them the news; but the little hypocrite affected to object.

"It will make so much trouble, pa," the young lady said, in a dissatisfied tone, "trouble for ma and me, I mean. I wish he wasn't coming."

Mr. Blair listened to the shocking fib with the greatest indifference. He didn't care whether she liked it or not, and said so, with paternal frankness.

So Miss Jo kissed everybody and departed, and Val translated his Lares and Penates to Mr. Blair's; at least, such of them as were not disposed of by public auction.

Speckport was just settling its nerves after this, when it was thrown into another little flutter by the unexpected return of Captain Cavendish.

Yes, Captain Cavendish, the defeated conqueror, came back to the scene of his defeat, rather swaggering than otherwise, and carrying things with a high hand. Perhaps the gallant captain wanted to show Speckport how little he cared for being jilted; perhaps he wanted to see what kind of life Mr. and Mrs. Wyndham would lead

together; perhaps he found himself too well known as a
roué and gambler in Montreal; or perhaps he was not
tired bleeding young Alick McGregor and young Speckport generally, in that quiet house in Prince Street. He
was back, anyway, handsome, and nonchalant, and unprincipled as ever.

Miss Blair received a letter from her friend three
weeks after her departure, dated Niagara. Mrs. Wyndham was not a good correspondent, it seemed; her letter
was very brief and unsatisfactory, and she only mentioned
her husband once, and then merely to say Mr. Wyndham
was well. She signed the letter simply, "Olive," not
using her real name, and told Laura that Montreal was
tiresome and the Canadians stupid. Miss Blair sent her
half a quire of note-paper by way of answer, recording
every item of information, and every possible scrap of
news, and imploring a speedy reply. But Olive never
replied, although August wore itself out while Laura
waited. On the last day of that month, Mrs. Hill received a telegram from Portland, Me., from Mr. Wyndham, informing her her master and mistress would arrive
next day.

It was a glorious September afternoon that on which the
wedded pair returned from their short bridal-tour. The
steamer swept up to the crowded wharf in a sort of sun-
burst of glory, and the air was opaque with amber mist,
as if it were raining impalpable gold-dust. Not a sign of
fog in the cloudless blue sky; it might have been Venice
instead of Speckport, so luminously brilliant was sky and
earth that afternoon.

The passengers poured out of the steamer, and came
up the bustling floats, where cabmen, porters, hotel-run-
ners and the steamer-hands were making a Babel of dis-
cord, and the passengers wondered to see the crowd of
people looking curiously down upon them from the wharf
above. Laura Blair stood straining her eyes for a sight
of her friend. Olive Henderson, with her dangerous
gift of fascination, had won the girl's love as it had never
been won before, and Laura had missed her sadly during
these two last months. As she stood impatiently waiting,

she was thinking of that pleasant March evening when Olive Henderson had first come to Speckport, and they had watched her walk up these very floats, stately and tall, leaning on Mr. Darcy's arm, and wearing a vail over her face. And while Laura thought of it, and could scarcely believe it was only six months ago, she saw the same Olive—Olive Wyndham now—coming toward her on her husband's arm. She was not vailed this time, although a long drab gossamer vail floated back from the pretty jockey-hat she wore, and Laura saw how pale and fagged and spiritless she looked. The next moment, she had thrown her arms impetuously around her, and was kissing her rapturously.

"My darling Olly! my darling Olly!" she was crying out. "Oh, how glad I am to see you again!"

Her darling Olly did not return the embrace very enthusiastically, though her face lit up at sight of her friend. Laura shook hands with Mr. Wyndham, who was smiling at her effusions, and then turned again to the friend she loved.

"Oh, Olly! how dull it has been since you went away, and how cruel of you never to write to me! Why didn't you write?"

"Writing is such a bore," Olive said, drearily. "I hate writing. Is that the carriage waiting up there?"

"Yes," said Laura; "and how did you enjoy your travel? You look pale and tired."

"I am tired to death," Mrs. Wyndham said, impatiently, "and I have not enjoyed myself at all. Every place was stupid, and I am glad to be home! Do let us get out of this mob, Mr. Wyndham!"

Mr. Wyndham had paused for a moment to give some directions about the baggage, and his wife addressed him so sharply that Laura stared. Laura noticed during the homeward drive how seldom she spoke to her husband, and how cold her tone always was when she addressed him. But Mr. Wyndham did not seem to mind much. He talked to Laura—and Mr. Wyndham knew how to talk—and told her about their travels, and the places they

15*

had been, and the people they had met, and the adventures they had encountered.

"Olive reigned Lady Paramount wherever we went," he said, smiling (he never called her Mrs. Wyndham or "my wife," always Olive). "Our tour was a long succession of brilliant triumphs for her."

Olive merely shrugged her shoulders disdainfully, and looked at the swelling meadows as they drove along Redmon road. A beautiful road in summer time, and the Nettleby cottage was quite lost in a sea of green verdure, sprinkled with red stars of the scarlet-runners. Ann Nettleby stood in the door as they drove by in a cloud of dust—in that doorway where pretty Cherrie used to stand, pretty, flighty little Cherrie, whom Speckport was fast learning to forget.

And Redmon! Could Mrs. Leroy have risen from her grave and looked on Redmon, she might well have stared aghast at the magical changes. A lovely little villa, with miniature peaks and turrets, and a long piazza running around it, and verdant with climbing roses and sweetbrier. A sloping velvety lawn, on which the drawing-room and dining-rooms windows opened, led from the house to the avenue; and fair flower-gardens, where fountains played in marble basins, and bees and butterflies disported in the September sunshine, spread away on all sides. Beyond them lay the swelling meadows, the dark woods; and, beyond all, the shining sea aglitter in the summer sunshine. The groom came up to lead away the horse, and Mrs. Hill, in a black silk dress and new cap, stood in the doorway to receive them. The dark, sunless face of Olive lit up and became luminous for the first time as she saw all this.

"How pretty it is, Laura!" she said. "I am glad I am home."

The servants were gathered in the hall to welcome their master and mistress as they entered arm-in-arm. The upholsterer had done his work well, the drawing-room was one long vista of splendor, the dining-room almost too beautiful for eating in, and there was a conservatory the like of which Speckport had never seen before.

Mrs. Wyndham had a suite of rooms, too—sleeping-room, dressing-room, bath-room, and boudoir—all opening into one another in a long vision of brightness and beauty, and there was a library which was a library, and not a mockery and a delusion, and was lined with books from floor to ceiling. Speckport had been shown the house, and pronounced it perfection.

Olive Wyndham forgot her languor and weariness, and broke out in her old delighted way as she went through it.

"How beautiful it all is!" she cried, "and it is all mine—my own! I am going to be happy here—I will be happy here!"

Her black eyes flashed strangely upon her husband walking by her side, and the hand clenched, as if she defied Fate from henceforth.

"I hope so," Paul Wyndham said, gravely. "I hope, with all my heart, you may be happy here."

Laura looked from one to the other in silent wonder. Mr. Wyndham turned to her as they finished the tour of the house.

"I suppose Rosebush Cottage is hardly equal to this, Miss Laura? Have you been there lately?"

"Yes," said Laura. "Val and I—he stops with us now, you know—went through it last week. The rooms are very pretty, and the garden is one wilderness of roses; and Midge reminds me of Eve in Eden, only there is no Adam."

"And Midge does not exactly correspond with our ideas of our fair first mother," laughed Mr. Wyndham. "I must go there to-morrow and see the place. Will you come, Olive?"

"No, thank you," she said, coldly. "Rosebush Cottage has very little interest for me."

Again Laura stared.

"Why is she so cross?" she thought. "How can she be cross, when he seems so kind? How soon do you expect your mother, Mr. Wyndham?" she said aloud.

"This is Friday—I shall leave on Monday morning for New York to fetch her."

There was an announcement that dinner was ready, and nothing more was said of Mr. Wyndham's mother. He rode over to Rosebush Cottage early next morning, attended only by a big Canadian wolf-hound, of which animals he had brought two splendid specimens with him, and told Midge he was going to leave him as guardian of the premises. Before he left the cottage, he called Midge into the pretty drawing-room, and held a very long and very confidential interview with her, from which she emerged with her ruddy face blanched to the hue of a sheet. Whatever was said in that long conversation, its effect was powerful on Midge; for she remained in a dazed and bewildered state for the rest of the day, capable of doing nothing but sitting with her arms folded on the kitchen-table, staring very hard at vacancy with her little round eyes.

Mr. Wyndham departed for New York on Monday morning, taking the other big dog, Faust, with him. Mrs. Wyndham took his departure with superb indifference—it was nothing to her. John, the coachman, was of as much consequence in her eyes as the man she had promised to love, honor, and obey. She did not ask him when he was coming back—what was it to her if he never came?—but he volunteered the information. "I will be back next week, Olive," he said. "Good-bye." And Olive had said good-bye, icily, and swept past him in the hall, and never once cast a look after him, as he drove down the long avenue in the hazy September sunshine.

The house-warming at Redmon could not very well come off until Mr. Wyndham's return; and the preparations for that great event being going on in magnificent style, and Olive eager for it to take place, she was not sorry when, toward the close of the following week, she learned her husband had returned. It was Miss McGregor who drove up to the villa to make a call, and related the news.

"The boat got in about two o'clock, my dear Mrs. Wyndham," Jeannette said, "and Mr. Wyndham and his mother came in her. I chanced to be on the wharf, and

I saw them go up together, and enter a cab and drive off.
I am surprised they are not here."

" They drove to Rosebush Cottage, I presume," Olive
said, rather haughtily. " Everything is in readiness for
Mrs. Wyndham there."

" What is she like, Jeannette?" asked Laura, who was
always at Redmon, familiarly. " I suppose she was dressed
in black?"

" Yes," Miss McGregor said, "she was dressed in
black, and wore a thick black vail over her face, and they
had driven off before any one had time to speak to them.
No doubt, she would be present at the house-warming,
and then they could call on her afterward."

But Mrs. Wyndham, Senior, did not appear at the
house-warming; and society was given to understand,
very quietly, by Mr. Wyndham, that his mother would
receive no callers. Her health forbade all exertion or excitement, it appeared. She seldom, if ever, crossed her
own threshold, from week's end to week's end; and it
was her habit to keep her room, and she did not care to
be disturbed by any one. Her health was not so very
poor as to require medical attendance; but Mr. Wyndham
owned she was somewhat eccentric, and he liked to humor
her. Speckport was quite disappointed, and said, it
thought Mr. Wyndham's mother was a very singular
person, indeed!

CHAPTER XXX.

VERY MYSTERIOUS.

HE house-warming at Redmon was such a
house-warming as Speckport never saw before; for, as Mr. Blake with his customary
good sense remarked, "When Mrs. P. Wyndham did that sort of thing, she did do it." In
the luminous darkness of the September evening, the

carriages of the guests drove through the tall iron gates
up the back avenue, all aglow with red, and blue, and
green lamps, twinkling like tropical fireflies among the
trees.   The whole front of the beautiful villa blazed with
illumination, and up in the gilded gallery the musicians
were filling the scented air with delicious melody.   It
was not Redmon, this; it was fairy-land; it was a scene
out of the Arabian Nights, and the darkly-beautiful lady
in ruby velvet and diamonds, welcoming her friends, was
the Princess Badelbradour, lovely enough to turn the
heads of a brigade of poor Aladdins.   Society went
through the house that night, and had the eyes dazzled
in their heads by the blinding radiance of light, and the
glowing coloring and richness of all.   The ladies went
into raptures over Mrs. Wyndham's rooms, and the literary
people cast envious eyes over the book-lined library, with
its busts of poets, and pictures of great men, dead and
gone.   There was a little room opening off this library
that seemed out of keeping in its severe plainness with
the magnificence of the rest of the house—a bare, severe
room, with only one window, looking out upon the velvety sward of the lawn at the back of the villa; a room
that had no carpet on the floor, and very little furniture,
only two or three chairs, a baize-covered writing-table, a
leather-covered lounge under the window, a few pictures
of dogs and horses, a plaster head of John Milton, a se-
lection of books on swinging shelves, a bureau, a dress-
ing-table, a lavatory, a shaving-glass, and a sofa-bedstead.
Except the servants' apartments, there was nothing at all
so plain as this in the whole house; and when people
asked what it was, they were told by Mrs. Hill, who
showed the house, that it was Mr. Wyndham's room.
Yes, this was Mr. Wyndham's room, the only room in
that house he ever entered, save when he went to dinner,
or when visitors required his presence in the drawing-
room or library.   His big dog Faust slept on a rug beside
the table, his canaries sung to him in their cages
around the window, he wrote in that hard leathern arm-
chair beside the green-baize table, he lay on that lounge
under the open window in the golden breeze of the

September weather, and smoked endless cigars; late
into the night his lamp glimmered in that quiet
room; and when it went out after midnight, he
was sleeping the sleep of the just on the sofa-bedstead.
The servants at Redmon talked, as servants will talk, about
the palpable estrangement between master and mistress,
about their never meeting, except at dinner, when there
always was company; for Mrs. Wyndham breakfasted in
the boudoir, and Mr. Wyndham never ate luncheon. He
was quite hermit-like in his habits, this pale, inscrutable
young author—one glass of wine sufficed for him—he
was out of bed and at work before the stable-boys or
scullery-maids were stirring, and his only extravagance
was in the way of cigars. From the day he had married
Olive Henderson until this, he had never asked or received
one stiver of her money; he had more than sufficient of
his own for his simple wants and his mother's, and had
Olive been the hardest virago of a landlady, she could
hardly have brought in a bill against him, even for board
and lodging, for he more than repaid her for both. He
was always courteous, genial, and polite to her—too polite
for one spark of her affection; always deferring to her
wishes, and never attempting in the smallest iota to interfere with her caprices, or thwart her desires, or use his
husbandly authority. She was in every way as much
her own mistress as she had ever been; so much so that
sometimes she wondered, and found it impossible to realize
that she was really married. No, she was not married;
these two had never been united either in heart or desire;
they were bound together by a compact never mentioned
now. What had he gained by this marriage? Olive sometimes wonderingly asked herself. He told her, or as good
as told her, he wanted her for her money; but now that
money was at his disposal, and he never made use of it.
What had he married her for?

"How proud you must be of your husband, Mrs.
Wyndham!" other women had said to her, when abroad;
and sometimes, in spite of herself, a sharp pang cut to the
center of her haughty heart at the words. Why, these
very women had as much right to be proud of him, **to**

speak to him, to be near him, as she had. Proud of him! She thought she had cause to hate him, she was wicked enough to wish to hate him, but she could not. Neither could she despise him; she might treat him as coldly as she pleased, but she never could treat him with contempt. There was a dignity about the man, the dignity of a gentleman and a scholar, that asserted itself, and made her respect him, as she never had respected any other man. Once or twice a strange thought had come across her; a thought that if he would come to her and tell her he was growing to love her, and ask her not to be so cruelly cold and repellent, she might lay her hand on his shoulder with the humility of a little child, and trust him, and yield herself to him as her friend and protector through life, and be simply and honestly happy, like other women. But he never did this; his manner never changed to her in the slightest degree. She had nothing to complain of from him, she had every cause to be grateful for his kindness and clemency. And so she shut herself up in her pride, and silenced fiercely her mutinous heart, and sought happiness in costly dress and jewelry, and womanly employment, and incessant visiting, and party-giving, and receptions, and money-spending—and failed miserably. Was she never to be happy? She had everything her heart could desire—a beautiful house, servants to attend her, rich garments to wear, and she fared sumptuously every day; but for all that, she was wretched. I do not suppose Dives was a happy man. There is only one receipt in this wide world for happiness, believe me, and that is goodness. We may be happy for a brief while, with the brief happiness of a lotus-eater; but it cannot last—it cannot last! and the after-misery is worse than anything we ever suffered before. Olive Henderson had said she would be happy, she had tried to compel herself to be happy; and thought for a few poor minutes, sometimes, when she found herself the belle of some gay party, dancing and laughing, and reigning like a queen, that she had succeeded. But "Oh, the lees are bitter, bitter!" Next day she would know what a ghastly mockery it had all been, and she would watch Paul Wyndham, mounted on his pony, with his dog behind him, riding away to his mother's cottage, with a passionately rebellious and bitter heart, and wonder if he or any one else in the wide world would really care if they found her lying on the floor of her costly boudoir, stark and dead, slain by her own hand.

Paul Wyndham appeared to be very fond of his mother, if he was not of his wife. He rode over to Rosebush Cottage every day, rain or shine, and sometimes staid there two or three days together.

Mr. Wyndham's mother, for all her age and her ill-health, could play the piano, it seemed. People going past Rosebush Cottage had often heard the piano going, and played, too, with masterly skill. At first, it was thought to be Mr. Wyndham himself, who was quite a musician, but they soon found out the piano-playing went on when he was known to be at Redmon. Olive heard all this, and, like Speckport, would have given a good deal to see Mr. Wyndham's mother; but she never saw her. She had asked him, carelessly, if his mother would come to the house-warming, and he had said "No, she never went out;" and so the house-warming had come off without her.

There was one person present on that occasion whom Speckport was surprised to see, and that was Captain Cavendish. Captain Cavendish had received a card of invitation, and, having arrayed himself in his uniform, made his appearance as a guest, in the house he once hoped to call his own. Those floating stories, whispered by the servants, and current in the town, of the cold disunion between husband and wife, had reached him, and delighted him more than words can tell. After all, then, she had loved him! Doubtless she spent her nights in secret weeping and mourning for his loss, fit to tear her black hair out by the roots, in her anguish at having lost him. He was very late in arriving at Redmon, purposely late; and he could imagine her straining her eyes toward the drawing-room door, her heart throbbing at every fresh announcement, and turning sick with disappointment when she found it was not he. Would she betray any

emotion when she met him? Would her voice falter, her
eyes droop, her color rise, or her hand turn cold in his
own?

Oh, Captain Cavendish! you might have spared yourself the trouble of all these conjectures. Not one poor
thought had she ever given you; not once had your image
crossed her mind, until you stood bowing before her; and
then, when she spoke to you, every nerve was as steady as
when, an instant later, she welcomed old Squire Tod. Her
eyes were following furtively another form, nothing like
so tall, or stately, or gallant as your own, Captain Cavendish; another form that went in and out through the
crowd—the form of her husband, who welcomed every
one with a face infinitely kind and genial, who found
partners for forlorn damsels, who stopped to talk cour-
teously to neglected wall-flowers, and who came to where
his wife stood every now and then, and addressed her as
any other gentleman in his own house might address his
wife, showing no sign of coldness or disunion on his part,
at least.

Captain Cavendish was disappointed, and all Speckport with him. Where was the cold neglect on Mr. Wyndham's part, they had come prepared to see and relish? where
the haughty disdain of the neglected and resentful wife?
They were calmly polite to one another, and what more
was required? As long as Mr. Wyndham did not beat
her, or Mrs. Wyndham showed no sign of intending to
elope with any other man, Speckport could see no reason
why it should set them down as other than a very well-
matched couple.

It was noticeable that Mr. Wyndham that night paid
rather marked attention to one of the lady guests present;
but as the lady wore black bombazine and crape, a widow's
cap, and was on the frosty side of fifty, no scandal came
of it. The lady was poor Mrs. Marsh, who had come,
nothing loth, and who simpered a good deal, and was
fluttered and flattered to find herself thus honored by the
master of Redmon.

"Her story is a very sad one, Olive," he said; "I

am glad you settled that annuity upon her; it does you credit."

Olive said nothing; but a dark red streak flashed across her face—a burning glow of shame. She was thinking of Mrs. Major Wheatly's governess—what would Paul Wyndham say of that pale little girl if he knew all? Mrs. Wyndham had repeatedly invited Miss Rose to Redmon; and Miss Rose had come two or three times, but never when there was company.

Mr. Wyndham led Mrs. Marsh in to supper, and sat beside her, and filled her plate with good things, and talked to her all through that repast. His wife, sitting between Major Wheatly and the Rev. Augustus Tod, still watched him askance, and wondered what he could find to say to that insipid and faded nonentity, who simpered like a school-girl as she listened to him. But shortly after conducting Mrs. Marsh back to the ballroom, and seeing her safely seated at a card-table, he disappeared, and was nowhere to be seen. Every one was so busy dancing, and flirting, and card-playing, that his absence was quite unnoticed—no, not quite, his wife had observed it. It was strange the habit she had insensibly contracted, of watching this man, for whom she did not care—or persuaded herself she did not—of listening for his voice, his step, and feeling better satisfied, somehow, to see him in the room. Where had he gone to? What was he doing? How could he be so rude as to go and leave their guests? She grew distrait, then fidgety, then feverishly and foolishly anxious to know what he could be about, and who he was with; and gliding unobserved from the crowded ballroom, she visited the dining-room, the library, peeped into his own room, which she never condescended to enter; all in vain. Mr. Wyndham was nowhere to be seen.

"It is very strange!" said Mrs. Wyndham to herself, knitting her black brow—always her habit when annoyed. "It is most extraordinary conduct! I think he might show a little more attention to his guests."

The library windows opened on the velvet lawn, and were opened now to their widest extent, to admit the cool night air. She stepped out into the pale starlit night, her

rich ruby velvet dress and starry diamonds glowing dimly
in the luminous darkness.   As she walked across the lawn,
glad to be alone for a moment, a figure all in white flew
past her with a rush, but not before she had recognized
the frightened face of Laura Blair.

"Laura!" she said, "is it you? What is the matter?"

Laura stopped, and passed her hands over her beating
heart.

"I have had such a scare! I came out of the conservatory five minutes ago, on to the lawn to get cool, when
I saw a figure that had been standing under the trees dart
behind one of them, as if to hide.   The person seemed to
have been watching the house, and was trying to hide from
me. It frightened me, and I ran."

Olive Wyndham was physically as brave as a man:
she never screamed, or ran, or went into hysterics, from
palpable terror. Now, she drew Laura's arm within her
own, and turned in the direction that young lady had
come.

"You little goose," she said, "it was some of the people here, out to get cool like yourself. We will go and
see who they are."

"I don't believe it is any of the people here. I think
it was a woman in a long cloak, with the hood over her
head. Oh, I had rather not go!"

"Nonsense! it was some of the servants, or some curious, inquisitive straggler, come to——"

She stopped, for Laura had made a warning gesture,
and whispered, "Look there!" Olive looked. Directly
opposite the house, and shrinking behind a clump of cedar
trees, on the edge of a thickly-wooded portion of the
grounds, she could see a figure indistinctly in the star-
light—the figure of a female it looked, wearing, as Laura
said, a long cloak, with the hood drawn over the head and
shrouding the face. They were in deep shadow themselves, and Laura hid her white dress behind some laurel
bushes. Olive's curiosity was excited by the steadfast
manner in which the shrouded figure watched the house
—through those large, lighted windows, Olive knew the

person could distinctly see into the drawing-room, if not distinguish the people there.

"Laura," she whispered, "I must find out who that is. I can get round without being seen—you remain and wait for me here."

Keeping in the shadow, Olive skirted the lawn and round the cedar clump, without being seen or heard by the watcher. She glided behind the stunted trees; but though she was almost near enough to touch the singular apparition, she could not see its face, it was so shrouded by the cowl-like hood. While she stood waiting for it to turn round, a man crossed the lawn hurriedly, excitedly, and, with a suppressed exclamation, clasped the cloaked figure in his arms. Olive hardly repressed a cry—the man was her husband, Paul Wyndham!

"My darling!" she heard him say, in a voice she never forgot—a voice so full of infinite love and tenderness, that it thrilled to her very heart—"my darling, why have you done this? I have been searching for you everywhere since I heard you were here. My love! my love! how could you be so rash?"

"I was so lonely, Paul, without you!" a woman's voice answered—a voice that had a strangely-familiar sound, and Olive saw the cloaked figure clinging to him, trustingly. "I was so lonely, and I wanted to see them all. But I am very cold now, and I want to go home!"

"I shall take you home at once, my darling! Your carriage is waiting at the gate. Come, I know a path through this wood that will lead us out—it will not do to go down the avenue. Oh, my dearest! never be so rash again! You might have been seen."

They were gone; disappearing into the black cedar woods, like two dark specters, and Olive Wyndham came out from her place of concealment, and stood an instant or two like one who has been stunned by a blow. Laura Blair rose up at her approach with a startled face, and saw that she was ghastly white.

"Olly!" Laura said, in a scared voice, "wasn't that Mr. Wyndham who went away with—with—that person?"

Olive Wyndham turned suddenly upon her, and grasped her arm, with a violence that made Laura cry out with pain.

"Laura Blair!" she cried, with passionate fierceness in her voice, "if ever you say a word of what you have seen to-night, I will kill you!"

With which remark, Mrs. Wyndham walked away, stepped through the library window, and into the house. She was in the drawing-room when poor Laura ventured in, sitting at the piano, enchanting her guests with some new and popular music, but with a face that had blanched to a sickly white. She might play, she might talk, she might laugh and dance, but she could not banish that frozen look from her face; and her friends, looking at her, inquired anxiously if she was ill; no, she said she was not ill; but she had been out in the grounds a short time before, and had got chilled—that was all.

Half an hour later, Mr. Wyndham re-appeared in the drawing-room, with a calm face that hid his secret guilt well. Some of the people were already beginning to depart, and his absence was unknown to all save two. Once he spoke to his wife, remarking on her paleness, and telling her she had fatigued herself dancing; and she had laughed strangely and answered, yes, it had been a delightful evening all through, and she had never enjoyed herself so much. And then she was animatedly bidding the last of her guests good-night, and the lights were fled, the garlands dead, and the banquet-hall deserted. And Paul Wyndham bade her good night, and left her alone in her velvet robes and diamond necklace, and splendid misery, and never dreamed that he was found out.

Mr. and Mrs. Wyndham did not meet again until Sunday. The next day, Friday, the young author had gone over to Rosebush Cottage with his MSS. and fishing-rod, and there spent the rest of the week. The dissipation at Redmon, the constant round of dressing, and visiting, and party-giving, knocked him up, he told Val Blake, and unfitted him for work; and, at the cottage, he could recruit, and smoke, and get on with his writing.

Speckport saw Mrs. Wyndham driving, and riding, and

promenading through its streets, that day and the next, beautifully dressed and looking beautiful, but Speckport never once dreamed of the devouring jealousy that had eaten its way to her inmost heart, and must hitherto be added to her other tortures. Yes, Olive Wyndham was jealous, with the fierce jealousy of such natures as hers— and your dark women can be jealous of your fair women with a vengeance. And as real jealousy without love is simply an impossibility, the slow truth broke upon Olive Wyndham that she had grown to love her husband.

How it had come about, Heaven only knows; she had honestly done her best to hate him. But that mischievous little blind god, flying his arrows at random, had shot one straight to her haughty heart. This, then, was the secret of all her anxiety and watchfulness, though she had never suspected it—she might have been a long time in suspecting it, but for the discovery made in the grounds that night. She loved him who would never love her. She knew him indifferent to herself; but while she thought him equally indifferent to every one else, she had not cared much; but now, but now! Who was this woman who had stepped between her and the man to whom she was married?

Who was she? who was she? she asked herself the miserable question a hundred times a minute—she could think of nothing else—but she never could answer it. In all Speckport she could not fix upon any one she knew Paul Wyndham was likely to address such words as she had heard to. How their memory thrilled her—those tones so full of passionate love—it made her grind her teeth to think of them.

"If I had her here, whoever she is," she thought, "I could tear the eyes out of her head, and send her back to him streaming blood! Oh, who can she be? who can she be?"

It was Catty Clowrie who first changed the course of her ideas, and set her off at a new tangent. Catty was sewing at the villa; and, as Mrs. Wyndham, in her miserable restlessness, wandered from room to room, she came at last to a pleasant vine-grown glass porch at the back of the house, where Miss Clowrie sat stitching away in the afternoon sunshine. An open book lay beside her, as if she had just been reading, and Olive saw it was Mr. Wyndham's volume of travels. She took it up with a strange contradictory feeling of tenderness for the insensate thing.

"How do you like it?" she asked, looking at his portrait in front, the deep, thoughtful eyes gazing back at her from the engraving, with the same inscrutable look she knew so well.

"I think it is lovely," said Catty. "I wish I could finish it, but I must get on with my work. Mr. Wyndham must be wonderfully clever; his descriptions set the places before you as if you saw them."

Olive sat down, and began talking to this girl, whom she instinctively disliked, about her husband and her husband's books. Catty, snapping off her thread, asked at last:

"Mr. Wyndham is not at home to-day, is he? I haven't seen him."

"No," said his wife, carelessly, "he has gone over to Rosebush Cottage."

Miss Clowrie gave an unpleasant little laugh.

"Of course he is at Rosebush Cottage! Every one knows Mr. Wyndham never goes anywhere else! If he had a Fair Rosamond shut up there, he could not be fonder of going there. Mr. Wyndham must be very much attached to his mother."

There was a long blank pause after her cruel speech, during which the mistress of Redmon never took the book from before her face. She felt that she was deadly pale, and had sense enough left not to wish Catty Clowrie to see it. She rose up presently, throwing the book on the ground as she did so, and walked out of the porch with such fierce rebellious bitterness in her heart, as never at her worst of misery had she felt before. A Fair Rosamond! Yes, the secret was out! and what a blind fool she must have been not to have seen it before! It was no sickly old mother Paul Wyndham had shut up in Rosebush Cottage, but a fair inamorata. It was she, too, whom they had seen in the grounds the previous night; she who,

wearied of her pretty prison without him, and full of curiosity, doubtless, had come to Redmon. "I was so lonely
without you, Paul!"—she remembered the sweet and
strangely-familiar voice that had said those words, and the
tender caress which had answered them; and she sank
down in her jealous rage and despair in her own room,
hating herself and all the world. Oh, my poor Olive!
Surely retribution had overtaken you, surely judgment
had fallen upon you even in this life, for your sins of ambition and pride!

Mrs. Wyndham was not much of a church-goer, but
rather the reverse. She had a heathenish way of lolling
in her boudoir Sundays, and listening with a dreamy sensuous pleasure to the clashing of bells, and falling asleep
when they ceased, and awakening to read novels until
dinner-time.

But sometimes she went to the fashionable Episcopal
church, and yawned in the face of the Rev. Augustus
Tod, expounding the word rather drawlingly in his white
surplice, and sometimes she went to the cathedral with
Laura Blair. She took the same sensuous, dreamy pleasure
in going there that she did in listening to the bells, or in
reading Owen Meredith's poetry. She liked to watch the
purple, and violet, and ruby, and amber glows from the
stained-glass windows on the heads of the faithful; she
liked to listen to the grand solemn music of the old church,
to inhale the floating incense, and listen to the chanting
of the robed priests. And best of all she liked to see the
Sisters of Charity glide noiselessly in through some side-
door, with vailed faces and bowed heads, and to weave
romances about them all the time high mass was going on.
Matter-of-fact Catholics about her wondered why Mrs.
Wyndham stared so at the Sisters, and it is probable the
Sisters themselves would have laughed good-naturedly had
they known of the tale of romance with which the dark-
eyed heiress invested them. But it was not to look at the
nuns—though she did look at them, almost wishing she
were one too, and at rest from the great world-strife—it
was not to look at them she had come to the cathedral to-
day, but to listen to a celebrated preacher somewhere from

16

the United States. Laura had told her he was a Jesuit—those terrible Jesuits!—and Olive had almost as much curiosity to see a Jesuit as a nun. So she drove to the cathedral in her carriage, and sat in Mr. Blair's cushioned pew, and watched the people filling the large building, and listened to the grand, solemn strains of the organ touched by the masterly hand; and all listlessly enough. But suddenly her heart gave a quick plunge, and all listlessness was gone. There, coming up the aisle, behind the sexton, was a gentleman and a lady; a gentleman whose step she would have known the wide world over, and a lady she was more desirous of seeing than any other being on earth. It was Mr. Wyndham and his mother, and dozens of heads turned in surprise and curiosity, to look at that hitherto invisible mother. But she was invisible still, at least her face was, for the long black crape vail she wore was so impenetrably thick, no human eyes could pierce it. They saw she was tall and very slender, although she wore a great double black woolen shawl that would have made the slightest girlish form look clumsy and stout. She bent forward slightly as she walked, but the stoop was not the stoop of age—Olive Wyndham saw that. Mr. Wyndham, hat in hand, his mother hanging on his arm, his pale face gravely reverent, entered the pew the sexton indicated, after his mother.

It was directly in front of Mr. Blair's, facing the grand altar, and the jealous wife had an excellent chance of watching her husband and his companion.

Paul Wyndham was not a Catholic—he did not pretend to be anything in particular, a favorite creed with his countrymen, I think—but he was a gentleman; so he rose and sat and knelt as the worshipers about him did, and never once turned his back to the altar to stare at the choir.

Mrs. Wyndham, Senior, made no attempt to raise her vail during the whole service. She knelt most of the time with her face lying on the front rail of the pew, as if in prayer—a good deal to the surprise of those who saw her and imagined her not of their faith.

Olive never took her eyes off her—the Sisters of

Charity, the swinging censers, the mitred bishop, the robed priests, the solemn ceremonies, the swelling music, were all unheard and unseen—that woman in front absorbed every sense she possessed. Even when the Jesuit mounted to the pulpit, she only gave him one glance, and saw that he was tall and thin and sallow, and not a bit oily and Jesuit-like, and returned to her watching of Mr. Wyndham's mother. That lady seemed to pay attention to the sermon, if her daughter-in-law did not, and a very impressive sermon it was, and one Olive Wyndham would have done well to heed. He took for his text that solemn warning of our Lord, "What will it avail a man to gain the whole world and lose his own soul?" and the hearts of his hearers thrilled within them with wholesome fear as they listened to the discourse which followed. "You are here to-day, but you may be gone to-morrow. O my brethren!" the sonorous voice, which rang from aisle to aisle, like the trump of the last angel, cried; "the riches you are laboring so hard to amass you may never enjoy. The riches for which you toil by day and by night mean nothing if your poor span of existence permits you to accomplish them. Stop and think, oh, worldlings, while time remains. Work while it is yet day, for the night is at hand, and work for the glory which shall last for eternity. The road over which you are walking leads nowhere, but ends abruptly in the yawning grave. The fame for which you suffer and struggle and give up ease and rest, will be when over but a hollow sound, heard for one poor, pitiful moment, ere your ears are stilled in death, and your laurel crown dust and ashes. The great of this world—who made kings their puppets, and the nations of the earth their toys—have lived their brief space and are gone, and what avails them now the glory and the greatness they won? The fame of Shakespeare, of Alexander, of Napoleon of France, of a Byron, and a Milton, and all other great men—great in this life—remains to posterity, but what availed it all to them at the judgment-seat of God. There, at that awful tribunal, where we all must stand, nothing but their good works—if they ever did good works—could soften the rigor of Divine Justice.

The world is like an express-train, rushing madly on, with
a fathomless precipice at the end ; and you laugh and sing
on your way to it, consoling yourself with the thought,
'At the last moment I will repent, and all will be well.'
But the Divine Justice has answered you beforehand—
terribly answered you—'You shall seek me and you shall
not find me, and you shall die in your sins!'"

The sermon was a very long one, and a very terrible
one, likely to stir the dead souls of the most hardened sin-
ner there. It was noticeable that Mr. Wyndham's mother
never lifted her head all the time, but that it lay on the
pew-rail, and that she was as immovable as a figure carved
in ebony. Olive Wyndham had to listen, and her cheek
blanched as she did so. Was this sermon preached for
her? Was she bartering her immortal soul for dross, so
soon to be taken from her? And then a wild terror took
possession of her, and she dared think no longer. She
could have put her fingers to her ears to shut out the
inexorable voice, thundering awfully to her conscience:
"You shall seek me and you shall not find me, and you
shall die in your sins." There was a dead silence of
dumb fear in the cathedral when the eloquent preacher
descended, and very devout were the hearers until the
conclusion of mass. Then they poured out, a good deal
more subdued than when they had entered, and Olive had
to go with the rest. Mr. Wyndham and his mother
showed no sign of stirring, nor did they leave their pew
until the last straggler of the congregation was gone. The
carriage from Rosebush Cottage was waiting outside the
gates, and Mr. Wyndham assisted his mother in, and they
drove off.

Olive dined at Mr. Blair's that day, and heard them
discussing the sermon, and the unexpected appearance of
Mr. Wyndham and his mother. Olive said very little—
the panic in her soul had not ceased. The shortness of
time, the length of eternity—that terrible eternity!—had
never been brought so vividly before her before. Was
the express-train in which she was flying through life near
the end—near that awful chasm where all was blackness
and horror? Human things frittered away—earthly

troubles, gigantic before, looked puny and insignificant seen in the light of eternity—so soon to begin, never to end! She had been awakened—she never could sleep again the blind, heathenish sleep that had been hers all her life, or woe to her if she could.

Mr. Blake and Miss Blair walked home with her in the hazy September moonlight. They found Mr. Wyndham sitting in one of the basket-chairs in the glass porch, looking up at the moon as seen through the smoke of his cigar, and Olive's inconsistent heart throbbed as if it would break from its prison and fly to him. Oh, if all this miserable acting could end; if he would only love her, and let her love him, she would yield forever the wealth that had never brought her happiness, and be his true and loving wife from henceforth, and try and atone for the sins of the past. She might be a good woman yet, if her life could only be simple and true like other women, and all this miserable secresy at an end. But, though the silken skirt of her rich robe touched him, they could not have been further apart if the wide world divided them. She could have laid her head down on the table there, and wept passionate, scalding tears, so utterly forlorn and wretched and lonely and unloved did she feel. She could not talk—something rose in her throat and choked her—but she listened to Mr. Wyndham telling in his quiet voice how he had persuaded his mother to go out that day to hear the famous preacher, and how he thought it had done her good.

Val and Laura did not stay long, but set out on their moonlit homeward way. Ann Nettleby sat in her own doorway, and Val paused to speak to her.

"No news of Cherrie, yet, Ann?"

Ann made the usual reply, "No," and they walked on, talking of lost Cherrie.

"I'll find her out yet," Mr. Blake said, determinedly. "I don't despair, even though—well, what's the matter?"

Laura had uttered an exclamation, and clung suddenly to his arm. Redmon road was lonely, as you know, and not a creature was to be seen; but Laura was pointing to where, under the trees, in the moonlight, a woman was standing still. A woman or a spirit, which? For it was robed in white from head to foot, and a shower of pale hair drifted over its shoulders. The face turned toward them as they approached, a face as white as the dress, and Laura Blair uttered a loud shriek as she saw it, reeled and would have fallen, had not Val caught her in his arms.

Val had turned white himself, for the pale shadow under the trees had worn the dead face of Nathalie Marsh! As Laura shrieked it had vanished, in a ghostly manner enough, among the trees, and Val Blake was left standing gaping in the middle of Redmon road, holding a fainting lady in his arms.

CHAPTER XXXI.

VAL'S DISCOVERY.

MR. BLAKE was in a predicament. Some men there are who would by no means turn aghast at being obliged to hold a fair, fainting damsel in their arms, but Mr. Blake was none of these. Should he lay her down on the road while he went for help, or should he carry her to the Nettleby Cottage? Yes, that was the idea; and Mr. Blake lifted the fair fainted in his stalwart arms, and bore her off like a man. The cottage was very near, and Mr. Blake was big and strong; but for all that he was in a very red and panting state when he gave a thundering knock at the cottage-door. One hundred and twenty pounds of female loveliness is no joke to carry, even for a short distance; and he leaned Miss Blair up against the door-post in such a way that she nearly toppled over on Miss Ann Nettleby's head, when that young lady opened the door. Ann screamed at the sight, but Mr. Blake pushed past her with very little ceremony.

"She's only fainted, Ann! Don't make a howling. Get some water, or hartshorn, or something, and bring her to."

Miss Ann Nettleby was a young lady of considerable presence of mind, and immediately began to apply restoratives. Whether it was that nature was coming round of her own accord, or from the intrinsic merit of burnt feathers held under her nose, and cold water doused in her face, Miss Blair, with a long, shivering sigh, consented at last to come to, and looked around her with a blank, bewildered stare.

"Well, Laura," said Val, stooping over her, "how do you find yourself, now?"

At the sound of his voice, recollection seemed to flash vividly across Laura's mind. She was lying on the couch in the front room; but she started up with a scream, her eyes dilating, and, to Mr. Blake's dismay, flung herself into his arms.

"Oh, Val!" she cried, clinging wildly to him, "the ghost! the ghost! I saw the ghost of Nathalie Marsh."

Ann Nettleby's eyes grew as round as saucers.

"The ghost of Nathalie Marsh!" she repeated. "Lor! Miss Laura, you haven't seen her ghost, have you?"

"Come, Laura, don't be frightened," said Val, soothingly, though sorely perplexed himself. "There is no ghost here, at all events. Perhaps you had better go back to Redmon, and stay with Mrs. Wyndham all night."

But Laura, gasping and hysterical, protested she would not venture out that night again for all the world, and ended the declaration by falling back on the lounge in a violent fit of hysterics. Val seized his hat and made for the door.

"You look after her, Ann," he said, "and I'll run up to Redmon for Mrs. Wyndham. She'll die before morning if she keeps on like this."

Mr. Blake's long limbs never measured off the ground so rapidly before, as they did now the distance between the cottage and the villa. In the whole course of his

life, Val Blake had never received such a staggerer as he
had this night. He did not believe in ghosts; he was as
devoid of imagination as a pig; he had not eaten a heavy
supper, nor drank, one single glass of wine, yet he had
seen the ghost of Nathalie Marsh! They had not been
talking of the dead girl; they had not been thinking of
her; yet she had stood before them, wearing the face,
and looking at them out of the blue eyes they knew so
well. It was all very fine to talk of the freaks of the
sense of vision, of optical illusions, and all that sort of
thing. It was no illusion, optical or otherwise. Nathalie Marsh was dead and buried, and they had seen her
ghost on Redmon Road.

The servant who answered Mr. Blake's ring looked
rather surprised, but showed him into the library, and
went in search of his mistress. Olive came in, wearing
the dress in which they had left her, and Val told his
story with blunt straightforwardness. Olive's black eyes
opened to their widest extent.

"Seen a ghost! My dear Mr. Blake, do I understand
you aright?"

Mr. Blake gave one of his nods.

"Yes. It was a ghost, and it frightened Laura into a
fit; and she's in one still, down there at Nettleby's. It
was a ghost, I'll take my oath of it; for it had Nathalie
Marsh's face, and Nathalie Marsh is dead and buried."

There was a slight noise at the door. Olive Wynd-
nam's quick ear recognized it, and she turned round.
Mr. Blake followed her eyes, and saw Paul Wyndham
standing in the doorway. But what ailed him? His face
was always pale; but it looked ghastly at this moment, turning from its natural hue to an awful ashen
white.

"Hallo, Wyndham!" cried Val, "what's gone wrong
with you? You look as if you had seen a ghost yourself."

"There is nothing the matter with me," said Mr.
Wyndham, coming quietly forward. "What is that
about ghosts, and where have you left Miss Blair?"

"At Nettleby's, fit to die of fright. We saw a

woman who has been dead for more than a year, on the road; and Laura screamed out, and dropped down like a stone!"

"My dear Blake!"

"I wanted her to come up here," pursued Val, "and stay all night, but she went off into strong hysterics in the middle of what I was saying; so I left her with Ann Nettleby, and came up here for Mrs. Wyndham."

"I will go to her at once," Olive said, ringing the bell; "but, Mr. Blake, I don't understand this at all. Seen a ghost! It is incomprehensible!"

"Just so!" said Mr. Blake, with constitutional composure, "but it's true, for all that. Nathalie Marsh is dead, and buried over there in the cemetery; but, for all that, I saw her as plainly this night on Redmon road as ever I saw her in my life!"

There was something in Mr. Blake's manner that carried conviction with it, and Mr. Blake was not the man to tell a cock-and-bull story, or let himself be easily deceived. Had Laura Blair, a fanciful and romantic girl, alone told the story, every one would have laughed incredulously, but Val Blake was another story. Matter-of-fact Val had no fancies, natural or supernatural, and told his story with a resolute air of conviction now that perplexed his hearers. Mr. Wyndham affected to laugh; but, somehow, the laugh was mirthless, and his face and lips remained strangely colorless.

"It was some one playing a practical joke, depend upon it," he said; "perhaps that imp of mischief, Sam's brother. As to ghosts—why, Blake, where have your wits gone to?"

"All right," said Val; "I don't ask you to believe it, you know; but if it wasn't Nathalie Marsh's spirit, then it was Nathalie Marsh in the flesh, and we have all been deceived, and the woman buried in Speckport cemetery is not the woman I took her to be."

Paul Wyndham turned round suddenly, and walked to the window and looked out. He turned round so suddenly that neither his wife nor his friend saw the awful change that came over his face when these words were

10*

said. A servant brought Mrs. Wyndham her hat and shawl, and he did not turn round again until they were leaving the room. Olive's heart stood still at sight of the white change in his face.

"You are ill, Mr. Wyndham," she said, looking at him sharply and wistfully.

"You're as pale as a ghost," said Mr. Blake; "don't come with us—what's the matter?"

Mr. Wyndham gave them his former answer, "Nothing," and watched them walking down the moonlit avenue together, until they were out of sight. Then he left the room, put on his hat and overcoat, locked his own door, and dropped the key in his pocket, and followed them. Half an hour later, while Olive and Val were persuading Laura to come with them to Redmon, he was knocking at the door of Rosebush Cottage, and being admitted by Midge, whose ruddy face wore a look of blanched consternation at sight of him.

Mr. Val Blake walked home in the moonlight alone. As he passed the spot where, under the tree, the ghostly-white figure with the hazy hair and deathlike face had stood, he felt a cold thrill in spite of himself; but the spot was vacant now—not a soul, in the flesh or out of it, was to be seen on Redmon road. Mr. Blake, as I said, walked home in the moonlight alone, and astounded the whole Blair family by the unearthly tidings. For good Mrs. Blake's sake he omitted that part concerning Laura's fainting-fits—merely saying she was frightened, and he had thought it best to leave her at Redmon. Mrs. Blair turned pale, Master Bill grinned, and Mr. Blair pooh-poohed the story incredulously.

"A ghost! What nonsense, Blake! I always thought you a sensible man before; but if you draw the long bow like that, I shall have to change my opinion."

"Very well," said Val, in nowise disturbed at having his veracity doubted, "seeing's believing! You may think what you please, and so shall I!"

Before it took its breakfast next morning, Speckport had heard the story—the astounding story—that the ghost of Nathalie Marsh had appeared to Mr. Blake and Miss

Blair on Redmon road, and had frightened the young lady nearly to death. Speckport relished the story amazingly—it was nothing more than they had expected. How could that poor suicide be supposed to rest easy in her grave! Mrs. Marsh, over her eternal novels, heard it, and cried a little, and wondered how Mr. Blake could say such cruel things on purpose to worry her. Captain Cavendish heard it, and laughed incredulously in Mr. Blake's face.

"Why, Val," he cried, "are you going loony, or getting German, or taken to eating cold pork before going to bed? Cold pork might account for it, but nothing else could ever excuse you for telling such a raw-head-and-bloody-bones story as that, and expecting sensible people to believe it. As to Laura, any gatepost or white birch tree in the moonlight would pass for a ghost with her."

Mr. Blake was entirely too much of a philosopher to waste his time in controversy with these unbelievers. He knew well enough it was no gatepost or white birch he had seen, but the subject was full of mystery and perplexity, and he was glad to let it drop. It could not be Nathalie Marsh; he had seen her dead and buried; and ghosts were opposed to reason and common sense, and all the beliefs of his life. It was better to let the subject drop then; so he only whistled when people laughed at him, or cross-questioned him, and told them if they didn't believe him the less they said about it the better.

But the strange story was not so soon to die out. Mr. Blake, about a fortnight after, was suddenly and unexpectedly confirmed. The ghost of Nathalie Marsh had been seen again—this time in Speckport Cemetery, kneeling beside her own grave; and the person who saw it had fled away, shrieking and falling in a fit at the sexton's door. It was the sexton's nephew, a lad of fifteen or thereabouts, who, going at nightfall to close the cemetery gates, had seen some one kneeling on one of the graves. This being nothing unusual, the boy had gone over, to desire the person to leave, when, to his horror, it slowly turned round its face—the face of one buried there a twelvemonth before. With an unearthly yell, the boy turned tail and fled, and had been raving delirious ever since. The alarmed sexton had gone out to prove the truth of the incoherent story, but had found the cemetery deserted, and no earthly or unearthly visitant near the grave of the doomed girl.

Here was a staggerer for Speckport! People began to look blankly at each other, and took a sudden aversion to being out after nightfall. The "Snorter" and the "Bellower" and the "Puffer" reluctantly recorded this new marvel, confirming, as it did, the truth of Mr. Blake's story; but opined some evil person was playing off a practical joke, and hinted to the police to be on the look-out, and pin the ghost the first opportunity. It was the talk of the whole town—the boy was dangerously ill, and young ladies grew nervous and hysterical, and would not stay a moment in the dark, for untold gold. Laura Blair was worst of all; she was hysterical to the last degree, and shrieked if a door shut loudly, and fell into hysterics if they left her alone an instant night or day. Olive Wyndham's dark face paled with terror as she listened. Was the dead and defrauded heiress rising from her grave because her earthly wrongs would not let her rest there? Would she appear to her next?

Was it superstitious fear that had taken all the color —and he never at best had much to spare—out of Paul Wyndham's face, and left him the ghost of his former self. The servants at Redmon could have told you how little he ate, and perhaps that accounted for his growing as thin as a shadow. A dark look of settled gloom overshadowed his pale face always now. He spent more of his time than ever at his mother's cottage, and when asked what was the matter—was he ill?—he answered no, but his mother was. Why, then, did he not have medical advice, sympathizers asked; and Mr. Wyndham replied that his mother declined—she was very peculiar, and positively refused. What did he suppose was the matter with her? and Mr. Wyndham had told them it was her nervous system—she was hypochondriacal—in fact; and he made the admission very reluctantly, and with a pain-

ful quivering about the mouth—she was not quite herself—her mind had lost its balance. And the sympathizers going their way, informed other sympathizers that
all old Mrs. Wyndham's oddities were accounted for—the
woman was mad!

Speckport pitied poor Mr. Wyndham, saddled with
an insane mother, very much, when they saw his pale,
worn face, and that gloomy look that never left it. Olive
pitied him, too; and would have given the world, had it
been hers to give, to comfort him in his great trouble;
but she was nothing to him, and her heart turned to gall
and bitterness, as she thought of it. No, she was nothing
to him, she scarcely ever saw him at all now, and he
seemed unconscious of her presence when they were together. But it was a relief to know the secret of Rosebush Cottage—however dreadful that secret was, it were
better than the first diabolical thought suggested by Catty
Clowrie. Once Olive Wyndham, in the humility born of
this new love, had descended from the heights of high and
mightydom on which she dwelt, and ate humble pie at
her cold lord's feet. She might have left the unsavory
dish alone—her humility was no more to him than her
pride, and she had been repulsed. Not rudely, or un-
kindly. Mr. Wyndham was a gentleman, every inch of
him, and would not be harsh to a woman; but still she
was repulsed, and her proud heart quivered to its inmost
core with the degradation.

She had found him, one evening on entering the
library, sitting alone there, his forehead bowed on his
hand, a look that was so like despair on his face; but she
forgot everything but that she loved him, and that he was
suffering a sorrow too great for words to tell. Had she
not a right to love him, to comfort him—was she not his
wife? She would not listen to her woman's nature,
which revolted, and ordered her sternly back. She only
knew that she loved him; and she went over and touched
him lightly on the shoulder. It was the first time they had
ever so met—therefore the look of surprise which came
into his eyes when he looked up, was natural enough. He

rose up, looking with that quiet air of surprise on the downcast eyes and flushed face, and waited silently.

"Mr. Wyndham," she said, her voice trembling so, her words were scarcely intelligible. "I—I am sorry to see you in such trouble? Can—can I do anything to alleviate it?"

"Thank you!" he said, "No!"

"If," still tremulously, "if I could do anything for your mother—visit her——"

She broke down entirely. In Mr. Wyndham's face there was nothing but cold surprise.

"You are very good," he said, "but you can do nothing."

He bowed and left the room. And Olive, humbled, repulsed, mortified to death, hating, for the moment, herself and him and all the world, flung herself upon a sofa, and wept such a scalding rush of tears, as only those proud, sensitive hearts can ever shed. They might have been tears of blood, so torn and wounded was the poor heart from whence they sprang; and when they dried, and she rose up, they had left her like a stone.

Between Nathalie Marsh's ghost and Mr. Wyndham's mad mother, Speckport was kept so busy talking, it had scarcely time to canvas the movement, when Captain George Cavendish announced his intention of selling out and going home. Mr. Blake was the only one, with the exception of some milk-and-water young ladies who were in love with the dashing Englisher, whom the announcement bothered; and it was not for the captain's sake, but for poor lost Cherrie's. Where was Cherrie? Val had vowed a vow to find her out, but this turn of affairs knocked all his plans in the head.

"If he does go," said Val to himself, "I'll send him off with a flea in his ear! I must find Cherrie, or Charley Marsh will be an exile forever!"

"But how?" Mr. Blake was at his wit's end thinking the matter over, and trying to hit on some plan. He was still thinking about it, when he sallied off to the post-office for his papers and letters, and encountered Mr. Johnston, the captain's man, coming out with a handful of letters. He was sorting them as he walked, and never noticed that he dropped one as he passed Mr. Blake. Val picked it up to return it, glancing carelessly at the superscription as he did so. His glance was magical—a red flush crimsoned his sallow face, and he turned it over to look at the postmark. Then he saw Mr. Johnston had missed it, and was turning round—he dropped it again, and walked on, and the captain's valet pounced upon it and walked off.

Blake strode straight to his boarding-house, informed Mr. Blair sudden business required him to go up the country for a week or so, scrawled off a note to his foreman, flung a few things into a valise, and started for the cars. He was just in time to take a through ticket to S——, before the evening train started, and was whirled off in the amber haze of a brilliant September sunset.

It was past midnight when the train reached the terminus, but Mr. Blake was not going to stop at S——. The steamer which started at eight next morning for Charlottetown, Prince Edward's Island, lay at the wharf, and Mr. Blake went on board immediately, and turned in. When the boat started next morning, he was strolling about the deck, smoking a pipe and watching the passengers come on board. There were not many, and he knew none of them, which was just what he wanted. It was a long, delightful day on the Gulf; and in the yellow glory of another sunset, Mr. Blake landed in Charlottetown, and, valise in hand, sauntered up to one of the principal hotels.

Mr. Blake took his tea, and then set off for a ramble through the town. A quiet town, with grass-grown red-clay streets, and only a few stragglers abroad. A beautiful town, with a few quiet shops, and a drowsiness pervading the air, and a general stillness and torpor pervading everywhere. Val retired early; but he arose early also, and was out with his hands in his pocket and a cigar in his mouth, wandering about again, staring at the Government House and the Colonial Buildings, and the fly-specked books in the stationers' shops, and the deserted drygoods'-stores, and going into the cathedral where morn-

ing-service was going on, and contemplating the pretty
nuns of Notre Dame reading their missals with devoutly
downcast eyes, in their pew. He was out again the moment he had swallowed his breakfast and made a few inquiries of the clerk, traversing the town-streets once more.
These inquiries of his were concerning a lady, a young
lady, he told the polite clerk, a friend of his whom he was
most anxious to find out, but whose precise residence he
was ignorant of. He was pretty certain she was in Charlottetown, but he could not exactly tell where. Perhaps
the clerk had seen her—a black-eyed young lady with black
curls and red cheeks, and not tall? No!—the clerk did
not remember ; he had seen a good many black-eyed young
ladies in his time, but he did not know that he had seen
this particular one. Mr. Blake pursued these inquiries in
other places,—chiefly in drygoods' or milliners' stores, and
in one of these latter, the lady in attendance informed
him that she knew such a person, a young lady, a Miss
Smith, she believed, who used to shop there, and generally
walked by every afternoon.

Mr. Blake never went home to dinner that day. It
was a hot, sunshiny day, and he lounged about the milli-
ner's shop, attracting a good deal of curiosity, and suspicion
that he might have designs on the bonnets. But Val did
not care for their suspicions ; he was looking out for some
one he felt sure would be along presently, if she were living and well. The watch was a very long one, but he
kept it patiently, and about three in the afternoon he met
with his reward. There, swinging along the street, with
the old jaunty step he remembered so well, was a black-
eyed, black-ringleted young lady, turban on head, parasol
in hand. Mr. Blake bounced up, walked forward, and
accosted her with the simple remark—sublime in its simplicity—"How are you, Cherrie?"

CHAPTER XXXII.

CHERRIE TELLS THE TRUTH.

T was a fortunate thing, perhaps, that that quiet, grass-grown Charlotte Street was almost deserted; else the scream and recoil with which Cherrie—our old and long-lost-sight-of friend, Cherrie—received this salutation, might have attracted unpleasant attention.

Mr. Blake took the matter with constitutional phlegm.

"Oh, come now, Cherrie, no hysterics! How have you been all these everlasting ages?"

"Mis-ter Blake?" Cherrie gasped, her eyes starting in her head with the surprise. "Oh, my goodness! What a turn you gave me!"

"Did I?" said Val. "Then I'll give you another; for I want you to turn back with me, and take me to wherever you live, Mrs. Smith. That's the name you go by here, isn't it?"

"Who told you so?"

"A little bird! I say, Cherrie, you've lost your red cheeks! Doesn't Prince Edward's Island agree with you?"

Cherrie had lost her bright bloom of color; but save that she was much thinner and paler, and far less gaudily dressed, she was the same Cherrie of old.

"Agree with me!" exclaimed Cherrie, in rather a loudly-resentful tone, considering that they were on the street. "I hate the place, and I am nearly moped to death in it. I never was so miserable in all my life as I have been since I came here!"

"Then why didn't you leave it?" inquired Mr. Blake.

"Leave it!" reiterated Cherrie, like an angry echo. "It's very easy to say leave it; but when you have no money or nothing, it's not quite so easy doing it. I've been used shamefully; and if ever I get back to Speckport, I'll let some of the folks there know it, too! Did he send you?"

"Who?"

"You know well enough! Captain Cavendish!"

"He send me!" said Val. "I should think not. There isn't a soul in Speckport knows whether you are alive or dead; and he takes care they shan't, either. I have been trying to find you out ever since you left; and I have asked Captain Cavendish scores of times, but he always vowed he knew nothing about you—that you had run off after Charley Marsh. It was only by chance I saw a letter from you to him the other day, posted here, and I started off in a trice. Why didn't you write to your folks, Cherrie?"

"I daren't. He wouldn't let me. He told me, if I didn't stay here and keep quiet, he never would have anything more to say to me. I have been shamefully used!" —and here Cherrie began to cry on the street—"and I wish I was dead. There!"

"Perhaps you will before long," said Val, significantly.

Cherrie looked at him.

"What?"

"Perhaps you won't be let live long! You'll have to stand your trial when you go back, for helping in the murder of Mrs. Leroy; and maybe they'll hang you! Now, don't go screaming out and making such an infernal row on the street—will you?"

Cherrie did not scream. She suppressed a rising cry, and turned ashen white.

"I had nothing to do with the murder of Mrs. Leroy," she said, with lips that trembled. "You know I hadn't. You know I left Speckport the afternoon it happened. You have no business saying such things to me, Val Blake."

She laid her hand on her heart while she spoke, as if to still its clamor. Val saw by her white and parted lips how that poor, fluttering, frightened heart was throbbing.

"Oh, yes; I know you left Speckport that afternoon, Cherrie; but you and Cavendish had it all made up beforehand. You were to write Charley that note, and appoint

a meeting in Redmon grounds, promising to run away
with him, and making him wait for you there, while Cavendish got in through the window, and robbed the old
woman. You never intended meeting Charley, you know;
and you are just as much accessory to the murder as if
you had stood by and held the lamp while he was choking Lady Leroy."

They had left the dull streets of the town, and were
out in a lovely country road. Swelling meadows of golden
grain and scented hay spread away on either hand, until
they melted into the azure arch; and the long, dusty road
wound its way under pleasant, shadowy trees, without a
living creature to be seen. Cherrie, listening to these
terrible words, spoken in the same tone Mr. Blake would
have used had he been informing her the day was uncommonly fine, sank down on a green hillock by the roadside,
and, covering her face with her hands, broke out in a
passion of tempestuous tears. He had taken her so by
surprise—he had given her no time to prepare—the sight
of him had brought back the recollection of the old pleasant days, and the wretched dullness of the present. She
was weak, and sick, and neglected, and miserable; and
now this last turn was coming to crush her. Poor Cherrie
sat there and cried the bitterest tears she had ever shed in
her life; her whole frame shaking with her convulsive
sobs. Her distress touched Val; for pretty Cherrie had
always been a favorite of his, despite her glaring faults
and folly; and a twinge of remorse smote his conscience
at what he had done.

"Oh, now, Cherrie, don't cry! People will be coming
along, and what will they think? Come, get up, like a
good girl, and we'll talk it over when we get to your house.
Perhaps it may not be so bad after all."

Cherrie looked up at him with piteous reproach
through her tears.

"Was it for this you wanted to find me out so bad,
Mr. Blake? Was it to make me a prisoner you came over
here?"

"Well," said Val, with another twinge of conscience,
"ye-e-es, it was partly. But you must recollect, Cherrie,

you have done worse. You let Charley Marsh—poor Charley! who loved you a thousand times better than that scamp of an Englishman—be sentenced for a deed he never committed, when you could have told the truth and freed him. Worse still, you helped to inveigle him into as horrible a plot as ever was concocted."

"I couldn't help it!" sobbed Cherrie. "I didn't want to do it, but he made me! I wish I had ran away with Charley that night. He never would have left me like this!"

"No; that he wouldn't! Charley was as true as steel, poor fellow! and loved you as no one ever will love you again, in this world! He is a soldier now, fighting down South; and perhaps he's shot before this; and if he is, his death lies at your door, Cherrie."

Cherrie's tears flowed faster than ever.

"As for Cavendish," went on Val, "he's the greatest villain unhung! Not to speak of his other atrocities—his gambling, his robbing, his murdering, his breaking the heart of Nathalie Marsh—he has been the biggest rascal that ever lived, to you, my poor Cherrie."

"Yes, he has!" wept Cherrie, all her wrongs bleeding afresh. "He's a villain, and I hate him. Oh dear me, I wish I was dead!"

"You don't know half the wrong he has done you and means to do," said Val. "Come, Cherrie, get up, and I'll tell you about it as we go along. Do you live far from this?"

"No; it's the first house you meet; the dullest old place on the face of the earth! He wouldn't let me leave it; and I know they despise me, and think I'm no better than I ought to be. There never was a girl in this world so ill-used as I have been! Why did he marry me, if he is ashamed of me? Why can't he stay with me as he ought to stay with his wife?"

"His wife!" repeated Val, staring at her as they walked along. "Why, Cherrie, is that all you know about it? Hasn't he told you that you are not his wife?"

"Not his wife!" shrieked Cherrie. "Val Blake, what do you mean?"

"Bless my soul!" cried Mr. Blake, appealing in dismay to the scarecrows in the fields, "I thought he had told her. Why, you unfortunate Cherrie, don't you know the marriage was a sham one?"

Cherrie gasped for breath. The surprise struck her speechless.

"I thought you knew all about it!" said Val; "I'll take my oath I did! Why, you poor little simpleton, how could you ever be idiot enough to think a fellow like Cavendish would marry the like of you! If you had two grains of sense in your head," said Mr. Blake, politely, "you must have seen through it. He planned the whole thing himself—a sham from beginning to end!"

"It isn't! it can't be! I don't believe it! I won't believe it!" panted Cherrie, recovering her breath. "You helped him, and the minister was there; and I am his wife, his lawful wedded wife. You are only trying to frighten me to death."

"No, I'm not," said Val; "and you're no more his wife than I am. The minister wasn't a minister, but a fellow who played the part. If you hadn't been the greatest goose that ever lived, Cherrie, you couldn't have been so taken in!"

Cherrie's breath went and came, and her tears seemed turned to sparks of fire, as she turned her eyes upon her companion.

"And you helped him to do this, Mr. Blake?"

"Well, Cherrie, what could I do? If I hadn't helped him, some one else would; and, anyhow, you would have run away with him, marriage or no marriage. Now, don't deny it—you know you would!"

"And you mean to say I'm not married to Captain Cavendish?"

"Yes, I do. I only wonder he hasn't let you find it out long ago. He came to me and persuaded me to help him, telling me you were ready to run off with him any time he asked you, which I knew myself. I'm sorry for it now, but it can't be helped."

"Very well, Mr. Blake," said Cherrie, whose cheeks were red, and whose eyes were flashing, "you may both

be proud of your work. You are fine gentlemen, both of
you, to distress a poor girl like me, as you have done. But
I'll go back to Speckport, and I'll tell every soul in it how
I have been taken in; and I hope they'll tar and feather
the two of you for what you have done."

"Well," said Mr. Blake, in a subdued tone, "we deserve it, I dare say, but Cavendish is the worst after all.
Why, Cherrie, my girl, you don't know half the wrong he
has done you. He would have been married three months
ago, if the lady had not changed her mind and married
another man."

"Would he?" said Cherrie, vindictively, between her
closed teeth. "Oh, if ever I get a chance, won't I pay
him off! Who was the lady?"

"The new heiress of Redmon—Miss Henderson she
was then, Mrs. Wyndham she is now. He was crazy about
her, as all Speckport can tell you; and he asked her to
marry him; and she consented first, and backed out afterward. You never saw any one in the state he was in,
Cherrie; and he started off to Canada, because he couldn't
bear to stay in the place and see her married to another
man."

"But he's back, now," said Cherrie. "I had a letter
from him two weeks ago, with a couple of pounds in it.
He's the meanest, stingiest miser on the face of the earth,
and I have to write and write, before I get enough from
him to pay my board. I haven't had a decent dress these
six months; and I can't leave the place, because I never
have enough to pay my way back. I'm the worst-treated
and most unfortunate creature in the whole world!"

And here poor Cherrie's tears broke out afresh.

"And that's not the worst, either," pursued Mr. Blake.
"Do you know what has brought him back to Speckport,
as you say? Of course, you don't—you are the last he
would tell; but it is because he is selling out of the army,
and going back to England for good. He wants to be rid
of you entirely; and once he is there, and married to some
one else with a fortune, many a fine laugh he will have at
you."

"Never!" cried Cherrie, wrought up to the right pitch

of indignation; "never shall he leave Speckport, if I can
help it! I'll tell all, if I was to hang for it myself, sooner
than let him get off like that, the villain!"

"But you won't hang for it, Cherrie, if you tell; it's
only if you refuse to tell, that you are in danger. Whoever turns Queen's evidence gets off scot free, you know;
and if you only do what is right, and take my advice,
which means the same thing, you may triumph over Captain George Percy Cavendish yet."

"I'll do it!" said Cherrie, her lips compressed and her
eyes flashing, and the memory of all her wrongs surging
back upon her at once. "I'll do it, and be revenged on
the greatest scoundrel that ever called himself a gentleman! But, mind, Val Blake, I must be sure that this is
all true—I must be sure that I am not his wife."

"It will be very easy convincing you of that, once you
are back in Speckport. You shall hear it from his own
lips, without his knowing you are listening. Oh, is this
the place?"

For Cherrie had stopped before a little farmhouse,
garnished with a potato garden in front, and adorned with
numerous pigsties on either hand. She led the way to
the front room of the establishment; which was carpetless,
and curtainless, and unfurnished, and impoverished-look-
ing enough.

"Well," Val said, "this is rather different, Cherrie,
from the days when you used to dress in silks and sport
gold chains, and do nothing but flirt, and be petted and
made love to from week's-end to week's-end. But never
mind—the worst's over, now that I've found you out, and
you'll have good times yet in Speckport."

"If it hadn't been for you," sobbed Cherrie, "it
never would have happened. I hate you, Mr. Blake!
There!"

"Now, Cherrie, you know right well you would have
run away with Captain Cavendish that time, married or
not married. Oh! you may deny it, and perhaps you
think so now; but I know better. But he's the greatest
rascal that ever went unhung, to use you as he has; and

if you had the spirit of a turnip, you would be revenged.'

"I will !" cried Cherrie, clenching her little fist resolutely; "I will! I'll let him see I'm not the dirt under his feet! I've stood it long enough! I'll stand it no longer!"

Mr. Blake's eyes sparkled at the spirited declaration.

"That's my brave Cherrie! I always knew you were spunky! You shall hear from his own lips the avowal of his false marriage, and then you will go before a magistrate and swear to all you know about that night of the robbery and murder. There is a steamer to leave Charlottetown to-morrow, at nine. Will you be ready if I drive up here for you ?"

"Yes," said Cherrie; "I haven't so much to pack, goodness knows! and I'm sick and tired of this place. How's all our folks ? It's time to ask."

"They are all well, and will be very glad to get pretty Cherrie back again. Speckport's been a dull place since you left it. Cheer up, Cherrie! There's bright days in store for you yet."

Cherrie did not reply, and she did not look very hopeful. She was crying quietly; and Val's heart was touched as he looked at the pale, tear-stained face, and thought how bright and pretty and rosy and smiling it used to be. He bent over her, and—well, I shouldn't like Miss Blair to know it—but Mr. Blake deliberately kissed her!

"Keep up a good heart, little Cherrie; it will be all right yet, and we'll fix the flint of Captain G. P. Cavendish. I'll drive up here for you at eight to-morrow. Be all ready. Good-bye."

Cherrie was all ready and waiting at the gate, next morning, when Mr. Blake drove up through the slanting morning sunlight, dressed in her best. She was in considerably better spirits than on the previous day, and much more like the Cherrie of other days, glad to get home and eager for the journey. The lady passengers, during the day, asked her if "the tall gentleman" was her husband. That gentleman had a great deal to tell her; of poor Nathalie's death, and Charley's flight; of the new heiress,

who had turned so many heads, and had given the worst
turn of all to Captain Cavendish; of that gentleman's despair when she married Mr. Wyndham; of the changes
and gay doings at Redmon; and lastly, of Nathalie's ghost.
This last rather scared Cherrie. What if Nathalie should
appear to her—to her, who had wronged her so deeply
through her brother.

"Oh, no!" said Mr. Blake, to whom she imparted her
fears; "I don't think she will, if you tell the truth; or,
at all events, she will be a most unreasonable ghost if she
does. You tell all, Cherrie, and Charley will come back
to Speckport; and by that time you'll have got your red
checks back again, and who knows what may happen?"

Mr. Blake whistled as he threw out this artful insinua
tion; but Cherrie caught at it eagerly, and her face lit up.
Charley's handsome visage rose before her—blue-eyed,
fair-haired Charley—who had always loved her, and never
would have treated her as Captain Cavendish had done.
Who knew what might happen! Who, indeed!

"I'll tell the whole truth," said Cherrie, aloud. "I'll
tell everything, Mr. Blake, when I'm once sure I'm not
Captain Cavendish's real wife. I know I did wrong to
treat poor Charley as I did; but I will do all I can now
to make up for it."

They reached S—— at dark, and remained there all
night and the following morning. They might have gone
down to Speckport in the eight P.M. train; but Val preferred to remain for the two A.M., for reasons of his own.

"If we land in Speckport at noon, Cherrie," he said,
"we may be seen and recognized. We will go down in
the afternoon and get there about nine, when it will be
dark, and you can pass unnoticed. I don't want Captain
Cavendish to find out you are there, until I am ready."

So Cherrie, thickly vailed, took her place in the car,
after dinner; and was whirled through the pleasant country, with its fields and forests and villages, toward good
old Speckport—that dull, foggy town that her heart had
grown sick with longing many a time to see.

There were no lamps lit in the streets of Speckport
that night. When the waning September moon shone

17

out in such brilliance, surrounded by such a crowd of stars as persuaded one to believe all the constellations were flaming at once, gas became superfluous, and the city fathers spared it. The vailed lady was handed out by Mr. Blake; a proceeding which considerably excited the curiosity of some of Mr. Blake's friends, loafing around the platform.

" Blake can't have got married up the country, can he ?" drawled out Lieutenant the Honorable L. H. Blank to young McGregor. " Who's the woman ?"

" Blessed if I know," replied Alick.

Val hurried his charge into a cab, sprang in after her, and gave the order, " Wasson's Hotel."

" It's a new place, and not much patronized," he explained to Cherrie. " You won't be recognized there; and I'll tell them to fetch you your meals up to your room. And to-morrow, Cherrie, I want you to come round to my office at about eleven. Come in the back way off Brunswick street, you know; so you won't have to pass through the outer office, and be recognized by Clowrie and Gilcase, and the rest of 'em. I'll be waiting for you; and if Cavendish doesn't drop in, which he does to kill time about that hour every day, I'll send for him, and you'll hear his confession without being seen."

Mr. Blake walked home that night, chuckling inwardly all the way.

" I said I would pay you off, Cavendish," he soliloquized, " for leading Charley Marsh astray, and cutting up those other little cantrips of yours; and I think the time has come at last—I really think, my dear boy, the time has come !"

It was some time after ten when Mr. Blake presented himself at Mr. Blair's, and found the family about retiring for the night. Laura was not at home, she was up at Redmon—Laura's mamma said—stopping with Mrs. Wyndham, who seemed to be very unhappy.

" What was she unhappy about ?" Mr. Blake inquired. But Mrs. Blair only sighed, and shook her head, and hinted darkly about hasty marriages.

" Eh ?" said Val, " Wyndham doesn't thrash her, does

he ? She's big and buxom, and he's only a little fellow; and I think, on the whole, she would be a match for him in a free fight !"

Mr. Blair laughed, but Mrs. Blair looked displeased.

"My dear Mr. Blake, how can you say such things? Mr. and Mrs. Wyndham are not a happy couple, that is clear ; but whose is the fault I cannot undertake to say. He is greatly changed of late. I suppose he worries about his mother."

"Oh, his mother! Has anybody seen that most mysterious lady yet ?"

"Not that I am aware of ! He has not even called in medical advice."

"And the ghost," said Val, lighting his bedroom-lamp, "has it been figuranting since ?"

"No," said Mr. Blair; "the ghost hasn't showed since you left. I say, Blake, did you settle your country-business satisfactorily ?"

"Very !" replied Mr. Blake, with emphasis. "I never settled any business more to my satisfaction in the whole course of my life !"

Mr. Blake was in his office bright and early next morning, hard at work. At about eleven he descended the stairs, and opened the back door, which fronted on a dull little street, through which a closely-vailed female figure was daintily picking her way. Val admitted the lady, and ran before her up-stairs.

"Up to time, Cherrie, there's nothing like it ! I sent Bill Blair round to Cavendish's rooms to tell him to look in before twelve, and I expect them back every moment. By Jove! there's his voice outside now. Get in here quick, and sit down ! There's a crack in the partition, through which you can see and hear. Not a chirp out of you, now. Come in !"

Mr. Blake raised his voice ; and in answer, the door opened, and Captain Cavendish, smoking a cigar, lounged in. Val gave one glance at the buttoned door of the little closet in which he had hidden Cherrie, and nodded familiarly to his visitor.

"Good-morning, captain ! find a chair. Oh, pitch

the books on the floor—they're of no account. I'm to notice them all favorably in the 'Spouter'—the author sent a five-dollar bill for me to do it!"

"Young Blair said you wanted to see me," remarked the captain, tilting back his chair, and looking inquiringly through his cigar-smoke.

"Why, so I did. I heard before I went up the country a rumor that you were going to leave us—going to leave the army, in fact, and return to England. Is it so?"

"Yes. I'm confoundedly tired of Speckport, and this from-hand-to-mouth life. It is time I retired on my fortune, and I am going to do it."

"How?"

"Well, I mean to return home—run down to Cumberland, and saddle myself on my old uncle. He was always fond of me as a boy, and I know is yet, in spite of his new wife and heir. Perhaps I may drop into a good thing there—heiresses are plenty."

"I should think you had got your heart-scald of that," said Val, grinning. "You bait your hook for heiresses often enough, but the gold-fish don't seem to bite."

Captain Cavendish colored and frowned.

"All heiresses are not Miss Hendersons," he said, with a cold sneer. "I might know what to look for from your Bluenose and Quaker tradesmen's daughters. I shall marry an English lady—one whose father did not make his money selling butter or hawking fish."

"Oh, come now, Cavendish! You have been in love in Speckport. Don't deny it!"

"I do deny it," said the captain, coldly.

"Nonsense! You were in love with Nathalie Marsh."

"Never! Azure-eyed and fair-haired wax dolls never were any more to my taste than boiled chicken! I never cared a jot for Nathalie Marsh."

"Well, you did for Olive Henderson—you can't deny that! She is not of the boiled chicken order, and all Speckport knows you were mad about her."

"Speckport knows more than its prayers. I did admire Miss Henderson—I don't deny it; but she had the temper of the old devil, and I am glad I escaped her!"

"And Cherrie—have you quite forgotten Cherrie? You were spooney enough about her."

"Bah!" said Captain Cavendish, with infinite contempt; "don't sicken me by talking of Cherrie! I had almost forgotten there ever was such a little fool in existence!"

"And you never cared for Cherrie, either?"

Captain Cavendish broke into a laugh.

"You know how I cared for her. The woman a man can marry is another thing altogether!"

"Some far higher up in the world than Captain Cavendish have stooped to fall in love and marry girls as poor as Cherrie. You never could, I suppose?"

"Never! The idea is absurd! I wouldn't marry a girl like Cherrie if she had the beauty of the Venus de Medicis!"

"Did you ever undeceive Cherrie about that marriage affair? Did you let her know she was not your wife?"

"Not I," said Captain Cavendish, coolly. "I never took so much trouble about her! I was heartily sick of her before a week!"

"Well, it seems hard," said Val. "Poor little thing! She was very fond of you, too."

"Stuff! She was as fond of me as she was, or would be, of any other decently good-looking man. She was ready to run off with any one who asked her, whether it were I, or young Marsh, or any of the rest. I know what Cherrie was made of."

"And so she thinks she is still your wife?"

"I don't know what she thinks!" exclaimed the young officer, impatiently; "and what's more, I don't care! What do you talk to me of Cherrie Nettleby for? I tell you I know nothing about her!"

"And I tell you I don't believe it," said Val. "You have her hid away somewhere, Cavendish; and if you are an honorable man, you will tell her the truth, and provide for her before you leave Speckport."

Captain Cavendish might have flown into a rage with any other man, but he only burst into a loud laugh at Val.

"Tell her the truth and provide for her! Why, you blessed innocent, do you suppose Cherrie, wherever she is, has been constant to me all this time? I tell you I know nothing of her, and care nothing! Make your mind easy, old fellow! the girl is off with somebody else long before this! What's that?"

Captain Cavendish looked toward the buttoned door of the closet. There had been a strange sound, between a gasp and a cry, but Mr. Blake took no notice.

"It's only the rats! So you will leave Speckport, and do nothing for Cherrie? Cavendish, I am sorry I ever had a hand in that night's work!"

"Too late now, my dear boy!" laughed the Englishman. "Make your mind easy about Cherrie! She's just the girl can take care of herself! If ever she comes back to Speckport, give her my regards!"

He pulled out his watch, still laughing, and arose to go.

"Half-past eleven—I have an engagement at twelve, and must be off. By-by, Blake! don't fret about Cherrie!"

Mr. Blake did not reply, and his face was very grave as he shut and locked the door after his visitor.

"You're a greater villain, Captain Cavendish," he said to himself, "than even I took you to be! Come out, Cherrie—have you heard enough?"

Yes, she had heard enough! She was crouching on the floor, her hands clenched, her eyes flashing. She leaped up like a little tigress as he opened the door.

"Take me to a magistrate!" she cried. "Let me tell all I know! I'll hang him! I'll hang him, if I can!"

"Sit down, Cherrie," said Val, "and compose yourself. It won't do to go in such a gale as this before the authorities. Tell me first. By that time you will be settled!"

An hour afterward, Mr. Blake left his office by the back-door, accompanied by the vailed lady. Cherrie had told all.

CHAPTER XXXIII.

OVERTAKEN.

MR. BLAKE had made little notes of Cherrie's discourse, and had the whole story arranged in straightforward and business-like shape, for the proper authorities. He did not lead his fair companion straight to those authorities, as she vindictively desired, but back to her hotel.

"I think I'll hand over the case to Darcy, Cherrie," he said; "and he is out of town, and won't be back till to-morrow afternoon. There's no hurry—Cavendish won't leave Speckport yet awhile. We'll wait until to-morrow, Cherrie.

Cherrie had to obey orders; and passed the time watching the passers-by under her window. There were plenty of passers-by, for the window fronted on Queen Street, and Cherrie knew almost every one. It was hard sometimes to hide behind the curtain instead of throwing open the casement and hailing those old friends who brought back so vividly the happy days when she had been the little black-eyed belle, and Captain Cavendish was unknown. It seemed only like yesterday since she had tripped down that sunlit street, in glittering silk, with all the men bowing, and smiling, and tipping their hats jocosely to her; only yesterday since the good-looking young drygoods clerks vaulted airily over the counters to do her bidding. And now, and now! She never could be what she had been again. And to this man, this false and treacherous Englishman, for whom she had sacrificed noble-hearted Charley Marsh, she owed it all. She set her teeth vindictively, and clenched her little fist at the thought.

"But I'll pay him for it! I'll teach him to despise me! I only hope they may hang him—the villain! Hard labor for life would not be half punishment enough for him!"

They talk of presentiments! Surely, there never was such a thing, else why had George Cavendish no dim foreshadowing of the doom darkening so rapidly around him. He had told Val Blake he had an engagement. So he had; it was in Prince Street, with Mr. Tom Oaks, who had returned to Speckport, and who was going the road to ruin faster than any victim Captain Cavendish had ever in hand before. It was growing dusk when they left the gambling-hell; and Mr. Oaks was poorer and Captain Cavendish richer by several hundred pounds than when they entered. The gorgeous coloring of the sunset yet flared in the sky, though the crimson and amber were flecked with sinister black. Captain Cavendish drew out a gold hunting-watch, and looked at the hour. "Past six," he said, carelessly; "I shall be late at Redmon, I fear. The hour is seven, I believe. Do you drive there this evening?"

"No," said Mr. Oaks, with a black scowl, "I hope my legs will be palsied if ever they cross the threshold of that woman! I'm not a hound, to fawn on people who kick me!"

Captain Cavendish only smiled—he rarely lost his temper—and went off to his hotel, whistling an opera air. He passed under Cherrie's window; but no prescience of the flashing black eyes above troubled the serenity of his mind. He was walking steadily to his fate, as we all walk—blindly, unconsciously.

Captain Cavendish was the last to arrive at Redmon —all the other guests were assembled in the drawing-room when he entered, and they had been discussing him and his departure for the last quarter of an hour.

The dinner party at Redmon was a very pleasant one; and every one, except, perhaps, the stately hostess herself, was very gay and animated. Mr. Wyndham, despite the trouble he was in about his poor mad mother, was the most entertaining and agreeable of hosts. The ladies, when they flocked back to the drawing-room, enthusiastically pronounced Mr. Wyndham "a perfect love!" and declared they quite envied Mrs. Wyndham a husband who could tell such charming stories, and who was so de

lightfully clever and talented. And Olive Wyndham
smiled, and sat down at the piano to do her share of the
entertaining, with that dreary pain at her beating and rebellious heart that never seemed to leave it now. Yes, it
was a very pleasant evening; and Captain Cavendish
found it so, and lingered strangely, talking to his hostess
after all the rest had gone. Lieutenant the Honorable L.
H. Blank, who was waiting for him on the graveled drive
outside, grew savage as he pulled out his watch and saw
it wanted only a quarter of twelve.

"Confound the fellow!" he muttered, "does he mean
to stay all night talking to Mrs. Wyndham, and I am
sleepy. Oh, here he is at last! I say, Cavendish, what
the dickens kept you?"

Captain Cavendish laughed, as he vaulted into his
saddle.

"What's your hurry, my dear fellow? I was talking
to Mrs. Wyndham, and common politeness forbade my
cutting the conversation short."

"Common bosh! Mrs. Wyndham was yawning in
your face, I dare say! My belief is, Cavendish, you are
as much in love with that black-eyed goddess now as
ever."

"Pooh! it was only a flirtation all through; and I
would as soon flirt with a married lady any day as a
single one. She looked superb to-night, did not she, in
that dress that flashed as she walked—was it pink or
white—and that ivy crown on her head?"

"She always looks superb! I should like to fetch
such a wife as that back to old England. A coronet
would sit well on that stately head."

A strangely-bitter regret for what he had lost smote
the heart of Captain Cavendish. It might have been.
He might have brought that black-eyed divinity as his
wife to England, but for Paul Wyndham. Why had
she preferred that man to him?

"I wonder if she loves him?" he said aloud.

"Who?—her husband? Do you know, Cavendish,
she puzzles me there. She treats him with fearfully
frigid politeness, but she never ceases to watch him. If

17*

he were any kind of man but the kind he is, I should say she was jealous of him. He is a capital fellow, anyhow, and I like him immensely."

They rode through the iron gates as he spoke, which clanged noisily behind them. The night was not very bright, for the moon struggled through ragged piles of black cloud, and only glimmered with a wan and pallid light on the earth. The trees loomed up black against the clear sky, and cast vivid and unearthly shadows across the dusty road. A sighing wind moaned fitfully through the wood, and the trees surged and groaned, and rocked to and fro restlessly. It was a spectral night enough, and the young lieutenant shivered in the fitful blast.

"I feel as if I had taken a shower-bath of ice-water," he said. "Wasn't it somewhere near here that Val Blake saw the ghost? Good Heavens! What's that?"

As he spoke, there suddenly came forth from the shadow of the tree, as if it took shape from the blackness, a figure—a woman's figure, with long disordered fair hair, and a face white as snow. Captain Cavendish gave an awful cry as he saw it; the cry startled his horse— only a half-tamed thing at best—and, with a loud neigh, it started off like an arrow from a bow. The horse of Lieutenant Blank, either taking this as a challenge, or frightened by the sudden appearance of the woman, pricked up its ears and fled after, with a velocity that nearly unseated his rider. The lieutenant overtook his companion as they clattered through the streets of the town, and the face of Captain Cavendish was livid.

"For Heaven's sake, Cavendish!" cried the young man, "what was that? What was that we saw?"

"It was Nathalie Marsh!" Captain Cavendish said, in an awful voice. "Don't speak to me, Blank! I am going mad!"

He looked as if he was, as he galloped furiously out of sight, waking the sleeping townsfolk with the thunder of his horse's hoofs. He had heard the story of the ghost, and had laughed at it, with the rest; but he had heard it in broad daylight, and the most timid of us can laugh at ghost-stories then. He had not been thinking

of her, and he had seen her—he had seen her at midnight
—true ghostly hour—on the lonesome Redmon road,
with her death-white face and streaming hair! He had
seen her—he had seen the ghost of Nathalie Marsh!

Mr. Johnston, the sleepy valet, sitting up for his master, recoiled in terror as that master crossed the threshold
of the room. Captain Cavendish only stared vaguely as
the man spoke to him, and strode by him and into his
room, with an unearthly glare in his eyes and the horrible
lividness of death in his face. Mr. Johnston stood appalled
outside the door, wondering if his master had committed
a murder on the way home—nothing less could excuse his
looking like that. Once, half an hour after, Captain Cavendish opened his door, still "looking like that," and
ordered brandy, in a voice that did not sound like his own;
and Mr. Johnston brought it, and got the door slammed
in his face afterward.

The usually peaceful slumbers of Mr. Johnston were
very much disturbed that night by this extraordinary conduct on the part of his master. He lost at least three
hours' sleep perplexing himself about it, for never since he
had had the honor of being the captain's man, had that
gentleman behaved so singularly, or exhibited so ghastly
and deathlike a face. When, in the early watches of the
morning, he presented himself at his master's door with
towels and water, it was in a state of mingled curiosity
and terror; but he found there was no call for the latter
emotion. Beyond looking uncommonly pale and hollow-
eyed (sure tokens of a sleepless night), Captain Cavendish
was perfectly himself again; and whether this was owing
to the brandy he had drank or the exhilarating effect of
the morning sunshine, Mr. Johnston could not tell, but he
was inclined to set it down to the brandy. Even the paleness and hollow-eyedness was not noticeable after he had
shaved and dressed, and partaken of his breakfast, and
sauntered out, swinging his cane and smoking his cigar,
to kill thought in the bustling streets of the town. Val
Blake, standing in his office-door, hailed him as he
passed.

"How are you, Cavendish? Heavenly morning,

isn't it? Have you any particular engagement for this afternoon?"

"This afternoon? What hour?"

"Oh, about three. You must postpone your engagements to accommodate me."

"I have none so early. I dine with the mess at six. What is it?"

"A little surprise that I have in store for you. Drop into Darcy's office about five, and we'll give you a little surprise!"

"A little surprise! Of what nature, pray?"

"Honor bright!" said Val, turning to run up-stairs. "I won't tell. Will you come?"

"Oh, certainly! It will kill time as well as anything else."

He sauntered on unsuspiciously, never dreaming he was sealing his own fate. Val Blake had no compunctions about entrapping him. He was so artful a villain he must be taken by surprise, or he might baffle them yet.

"So slippery an eel," argued Mr. Blake to himself, "must not be handled with gloves. He may as well walk into Darcy's office himself, as be brought there by a couple of police-officers."

Captain Cavendish returned to his hotel early, and avoided all places where he was likely to meet Lieutenant Blank. Of all people, he wanted to shun him from henceforth; of all subjects, he never wanted to speak of the terrible fright he had received the previous night. So he returned to his rooms, and smoked and read, and wrote letters, and dined at two, and as the town clock was striking five, he was opening the door of Mr. Darcy's office. And still no presentiment of what was so near dawned darkly upon him; no weird foreboding thrilled in nameless dread through his breast; no dim and gloomy shadowing of the awful retribution overtaking him so fast, made his step falter or his heart beat faster as he opened that door. Perhaps it is only to good men that their angel-guardians whisper in that "still small voice" those mystic warnings, that tell us poor pilotless mariners on the sea of life of the shoals and quicksands ahead. Perhaps

it is only men like this man, whose souls are stone-blind,
that cannot see dimly the hidden shipwreck at hand. He
saw nothing, felt nothing; he walked in carelessly, and saw
Mr. Darcy, old Squire Tod, and Mr. Blake, sitting close
together and talking earnestly. He wondered why they
all looked so grave, and why two constables, who had
been looking out of a window, should place themselves
one on each side of the door, as if on guard, as he came in.
He wondered, but nothing more. Mr. Darcy arose very
gravely, very gravely bowed, and presented him with a
chair.

"Good afternoon, gentlemen," he said, indifferently,
"I have dropped in on my way to the mess-room, at the
request of Mr. Blake, who told me there was a surprise in
store for me here."

"There is, sir," replied Mr. Darcy, in a strange tone.
"There is a surprise in there for you, and not a very
pleasant one, either. Mr. Blake was quite right."

Something in his voice chilled Captain Cavendish, for
the first time; but he stared at him haughtily, and pulled
out his gold hunting-watch.

"I dine at six," he said coldly. "It is past five now.
I beg you will let me know what all this means, as fast as
possible. I have no time to spare."

"You will make time for our business, Captain Cavendish; and as for the mess-dinner, I think you must postpone that altogether to-day."

"Sir," cried Captain Cavendish, rising; but Mr. Darcy
returned his gaze stonily.

"Sit down, sir, sit down! The business that rendered
your presence here necessary is of so serious a nature—
so very serious a nature, that all other considerations must
yield before it. You will not go to the mess-dinner, I repeat. I do not think you will ever dine at the mess-table
again."

The face of Captain Cavendish turned ghastly, in spite
of every effort, and he turned with a look of suppressed
fury at Val Blake.

"You traitor!" he said, "you have done this. Your
invitation was only a snare to entrap me."

"Honest men, Captain Cavendish," said Mr. Blake, composedly, "fear no snare, dread no trap. It is only criminals, living in daily dread of detection, who need fear their fellow-men. I preferred you should enter here of your own accord, to being brought here handcuffed by the officials of the law."

Every drop of blood had left the face of the Englishman; but he strove manfully to brave it out.

"I cannot comprehend what you mean by these insults," he said. "Who dare talk to me, an English officer and a gentleman, of handcuffs and crimes?"

"We dare," replied Mr. Darcy. "We, in whom the laws of the land are invested. These laws you have vilely broken, Mr. Cavendish—for I understand you have sold out of the service, and have no longer claim to military rank. In the name of the law, George Cavendish, I arrest you for the willful murder of Jane Leroy!"

It was an utter impossibility for the white face of the man to grow whiter than it had been for the last ten minutes; but at the last words he gave a sort of gasp, and caught at the arms of the chair on which he sat. If they had wanted moral conviction before of his guilt, they wanted it no longer—it was written in every line of his bloodless face, in every quiver of his trembling lips, in every choking gasp of breath he drew. They sat looking at him with solemn faces, but no one spoke. They were waiting for him to recover from the shock, and break the silence. He did break it at last; but in a voice that shook so, the words seemed to fall to pieces in his mouth.

"It is false!" he said, trying to steady his shaky voice. "I deny the charge. Charley Marsh was tried and found guilty long ago. He is the murderer!"

"Charley Marsh is an innocent man—you are the murderer. Your own face is your accuser," said Mr. Darcy. "I never saw guilt betrayed more plainly in all my life. You murdered Jane Leroy—yes, strangled her for her pitiful wealth."

"Who has told you this infernal story?" exclaimed the infuriated captive, glaring upon the lawyer. "Has that d—d scoundrel found——" He stopped suddenly, nearly choking himself with his own words, and the phlegmatic lawyer finished the sentence.

"Found Cherrie?—yes! You see there is no hope for you now. Here, Cherrie, my girl, come out!"

There was a door standing ajar opposite them, that looked as if it led into some inner and smaller office. As the door opened wide, the prisoner caught a glimpse of two men, only a glimpse; for the next moment Cherrie stood before him. The last faint glimmer of hope died out in his breast at sight of her with that vindictive look in her face.

"Oh, you villain!" screamed Cherrie, shaking her fist at him, her black eyes flashing fire. "You mean, lying, deceitful villain! I'll fix you off for the way you have treated me! I'll tell everything—I have told it, and I'll tell it again, and again, and again; and I hope they'll hang you, and I'll go to see you hung with the greatest pleasure, I will!"

Here Cherrie, who had not drawn breath, and was scarlet in the face, had to stop for a second, and Mr. Darcy struck in:

"Hold your tongue, Cherrie! Not another word! Stick to facts—abuse is superfluous. You see, Captain Cavendish, with the evidence of this witness, nothing more is needed but drawing out a warrant for your arrest. She is prepared to swear positively to your guilt."

"I don't doubt it," said Captain Cavendish, with a bitter sneer; "such a creature as she is would swear to anything, I dare say. We all know the character of Cherrie Nettleby."

"Silence, sir!" thundered Mr. Darcy; "you are the very last who should cast a stone at her—you, who have deliberately led her to her ruin!"

"He told me I was his wife," sobbed Cherrie, hysterically, "or I never should have gone. I never knew it was a sham marriage, until Mr. Blake told me so down in Charlottetown. We were married in the Methodist meeting-house, and I thought it was a minister; and Mr. Blake was there, and I thought it was all right! Oh, dear me!" sobbed Cherrie, the hysterics growing alarming; "everybody was in a wicked plot against me, and I was only a poor girl, and not up to them; and I wish I had never been born—so there!"

Squire Tod and Mr. Darcy turned with looks of stern inquiry upon Mr. Blake.

"What does this mean?" asked old Squire Tod. "You never said anything about this, Blake."

"No," said Val, perfectly undisturbed; "I only told you Cherrie had run away with Captain Cavendish."

"That is my irreproachable accuser, you see," said Captain Cavendish, with sneering sarcasm. "What that woman says is true; I did inveigle her into a sham marriage, but Mr. Val Blake managed the whole affair—got the church and the sham clergyman, and deceived that crying fool there fifty times more than I did; for she trusted him!"

Squire Tod's face darkened into a look of stern severity as he turned upon Val.

"Mr. Blake," he said, "I am more astonished and shocked by this than anything I have heard yet. That you should be guilty of so base and unmanly an act—you, whom we all respected and trusted—as to entrap a poor weak-minded child (for she was only a child) to misery and ruin! Shame, shame on you, sir, for such a coward's act!"

Very few people ever suspected Val Blake of dignity. One would have thought he must have shrunk under these stern words, abashed. But he did not—he held his head proudly erect—he rose with the occasion, and was dignified.

"One moment!" he said, "wait one moment, squire, before you condemn me! Gentlemen," he rose up and threw wide the door of the room from which Cherrie had emerged, "gentlemen, please to come out."

Everybody looked, curious and expectant. Cherrie ceased the sobbing to look, and even Captain Cavendish forgot for a moment his supreme peril, in waiting for what was to come next.

Two gentlemen, the Reverend Mr. Drone, of the

Methodist persuasion, and another clerical and white neck-clothed gentleman, came out and stood before the company. Mr. Drone was well known, the other was a stranger, a young man, with rather a dashing air, considering his calling, and a pair of bright, roving dark eyes. Captain Cavendish had only seen him once in his life before, but he recognized him instantaneously.

"You all know Mr. Drone, gentlemen," said Val, "this other is the Reverend Mr. Barrett, of Narraville. Mr. Barrett, it is a year since you were in Speckport, is it not?"

"It is," replied Mr. Barrett, with the air of a witness under cross-examination.

"Will you relate what occurred on the last night of your stay in this town, on the occasion of that visit?"

"With pleasure, sir! I am a minister of the Gospel, gentlemen, as you may see," said Mr. Barrett, bowing to the room, "and a cousin of Mr. Drone's. I had been settled about two years up in Narraville last summer, when I took it into my head to run down here for a week or so on a visit to Mr. Drone. I had known Mr. Blake for years, and had a very high respect for his uprightness and integrity, else I never should have complied with the singular request he made me the day before I left."

"What was the request?" asked Mr. Darcy, on whom a new light was bursting.

"He came to me," said Mr. Barrett, "and having drawn from me a promise of strict secrecy, told me a somewhat singular story. A gentleman of rank and position, an English officer, had fallen in love with a gardener's pretty daughter, a young lady with more beauty than common sense, and wanted to entrap her into a sham marriage. He had intrusted the case to Mr. Blake, whose principles, he imagined, were as loose as his own, and Mr. Blake told me he would inevitably succeed in his diabolical plot if we did not frustrate him. Mr. Blake's proposal was, that I should marry them in reality, while letting him think it was only a mockery of a holy ordinance. He urged the case upon me strongly; he said the

man was a gambler, a libertine, and a fortune-hunter; that
he was striving to win for his wife a most estimable young
lady—Miss Marsh—for her fortune merely; that if he
succeeded, she would be miserable for life, and that this
was the only way to prevent it. He told me the man was
so thoroughly bad, that all compunctions would be thrown
away on him; and at last I consented. To prevent a great
crime, I married them privately in Mr. Drone's church.
Mr. Blake was the witness, and the marriage is inserted in
the register. I told Mr. Drone before I left, and he consented to keep the matter secret until such time as it was
necessary to divulge it. I married George Percy Cavendish and Charlotte Nettleby the night before I left Speckport, and took a copy of the certificate with me; and I
am ready to swear to the validity of the marriage at any
time and in any place. I recognize them both, and that
man and woman are lawfully husband and wife!"

Mr. Barrett bowed and was silent. Poor Cherrie,
with one glad cry, sprang forward and fell on her knees
before Mr. Val Blake, and did him theatrical homage on
the spot. Val lifted her up, and looked in calm triumph
at the baffled Englishman, and saw that that gentleman's
face was purple with furious rage.

"Liar!" he half screamed, glaring with tigerish eyes
as he heard Mr. Barrett, "it is false! You never performed it—I never saw you before!"

"You have forgotten me, I dare say," said Mr. Barrett, politely, "but I had the pleasure of marrying you to
this lady, nevertheless. It is easily proved, and I am prepared to prove it on any occasion."

"You may as well take it easy, Cavendish," said Val.
"Cherrie is your wife fast enough! Don't cry, Cherrie,
it's all right now, and you're Mrs. Cavendish as sure as
Church and State can make you."

"It's a most extraordinary story," said Squire Tod,
"and I hardly know what to say to you, Blake. How
came you to let him get engaged to Miss Henderson,
knowing this?"

"Oh," said Val, carelessly, "Miss Henderson never
cared a snap about him; and then Paul Wyndham came

along and cut him out, just as I was getting ready to tell the story. I meant to make him find Cherrie before he left Speckport, and publish the marriage; only Providence let me find her out myself, to clear the innocent, and bring this man's guilt home. I had to keep Cherrie in the dark, as I never would have got that confession out of her."

"Well," said Mr. Darcy, rising, "it is growing dark, and I think there is no more to be done this evening. Burke, call a cab. Captain Cavendish, you will have to exchange the mess-room for the town-jail to-night."

Captain Cavendish said nothing. His fury had turned to black, bitter sullenness, and his handsome face was disturbed by a savage scowl.

"You, gentlemen, and you, Mrs. Cavendish," said Mr. Darcy, bowing to Cherrie, and smiling slightly, "will hold yourselves in readiness to give evidence at the trial. I think we will have no difficulty in bringing out a clear case of willful murder."

An awful picture came before the mind of the scowling and sullen captain. A gaping crowd in the raw dawn of a cheerless morning, a horrible gallows, the dangling rope, the hangman's hand adjusting it round his neck, the drop, a convulsed figure quivering in the air in ghastly agony, and then—— Great beads of cold sweat broke out on his forehead, and his livid face was contracted by a spasm of mortal agony. Then he saw the two clergymen, Mr. Blake, and Cherrie standing up to go.

"I think I'll take you home, Cherrie," said Val, "I'll get another cab for you! Won't they open their eyes when they see you, though?"

Mr. Blake and Cherrie departed, followed by the two clergymen; and no one spoke to the ghastly-looking man, sitting, guarded by the constable, staring at the floor, with that black, desperate scowl, that so changed his face that his nearest friend would hardly have known it. Cherrie trembled and shrank away as she passed him, and did not breathe freely until she was safely seated in the cab beside Val, and rattling away through the streets on her way home.

Home! how poor Cherrie's heart longed for the peace
of that little cottage where those who loved her, and had
mourned her, dwelt. , She was crying quietly, as she sat
silently away in a corner, thinking what a long, and wretched, and forlorn, and dreary year the last had been, and
what a foolish girl she had been, and how much she owed
to Val Blake.

Mr. Blake did not disturb her reflections; he was
thinking of wronged Charley Marsh, exiled from home,
branded as a felon.

The cab, for which Mr. Darcy had sent one of the constables, drew up at the office door, as Mr. Blake's drove
away; and the prisoner, between the two officials, with
Mr. Darcy following close behind, came down-stairs.

Captain Cavendish had gone down-stairs very quietly
between his two guards, neither speaking nor offering the
slightest resistance; but his eyes were furtively taking in
everything, and the captive's instinct of flight was strong
upon him. One of the constables went forward to open
the cab-door, the other had but a slight grasp of his arm.
The murky darkness, the empty street, favored him.

With the rapidity of lightning, he wheeled round,
struck the constable a blinding blow in the face with his
fist, that forced him to release his hold, and, like a flash,
he sped off, turned sharp round a corner, and was gone!
The whole thing had been the work of two seconds. Before any one among them could quite comprehend he had
really gone, he was entirely out of sight.

The next instant, the still street was in an uproar, the
two constables and Mr. Darcy, shouting for assistance as
they went, started in pursuit. The corner round which
Captain Cavendish had cut, and which they now took, led
to a dirty waterside street, branching off into numerous
wharves, crowded with hogsheads, bales, barrels, and piles
of lumber, affording a secure and handy hiding-place for
any runaway. It was like looking for a needle in a hay-
stack even in daylight; and now, in the thick fog and
darkness, it was the wildest of wildgoose-chases. They
ran from one wharf to another, collecting a crowd about
them wherever they went; and all the time, he for whom

they were searching was quietly watching them in a black
and filthy alley, that cut like a dirty vein of black mud
from that waterside street to the one above.

Drawing his hat far down over his eyes, Captain Cavendish started up the alley, and found himself again in
the street he had left. The cab still stood before the office
door of Mr. Darcy; he gave it one derisive glance as he
strode rapidly along, and struck into another by-street.
If he could only make good his escape; if he could baffle
them yet! Hope sent his heart in mad plunges against
his side—if he could only escape!

Suddenly, a thought flashed upon him—the cars.
There had been a picnic that day, and an excursion-train,
he knew, left at half-past seven to fetch the picnickers
home. If he could only get to the depot in time, he might
stay in hiding about the country until the first hue and
cry was over, then, in disguise, make his way to S——,
and take the steamer for Quebec. He had a large sum of
money about him; he might do it—he might escape yet.

He pulled out his watch as he almost ran along, twenty-
five minutes past seven; only five minutes, and a long
way off still. He fled through the dark streets like a madman, but no one knew him, and reached the depot at last,
panting and breathless. A crowd lingered on the platform, a bell was clanging, and the train was in motion.
Desperation goaded him on; he made a furious leap on
board, and—there was a wild cry of horror from the bystanders, an awful shriek of " O my God!" from a falling
man, and then all was uproar, and confusion, and horror,
and dismay. Whether in his blind haste he had missed
his footing, whether the darkness of the night deceived
him, whether the train was moving faster than he had
supposed, no one ever knew; but he was down, and ground
under the remorseless wheels of the terrible Juggernaut.

The train was stopped, and everybody flocked around
in consternation. Two of the brakemen lifted up something—something that had once been a man, but which
was crushed out of all semblance of humanity now. No
one there recognized him; they had only heard that one
agonized cry wrung from the unbelieving soul in that hor-

rible moment—giving the lie to his whole past life—but
they had heard or knew nothing more Some one brought
a door; and they laid the bloody and mangled mass upon
it, and now raised it reverentially on their shoulders, and
carried it slowly to the nearest house. A cloth was thrown
over the white, staring face, the only part of him, it seemed,
not mangled into jelly; and so they carried him away from
the spot, a dreadful sight, which those who saw never
forgot.

CHAPTER XXXIV.

THE VESPER HYMN.

E was not dead. He was not even insensible.
While they carried him carefully through the
chill, black night, and when they carried him
into the nearest house, and laid him tenderly
on a bed, the large, dark eyes were wide open
and fixed, but neither in death nor unconsciousness.   It
was a hotel they had carried him to; and one of the pretty
chambermaids, who owned a sentimentally-tender heart,
and read a great many novels, cried as she looked at him.

"Poor fellow!" she said, to another pretty chambermaid; "it's such a pity, ain't it—and he so handsome?"

"Who is he, I wonder?" the other chambermaid wanted to know; but no one could tell her.

"He looks like an officer," some one remarked; "I
think I've seen him in the town before, and I'm pretty
sure he's one of the officers."

"The doctor will know, maybe," suggested the land-
lord. "Poor fellow! I'm afraid it's all up with him. I
don't think he can speak."

He had never spoken but that once, when the soul of
the infidel, in that supreme moment of mortal agony, in
spite of the infidel creed of his life, had uttered that awful

invocation—"O my God!" But the power of speech was not gone, nor of hearing; he retained all his senses, and, strangely enough, did not seem to suffer much. He lay quiescent, his dark eyes wide open, and staring vacantly straight ahead, his dark hair, dabbled with blood, falling loose on the pillow and around his bloodless face. They had drawn a white spread over him; and he had a strangely corpse-like look, with his white set face, and marble-like rigidity. But life burned yet in the strained, wide-open eyes.

The doctor came—it was Dr. Leach; and he knew him immediately, and told the gaping and curious bystanders who he was. He was very much shocked, and more shocked still when the white spread was drawn away, and the terrible truth revealed. The eyes of the wounded man followed him as he made his examination, but with no eagerness or hopefulness—only with a dull and awful sort of apathy.

"Do you know me, Captain Cavendish?" Dr. Leach asked, tenderly touching the heavy, dark hair falling over his face.

"Yes. How long—— ?"

He did not finish the sentence, not because he was unable to do it, but that he evidently thought he had finished it, and his eyes never once left the physician's face.

Dr. Leach looked very sadly down-in the dark, inquiring eyes.

"My poor fellow!" he said, "it is hard, I know, and for one so young and so far from all your friends. It is hard to die like this; but it is Heaven's will, and we must submit."

"How long?" repeated the sufferer, as if he had not heard him, and with that steady, inquiring gaze.

"You mean, how long can you last? I am afraid—I am afraid, my poor boy, but a short time; not over three hours at the most."

The dark, searching eyes turned slowly away from his face, and fixed themselves on vacancy as before; but he showed no signs of any emotion whatever. Physical and mental sense of suffering and fearing seemed alike to have forsaken him in this last dreadful honr. He had been a bad man; the life that lay behind him was a shameful record. He had been a gamester, a swindler, a libertine, a robber, and a murderer; and now he was dying in his sins, in a dull stupor, without remorse for the past or fear of the awful future. Dr. Leach stooped over him again, wondering at his unnatural apathy.

"Would you like a clergyman, my poor boy?" he said.

"No!"

"Is there any one you would like to see? Your time is very short, remember."

Captain Cavendish turned to him with something like human interest in his glance, for the first time.

"I should like to see Val Blake," he said, "and Mr. Darcy."

"I'll send for them," said the doctor, going out, and dispatching a couple of messengers in hot haste. "He wants to make his will, I suppose," Dr. Leach thought, as he returned to the bedroom. "Poor fellow; and Val Blake was his friend!"

Dr. Leach had requested one of the messengers to go for the army-surgeon before he came back. He knew the case was utterly hopeless, but still it was better to have the surgeon there. He found his patient lying as he had left him, staring blankly at a lamp flaring on a table under the window, while the slow minutes trailed away, and his short span of life wore away. His last night on earth! Did he think of it as he lay there, never taking his eyes from the lamp-flame, even when the doctor came to his bedside again and held something to his lips.

"My dear," Dr. Leach said, feeling as though he were speaking to a woman, and again stroking back his hair with a tender touch; "hadn't you better see a clergyman? You are dying, you know."

"Did you send for them?" said Captain Cavendish, looking at him.

"For Blake and Darcy? Yes. But will I not send for a clergyman too?"

"No."

"Would you like me to read to you, then? There is a Bible on the table?"

"No."

He sank back into his lethargic indifference once more and looked at the lamp again. Dr. Leach sighed as he sat down beside him, to watch and wait for the coming of the others.

They came at last—Val Blake and Mr. Darcy—knowing all beforehand. Their presence seemed to rouse him. Dr. Leach would have left the room, but the lawyer detained him.

"You may as well stay," he said, "it can make no difference to him now if all the world hears him. It is not his will—it is a confession he has to make."

Mr. Darcy was right. Strangely enough he wanted to do that one act of justice before he went out of life, and he seemed to make an effort to rally, and rouse himself to do it. The doctor gave him a stimulant, for he was perceptibly sinking, and the lawyer sat down to write out the broken sentences of that dying confession. It was not long; but it was long enough to triumphantly vindicate Charley Marsh before any court in the world, and just as it was completed the surgeon came. But a more terrible visitor was there too, before whom they held their breath in mute awe. Death stood terrible and invisible in their midst, and no word was spoken. They stood around the bed, pale and silent, and watched him go out of life with solemn awe at their hearts. There was no frightful death struggles—he died peacefully as a little child, but it was a fearful deathbed for all that. The soul of the unbeliever had gone to be judged. "God be merciful to him!" Dr. Leach had said, and they had all answered, "Amen." They drew the counterpane over the marble face, beautiful in death, and left the room together. All were pale, but the face of Val Blake was ghastly. He leaned against an open window, with a feeling of deadly sickness at his heart. It was all so awful, so suddenly awful; they, poor erring mortals, had judged and condemned him, and now he had gone before the

18

Great Judge of all mankind—and the dark story had ended in the solemn wonder of the winding-sheet.

"Speak nothing but good of the dead," a pitiful old proverb says. "We were friends once," Val Blake thought. "I never want to speak of him again."

The body of the dead man was to be taken to his hotel. The surgeon and Mr. Darcy volunteered to arrange it, and Dr. Leach and Val left. The doctor had his patients to attend to, and Val was going to tell Cherrie. She was his wife and ought to know, and Val remembered how she had loved the dead man once. But that love had died out long ago, under his cruel neglect; and though she cried when she heard the tragic end of the man to whom she had been bound by the mysterious tie of marriage, they were no very passionate tears. And before the Nettleby family had quite learned to comprehend she was a wife they found that Mrs. Cherrie Cavendish was a widow!

Of all the shocks which Speckport had received within the last twenty years, there was none to equal this. Charley Marsh innocent, Captain Cavendish guilty! Cherrie Nettleby come back, his wife, his widow! And still it spread, and "still the wonder grew;" and it was like a play or a sensation novel, and the strange old proverb, "Truth is stranger than fiction," was on the tongues of all the wiseacres in the town.

And while the good people talked and exclaimed and wondered, and told the story over and over and over again to one another, and found it ever new, the dead man lay in his own elegant room in the hotel, and Cherrie, his widow, sat at his bed head, feeling she had become all at once a heroine, and making the most of it.

Among the visitors to that darkened room were Mr. and Mrs. Wyndham, Miss Blair, and Mr. Blake. Olive Wyndham, stately and beautiful as ever, but paler and thinner, and less defiantly bright than of old, stood beside the bed of death, and looked down on the white, beautiful face of the dead man, with a strange, remorseful pang at her heart. How her soul bowed down before the disembodied spirit, and how touching was the marble beauty of that rigid face! If he had been old and ugly, perhaps people would not have felt so sadly pitiful about his dreadful fate; but he was so young and so handsome, that tears came into their eyes, and they forgot he had been a villain in life, and went away shaking their heads and saying, "Poor fellow! Poor fellow! It's such a pity!"

Laura Blair—but Laura was always tender-hearted—cried as she looked at him, and thought how much she had liked him, and what pleasant hours they had spent together, He was very bad, of course, but still—— Laura never could get any further, for the tears came so fast they choked her words.

She actually kissed Cherrie, who cried from sympathy, and Val Blake looked at her with a more tender glance than any one had ever seen in Val's unsentimental eyes before.

The pony-phaeton from Redmon was in waiting at the hotel door. Mr. Wyndham assisted the ladies in, and touched his hat as if in leave-taking.

"Are you not going back?" his wife asked, with strange timidity. She was in the habit now of speaking to him, and always in that strangely-hurried tone so foreign to her character.

"No," Mr. Wyndham said, "not just now. I shall return before dinner."

The carriage drove off. Mr. Wyndham took Val's arm, lit a cigar, and strolled with him down Queen Street. "It's a very sad business!" he said, thoughtfully. "I am sorry for him, poor fellow!—one can't help it; but, after all, I don't know that it is not a merciful deliverance. The public disgrace, the imprisonment, the trial, the sentence, would have been to him far more terrible. There are worse things than death!"

He said the last words with a sudden bitterness that made Val look at him. "It's his mother he is thinking of," said Mr. Blake to himself. "Poor woman, she's mad!"

"And it is really true that he confessed all before he

died?" Mr. Wyndham asked; "and exculpated, beyond
all doubt, Charley Marsh?"

"Yes," said Val; "Charley Marsh is free to return to
Speckport whenever he pleases now. I always knew he
was innocent. I had a letter from him last night, too, in-
closing one to his mother."

"Indeed!" Mr. Wyndham said, with a look of interest. "Is he well? Is he still in the army?"

"Yes; but his time is nearly up, it appears. I shall
write to him to-day, and tell him to come back to us. I
have a note—she called it a note, though it's four sheets
of paper closely written, and she sat up until three this
morning to finish it—from Laura Blair, to inclose to him.
If he is proof against four sheets of entreaty from a lady,
all I can say to him will not avail much."

"Laura is a good little girl," said Mr. Wyndham,
"and very much in earnest about all her friends. You
ought to marry her, Blake."

"Eh!" said Mr. Blake, aghast.

"You ought to marry her," repeated Mr. Wyndham,
as composedly as though he were saying, "You ought to
smoke another cigar." "I am sure you will never come
across one more suited to the purpose, if you live to be as
old as Methuselah's cat!"

"My dear Wyndham," expostulated Mr. Blake, rather
shocked than otherwise, "what are you talking about? I
give you my word I never thought of such a thing in my
life."

"I don't doubt it, in the least; but you know the proverb, 'Better late than never.'"

"Nonsense! What do I want with a wife?"

"A good deal, I should think; if only to save the
trouble of boarding out, and securing some one to darn
your stockings and button your shirt-collar. Have you
never indulged in any vision, O most prosaic of men! of
a quiet domestic fireside, garnished on one side by yourself, with your feet in slippers, and on the other by a do-
cile cat and a Mrs. Blake?"

"Never!" responded Mr. Blake, emphatically.

"Then it's time you did! Your hair's turning gray,

man, and your sister has left you! Come, rouse up, old
fellow, and secure that little prize, Laura Blair, before
some more ardent wooer bears her off, and leaves you in
the lurch."

Mr. Blair stared at him.

" I say, Wyndham, what crotchet have you got in your
head to-day? Marry Laura Blair! What should I marry
her for, more than any one else?"

" Well, for pure innate artlessness, Mr. Blake," he
said, " I'll back you against the world! Why should you
marry Laura Blair, indeed! Why, you overgrown infant,
because you are in love with her! That's why!"

" Am I?" responded Mr. Blake, helplessly. " I didn't
know it. Is she in love with me, too?"

" Ask her," said Mr. Wyndham, still laughing. " Here
we are at the office. Good-morning to you."

" Won't you come in?"

" Not this morning; I am going to Rosebush Cottage."

" Oh," said Val, hesitatingly, for it was an understood thing the subject was very painful, " how is your
mother?"

" She is no better," said Mr. Wyndham, briefly.
" Good-morning!"

Mr. Blake went into his sanctum, and the first thing
he did was to write to Charley and tell him all.

" Come back to Speckport, dear old boy," wrote Val,
" everybody is in a state of remorse, you know, and dying
to see you. Come back for your mother's sake, and we
will give you such a reception as no man has had since the
Prince of Wales, long life to him! visited our town. Come
back, Charley, and cheer us again with the sight of your
honest sonsie face."

It took some time for Speckport to recover thoroughly
from the severe shock its nervous system had received in
the death of Captain Cavendish, and the various wonderful facts that death brought to light. It was fully a month
before the wonder quite subsided, and people could talk
of other things over the tea-table.

Cherrie, the bereaved, was safely back again in the

parental nest. Creditors had flocked in with the dead man's long bills; and when all was settled, nothing was left for the widow. But some good men among them made up two hundred pounds, and Mrs. Wyndham added another hundred, and the three were presented to Mrs. Cavendish, with the sympathy of the donors. It was a little fortune for Cherrie, though a pitiful ending of the brilliant match she had made; and she took it, crying very much, and was humbly thankful. Once more she tripped the streets of her native town, and her crape, and bombazine, and widow's cap, were charmingly becoming; and when the roses began to return to her cheeks, she was prettier than ever.

The town was quiet, and October was wearing away. The last week of that month brought a letter from Charley Marsh—a letter that was not like Charley, but was very grave, almost sad.

"Under God, my dear Val," he wrote, "I owe the restoration of my good name to you. I know all you have done for me and mine—my poor mother has told me; but I cannot thank you. I am sure you do not want me to thank you; but it is all written deep in my heart, and will be buried with me. I am coming back to Speckport—ah! dear old Speckport! I never thought it could be so dear! I shall be with you in November, and perhaps I may say to you then what I cannot write now. I am coming back a man, Val; I went away a hot-headed, passionate, unreasoning boy. I have learned to be wise, I hope, and if the school has been a hard one, I shall only remember its lessons the longer. I am coming back rich; blessings as well as misfortunes do not come alone. I have been left a fortune—you will see an account of it in the paper I send you. Our colonel, a gallant fellow, and a rich Georgian planter, has remembered me in his will. I saved his life shortly after I came here, almost at the risk of my own, I believe. They promoted me for it at the time, and I thought I had got my reward; but I was mistaken. He died last week of a bayonet-thrust, and when his will was read, I found I was left thirty thousand dollars. He was a childless widower, with no near relatives; so no one is wronged. You see I shall not have to fall back upon Dr. Leach's hand on my return, and my mother need depend no more on Mrs. Wyndham's generosity. I am very grateful to that lady all the same."

"I believe I'll show this letter to Father Lennard," said Val to himself; "he asked me on Sunday if I had heard from Charley lately, and told me to let him know when I did. Charley was always a favorite of his, since the day when he was a little shaver and an acolyte on the altar."

Mr. Blake was not the man to let grass grow under his feet when he took a notion in his head; so he started off at once, at a swinging pace, for the cathedral. The October twilight was cold and gray. A dreary evening, in which men went by with pinched noses and were buttoned up in greatcoats, and women had vails over their faces, and shivered in the street—a melancholy evening, speaking of desolation, and decay, and death, and the end of all things earthly.

Mr. Blake, to whom it was only a rawish evening, strode along, and reached the cathedral in the bleak dusk. The principal entrances were all closed, but he went in through a side door, and looked into the side chapel for the priest. Not finding him, he entered the cathedral through one of the transepts, but neither was Father Lennard there. The gray twilight shone but dimly through the painted windows, and the long and lofty aisles were very dim and shadowy. There was but one light in the great church—a tiny lamp burning on the grand altar—a lamp that never went out by night or day. Two or three shadowy female figures knelt around the altar-rails in silent prayer, and Val thought one of them looked like Miss Rose. He knew she was in the habit of coming in the twilight here; but something else had caught his attention, and he turned away and went on tiptoe down the echoing nave, staring up at the choir. Some one was singing softly there—singing so softly that it seemed but the sighing of the autumn-wind, and seemed to belong to it. But Val had a quick ear, and the low melancholy cadences struck him with a nameless thrill. What was there that sounded so strangely familiar in that voice? It was a woman's voice—a sweet, full soprano, that could rise to power at its owner's will. But what did it remind him of? A thought flashed through him—a sudden and startling thought—that brought the blood in a red gush to his face, and then left him cold and white. He softly ascended the stairs, the low, mournful voice breaking into a sweetly-plaintive vesper hymn as he went.

Val Blake trembled from head to foot, and a cold sweat broke out on his face. He paused a moment before he entered into the choir, his heart beating faster than it ever had beat before. A woman sat before the organ, not playing, but with her fingers wandering noiselessly over the keys, her face upraised in the ghostly light. She looked like the picture of St. Cecilia, with a cloud of tressed hazy golden hair falling about that pale, earnest, upraised face. Her mantle had fallen back—a white cashmere mantle, edged with ermine and lined with blue satin—and she sung, unconscious, as it seemed, of all the world. Val Blake stood like a man paralyzed—struck dumb and motionless—and the sweet voice sang on:

> "Ave Maria! Oh, hear when we call,
> Mother of Heaven, who is Saviour of all;
> Feeble and fearing, we trust in thy might;
> In doubting and darkness thy love be our light.
> Let us sleep on thy breast while the night-taper burns,
> And wake in thine arms when the morning returns!
> Ave Maria! Ave Maria! Ave Maria! audi nos!"

The singing ceased, the fingers were motionless, and the pale face drooped and sunk down on the pale hands. And still Val Blake stood mute, motionless, utterly confounded. For there before him, with only the moonlight shadow of her former loveliness left, sat and sang, not the dead, but the living, Nathalie Marsh!

CHAPTER XXXV.

"QUOTH THE RAVEN, 'NEVERMORE!'"

OW long Mr. Val Blake stood there, staring at that sight of wonder, neither he nor I ever knew; but while it drooped in a strange, heartbroken way over the instrument, and he stood looking at it, powerless to speak or move, a hand was laid on his shoulder, and looking round he saw the pale face of Paul Wyndham. Pale always, but deadly white, Mr. Blake saw, in the spectral October gloaming.

"Blake," he said, in a hoarse whisper, that did not sound like Paul Wyndham's peculiarly clear and melodious voice, "if ever you were my friend, be silent now! Help me to get away from here unseen."

Some dim foreshadowing of the truth dawned on the slow mind of Val Blake. The ghost of Nathalie Marsh— the invisible and mysterious woman shut up in Rosebush Cottage—could they, after all, be connected, and was the mad mother only a blind. The question passed through Val's mind in a vague sort of way, while he watched Paul Wyndham bend over the drooping figure, as tenderly as a mother over the cradle of her first-born. His voice too, had changed when he spoke to her, and was infinitely gentle and loving.

"My darling," he said, "you must not stay here. I have come to fetch you home."

She lifted up her head at once, and held out her arms to him, like a little child that wants to be taken. All the pale, misty hair floated softly back from her wan face. Oh! how altered from the bright face Val Blake once knew, and the blue eyes she lifted to his face had a strange, meaningless light, that chilled the blood in the veins of the looker-on.

"Yes, take me away," she said, wearily; but in Natha-

17*

lic Marsh's own voice.   "I knew you would come.
Where's Midge?   I am cold here."

"Midge is at home, my darling.   Here is your mantle
—stand up while I put it on."

She arose; and Val saw she was dressed in white—a
sort of white cashmere morning-gown, lined with quilted
blue silk.   Mr. Wyndham arranged the long white mantle
around the wasted figure, drawing the hood over the head
and face.   Ghostly enough she looked, standing there in
the gloom; and Val knew she must have been dressed
in the same manner on the night she so startled him and
Laura.   But Mr. Wyndham, who wore a long black cloak
himself these chilly evenings, took it off and arranged it
over her white robes, effectually concealing them, as he
drew her forward.

"Go down-stairs, Blake," he said, "a cab is waiting
outside the gates.   Come with us, and I will tell you
everything."

Mr. Blake mechanically obeyed.   He was not quite
sure it was not all the nightmare, and not at all certain
he was not asleep in his own room, and dreaming this
singular little episode, and would awake presently to smile
at it all.   He went down-stairs in silent bewilderment,
never speaking a word, and hardly able to think.   Nathalie Marsh was dead—or at least some one was dead, and
buried out there in the cemetery, that he had taken to be
Nathalie Marsh—how then did she come to be walking
down-stairs behind him, supported by that extraordinary
man, Paul Wyndham?

The cathedral was quite deserted when they got down,
and the sexton was just locking it up for the night.   He
stared a little at the three forms going by him; but he
was an old man, with sight not so good as it might be,
and he did not recognize them.   They met no one within
the inclosed grounds.   At the side gate a cab stood waiting; Mr. Blake opened the door, and Mr. Wyndham
helped in his silent companion, who yielded herself, "passive to all changes."

"Come with us, Blake," Mr. Wyndham said, as he

entered and seated hi nself by the lady. "Rosebush Cottage, driver. Make haste!"

Not a word was spoken during the drive. The slight figure of the woman lay back in a corner, her head drooping against the side of the carriage. Paul Wyndham sat by her, looking at her often, but not addressing her; and Mr. Blake, in a hopeless morass of doubt and mystification, sat staring at the living ghost, and wondering when he was going to wake from his dream.

The distance was short. In ten minutes they stopped in front of the pretty cottage, from whose curtained windows a bright light shone. The roses in the garden were dead long ago, and only gaunt stalks and bare vines twined themselves, like ugly brown snakes, where the climbing roses grew. A queer figure stood at the gate— an ugly, dwarfed, and unwieldy figure, with a big head set on no neck at all, and a broad, florid face, and little pin-hole eyes. But the eyes were big enough to express a great deal of anxiety; and she flung the gate open and rushed out as the carriage door opened and Mr. Wyndham got out.

"Have you found her?" she cried. "Oh, dear! oh, dear! Where was she, now?"

Mr. Wyndham did not notice her.

"Get out, Blake," he said; and Midge recoiled with a cry of consternation at sight of Val's towering form. The next instant, he had lifted the lady out in his arms, as if she were a baby, and carried her within the gate. "Take her into the house," he said, sternly. "I shall talk to you about this again!"

Midge obeyed meekly—Val wondered as much at that meekness as at anything he had seen yet—and led the passive girlish creature into the house. Mr. Wyndham paid and dismissed the cabman, and held the gate open for Val.

"Come in, Blake," he said gravely; "the time has come when my secret can be no longer kept, and I would sooner tell it to you than to any other human being in existence."

"Tell me," said Val, finding voice for the first time, "is that really Nathalie Marsh?"

"She was Nathalie Marsh—she is Nathalie Wyndham now. She is my wife!"

Mr. Blake fairly gasped for breath.

"Your wife!" he exclaimed, "are you going mad, Mr. Wyndham? Olive is your wife!"

"No," said Paul Wyndham, with cold sternness, "she is not—she never has been. The compact I made with her was a formal matter of business, which gave me the right to dwell under the same roof with her, but never made me her husband. She and I understand each other perfectly. Nathalie is my wife—my dear and cherished wife, and was so before I ever came to Speckport."

"Then, Mr. Wyndham," said Val, with gravity, "you are a scoundrel!"

"Perhaps so. Come in."

Val Blake took off his hat and crossed the threshold of Rosebush Cottage for the first time since it was inhabited.

"And your mother was only a myth?" he asked, as Mr. Wyndham closed and locked carefully the front door.

"Only a myth. My mother is in Westchester County yet."

Val asked no more questions, but looked around him. The hall was long, with beautiful proof-engravings, and lit by pendant chandeliers. There was a door to either hand—Midge came out of the one to the left, still wearing that anxious face.

"Now, then," said Mr. Wyndham, sternly, "how did this happen?"

"It wasn't my fault," snapped Midge, her usual manner returning. "I did my best, and she'd behaved herself for so long, I'd no idee she was going to scud off again. The door wasn't open ten minutes, and I was out in the kitchen bakin' the pies, and when I came back she was gone. I put after her and met you, and I couldn't help it now; so talk's of no use. Where did you find her?"

"In the cathedral. She was speaking of it this morning, and asking me to take her there, so I knew she would make for that."

"What made you fetch him here?" inquired Midge, poking one stubby index-finger at Mr. Blake.

"He saw her and recognized her before I did. Get out of the way, Midge, we are going in."

Midge went away, snorting to herself, and Mr. Wyndham opened the door, and preceded Mr. Blake into the drawing-room of the cottage. Such a pretty drawing-room, lit by the rosy blaze of a clear coal-fire in a grate of shining steel, and pendent chandeliers of glittering glass and frosted silver. A small, high-ceilinged room, the walls hung with white and gold paperhangings, and adorned with perfect gems of art. The windows were draped in blue satin and white lace, and there was a Brussels carpet on the floor, where violets, and bluebells, and morning-glories ran wild on a white ground, and looked like pale spring flowers blooming in a snow bank. The chairs were of white enameled wood—the legs and back touched up with gold, and cushioned in blue satin. There were inlaid tables, laden with superbly bound books of beauty, annuals, albums, and portfolios of engravings; and a rosewood piano stood in one corner, with the music scattered about. There was an open door to the left, leading into a bed-room furnished in much the same style; but Val scarcely looked at it—all his attention was taken by the white girlish form lying back in a great carved and gilded chair in front of the fire. What a wreck she was! The transparent skin, the hollow cheeks, the sunken eyes, the wasted little hands, the shadowy figure—what a wreck of the blonde loveliness of other days. Her head lay back among the blue satin pillows, her hands dropped listless over the arms of the chair, and her eyes were fixed on the leaping jets of flame, in a meaningless stare. She never turned to look at them whey they came in; she did not even turn when Val Blake crossed over and bent above her.

"Nathalie," he said, a little tremor in his voice; "Nathalie, don't you know me?"

She lifted her blue eyes vacantly to his face, murmured an inarticulate something, moved her head restlessly, and then went back to staring at the fire. Val rose
up, white even to his lips.

"Wyndham, what is it?" he asked, afraid, while he
spoke, to hear the answer. "Why does she look like
that?"

Paul Wyndham was leaning against the mantel, his
head drooping. Now he lifted it, and Val saw the dark
despair that filled his eyes.

"Its meaning," he said, "has nearly broken my heart.
If I have done wrong, I have been terribly punished, and
even you, Blake, might be merciful now. My poor darling's mind is gone!"

There was a pause, a pause of mute consternation on
Val's part. Mr. Wyndham bent over Nathalie, with that
look of unspeakable tenderness that made his face something new to Val—a face entirely new.

"My darling, you are tired, I know," he said, "and
want to go to bed. Don't you, Natty?"

The old name! It brought a pang to Val's heart to
hear it. Paul Wyndham spoke to her as he would have
spoken to a child of three years; and Val thought he
would sooner she were indeed lying under the sods in the
cemetery than see her as he saw her now—dead in
life.

"Yes, Paul," she said, rising wearily, but at once.

"Or, perhaps," Mr. Wyndham said, looking at her
thoughtfully, "you would like to sing before you go.
You told me the other day, you know, you always slept
better if you sang before going to bed."

"Oh, yes!" Nathalie said, her face lighting suddenly
with animation. "What shall I sing, Paul?"

"Anything you like, my dearest."

He led her to the piano, and opened it, while she took
her seat on the stool, and ran her fingers lightly over the
keys at random. Val Blake closed his eyes to listen.
How long—how long ago it seemed since he had heard
Nathalie Marsh's melodious voice ringing through the
cathedral-aisles! The thin fingers wandered off into a

plaintive little prelude, that had something wild and melancholy in its wailing minor key. The song was as sadly-sweet as the air, and the voice that sung was full of pathos.

*   *   *   *   *

The song died out as mournfully as the last cadence of a funeral-hymn, and the pale singer arose.

"I am very tired, Paul," Nathalie said, in a spiritless sort of way, "and I think my head is aching. Tell Midge to come."

He rang the bell and put his arm round her to lead her away.

"Say good night to Mr. Blake, Nathalie. You remember Val Blake, don't you, my darling?"

"Yes," she said; but the smile she turned upon him was meaningless, and as cold as moonlight in snow. "Good-night!"

Something was choking Val's voice, and his answering good-night was very husky. Paul Wyndham led her into the inner room, and Midge bustled in after the old fashion, and Nathalie was left in her charge to be undressed for the night. Mr. Wyndham left the room and returned presently, bearing wine and cigars.

"If I am what you called me a while ago, Blake," Mr. Wyndham said, with a smile that had very much of sadness in it, "there are extenuating circumstances that may lighten my guilt."

"Wrong is wrong," said Mr Blake, gravely, "and no extenuating circumstances can make it right. You are a bigamist, by your own confession, and you know how the civil law punishes that."

"Yes, Blake, I know it," said Mr. Wyndham, "and, knowing it, I have risked all to win her, my poor lost darling within that room! Heaven knows, I have hardly had a day's peace since. The broad road may be strewn with roses, as preachers say it is, but the thorns in the flowers sting very sharply sometimes, too."

Mr. Blake made no reply to this aphorism. He was lighting his cigar, with a listening face, waiting for the story his companion had to tell. Midge came out of the bed-room while he waited, threw more coal on the fire, and left the room. But still Paul Wyndham did not begin. He was smoking, and looking thoughtfully into the red fire and the falling cinders, and the ticking of an ormolu clock on the chimney-piece, and the dreary sighing of the night-wind without alone broke the silence. The clock struck eight, and Val lost patience.

"Well, Wyndham, why wait? Go on. I am waiting to hear this most extraordinary affair explained."

"You all here in Speckport thought Nathalie Marsh committed suicide—did you not?" said Mr. Wyndham, looking up. "It is such a charitable place this town of yours, and your good people are so wonderfully ready to place the worst construction on everything, that you never thought she might have fallen in by accident—did you?"

"It looked very suspicious," said Val. "Heaven knows how some of us pitied her, poor girl! but still——"

"But still you gave her credit for suicide. Let me restore her character. She never for a moment thought of self-destruction. I have her own solemn word for it. She was heart-broken,—despairing—my own injured darling!—but all the teachings of her life told her suicide was the only crime for which God has no mercy. She never thought of suicide on the night she wandered down to the old wharf. Most miserable she was. Perhaps the wretched night was in harmony with her great trouble; but she did not go there to look for death. She missed her footing on the slimy, rotten plank, and fell in, and from that moment her story—as far as you know it—ends."

Val nodded. He was smoking, and it was too much trouble to remove the cigar to speak.

"She was saved almost by a miracle. A passing boat heard the splash and her cry for help, and rowed to the spot. They saw her as she arose, and saved her, and one man on board recognized her. The man's name was Captain Locksley. Do you remember it?"

"Locksley!" cried Val. "Captain Frank Locksley of the

'Southern Cross?' Know him? Yes, as well as I know you! He was over head and ears in love with Nathalie, himself."

"Yes, I know. He recognized her, and would have returned with her to the shore; but she positively refused to go. She would die, she cried out, if she did not get away from this horrible place. Captain Locksley took her on board of his ship. There was a woman there, the wife of the steward, and she took charge of the poor, deranged girl. Captain Locksley sailed that night. He was off on a three-years' voyage; but on his way he was to touch at New York. The evening before they reached that city, he made an offer of his hand to the poor girl he had saved. He knew her story. He loved her and pitied her; but she refused. She only wanted to be away from Speckport. She would remain in New York. One place was as good as another, and a great city the best of all; but her lot was dust and ashes. She would never marry, she told him. Captain Locksley had a cousin, the wealthy manager of a fashionable Broadway theater, and, as a favor, the manager consented to receive Nathalie into his corps. Her rôle was a very simple one—walking lady at first, coming on only to stare at the audience at first. But my poor girl's beauty, though the shadow only of the brightness that had been, made her rise. She took minor parts, and they made her sing when they found what a superb voice she possessed. Her voice, the manager told me once, might make her fortune—at least it would have made the fortune of any other woman; but my darling had lost life, and with it all ambition. She never would be a good actress, but the audience looked at her a great deal; and the mournful melody of her voice, whether she talked or sang, had a charm for all. It paid the manager; so he kept her, and doled out her weekly pittance, and she took it uncomplainingly. I have sometimes wondered since how it was no one from Speckport ever saw and recognized her; but, I dare say, if they did, they would merely set it down as an odd chance resemblance. They were all so certain of her death, and then the false name and the disguising stage-dresses helped to baffle them. It was at

the theater I first met her. They took my dramas when
I turned dramatist, and I was always there. She attracted
me from the beginning. She interested me strongly the
first time I saw her, and I found myself pitying her somehow without knowing anything about her. I could not cease
thinking of her after. The pale face and mournful blue
eyes haunted me wherever I went. I found out she was
called Miss Johnson, and that she lodged in a shabby house
in a shabby street; and that was all any one heard. But of
my own knowledge I knew she was good and fair, and that
great sorrow, not sin, had darkened her young life. Why
it was I loved her, I never could tell. It was my fate, I
suppose; for my struggles were vain, and only left me
more helplessly entangled. The manager laughed at me;
my friends talked of acts of lunacy and genteel private
lunatic asylums for me; but it was all useless. I loved
her, and was not to be laughed out of it, and one night
the truth broke from me. I begged her to tell me who
she was and to become my wife; but she refused. She
refused, Blake, to do either; but she was very gentle and
womanly saying the cruel words. She was very grateful
to me, she said, my poor dear! but she could not be unjust enough to take me at my word. The fancy for her
would soon leave me. She was not worthy to be the wife
of any good man. I must forget her. I must never
speak to her like this again. Blake, I went home that
night in a sort of despair. I hated and despised myself
for my pitiful weakness. I tried to conquer myself, and
failed miserably. I could not stay away from the theater.
I could not forget her. I could not do anything I ought
to do. I went to the house where she lodged, and found
out all they knew about her there. It was very little;
but it was all good I made the manager tell me again
what his cousin, Captain Locksley, had told him of her,
and I ascertained that Captain Locksley was an honorable
and truthful man. He had said she had undergone a
great deal of trouble, and had met with heavy reverse of
fortune, but that she was the best and purest of beings,
and he trusted his cousin would always be her true friend.
He told him he had long loved her, and that he had asked

her to be his wife, and she had refused. I knew, therefore, there was nothing worse than worldly misfortune in
the past life of the woman I had loved. Once again I
sought her out, and implored her to leave her hard
life and be my wife, keeping her past life secret if she
chose; and once again I was refused.

"After that second refusal," Mr. Wyndham said,
throwing his smoked-out cigar in the fire, and lighting another, "I gave up hope entirely. There was such a steady,
inflexible resolution on her poor, pale, worn face, that a
despairing conviction of the uselessness of all further
attempts came upon me. Still I could not go away—I
despised myself for my pitiful weakness—but I could not,
Blake, I could not! I loved her, and I was a weak,
irresolute coward, and lingered about the theater only to
get a word from her, a look at her, as she went past, or
follow her at a distance through the city streets, to see that
she got safely home. I despaired, but I could not fly.
And one cold March morning, as I sat at the window of
my hotel, staring dreamily out, she passed by; trying to
fix my thoughts on the manuscript before me, and unable
to think of anything but the pale actress, a waiter came in
and handed me a letter. It was a very large letter, in a
strange female hand I had never seen before; but I knew
it was from her—my darling! I tore off the envelope;
it contained half a dozen closely-written sheets, and was
signed "Nathalie Marsh." I knew the actress only as
Miss Johnson; but I never thought it was her real name.
I knew now what it was. It was a very long letter; she
told me where she came from, and why she was here, an
actress. She told me her whole story; her sad, pitiful
story of wrong and suffering; the fortune she had lost;
the brother wrongfully condemned; and the treachery—
the false, cruel, shameful treachery—of the man she had
loved and trusted. She told me all, in a simple, truthful,
earnest way that went to my heart; and then she told me
her reasons for telling it. I was her only friend, she said.
I had always been good and kind to her—my poor, little,
forlorn lamb!—and she trusted and believed in me. She
did not love me; she never could love any one again; but

she honored and esteemed me, and if I could be content with that, she would be my wife—faithful and true until death—on one condition."

Paul Wyndham paused. He had been gazing dreamily into the fire whilst talking, but now he looked hesitatingly at Val Blake.

"I hardly know how to go on," he said, "without involving others, whom I have no right to name, but I must, I suppose; there is no alternative after the discovery you have made to-night. Another had become possessed of the fortune that should have been hers; a fortune that was hers by every law of right and justice. Another, who had no claim upon it, except, perhaps, that of mere chance—and the new heiress had been a fellow-lodger of hers in Minetta street. She was young and handsome, and had been a lady. I knew her by sight, for she had accompanied my darling often to the theater. She would go to Speckport; she would possess the thousands that should have been my Nathalie's—the fatal thousands for which her heart had been broken, her young life ruined. She would be honored and flattered and happy; she would marry, perhaps, the very man who had so wronged herself. He was a notorious fortune-hunter; she was sure he would be at her feet in a month, and was almost equally sure he would be accepted. She could not endure the thought—not that she loved him now—that had all gone long ago; but she wanted to baffle him, to make him suffer as he had made her suffer, and to possess after all a portion of the wealth which should have been all hers. She would be my wife, she said, if I would bring this about. She knew a secret in the life of this new heiress that placed her completely in her power, and she confided that secret to me. She would be my wife as soon as I pleased, if I would only help her in this scheme—if, after our marriage, I would go to Speckport, compel the heiress into a formal union with myself that should mean nothing but a business compact on either side, and so baffle Captain Cavendish, and win for my lawful wife after all the fortune that was hers by right. You stare, Blake; it sounds very extraordinary and improbable, but it is the simple truth, nevertheless, and I saw no reason to see why it could not be carried out. The secret I held placed the heiress utterly in my power and would force her to comply with my every wish. Mind, Blake, it was not the sort of secret that causes divorce cases; it was a crime committed, no doubt; a crime of falsehood and ambition, not of shame, else that woman at Redmon would never for one poor instant, under any temptation whatever, have borne my name.

"I read the strange letter over a half a dozen times, and Val, old boy, I consented. You don't need to tell me how miserably weak and despicable it was. I know it all, and knew it then just as well. But I want you to think of me at my best. If the heiress had been a good woman, I would have lain down and died sooner than disturb her; but I knew she was not. I knew she was a bad, bold, crafty, ambitious creature, without a heart; with only a cold, calculating brain, capable of committing a great crime for her own ends; and I had no pity for her. I consented, for I loved my poor, pale girl with a passionate devotion you never can realize, and felt all her wrongs burning in my own breast, and longed to take them upon myself and go forth and avenge her. I did not know then, as I do now, that it was a diseased brain that prompted that letter. I did not know that reason had left her throne, with that constant brooding on one theme, and that my love was mad when she asked me to commit a crime. I did not know. I wrote her a long answer, promising anything, everything, if she would be my wife. My poor girl! My poor, poor Nathalie!"

Mr. Blake sat staring stoically at the coals, making no comment whatever on anything he heard, even when Paul Wyndham made that pause, with a face full of tender pity and love.

"We were married, Val," he said, looking up again, "and the month that followed was the happiest I ever knew. Our marriage was very recent, and I took my darling on a Southern tour, hoping that would make her forget the past and be happy. But it did not. Nothing could ever make her happy, she said, but seeing retribution fall on the unjust, and returning to her native town. Not openly, that was out of the question—but in secret, where she could know for herself that her wrongs had been avenged. So I left her in New York, and came here, and, Blake, you know the rest. I did frustrate that bad man, of whom I do not wish to speak since he is dead. I did marry the heiress, or we went through the ceremony that our friends took to be such. We understood each other perfectly from the first. I found her precisely what I had thought her—a bold, ambitious woman, reveling in wealth that was the birthright of another; ready to marry a man for whom she did not care a jot, because she hoped he would some day place a coronet on her head. I had little pity for such a woman, and besides, I was bound by a solemn promise to my dear one, who never would see me again if I failed. I married the heiress of Redmon, and had a legal right to share the wealth that should have been all my own true wife's. I purchased this cottage—I brought Nathalie here—I secured the services of her faithful old servant, and Speckport thought it was my sick mother!

"Very slowly some dim shadow of the truth came into my mind —very slowly—for I turned cold with horror only at the thought. Her mind was going—I saw it now—and the horror and anguish and despair of that discovery is known only to Heaven and myself. I had been so happy in spite of all—happy in this cottage with my darling wife—and now my punishment was coming, and was heavier than I could bear. My own act brought on the crisis. I was always urging her to let me take her out—I knew it would do her good; but she had such a dread of discovery that I never could persuade her. You remember the Sunday you saw us at the cathedral. She had often said she would like to go there, and that day I persuaded her to go, to hear the popular preacher. The sermon was a fearful one—you recollect it—and it completed the work remorse and suffering had begun. My wife was a hopeless lunatic from that day. O my love! my love! surely your punishment was greater than your sin!"

Val did not speak. The white anguish on Paul
Wyndham's face was beyond all wordy consolation.

"It was after that she took to wandering out. She
was haunted by one idea now—the sin she had committed
against Olive ; and tormented by a ceaseless desire to find
her out, and kneel at her feet for forgiveness. She wandered to the Redmon road on the night you saw her first,
with some such idea, and fled in terror at Laura's scream.
Midge had followed and found her, and led her home.
From that time, Midge had to watch her ceaselessly to
keep her in ; but sometimes, in spite of all, she would
make her way out. She went to the cemetery to see her
own grave, poor child! and Midge found her there, too ;
she went to the cathedral this evening in the same way.
All the old familiar places drew her to them with an irresistible power of attraction, and I knew this discovery
must come, sooner or later. I am deeply thankful you
were the first to make it, for I can trust you, dear old
Val ! I dare not call in medical service, but I know her
case is quite hopeless. She is never otherwise than gentle
and patient—she is like a little child, and I know reason
has gone forever. Blake, I know I have done wrong. I
know I have deserved this, but it breaks my heart !"

"And this is the end of your story," said Val, looking
at him with a stony face.

"This is the end—a pitiful story of weakness and
wrong-doing, isn't it ?"

"Yes," said Val, rising, and flinging his smoked-out
cigar in the fire, "it is. A bad and cruel story as ever I
heard. A story I never should have given you the credit
of being the hero of, Paul Wyndham. You have profaned
a holy rite—you have broken the laws of God and man—
you have committed a felony, for which life-long imprisonment is the penalty. You are a bigamist, sir. The
laws of this matter-of-fact land recognize no romantic
glossing over of facts. You have married two wives—
that humbug about one marriage meaning nothing, being
only a business arrangement, is only bosh. You are a
bigamist, Mr. Wyndham, and you cannot expect me to
hoodwink your crime from the eyes of the land."

"No," said Mr. Wyndham, bitterly, "I expect nothing. You will turn Rhadamanthus, and have justice, though the heavens fall, I dare say. You will publish my misdoings on the house-tops, and at the street-corners. It will be a rare treat for Speckport, and Mr. Val Blake will awake all at once, and find himself famous!"

Mr. Blake listened with the same face of stone.

"I will do what is right and above-board, Mr. Wyndham. I will have no act or part in any plot as long as I live. The only one I ever had a hand in was that affair of Cherrie's, and I was sorry enough for that afterward. If Nathalie Marsh were my sister, I could scarcely care more for her than I do; but I tell you I would sooner know she was dead and buried out there, than living, and as she is. I am sorry for you, Mr. Wyndham, for I had some faith in you; but it is out of all reason to ask me to conceal such a crime as this."

"I ask for nothing," Paul Wyndham said, more in sorrow than in anger. "I am entirely at your mercy. Heaven knows it does not matter much what becomes of me, but it is hard to think of her name—my poor dear!—dragged through the slime of the streets."

Perhaps Val Blake was sorry for him in his secret heart—for it was a kindly heart, too, was Val's—but his face did not show it. He lifted his hat, and turned to go.

"I shall be as merciful as is compatible with justice," he said; "before I make this matter known to the proper authorities, you shall be warned. But there are others who must be told to-morrow. She must have medical advice at once, for she is evidently dying by inches; her mother must know, and—" His hand was on the lock of the door as he stopped, and faced round—"and the woman you have wronged. As to your secret power over her, you need not make such a mystery of it. I know what it is!"

"You!" Paul Wyndham said, turning his powerful gray eyes upon him. "You, Blake! Impossible!"

Mr. Blake nodded intelligently.

"She is not the true heiress! Ah! I see I am right!

I have had reason to think so for some time past; but I never was sure until to-night. Oh, yes! I know the secret, and I know more. I think I can put my hand on one who is the heiress, before to-morrow's sun goes down."

There flashed through Paul Wyndham's mind what Olive had said, in that first stormy interview they had held, about the true heiress, who had made over to her the true estate. What if it had been true?

"Who is it?" he asked. "You cannot! She is dead!"

"Not a bit of it. She is worth half a dozen dead people yet! I shall see her to-morrow, and find out if I am not right."

"See her to-morrow! Then she is in Speckport?"

"To be sure she is! I will visit the other one, too—Harriet, you know. She must be told at once."

"You know her name! Blake, who has told you all this?" .

"Not now!" said Val, opening the door; "some other time I will tell you. You are at liberty to make what use of your time you please. You have between this and to-morrow."

"I shall not make use of it to fly," said Mr. Wyndham, coolly; "whatever comes, I shall stay here and meet it. I have only one request to make—be as tender with that poor girl at Redmon as you can. I do not think she is happy, and I believe she is a far better woman than I took her to be. I am sorry for the wrong I have done her, but it is too late in the day for all that now. I do not ask you to spare me, but do spare her?"

"I shall not add to the truth—be sure of it. Good night!"

"Good night!" Paul Wyndham said, locking and closing the door after him, and returning to the room they had left. So it was all over, and the discovery he had dreaded and foreseen all along, had come at last. It was all over, and the scheme of his life was at an end. He had been happy here—oh, very, very happy! with the wife he loved, and who had trusted and clung to him,

as a timid child does to a father. How often he had sat
in this very room, reading to her dreamy, misty Shelley,
or Byron, or Owen Meredith, and she had sat on a low
stool at his feet, her blue eyes looking up in his face, her
hazy gold hair rippling loose about her, like a cloud of
sunlight, or with that golden head pillowed on his knee,
while she dropped asleep in the blue summer twilight,
listening. Yes, he had been unspeakably happy there,
while some one had sat unthought of at Redmon, eating
out her own heart in her grand miserable solitude. He
had been very happy here; but it was all over now, and
his life seemed closing black around him, like a sort of
iron shroud. It would all pass, and he would exist for
years, perhaps, yet, and eat, and drink, and sleep, and go
on with the dull routine of existence, but his life was at
an end. He had sinned, and the retribution that always
follows sin in this world, or the next, had overtaken him.
He had been happy here, but it was gone forever—nevermore to be—nevermore—nevermore!

CHAPTER XXXVI.

DRIFTING OUT.

IN Mrs. Major Wheatly's pretty drawing-room
in their new house in Golden Row sat Miss
Winnie Rose, the governess. She is dressed
in slight mourning, very simple, as becomes a
governess, but fitting the small, light figure
with exquisite neatness, and she is counting time for Miss
Wheatly, who sits strumming out her music-lesson at the
piano. Mrs. Wheatly lies on a sofa at the window, dawd-
ling over a novel and looking listlessly at the passers-by,
and wishing some one would call. She started up, thinking her mental prayer was granted, as a servant entered

with a card. But it was not for her. It was handed to
the governess.

"Mr. Blake!" said Miss Rose, hesitatingly. "This
cannot be for me, Margaret."

"O yes'm, it is! He requested particularly to see Miss
Rose."

"Is it Mr. Blake?" inquired Mrs. Wheatly. "What
can he want with you, I wonder?"

Miss Rose smiled as she got up.

"I am sure I don't know. I may go down, I sup
pose?"

"Oh, certainly, my dear!" said Mrs. Wheatly, yawning. "And ask him if he has heard from his sister
lately. Stop your strumming, Louisa, it makes my head
ache."

Mr. Blake was sitting in what was called the morning-
room, and shook hands with Miss Rose when she came in.
But how strangely grave he was! What could he want
with her? Her heart fluttered a little as she looked at
him.

"My dear young lady!" he began, with an ominously
grave face, "it is very serious business that brings me
here this morning. Are you quite sure no one can overhear us?"

Awful beginning! The little governess turned pale
as she listened.

"No one," she faltered. "What is it you mean, Mr.
Blake?"

"My dear," said Mr. Blake, as if he were speaking to
a young lady of ten years, "don't look so frightened. I
want to ask you a question, and you must pardon me if it
sounds impertinent. Is your name, your family-name,
really Rose?"

The governess uttered a low cry, and covered her face
with both hands.

"I am answered," said Val. "Your name is Henderson—Olive Henderson; and you should be heiress of
Redmon, instead of—of the person whose name is Harriet,
and who reigns there now. Oh, my dear young lady, how
is this? Is there no one in the world to be trusted?"

. She rose from her seat suddenly, and sank on her knees at his feet with a gushing sob.

"I have done wrong," she cried, "for all deceit is wrong; and though Rose is my name, it is not my father's. But oh, Mr. Blake! if you only knew all, I don't think you would blame me so much. It was not I who changed it. It has been the name by which I have gone for years, and I could not resume my rightful one without suspicion and explanation that involved the honor of the dead; and so I was silent. No one was wronged by it—no one in the wide world; and I did not think it so very wrong."

She sobbed out as she spoke, in a sudden outbreak of distress. Val stooped kindly and raised her up.

"My dear child, I only doubted you for a moment. You are too good to willfully deceive any one to their harm. But you must calm yourself and listen to me; for right must be done to all. Who is that woman at Redmon? Is she your stepsister?"

The governess's only reply was to clasp her hands piteously.

"Oh, Mr. Blake, what have you done? How have you found this out? Oh, I am so sorry, so very sorry; for you don't know the misery you will make!"

"Misery! Do you mean to yourself?"

"No, no! but to her. Poor Harriet! Oh, Mr. Blake, who can have told you this?"

"Sit down and calm yourself, my dear Miss Rose, and you shall hear all. Do you recollect one day, very shortly after your return here, visiting Miss Henderson at her cottage down the street here?"

"Yes, yes."

"You and she had a long conversation in her chamber that day, part of which was overheard. Miss Catty Clowrie was in the house at the time, and she overheard—how, I don't pretend to say; but she heard enough to excite her suspicions that all was not as it should be. She heard you addressed as 'Olly', and heard you call Miss Henderson 'Harriet.' She saw her down on her knees before you, pleading desparately for something, Miss

Clowrie could not quite make out what; and she heard you promise to comply with her request, on condition of her paying over to Mrs. Marsh a certain annuity. All this looked very odd, you know; and Miss Clowrie, who is a good deal of an attorney, they tell me, scented a criminal case. She consulted with her father on the subject, and was overheard by her brother Jacob, who is in my office. Jake communicated the story next morning in confidence to Bill Blair, and Bill related it in confidence to me. I cross-questioned Jake, and got out of him all he knew, and then pooh-poohed the story, and told them Catty must have been dreaming. But the annuity was paid, and I suspected the whole thing at once. It was none of my business, however, so I held my tongue; and as Mr. and Miss Clowrie hadn't facts enough to go upon, they held theirs, too, and waited for something to turn up. There is the story to you, Miss Rose; and now why on earth, if you are the true Olive Henderson, have you slaved here as a governess, while you let another, who had no right, usurp your place and wealth?"

She governess lifted her head with some spirit.

"It is no slavery, Mr. Blake! They are very kind to me here, Mr. Blake, and I have every reason to be happy; and Harriet has a right, a strong right, which I never mean to dispute, to possess whatever belongs to me. She is no usurper, for I have made over to her fully and sincerely the legacy bequeathed to Philip Henderson.

"I understand. You are very generous and self-sacrificing, Miss Rose—but still she has no right there, and—" But Miss Rose interrupted, clasping her hands in passionate appeal.

"Oh, Mr. Blake, what are you going to do? Oh, I entreat of you, if you have any regard for me or poor Harriet, not to reveal what you know. Indeed, indeed, I don't want it! What should I do with half that money? I have everything I want, and am as happy as the day is long. Do you think I could ever be happy again if I turned poor Harriet out; do you think I could ever live in that grand place, knowing I had made her miserable for life? Oh, no, Mr. Blake! You are good and kind-

hearted, and would not make any one unhappy, I know!
Then let things go on as they are; and don't say anything
about this?"

"But I cannot, my dear little martyr!" said Val, "and
I must speak of it to her, at least, because it is involved
in another story she must hear."

"In another story?"

"Yes, Miss Rose—for I suppose I must still call you
by that name—in another story, stranger than anything
you ever heard out of a novel. A cruel and shameful
story of wrong and revenge, that I have come here to tell
you this morning, and to which all this has been but the
preface."

The governess lifted her pale, wondering face in mute
inquiry, and Val began the story Paul Wyndham had related the night before. The brown eyes of the little governess dilated, and her lips parted as she listened, but she
never spoke or interrupted him until he had finished. She
sat with her clasped hands in her lap, her eyes never leaving his face, her lips apart and breathless.

"So you see, Miss Rose," Val wound up, "in telling
that unfortunate girl at Redmon that she is not, and never
has been, legally the wife of Paul Wyndham, it is of ab-
solute impossibility to shirk the other story. Had she
never falsely possessed herself of that to which she had no
claim, this dishonor would have been saved her. She might
have been poor, but not disgraced, as she is now."

"Oh, Mr. Blake! what have I heard? Nathalie Marsh
alive and here?"

"Not Nathalie Marsh—Nathalie Wyndham. What-
ever your stepsister may be, Nathalie at least is his lawful
wife!"

"Oh, my poor, poor, Nathalie! And is she really insane—hopelessly insane?"

"Hopelessly, I fear, but she does not look as if her
life would last long. She is only the shadow of what she
was—a poor, thin, frail shadow."

"And Harriet, who is so proud, what will she say when
this is told her? Oh, how could Mr. Wyndham do her
such a wrong? It was cruel! it was unmanly!"

'So it was," nodded Val, "and it's not like him, either; for Wyndham is a pretty honorable fellow, as the world goes. But man, even at the best," said Mr. Blake, modestly, thinking of his own short-comings, " is weak, and temptation is strong. I think he is sorry enough for it now—not selfishly sorry, either. And now, Miss Rose, what I want is this. I know you are a sort of unprofessed Sister of Charity where the sick are concerned, and you and poor Natty used to be friends. I want to know if you will come and stay with her for awhile; she hasn't a soul of the female kind but Midge. If Joanna were here, I wouldn't have to trouble you; but in her absence you are the only one I can think of. Of course, her mother must go; but poor Mrs. Marsh is of no more use in a sick room than a big wax doll. She will play propriety while you stay."

" Yes, yes; I will go at once !" exclaimed Miss Rose, starting up in womanly impulsiveness. " Wait one moment while I run and tell Mrs. Wheatley."

" Oh, there's no such hurry ! It will do this afternoon, when I will call for you, with Mrs. Marsh. Don't tell Mrs. Wheatley who it is you are going to see, mind—the secret will get out, of course, but we don't want everybody to know it just yet."

" I will not tell. What time will you call ?"

" About three. I am going to Redmon now. She ought to know at once !"

" My poor, poor Harriet ! Oh, Mr. Blake ! She is so proud and sensitive. You will spare her as much as you can ?"

Mr. Blake took the two little clasped hands between his own broad palms, and looked down kindly in the pale, pleading face.

" I think I could spare my worst enemy if you pleaded for him, my little friend. Don't be afraid of me, Miss Winnie. I don't think it is in me to strike a fallen foe— and that poor girl at Redmon never injured me. Good-bye, until then !"

Mr. Blake's composure, as we know, was not easily disturbed; but he rang the bell at Redmon with much the same sensation a miserable sufferer from toothache rings at a dentist's door.

Yes, Mrs. Wyndham was in, the servant said, taking the visitor's card and ushering him into the library, where a bright fire blazed, for the lady of Redmon liked fires. Val sat and stared at it, wondering how he would begin his disagreeable task, and how she would take it.

"She's such a flarer anyway!" thought Mr. Blake, "that I dare say she'll fly out at me like a wildcat! What a mess it is! I wish I never had got into it!"

The door opened while he was thinking, and Olive came in. She was dressed in a loose morning negligee, every fold showing how indifferently her toilet had been made. Val saw, too, how pale, and wan, and weary her dark face looked; how hollow, and earthen, and melancholy her large black eyes. She had had her own share of the suffering, and her pride and haughty defiance seemed subdued now.

"Does she know already?" wondered Val; "if not, why does she look like that? Have you been ill, Mrs. Wyndham?" he asked, aloud.

"Oh, no," she said, drearily; "but I have not been out much of late, and so have got low-spirited, I suppose. This wretched autumn weather, too, always makes me dismal."

"How shall I begin?" thought Val, staring moodily in the fire. But the cheering blaze gave forth no answer, and it was Olive herself who broke the ice.

"Has anything happened, Mr. Blake, to make you wear that serious face? Mr. Wyndham——"

She paused—her voice quivering a little. Val looked up.

"Mr. Wyndham is at Rosebush Cottage," he said. "Did you know it?"

"I thought he was. It is three days since he was here."

The tremor was in her voice again.

"What does it mean, at all?" thought Val; "it can't be that she cares for the fellow, surely!"

"Is his mother worse, do you know?" she asked, her

spirit rebelling against the question her torturing anxiety forced from her.

"Now it is coming!" thought Val; "bless my soul! but it is hard to get out! It sticks in my throat like Macbeth's amen! Madam," he said, aloud, facing round and plunging into the icy shower-bath at once, "there has been a terrible mistake, which only came to my knowledge last night. A great wrong has been done you by Mr. Wyndham, and it is to inform you of it I have come here to-day."

He pale face turnéd blood-red, and then ghastly white.

"You need not tell me," she cried, "I know it! She is not his mother!"

"She is not!" said Val, very much surprised; "but how in the world did you find it out?"

She did not speak. She sat looking at him with a dreadful fixed stare.

"Tell me all," she said; "tell me all! Who is she?" .

"She is his wife! I don't think you can know that. He was a married man before he ever saw you here."

A low cry of despair broke from Olive's white lips. This was not what she had expected—at the worst, she had never thought of this.

"His wife!" she cried, "and what, then, am I?"

Val sat dumb. It was not a very pleasant question to answer; and, to tell the truth, he was more than a little afraid of the lightning flashing from those midnight eyes.

"What am I?" she repeated, in a voice almost piercing in its shrillness. "What am I? If she is his wife, what am I?"

"My dear madam, it is a most wicked affair from beginning to end, and you have been most shamefully duped. Believe me, I pity you from the very bottom of my heart."

With a cry that Val Blake never forgot, in its broken-hearted anguish and despair, she dropped down on the sofa, and buried her face among the pillows, as if she would

18*

have shut out the world and its miseries, as she did the sight of the man before her.

Mr. Blake, not knowing any panacea for misery such as this, and fearing to turn consoler, lest he should make a mess of it, did the very best thing he could have done, let it alone, and began the story he had to tell. So, lying there in her bitter humiliation, this woman heard that her miserable secret was a secret no longer, and that the pale, silent actress of Mrs. Butterby's lodgings had been Nathalie Marsh, and was now Paul Wyndham's beloved wife. That was the misery—she scarcely heeded, in the supreme suffering of that thought, the discovery of her own trickery and deceit—she only knew that the man she had thought her husband, and who, in spite of herself, she had learned to love, had cruelly and shamefully deceived her. She had never for one poor moment been his wife, never for an instant had a right to his name; she was only the poor despised tool, whom he used at the bidding of the wife he loved. The horrible agony she suffered lying there, and thinking of those things, no human pen can tell —no heart conceive.

Mr. Blake rose up when he finished his narrative, thankful it was over. She had never moved or spoken all the time, but he knew she had heard him, and he paused, with his hand on the door, to make a last remark.

"I beg, my dear young lady, you will not be overcome by this unfortunate affair. It will be kept as close as possible, and you need not be disturbed in the possession of Redmon, since such is Miss Rose's wish. I have done my duty in telling you, though the duty has been a very unpleasant one. Good-morning, madam."

She never moved. Val looked at the prostrate figure with a vague uneasiness, and remembered it was just such women as this that swallowed poison, or went down to the river and drowned themselves. He thought of it all the way to Mrs. Marsh's, growing more and more uneasy all the time.

"Oh, hang it," thought Mr. Blake, "I wish Paul Wyndham had been at Jericho before I ever got mixed up in his dirty doings. If that black-eyed young woman goes and does something desperate, I shall feel as if I had a hand in her death. I am always getting into other people's scrapes, somehow! I suppose it's my luck!"

Val knocked at the cottage door, and was admitted to the pleased presence of Mrs. Marsh. And to her, once again, the story of plot and counterplot had to be told; but it was a long time before she could quite comprehend it. She cried a good deal when she fully took in the sense of the thing, said she wondered at Mr. Wyndham, and thought it was dreadful to have Nathalie restored, only to find she was out of her mind. She wanted to go to her at once, she said—poor dear Natty! and so Mr. Blake went for a cab without more ado, and found Mrs. Marsh shawled and bonneted, and all ready, upon his return. They drove up Golden Row and stopped at Mrs. Wheatly's for Miss Rose, whom Val handed in, in a few minutes, and then packed himself up beside the driver.

Midge opened the door of Rosebush Cottage to the visitors, and stared aghast upon seeing who they were.

"Is Mr. Wyndham in?" asked Val.

Midge nodded, and jerked her head toward the room he had been in the preceding night, and, unconscious Val tapped at it, and then walked in, followed by the two ladies.

Paul Wyndham stood up as they entered, pale and quiet as ever. Nathalie, wrapped in a loose white morning-dress, lay on a lounge, a pile of pillows under her head, and a mingled odor of vinegar and cologne and a number of saturated cloths showed he had been bathing her forehead when they came in. Mrs. Marsh never noticed him, but fell down on her knees beside the lounge, in an outburst of motherly grief and joy, raining kisses on the feverish face. Alas! that now-flushed, feverish face! the cheeks crimson, the forehead shining, and burning with raging fever, the golden hair all tossed and disordered over the pillows, and the hot, restless head turning ceaselessly from side to side, vainly trying to cool its fire. The blue eyes shone with fever's luster; but no light of recognition came into them at her mother's passionate words and kisses. Miss Rose, throwing off her hat and mantle, knelt beside

her and dipped the cloths in vinegar and water, and laid
them on the burning brow of the poor stricken girl. Val
looked inquiringly at Mr. Wyndham.

"She must have taken cold last evening in the church,"
he answered, in a low tone; "she became delirious in the
night, and has continued so ever since."

"I'll be off for the doctor at once," said Val, briskly;
"she's in a bad way, I know. I'll fetch Dr. Leach, he
was their family physician, and won't tell."

Energetic Mr. Blake stalked out of the room without
more ado. Paul Wyndham followed him to the door.

"They know?" he inquired, motioning toward the
room they had quitted.

"All about it," said Val, "and so does that unhappy
young woman at Redmon, and if she doesn't commit
suicide before night it will be a mercy. And oh, Wyndham, by the way, you had better not show yourself. It
isn't a very creditable affair, you know, to any of the
parties concerned, and the best atonement you can make
is to keep out of sight."

He strode off, without waiting for a reply, in search of
Dr. Leach, and had the good fortune to find that gentleman taking his dinner. Mr. Blake hurried him through
that meal with little regard to calm digestion, and on the
road had to relate, for the fourth time, the story, of which
he was by this time heartily sick.

Dr. Leach listened like a man who cannot believe his
own ears.

"Bless my soul!" he exclaimed, "is it a story out of
the Arabian Nights you are telling me? Nathalie Marsh
alive, and Mr. Wyndham's wife! The mother all a
hoax, and the young woman at Redmon a—what is she,
Blake?"

"Blamed if I know!" replied Mr. Blake; "but, whatever she is, Nathalie was the first wife. It's a very uncommon story, but it is true as preaching for all that, only
I am getting tired of telling it so often."

"Well, well, well! Wonders will never cease! Natty
returned to life, Cherry back in Speekport, and Charley

coming! Why, Val, we will have the old merry time all over again before long "

"I am afraid not! I am afraid poor Nathalie is beyond even your skill, doctor. She was almost at death's door before, and this fever will finish her."

Mr. Wyndham was not in the room when the doctor and Val returned. Mrs. Marsh and Miss Rose were still keeping cooling applications to the hot forehead, but nothing could cool the fever that consumed her. Val drew Miss Rose aside as the doctor bent over his patient.

"Where is Wyndham?" he asked.

"I don't know. He has not been here since you left."

"What do you think of her?" nodding toward the fever-stricken girl on the lounge.

The governess, whose experience among the sick poor made her no unskillful leech, looked out of the window through a mist of tears.

"We have found her to lose her again, I fear. Look at Dr. Leach's face! Can you not read his verdict there?"

The old physician certainly was looking seriously grave, and shook his head at Mrs. Marsh's eager questioning.

"We must hope for the best, ma'am, and do what we can. The result is in the hands of Providence."

"Then you think there is danger, doctor?" said Val, coming forward.

"Imminent danger, sir! It is typhoid fever, and a very serious case, too. A strong constitution would stand a chance, but she has no constitution at all. Gone, sir! gone! she is as feeble as an infant."

"Then there is no hope at all?"

"None!" replied Dr. Leach, solemnly; "she will never leave this room alive. And better so, better so than as she was."

"Yes," said Val, sadly; "it is better as it is! My dear Mrs. Marsh, don't distress yourself so. Think that her mind is entirely gone, and never could be restored, I believe, and you will be thankful that her earthly troubles are so nearly ended."

Dr. Leach was giving directions in a low tone to Miss Rose, and Val, at his desire, lifted the slight form of the sufferer in his strong arms, carried her into the inner room, and laid her on the bed.

"I will call in again before night," said the doctor. "Remember my directions, Miss Rose. Come, Blake; you're going, I suppose?"

"Yes; in a moment. I want to see Wyndham."

Paul Wyndham was walking up and down the hall as they came out, his pale face expressive of but one thing—intensest anxiety. Dr. Leach, with a stiff bow, passed on and went out, but Val halted.

"Well?" Mr. Wyndham asked, eagerly.

"No hope," said Val; "no earthly power can save her. It's typhoid—the most malignant kind. She will die, thank God!"

Paul Wyndham leaned against the wall and covered his face, with a bitter groan.

"As to you," pursued Val, sternly, "you must leave this house at once, and enter it no more. Do not forget that we are acting criminally in screening you from the law, and that we can enforce our commands. Go at once, and do not come here again until all is over!"

He left the house as he spoke, and joined the doctor, who had gained the highroad. Some people passing stared to see them coming from Rosebush Cottage, and surmised Mr. Wyndham's mad mother must be worse than ever."

"How long can she last, doctor?" Val asked, before they parted.

"Not over two weeks, I fancy, at the most. This fever will carry her off at once."

Late in the evening Dr. Leach returned, and found Nathalie worse. Mr. Wyndham had left the cottage, after taking one last look at the wife he loved so passionately. The agony in his face had gone to Mrs. Marsh's heart, and she cried now, as she spoke of it to the doctor.

"Yes; I dare say," the old man returned, shortly, "he's very sorry, no doubt, but he's a villain for all that; and, only for poor Natty's sake, I'd have him arrested for bigamy this minute!"

Miss Rose did not go home that night; she would never leave Nathalie now. She sent a note to Mrs. Wheatly by the doctor, explaining that it was a case of typhoid, and that she feared to bring the infection into the family. All further explanation she left to the doctor, only desiring that her clothes might be sent to her. Mrs. Marsh dispatched a similar message to Betsy Ann, and before night everybody knew that Mr. Wyndham's mother was very bad, that Dr. Leach and Val Blake had been there, and that Mrs. Marsh and Miss Rose were staying to take care of her.

And what did Speckport say to all this? Oh, Speckport had a great deal to say, and surmise, and inquire. How was it, Speckport wanted to know, in the first place, that Mrs. Marsh and Miss Rose should be especially selected as the sick woman's nurses? To which Dr. Leach replied that Miss Rose, being such a capital hand at the business, and so fond of it into the bargain, he thought that there was no one in the town so fitted for the task; and Mrs. Marsh, having nothing else to do, could play propriety and read novels there as well as in Cottage Street. What was Mr. Wyndham's mother like, was she a violent lunatic, and was her present disease infectious? Speckport further inquired. To which Dr. Leach said, Mrs. Wyndham was the wreck of a very handsome woman, that she was not violent, only imbecile, and that her fever was highly infectious, and made it extremely dangerous for any one but the physician and nurses to enter the house; on which account Mr. Wyndham would absent himself from Redmon, and Mrs. Olive from Rosebush Cottage, until all was over. After which ominous phrase the doctor would hurry away, and Speckport was satisfied.

Mr. Blake, to be consistent, took up his quarters elsewhere, and visited the cottage every day to inquire. Paul Wyndham, who was stopping at the Farmer's Hotel, very near the cottage, came two or three times a day to ask, but no one invited him to enter, and a sense of honor forbade his intruding. The answer to all inquiries was continually the same, "No better." No, Nathalie was no better—never would be better in this world! She lay tossing on her feverish bed, raving wildly, consumed with burning heat, never resting night or day. All the scenes of her life were acted over again in that burning chasm. Now she babbled of her schoolgirl-days, her mathematics and her music, or berrying and nutting frolics with Charley. Now she was with Captain Cavendish, loving and trusting and happy; and now she was shrieking out again that she saw the murdered woman, and covering her eyes to shut out the ghastly sight. Now the days of her misery had come; now she was at sea with Captain Locksley, and in the New York lodging-house; now on the stage, making rambling, incoherent speeches, and singing stage-songs. Now she was with Paul Wyndham, his wife; now she was in the cathedral listening to the stern preacher. And here she would shriek out, and toss her arms wildly, and ask them to take her to Redmon, that she must tell her all—she must! she must! And Miss Rose and her mother would have to hold her down by force to prevent her from rising from the bed in her excitement, and soothe her with promises that she should go there—only to wait a little while. And the poor sufferer would fall back exhausted, and perhaps go back to the old days when she played with Charley, a child.

CHAPTER XXXVII.

DIES IRÆ, DIES ILLA.

THE November day broke bleak and gloomy. The dismal dawn was laden with thick, sodden fog, and wretched, drizzling rain. The wind, full of the wail of coming winter, was cold and raw; and the sky, seen dimly through the fog-bank, was of sullen lead, the earth black and dreary; and the sea and the fog so mixed that you could hardly tell where one began and the other ended.

In the Farmers' Hotel, a rambling wooden building, standing by itself on a quiet country road, all was still as the grave at this early hour of the miserable November morning. Even in the kitchen and halls there was as yet no step, and the servants slept the sleep of the just in their own dormitories. Perhaps of all in the house the man who stood at his chamber window, blurred and smeared with clammy wet, and stared hopelessly out through the full blank of fog and mist, was the only one astir in the house.

In the murky dawn of this bad November morning, Paul Wyndham, with hollow creases under his eyes, and deep plowshares of silent suffering about his mouth and forehead, stood looking out of the stained window, at the flat waste of desolation without. It was hardly two poor weeks, but it seemed a lifetime; and a horrible numbness was coming over him and blunting all sense of pain. Would it always go on like this—this dull, dead blank in life—would it last forever? All things were beginning to look unreal, and lose their significance, nothing seemed palpable or as it used to be. He was conscious that the crisis had come; that in the long, black, sluggish watches of that wet November night a battle had been fought between life and death, in the cottage whose lighted window he could see from his own; but only con-

scious in a dull, numb sort of way, to which the sharpness
of the torture had given force.

The pale, cold dawn crept shining in while he stood
there blankly staring out at the hopeless dreariness, and
he roused himself from his torpor by a great effort at last.
A loud-voiced clock somewhere in the silent house struck
six as he put on his overcoat and hat and went down
stairs.

Paul Wyndham waded on through the sea of mud, in
the cold morning rain, not meeting a soul, until he stood
before Rosebush Cottage. The red light in the window
burned still; but had that other light, that light of a
beloved life, gone out in the night? It had been the
crisis of the fever—that low, miserable, burning, delirious
fever, in which for so many weary days and endless
nights, the poor, unconscious sufferer had tossed. Ah!
that dreary time of probation—when the faithful watchers
had seen her sink day by day; when they had to force her
clenched teeth apart to admit teaspoonfuls of beef-tea;
when they had listened with aching hearts to her meaningless babble, or the songs the weak voice sang. But that
sad time of waiting had dragged itself out, and the night
came which must end all suspense. Does hope ever entirely leave the human heart, until the blank face actually
grows rigid and the death-rattle sounds? Those sad and
silent watchers in that darkened room hoped against hope
through the slow lingering hours of that night. They
were all there—Dr. Leach, Val, Mrs. Marsh, Miss Rose,
and Midge, all mutely watching the pale shadow of
Nathalie lying so still and white on the bed. You might
have thought her dead had you entered, and looked at her
lying with closed eyes, and no perceptible respiration. But
she was only sleeping, and a faint breath still came from
the colorless lips—sleeping a sleep from which the doctor,
at least, knew she could only awake to die. He had a
strong hope she might awake free from fever, and that
reason might return before the last hour. He sat by the
bedside, holding her wrist in his fingers, never taking his
eyes off her face. Mrs. Marsh had fallen asleep quietly in
her chair, and Mr. Blake was dozing; so when, as the pale

morning broke, and the blue eyes opened to life once more, there was only the doctor and Miss Rose to bend over her.

"Nathalie, darling!" the governess said, with trembling lips, "don't you know me?"

The blue eyes turned upon the sweet face with the clear light of restored reason, and a faint smile dawned on the wasted face.

"Miss Rose," she said, in a voice so faint that it sounded scarcely above a whisper. "You here?"

"I am here, too, Natty," said the physician. "Don't you know the old doctor?"

Yes, she knew him—she knew them all when they came crowding around her, and looked up at them with faint wonder in her fever-dimmed blue eyes.

"I have been ill, haven't I?" she said, feebly, glancing at her poor, transparent, wasted hands. "Have I been ill long?"

"Not very long, Natty dear," her mother answered, kissing her, "only two weeks, and you will be better soon now, won't she, doctor?"

But Dr. Leach did not reply. How could he deceive that dying girl? She looked into his grave, sad face, and a solemn shadow fell on her own, a shadow of the dark truth.

"Oh, doctor!" she cried out, "am I dying?"

He bent over her, and stroked away tenderly the full dark hair off her forehead.

"My poor child! my dear child! God knows I would save you if I could; but the power of life and death lies in higher hands. Has this world been such a pleasant place to you that you should wish to stay in it? Think of that better world, my poor little girl, that lies beyond the grave. It would be cruel in me to deceive you now."

She drew the hand he held out of his suddenly, and turned her face away from them. Mrs. Marsh broke out into strong sobbing, but the doctor sternly hushed her. But the dulled, dying ear caught the sound, and she turned to them again.

'How long have I to live?" she asked.

He could not tell an untruth with those earnest eyes fixed on his face, and his voice was husky as he replied:

"Not long! not long, my poor girl! But long enough to prepare for the world to which you are going."

"Will I die to-day?"

Her mother's sobs broke out again; but Nathalie looked only at the doctor.

"Yes, dear child, you will last to-day, I think; but try and be calm, and not disturb yourself at the shortness of the time."

Her hands dropped in a kind of collapse of despair.

"So soon, so soon!" she said, "and so much to do—so much to atone for!"

"Shall we send for a clergyman?" the doctor asked.

"Shall I fetch you Father Lennard?" inquired Val, stooping over her.

Her face brightened a little. The gray old priest had baptized her, an infant, had confirmed her a young girl, and she had loved and reverenced him more than any one else on earth. •

"Yes, yes," she said, eagerly. "Bring Father Lennard. Oh, how short the time is, and so much to be done."

Mr. Blake found Father Lennard at home, and had to go over again the weary story of wrong-doings and false-hood. He was a very old man; his hair had grown gray in his holy calling, and he was long used to tales of sorrow and sin—sorrow and sin, that go so surely hand in hand. He had learned to listen to such recitals—as a pitiful doctor, who knows all the ailments poor human nature is subject to, does to stories of bodily suffering—tenderly, sadly, but with no surprise. He had known Nathalie Marsh from babyhood; he had had a father's affection for the pretty, gentle, blue-eyed little girl, who had knelt at his confessional so often, lisping out her childish faults; he had moaned for her tragic fate; and he had nothing but pity, and prayer, and sorrow for her now.

Mrs. Marsh and Miss Rose were in the room with the dying girl when they returned; Mrs. Marsh sitting at the foot of the bed, weeping incessantly, and the pale governess kneeling beside the pillows, holding the cold thin hands in hers, and reading prayers for the sick out of a missal. Both arose when the Father entered, and the dying face lit up with a sudden light of recognition and hope.

"My poor child! my poor baby!" the old man said, tenderly, bending over her. "Is it thus I find my little Natty again? Thank God that reason has returned to you in your last hours."

The mother and friend of the dying girl quitted the room, leaving the old priest alone to prepare the departing soul for its last great journey. Miss Rose knelt in silent, fervent prayer all the time; but Mrs. Marsh—poor weak soul!—could do nothing but sit and cry. Val had found Mr. Wyndham in the kitchen, leaning against the wooden chimney-piece, with a white, despairing face; and, pitying him in spite of his misdoings, turned comforter as best he could. He walked up and down the hall restlessly between whiles, feeling in the solemn hush of the house as if he were in the tomb. His watch, which he was perpetually jerking out, pointed to ten; and he was thinking he would have to run down to the office presently, when, opening the parlor-door to announce that intention, he saw Father Lennard come out of the sick-room.

"Well, Father?" Val said, anxiously.

"All is well, thank God! She is quite resigned now; and if sincere contrition ever atoned for sin, hers will surely be pardoned. Are you in a hurry, Val?"

"I should be very much hurried indeed, Father, if I could not do anything you or she may desire! What is it?"

"Will you go to Redmon, and fetch that unhappy young lady here. The poor child says she cannot die until she has heard her pardon her."

"I'll go," said Val, "but I'm not so sure Mrs. Wyndham will come. You see, she is one of your proud and high-stepping people, and is in such trouble herself that——"

"Let me go with you, Mr. Blake," cried Miss Rose, starting up; "I think she will come with me."

"All right, then! Put your bonnet on while I run round and make Peter get out the buggy."

The buggy came round to the front door, and Val assisted the governess in and drove off.

Father Lennard returned to the sick-room, and sat there holding the hand of the dying, whose sad, sunken blue eyes never left his face, and talking of that merciful Redeemer, who once said to another poor sinful creature, "Neither do I condemn thee!" Nathalie lay, clasping a crucifix to her breast, her pale lips moving in ceaseless inward prayer, while she listened, her face calm and beautiful in its holy hope. The hours that intervened seemed very short, and then the carriage wheels crunched over the gravel, and Nathalie caught her breath with a sort of gasp.

"Oh, Father, do you think she has come?"

"I trust so, dear child! I will go and see."

As he entered the drawing-room, the front door opened. Val stalked in, followed by Miss Rose and—yes, by a figure stately and tall, dressed very plainly, and closely vailed. The priest knew that majestic figure, although the face, seen dimly through the vail, was so changed that he hardly knew it.

"You may go in," he said, in reply to Miss Rose's appealing look; "she is waiting for you."

As the door closed upon the tall vailed form, and the two women, united to the same man, were face to face, Father Lennard took his hat to go.

"I shall return again in the afternoon," he said; "I would stay all day if I could, but it is impossible."

"I will drive you into town," said Val; "Peter can fetch the traps back. Oh, here's the doctor!"

Dr. Leach opened the garden-gate as they came out, and lifted his hat to the clergyman.

"How is she?" he asked.

"Failing fast," said Father Lennard. "I do not think she will wear the night through!"

"You are coming back, I suppose?"

"I shall endeavor to do so. I promised her I would, poor child!"

The doctor went into the drawing-room, where Mrs. Marsh, through her tears, told him who was with her The old doctor looked dissatisfied.

"They'll agitate her too much—I know they will, with their crying and taking on. If they stay long, I will go and turn them out!"

He waited for a quarter of an hour, watch in hand, frowning impatiently at the dial-plate, and then the chamber-door reopened and the half-sisters came out. The swollen eyes of the governess told how she had been weeping, but the other had dropped her vail once more, and was invisible. Dr. Leach bowed to her, but she passed on without seeming to see him. Miss Rose followed her to the door, and looked wistfully out at the wet, foggy November weather, and the hopeless slough of mud.

"You cannot walk back, Harriet. I will send Peter to Redmon for the carriage. You will get your death of cold to walk there, unused as you are to walking."

"What does it matter?" she said, in a strangely hollow voice, "the sooner I get my death the better. If I could only die like her, I should rejoice however soon it came!"

"But, Harriet——"

But Harriet was gone, even while she spoke, walking rapidly through the drizzling rain and clammy mud—she, who had had a fastidious horror of mud on her dainty boots —and knowing nothing of either. All that was best in her nature had been roused into life by that dying-bed, but still that utter sense of despair and desolation filled her soul. Her life was done—there was no future for her— in all the wide universe there was not such another miserable woman as herself, she thought—desolate, un-loved, and alone.

There were not many people abroad that bad November day; but those who were, and who recognized Mrs. Wyndham through her vail, and bowed ceremoniously, felt themselves outraged at receiving the cut direct. She never saw them—she walked straight forward to that stately home that was hers no longer, as people walk in sleep, with eyes wide open and staring straight before her, but seeing nothing.

Dr. Leach went into the sick-room as the others left it; but he returned presently, frowning again.

"Where is the fellow to be found?" he asked, impatiently; "she will excite herself in spite of all I can say. She must see him, she says, if only for ten minutes."

"Is it Mr. Wyndham?" asked Miss Rose; and the doctor nodded crossly.

It was the first time that the dying girl had spoken of him; and Miss Rose, who knew he was in the house, left the room without a word.

"Oh, he is here, is he?" said Dr. Leach. "I might have known it! Hem! Here he comes!"

Paul Wyndham followed the governess into the parlor, looking so haggard that even the old doctor pitied him.

"Now, Mr. Wyndham," he said, "my patient is not to be unnecessarily excited, remember! I give you just ten minutes, not a second more!"

Mr. Wyndham bowed his head and passed into the chamber; and Dr. Leach, watch in hand, planted himself at the door, and grimly counted the minutes. When the ten had passed, he opened the door.

"Time's up," he said; "say good-bye, Mr. Wyndham, and come out!"

They were all merciful enough not to look at him as he obeyed. Dr. Leach went in and found poor Nathalie lying with her eyes closed, clasping her crucifix, her lips still moving in voiceless prayer. She looked up at him with her poor, pleading eyes.

The old doctor departed, and the two women were left alone with the dying wife of Paul Wyndham. Miss Rose sat by the bedside, reading, in her sweet, low voice, the consoling prayers for the sick, while poor, weak, useless Mrs. Marsh only rocked backward and forward in the rocking-chair, moaning and crying in feeble helplessness. And Paul Wyndham, in the room on the other side of the hall, walking restlessly up and down, or stopping to gaze out of the window, or running to Midge every five minutes to go and inquire how she was—felt and suffered as men only can feel and suffer once in a lifetime.

The leaden hours of the twilight deepened into night —black, somber, starless. With the night came the wind and fell the rain. The storm had been gathering sullenly all day, and broke with the night fast and furious. The rain lashed the windows, and the melancholy autumn winds shrieked and wailed alternately around the cottage, waking a surging roar in the black cedar woods beyond. The feeble hands still fold themselves over the precious crucifix—that "sign of hope to man"—but the power of speech has gone. She cannot move, either; her eyes and lips are all that seem alive, but her sense of hearing remains. She hears the sound of carriage-wheels outside, and hears when Father Lennard, Dr. Leach, and faithful Val enter the drawing-room. The old priest takes Miss Rose's place, to administer the last solemn rites to the dying, and Nathalie smiles faintly up in his face and kisses the cross he holds to her lips. Val Blake goes into the room where he knows Paul Wyndham must be, and finds him lying as Midge found him a quarter of an hour before. He stoops down and finds he is asleep—Ah! when had he slept night or day before?— and his face looks so haggard and heart-broken in repose that Val says "Poor fellow!" and goes softly out.

And so, with death in their midst, the faithful watchers sit and keep vigil, while the stormy night wore on. Ah! Heaven strengthen us all for that dread death-watch, when we sit beside those we love, and watch and wait for the soul to take its flight. No one spoke, except in hushed whispers, and the roaring of the wild storm sounded awfully loud in the stillness. They can hear the voice of the old priest as he reads, or talks, or prays with that fluttering spirit, already in the shadow of the valley of death. As the watch of Val points to eleven. Miss Rose glides softly out, with a face like snow, and tells them to kneel, while Father Lennard reads the prayers for the dying. So they kneel and bow their heads with awe-struck spirits, while the solemn and

beautiful prayers of the old church are read, and thrill as
they hear that awful adjuration: "Depart, Christian
soul, out of this world!" and then, as it is finishing,
there is a pause. What does it mean? The service for
the dying is not ended. A moment later and they know
—Father Lennard goes on, but it is prayers for the dead
he renders now, and they know all is over; and Val
Blake leans his head on his arm and feels it grow wet,
while the sad and solemn voice of the old priest goes on.
Then they all arise, Father Lennard reverentially closes
the blue eyes, that have looked their last on this mortal
life, and there is a wild outbreak of motherly love from
poor Mrs. Marsh; and Miss Rose, with her face buried in
the pillow, is crying as she has not cried for many a day;
and Val and the old doctor go softly in and look on the
beautiful dead face, and think of the bright, happy
Nathalie Marsh of last year—for whom all the world
might have prophesied a long and happy life—and feel
that neither youth, nor health, nor beauty, nor all the
glory of the world, can save us one hour from death.

CHAPTER XXXVIII.

OUT OF THE CROOKED WAYS.

AND so all was over; and Speckport found out
that the poor, miserable creature, Mr. Wyndham's mother, was dead. It must have been
a merciful release for her, poor soul! they
said; but the fever was infectious, and they
sympathized at a respectful distance. But Mr. Wyndham's wife left Redmon and went to the cottage as soon
as she heard it, and staid there through all the weary
time that intervened between the death and the burial.
There had been a consultation about the funeral and the

grave, and it was decided that that other grave, marked with the white cross, and bearing the name of Nathalie Marsh, should not be disturbed. By-and-by, Val said, the name can be erased; to disturb it now would involve the telling of the whole story. Let Mr. Wyndham erect what sort of monument he pleases. So the grave was dug in a sunny inclosure, under a tamarack tree, and the funeral-service was held in the cathedral, and a long file of carriages followed the hearse to the cemetery. Paul Wyndham, in his deep mourning, stood bareheaded in the cold November sunlight while the coffin was being lowered and the sods rattled heavily on the lid; and Speckport, as represented by the funeral cortege, whispered that Mr. Wyndham looked ten years older since his mother's death.

So Rosebush Cottage was left once more to the sole care of Midge, and Mr. Wyndham returned to his late quarters at the "Farmer's Hotel." Mrs. Marsh was driven to Cottage Street, and Mr. Blake, having fumigated himself thoroughly, delighted the home of Miss Laura Blair once more with the light of his presence. Poor Laura had led rather a lonely life of late; for her darling Olly, wrapped up in her own troubles, had no time to attend to her, and Val had deserted them altogether. She was sitting, pale and listless, turning over the leaves of a new and popular novel, with an indifference not very flattering to the author, when the opening of the door made her start up, with a flush on her pretty face and a light in her bright eyes, to whose flattering interest even Mr. Blake could not be insensible.

"Yes, I've come back to poor Laura," Mr. Blake said, shaking hands with more warmth than perhaps there was any real necessity for. "I find I can't stay away from you somehow. How's everybody?"

"Pa and ma are well, if you mean them by 'everybody.' So poor Mr. Wyndham's mother has gone?"

Mr. Blake nodded.

"And what is Mr. Wyndham going to do with that love of a cottage now, I wonder?"

"I," said Mr. Blake, imperiously, "am going to purchase that love of a cottage myself!"

"You! Why, Val! What will you ever do with a house?"

"Live in it, Miss Blair, like any other Christian!"

"Oh, yes; of course; I suppose you will send for Miss Jo to keep house for you again?"

"Why, no," said Mr. Blake, thoughtfully. "I think not. Do you know, Laura, what I have been thinking of lately?"

"No; how should I?"

"Well, then," said Val, in a confidential tone, "I have been thinking of getting married! You need not mention it just yet, until I see more about it. In fact, I have not asked the lady yet, and don't know what she may say."

"And who is the happy lady, pray?"

"A particular friend of mine," nodded Val, sagely, "and of yours, too, Laura. The nicest girl in Speckport."

"It is Miss Rose," thought Laura, with a sudden sinking of the heart. "He always admired her, and they have been so much together lately!"

"I'll buy the cottage from Wyndham as it stands," pursued Val, serenely unconscious of the turn Miss Blair's thoughts had taken, "and fetch my wife there, and live in clover all the rest of my life. So hold yourself in readiness, Miss Laura, to dance at the wedding."

Miss Laura might have replied but for a sudden choking sensation in the throat, and the entrance of her portly mamma. Under cover of that lady's entrance, she made her exit, and going up to her room, flung herself, face downward, on the bed, and cried until her eyes were as red as a ferret's. And all the time Mr. Blake was in a state of serene complacency at the artful way in which he had prepared her for what was to come.

"I couldn't speak much plainer," he thought, blandly. "How pretty she looked, blushing and looking down. Of course I'll get married. I wonder I never thought of it before. Dear little Laura! I'll never forget the first time I heard her sing, 'We won't go home till morning!' I thought her the jolliest girl then I ever met."

Mr. Blake was a gentleman in the habit of striking while the iron was hot. He called round at the office, rapped Master Bill Blair over the head with the tongs for standing on his hands instead of his feet, and then started off for the Farmer's Hotel, without more ado, and was ushered by a waiter into Mr. Wyndham's room.

"Blake, I owe you more than I can ever repay," he said; "you have been my true friend through all this miserable time; and believe me, I feel your goodness as much as a man can feel, even though I cannot express it! Please God, this trouble of my life shall make me a better man, if I can never be a happy one."

"Oh, you'll be happy," said Mr. Blake. "Get into the straight path again, Wyndham, and keep there. I don't set up for a preacher, goodness knows! but you may depend there is nothing like it."

"The straight path!" Paul Wyndham repeated, with a weary, regretful sigh; "yes, I have been straying sadly out of the straight path of truth and honor and rectitude into the crooked ways of falsehood and treachery and deceit. Heaven help me, it never was with a contented heart! No one on this earth could ever despise me half so much as I despised myself all the time!"

"All right," cried Val, cheerily, "it's never too late to mend. Keep straight now, and we can all forgive and forget the past. I suppose you will be for leaving us shortly now?"

"Immediately. This is Tuesday—I shall depart in Thursday's boat."

"Will you," said Val, lighting a cigar; "that soon! What are you going to do with Rosebush Cottage?"

"The cottage! Oh, I shall leave it as it is—that is, shut it up. In time—a year or two, perhaps—I may return and sell it, if any one will purchase."

"Don't wait a year or two. Sell it now."

"Who wants it?"

"I do," said Val, with one of his nods.

"You! What do you want of the place, may I ask."

"Well, now, I don't see any just cause or impediment to my possessing a house any more than the rest of mankind, that everybody should be so surprised. I want the house to live in, of course—what else?"

Paul Wyndham looked at him and smiled. The great trouble of his life had changed him to a grave, sad man; but being only human, he could still smile.

"I wish you joy with all my heart! Laura has said yes, then?"

"Why, no, not exactly—that is to say, I haven't asked her out-and-out yet. I wanted to settle about the house first. But I gave her a pretty broad hint, and I guess it's all right. I think I should like to live there particularly, and now what will you take for it as it stands?"

Mr. Wyndham arose, opened a desk, and took out a bundle of papers, which he laid before Val.

"Here is the deed and all the documents connected with the place. You can see what it cost me yourself. Here is the upholsterer's bill, but you must deduct from that, for it is only second-hand furniture now. I leave the matter entirely to yourself."

With such premises, bargaining was no very difficult matter; and half an hour after, Val had the deed in his pocket, and was the happy owner of Rosebush Cottage.

"You stay here, I suppose, until Thursday," he said, rising to go.

"Yes."

"And how about that poor girl at Redmon? What is to become of her?"

Mr. Wyndham laid his hand on Val's shoulder, and looked very gravely up in his face.

"Val, before she died, in that last brief interview, she spoke of Harriet, and I gave her a promise then which I shall faithfully keep. The devotion of a whole life can scarcely atone to her for the wrong I have done her; but if she will accept that atonement, Heaven knows it will make me happier now than anything else on earth. If she does not utterly loathe and hate me—if she will be my wife in reality, as she has hitherto been in name—we will leave this place together; and whether my life be long or short, it shall be entirely devoted to her alone."

Val's face turned radiant. He seized Mr. Wyndham's other hand, and shook it with crushing heartiness.

"My dear Wyndham! My dear old boy! I always knew your heart was in the right place, in spite of all your shortcomings. Oh, you'll be all right now! You've got the stuff in you that men are made of!"

With which Mr. Blake strode off, fairly beaming with delight, and whistling all the way home. He sprang up the outer steps at a bound, rang the bell with emphasis, and shooting past the astonished servant, bolted whirlwind-fashion into the dining-room. At first he thought there was no one there, but, disturbed by the noisy entrance, from a sofa before the fire, and from out a heaving sea of pillows, Laura lifted up her head and looked at him. Poor Laura! That feminine luxury, a "real good cry," had brought on a raging headache, and now her face was flushed, her eyes dim and heavy, and her head throbbing and hot. She dropped that poor but aching head again as she saw who it was, with a rebellious choking in the throat, and a sudden filling of the eyes.

"Oh, I say, Laura," cried Mr. Blake, in considerable consternation, "you're not sick, are you? What's the matter?"

"My head aches," Laura got out, through her tears.

"Poor little head!" Mr. Blake piteously remarked, and Laura sobbed outright; "don't cry, Laura, it will be better before you are twice married. Look, here's a plaster I've brought you for it!"

He put the deed of Rosebush Cottage in her feverish hand. Laura stayed her tears, and looked at it, blankly.

"What is it?" she asked.

"Can't you see? It's the deed of Rosebush Cottage. I've bought it, furniture and all—and the furniture is very pretty, Laura—from Paul Wyndham. I'll let you keep that paper, if you'll promise to take good care of it."

"I don't understand you! Oh, Val!" cried Miss Blair, her heart beginning to flutter wildly again, "what is it you mean?"

"Why, didn't I tell you this morning? I'm going to be married—that is, if you will have me, Laura!"

Happy Laura! Such a rosy tide swept over her fair face, and dyed it radiant red to the roots of her hair.

"Oh, Val! I thought it was Miss Rose."

Val stared.

"Miss Rose! What the dickens put that in your head? I never thought of Miss Rose—I meant you all the time. Is it all right, Laura?"

All right! He need hardly have asked that question, seeing the radiant face before him. Laura laughed and cried, and blushed, and forgot all about her headache, and for the next fifteen minutes was completely and perfectly happy. It was one of those little glimpses of Eden that we poor pilgrims of the desert sometimes catch fleetingly as we wander wearily through long dreary wastes of sand, of sluggish marshes, or briery roads. Transient gleams of perfect joy, when we forget the past, and ask nothing of the future—when we hold the overflowing cup of bliss to our lips and drink to our heart's content.

"Dinner on the table!" Somebody made this announcement in a stentorian voice, and Val insisted on Laura's taking his arm, and accompanying him to the dining-room. Papa and Mamma Blair and Master Bill were waiting there; and Mr. Blake, ever prompt and business-like, led the blushing and shrinking fair one to the parental side, and boldly demanded their blessing. To say that Mr. and Mrs. Blair were astonished, would be doing no sort of justice to the subject; to say they were delighted, would be doing still less; and Miss Laura was formally made over to Mr. Blake before grace was said. Dinner was only a matter of form that day with Miss Blair —her appetite was effectually gone; and even Val—matter-of-fact, unromantic, unsentimental Val—ate considerably less underdone roast-beef than usual, and looked a good deal more across the table at the rosy, smiling face of his vis-a-vis than at the contents of his plate. But dinner was over at last, and an extra bottle of crusty old port drank to the happy event; and then Papa Blair buttoned up his overcoat and set off to business again, and Master

Bill started full gallop for the office, to retail the news to Mr. Clowrie; and Mamma Blair went about her domestic concerns, and the lovers were alone together. But Mr. Blake was not at all "up" in the rôle of Romeo, and stood beside Laura at the window, looking at the pale moon rising, and using his toothpick.

"What a lovely night!" Laura said; for all the world, so lately a howling wilderness, was moonlight and couleur de rose to her now, with plain Val Blake standing by her side. "How beautifully the moon is rising over the bay!"

"Yes," said Mr. Blake, eying it with the glance of a connoisseur in moonshine. "It's rather a neat thing in the way of moonrise. What whistle's that?"

"It's the American boat getting in. Suppose we go down, Val, and see who's coming?"

"All right!" said Val. "Run and put your things on, and don't be an hour about it, if you can help it."

Laura ran off, and reappeared in a quarter of the allotted time, turbaned and mantled, and furred, and tripped along through the moonlit and gaslit streets, with her new fiancé down to the wharf. The fine night had, as usual, drawn crowds down there, and the wharf was all bustle, and excitement, and uproar. Miss Blair, clinging confidingly to Mr. Blake's arm, watched the passengers making their way through the tumult to where the cabs were waiting, when all of a sudden she dropped the arm she held, with a little shrill feminine scream, and darting forward, plumped head foremost into the arms of a gentleman coming up the wharf, valise in hand. To say that Mr. Blake stared aghast would be a mild way of putting it; but stare he undoubtedly did, with might and main. The gentleman wore a long, loose overcoat, heavily furred, and his face was partially shaded by a big, black, California hat; but Val saw the handsome, sun-browned face beneath for all that, with its thick, dark mustache and beard. Could it be? surely not, with all those whiskers and that brown skin; and yet—and yet, it did look like: but by this time Laura had got out of the mustached stranger's coat-sleeves, and was back, breathless with excitement, beside the staring editor.

20*

"Oh, Val! it's Charley!—it's Charley Marsh! Charley. Marsh!" Charley, sure enough, in spite of the whiskers and the sun-brown. Val was beside him in two strides, shaking both hands as if he meant to wrench the arms from their sockets.

"My dear boy! my dear boy! my dear boy!" was all Mr. Blake could get out, while he spoke. and shook poor Charley's hands; and Laura performed a little jig of ecstasy around them, to the great delight of sundry small boys looking on. As for Charley himself, there were tears in his blue eyes, even while he laughed at Val.

"Dear old Val!" he said, "it is a sight for sair een to look at your honest face again! Dear old boy! there is no place like home!"

"Come along," cried Val, hooking his arm in Charley's. "The people are gaping as if we had two heads on us! Here's a cab; get in, Laura; jump after her, Charley. Now, then, driver, No. 12 Golden Row!"

"Hold on!" exclaimed Charley, laughing at his phlegmatic friend's sudden excitement, "I cannot permit myself to be abducted in this manner. I must go to Cottage Street."

"Come home with us first," said Val, gravely. "I have something to tell you—something you ought to know before you go to Cottage Street."

"My mother!" Charley cried, in sudden alarm; "she is ill—something is wrong."

"No, she's not! Your mother is well, and nothing is wrong. Be patient for ten minutes, and you'll find out what I mean!"

The cab stopped with a jerk in front of Mr. Blair's; and, as they got out, a gentleman galloped past on horseback, and turned round to look at them. Val nodded, and the rider, touching his hat to Laura, rode on.

"Where is Mr. Wyndham going, I wonder?" said Laura.

"To Redmon, I think," Val answered. "Come in, Charley! Won't the old folks stare, though, when they see you?"

Miss Rose—her name is Rose, you know—had gone from Rosebush Cottage to Redmon, at the earnest entreaties of her half-sister. She had wished to return to Mrs. Wheatly's, and let things go on as before; but Harriet Wade—the only name to which she had any right—had opposed it so violently, and pleaded so passionately, that she had to have her way.

"Stay with me, Olive, stay with me while I am here!" had been the vehement cry. "I shall die if I am left alone!"

"Very well, I will stay," her sister said, kissing her; "but, please, Harriet, don't call me Olive, call me Winnie. I like it best, and it is the name by which they know me here."

So Winnie Rose Henderson went to Redmon—her own rightful home, and hers alone—and on the night of Charley Marsh's return, when Paul Wyndham entered the house, her small, light figure crossing the hall was the first object he saw. She came forward with a little womanly cry at sight of him.

"Oh, Mr. Wyndham, I am so glad you have come! I want you to talk to Harriet. She is going away."

"Going away! Where?"

"Back to New York, she says—anywhere out of this. Back to the old life of trouble and toil. Oh, Mr. Wyndham, talk to her. All I say is useless. But you have influence over her, I know."

"Have I?" Mr. Wyndham said, with a sad, incredulous smile. "What is it you want her to do, Miss Henderson?"

"I want you to make her stay here. I want you to persuade her to let everything go on as before. I mean," the governess said, coloring slightly, "as regards myself and her, of course."

Mr. Wyndham took her hand and looked down at her, with that grave, sad smile still on his face.

"My dear Miss Henderson," he said, "—for by that name I must call you—you are the best and noblest woman in the world, and I shall venerate all womankind henceforth for your sake. But we would be as selfish as you are noble did we accept the sacrifice you are sc wil. ing to make. I have come to offer the only atonement it is in my power to make for the wrong I have done her. On the result depends what her future life shall be."

The governess understood him, and the co.or deepened on her face.

"She is in the library." she said, withdrawing her hand and moving away. "You have my best wishes."

Paul Wyndham tapped at the library-door, and the familiar voice of the woman he sought called "Come in!" She was lying on a lounge, drawn up before a glowing coal-fire, listlessly lying there, its ruddy glow falling on her face, and showing how wan and worn it was. At sight of him, that pale face turned even paler, and she rose up and looked at him, as some poor criminal under trial for her life might look at her judge.

"Have I frightened you?" he said, noticing that startled glance. "Pray resume your seat. You hardly look well enough to stand up."

She sank back on the lounge, holding one hand over her throbbing heart. Paul Wyndham stood leaning against the marble mantel, looking down at the fire, and thinking of that other interview he had held with this woman, when he had to tell her she must be his wife. How few months had intervened since then, but what a lifetime of trouble, and secrecy, and suspicion, and guilt it seemed; and how she must hate and despise him! She had told him so once. How useless, then, it seemed, for him to approach her again! But, whether refused or not, that way duty lay; and he had deserved the humiliation. She sat before him, but not looking at him. He could not see her face, for she held up a dainty little toy of a hand-screen between it and the firelight; but he could see that the hand which held it shook, and that the lace on her breast fluttered, as if with the beating of the heart beneath. And seeing it, he took courage.

" I scarcely know," he began, " how I can say to you what I have come here to-night to say. I scarcely know how I dare speak to you at all. Believe me, no man **could be more penitent** for the wrong I have done you than I am. If my life could atone for it, I would give it, and think the atonement cheaply purchased. But my death cannot repair the sin of the past. I have wronged you—deeply, cruelly wronged you—and I have only your woman's pity and clemency to look to now. I can scarcely hope any feeling can remain for me in your heart but one of abhorrence, and that abhorrence I have deserved; but I owe it to you to say what I have come here to utter. You know all the story of the past. You heard it from the lips that are cold in death now, and those dying lips encouraged me to make this poor reparation. Harriet, my poor, wronged girl, if you will take her place, if you will be to me what the world here has for so many months thought you—what she really was—if you will be my wife, my dear and cherished wife, I will try what a lifetime of devotion will do to atone for the sorrowful past. Perhaps, my poor dear, you will be able to care for me enough in time to forgive me—almost to love me—and Heaven knows I will do my best to be all to you a husband should be to a beloved wife!"

He stopped, looking at her; but she did not stir, only the hand holding the screen trembled violently, and the fluttering breast rose and fell faster than ever.

"Harriet," he said, gently, "am I so hateful to you that you will not even look at me? Can you never forgive me for what I have done?"

She dropped the screen and rose up, her face all wet with a rain of happy tears, and held out both hands to him—all pride gone forever now.

"I do not forgive you," she said. "I love you, and love never has anything to forgive. O Paul, I have loved you ever since you made me your wife!"

So Paul Wyndham found out at last what others had known so long, and took his poor, forlorn wife to his arms with a strange, remorseful sort of tenderness, that, if not love, was near akin to it. So, while the fire burned low, and cast weird shadows on the dusky, book-lined walls, and the November wind wailed without, these two, never united before, sat side by side, and talked of a future that was to be theirs, far from Speckport and those who had heard the sinful and sorrowful story of the past.

By and by, a servant coming in to replenish the fire found them sitting peacefully together, as he had never seen his master and mistress sit before, and was sent to find Miss Rose and bring her to them. And I think Harriet herself was hardly happier in her new bliss than her gentle stepsister in witnessing it.

So, while Charley Marsh, up in Val Blake's room, that cold November night, listened in strange amazement to all that had been going on of late—to the romance-like story in which his unhappy sister had played so prominent a part—the two sat in the luxurious library at Redmon in this new happiness that had come to them from Nathalie Marsh's grave!

* * * * *

CHAPTER XXXIX.

IN HOPE.

IN the pale November sunlight of the next morning, in the plain, dark traveling-carriage from Redmon, a little party of four persons drove rapidly along the country-roads to a quiet little out-of-the-way church, some fifteen miles out of town. They were Mr. and Mrs. Paul Wyndham, Mr. Blake, and Miss Rose Henderson; and in the quiet church a quiet ceremony was performed by special license, which made Paul Wyndham and Harriet Wade man and wife, beyond the power of earthly tribunals to dispute. The clergyman was quite young, and the parties were all strangers to him, and he had a private opinion of his own that it was a runaway match. There were no witnesses but the two, and when it was over they drove back again to Redmon, and Harriet's heart was at peace at last. She had a trial to undergo that day—a great humiliation to endure—but it was a voluntary humiliation; and with her husband—hers now—she could undergo anything. The old, fierce, unbending pride, too, that had been her sin and misfortune all her life, had been chastened and subdued, and she owed to the society she had deceived the penance self-inflicted.

Val Blake had all the talking to himself on the way home, and, to do him justice, there wasn't much silence during the drive. He was talking of Charley Marsh, who had come home a far finer fellow than he had gone away, a brave and good and rich man.

They were all to meet that evening at a quiet dinner-party at Redmon—a farewell dinner party, it was understood, given by Mr. and Mrs. Wyndham, before their departure from Speckport to parts unknown. The invited guests were Mrs. Marsh and her son, Dr. Leach, Mr. Blake, and Miss Blair, Father Lennard (the old priest), and Mr. Darcy (the lawyer). A very select few, indeed, and all but Mr. Darcy acquainted with the story of the woman who had died at Rosebush Cottage, and the other story of the true and false heiress. He, too, was to be enlightened this evening, and Harriet Wyndham was publicly to renounce and hand over to her half-sister, Winnifred Rose Henderson, the fortune to which she never had possessed a claim. That was her humiliation; but with her husband by her side, she was great enough for that or anything else.

So the wedding-day passed very quietly at Redmon, and in the pale early twilight the guests began to arrive. Among the first to arrive was Mrs. Marsh and her son; the next to appear was Val, with Laura tucked under his arm; and Laura, with a little feminine scream of delight, dropped into Mrs. Wyndham's arms, and rained upon that lady a shower of gushing tears.

"Oh, what an age it is since I have seen my darling Olly before!" Miss Blair cried, "and I have been fairly dying for this hour to arrive."

Mrs. Paul Wyndham kissed the rosy rapturous face,

with that subdued and chastened tenderness that had come
to her through much sorrow ; and her dark eyes filled
with tears, as she thought, perhaps, loving little Laura
might leave Redmon that night with all this pretty girlish love gone, and nothing but contempt in its place.

Half an hour after, all the guests had arrived, and
were seated around the dinner table ; but the party was
not a very gay one, somehow. The knowledge of what
had passed was in every mind ; but Mr. Darcy was yet in
ignorance, and he set the dullness down to the recent
death of Mr. Wyndham's mother. Once, too, there was a
little awkwardness—Wyndham, speaking to Miss Rose, had
addressed her as Miss Henderson, and Mr. Darcy stared.

" Henderson !" he exclaimed, " you are talking to Miss
Rose, Wyndham ! Are you thinking of your courting
days and Miss Olive Henderson ?"

But Mrs. Wyndham and her half-sister colored, and
everybody looked suddenly down at their plates. Mr.
Darcy stared the more ; but Paul Wyndham, looking
very grave, came to the rescue.

" Miss Rose is Miss Rose Henderson ! Eat your
dinner, Mr. Darcy ; we will tell you all about it after."

So, when all returned to the drawing-room, Val
Blake told Mr. Darcy how he had been outwitted by a
girl. Not that Mr. Blake put it in any such barbarous
way, but glossed over ugly facts with a politeness that
was quite unusual in straightforward Val. But Mrs. Paul
Wyndham herself rose up, very white, with lips that
trembled, and was brave enough and strong enough to
openly confess her sin and her sister's goodness. She
looked up, with pitiful supplication, in the face of her
husband, as she finished, with the imploring appeal of a
little child for pardon ; and he put his protecting arm
around her, and smiled tenderly down in the mournful
black eyes, once so defiantly bright to him. Mr. Darcy's
amazement was beyond everything.

" Bless my soul !" was his cry, " and little Miss Rose
is Miss Henderson, after all, and the heiress of Redmon."

Miss Henderson, on whom all eyes were admiringly

bent, was painfully confused, and shrank so palpably, that the old lawyer spared her, and no one was sacrilegious enough to tell the little heroine what they thought of her noble conduct. And when Mrs. Marsh burst unexpectedly out in a glowing eulogy on all her goodness, not only to herself and Nathalie, but to all who were poor and friendless in the town, the little heiress broke down and cried. So no more was said in her hearing, and the gentlemen gathered together, and talked the matter over apart from the ladies, and settled how the news was to be taken to Speckport.

It was late when the party broke up, and good-night and good-bye was said to Mr. and Mrs. Wyndham, who were to leave to-morrow at eight. Val and Laura promised to be at the boat to see them off; and they were down true to their word, before the Redmon carriage arrived. Charley was there, too, and so was Cherrie, in crape to the eyes, looking very pretty in her widow's weeds, and all in a flutter at the thought of seeing Charley again. But this bearded and mustached and grave-looking young man was not the hot-headed, thoughtless Charley her pretty face had nearly ruined for life; and as he held out his hand to her, with a grave, almost sad smile, Cherrie suddenly recollected all the evil she had caused him, and had the grace to burst into tears, much to the horror of Mr. Blake, who had a true masculine dread of scenes.

"Don't cry, Cherrie," Charley said, "it's all over now, and it has done me good."

If any lingering hope remained that the old time might be renewed, that question and the smile that accompanied it banished it forever from poor Cherrie's foolish heart and her punishment that moment was bitterer than all that had gone before.

Miss Henderson was in the carriage with Mr. and Mrs. Wyndham, and went on board with them, as did the rest of their friends, and lingered until the last bell rang. Then, as Mrs. Wyndham threw back her vail for a parting kiss, they all saw that her eyes were swollen with crying. Paul Wyndham held both the little hands of the heiress in his own, and looked down in the gentle face with tender reverence.

"Good-bye, little sister," he said; "good-bye, and God bless you!"

The others were crowding around, and hasty farewells were spoken; and then the steamer was moving away from the wharf, and Charley led Miss Henderson, who was crying behind her vail, ashore; and they stood on the wharf to watch the steamer out of sight. They saw Paul Wyndham with his wife on his arm, waving a last farewell from the deck; and then the steamer was down the bay, and all the people on the wharf were going home. Charley Marsh assisted Miss Henderson into her carriage, and she was driven away to her new home.

Speckport knew everything—the murder was out, and Speckport, from one end to the other, was agape at the news. There was one thing about the affair they could not understand, and that was, how the rightful heiress, knowing herself to be so, and perfectly able to prove it, could wear out her life as a pitiful governess, and leave a princely fortune in the hands of a usurping stepsister. Speckport could not understand this—never could understand it, and set her down as an insipid little nonentity, with no will of her own, and easily twisted around the finger of that bold, bad, ambitious woman, Mrs. Paul Wyndham. Speckport did not spare its late enchantress, and for all their contempt of that "insipid thing" the present heiress, were very well satisfied to be noticed by her in public, and only too happy to call at Redmon. It was in her favor, they said, that she put on no airs in consequence of her sudden rise in the world, but was as gentle, and humble, and patient, and sweet, as heiress of Redmon as she had been when Mrs. Wheatly's governess. A few there were who understood and appreciated her; and when old Father Lennard laid his hand on her drooping head and fervently exclaimed, "God bless you, my child!" her eyes filled, and she felt more than repaid for any sacrifice she had ever made. Speckport said—but

Speckport was always given to say a good deal more than
its prayers—Speckport said Mr. Charles Marsh appreciated her, too, and that the estate of Redmon would
eventually go, in spite of Mrs. Leroy's unjust will, to the
Marsh family. But it was only gossip, this, and nobody
knew for certain, and Mrs. Marsh and Miss Rose Henderson had always been the best of friends.

And just about this time, too, Speckport found something else to talk about—no less a matter, indeed, than
the marriage of Valentine Blake, Esq., to Miss Laura
Amelia Blair. Such a snapper of a day as the wedding-
day was—cold enough to freeze the leg off an iron pot,
but for all that, the big cathedral was half filled with
curious Speckportonians, straining their necks to see the
bride and bridegroom, and their aiders and abettors. Mr.
Blake stood it like a man, and looked almost good-looking
in his neatly-fitting wedding suit ; and Charley Marsh
by his side looked like a young prince—handsomer than
any prince that ever wore a crown, poor Cherrie thought,
as she made eyes at him from her pew.

There was a wedding-breakfast to be eaten at Mr.
Blair's, and a very jolly breakfast it was. And then Mrs.
V. Blake exchanged her bridal-gear for a traveling-dress,
and was handed into the carriage that was to convey her
to the railway station, by her husband ; and the bridemaids were kissed all round by the bride, and good-bye
was said, and the happy pair were fairly started on their
bridal tour.

It took Speckport a week to fairly digest this matter,
and by the end of that time it got another delectable mor-
sel of gossip to swallow. Charley Marsh was going away.
He was a rich man, now ; but for all that he was going
to be a doctor, and was off to New York right away, to
finish his medical studies and get his diploma.

It was a miserably wet and windy day, that which
preceded the young man's departure. A depressing day,
that lowered the spirits of the most sanguine, and made
them feel life was a cheat, and not what it is cracked up
to be, and wonder how they could ever laugh and enjoy

themselves at all. A dreary day to say good-bye; but Charley, buttoned up in his overcoat, and making sunshine with his bright blue eyes and pleasant smile, went through with it bravely, and had bidden his dear five hundred adieu in the course of two brisk hours. There was only one friend remaining to whom he had yet to say "that dear old word good-bye;" and in the rainy twilight he drove up the long avenue of Redmon, black and ghastly now, and was admitted by Mrs. Hill herself.

"Oh, Mr. Charley, is it you?" the good woman said. "You're going away, they tell me. Dear me, we'll miss you so much!"

"That's right, Mrs. Hill! I like my friends to miss me; but I don't mean to stay away forever. Is Miss Henderson at home?"

"She is in the library. Walk right in!"

Charley was quite at home in Redmon Villa. The library door stood ajar. Some one was playing, and he entered unheard. The rain lashed and blustered at the windows: and the wail of the wind, and sea, and woods made a dull, roaring sound of dreariness without; but a coal-fire glowed red and cheery in the steel grate; and curtained, and close, and warm, the library was a very cozy place that bad January day. The twilight shadows lurked in the corners; but, despite their deepening gloom, the visitor saw a little, slender, girlish shape sitting before a small cottage-piano and softly touching the keys. Old, sad memories seemed to be at work in her heart; for the chords she struck were mournful, and she broke softly into singing at last—a song as sad as a funeral-hymn:

"Rain! rain! rain!
  On the cold autumnal night!
Like tears we weep o'er the banished hope
  That fled with the summer light.

"O rain! rain! rain!
  You mourn for the flowers dead;
But hearts there are, in their hopeless **woe**,
  That not even tears may shed!

"O rain ! rain ! rain !
   You fall on the new-made grave
Where the loved one sleeps that our bitter prayers
   Were powerless to save !

"O fall ! fall ! fall !
   Thou dreary and cheerless rain !
But the voice that sang with your summer-chime
   Will never be heard again !"

The song died away like a sigh ; and she arose from the instrument, looking like a little, pale spirit of the twilight, in her flowing white cashmere dress. The red firelight, flickering uncertainly, fell on a young man's figure leaning against the mantel, and the girl recoiled with a faint cry. Charley started up.

"I beg your pardon, Miss Henderson—Winnie" (they had all grown to call her Winnie of late)." "I am afraid I have startled you ; but you were singing when I came in, and the song was too sweet to be broken. I am rather late, but I wanted to say good-bye here last."

"Then you really go to-morrow ?" she said, not looking at him. "How much your mother will miss you !"

"Yes, poor mother ! but," smiling slightly, "I shall send her a box full of all the new novels when I get to New York, and that will console her. I wish somebody else would miss me, Winnie."

Is a woman ever taken by surprise, I wonder, in these cases ? Does she not always know beforehand when that all-important revelation is made that it is coming, particularly if she loves the narrator? I am pretty sure of it, though she may feign surprise ever so well. She can tell the instant he crosses the threshold what he has come to say. So Winnifred Rose Henderson knew what Charles Marsh had come to tell her from the moment she looked at him ; and sitting down on a low chair before the glowing fire, she listened for a second time in her life to the old, old story. What a gulf lay between that time and this—a girl then, a woman now ! And how different the two men who had told it !

Worthy Mrs. Hill, trotting up-stairs and down-stairs, seeing to fires and bed-rooms, and everything proper to be seen to by a good housekeeper, suddenly remembered the fire in the library must be getting low, and that it would be just like the young people saying good-bye to one another to forget all about it, rapped to the door some half an hour after. "Come in!" the sweet voice of Miss Henderson said, and Mrs. Hill went in and found the young lady and Mr. Marsh sitting side by side on a sofa, and both wearing such radiant faces, that the dear old lady saw at once through her spectacles how matters stood, and kissed Miss Henderson on the spot, and shook hands with Mister Charley, and wished him joy with all her honest heart. So the momentous question had been asked and answered, and on Miss Henderson's finger glittered an engagement-ring, and Charley Marsh, in the bleak dawn of the next morning, left Speckport once more, the happiest fellow in the universe.

* * * * * *

The story is told, the play played out, the actors off the stage, and high time for the curtain to fall. But the audience are dissatisfied yet, and have some questions to ask. "How did Val Blake and Laura get on, and Mr. and Mrs. Wyndham? What became of Cherrie and Catty Clowrie? and have Charley and Miss Henderson got married yet? and who was at the wedding? and who were the bridemaids? and what did the bride wear?" Well, let me see. I'll answer as they come. It is six months after, red-hot July—not a sign of fog in Speckport, picnics and jollifications every day, and the blessed little city (it is a city, though I have stigmatized it as a town) out in its gala-dress. Do you see that handsome house in Golden Row? There is a shining door-plate on the front door, and you can read the name—"V. Blake." Yes, that is Mr. Blake's house, and inside it is sumptuous to behold; for the "Spouter" increases its circulation every day, and Mr. B. keeps his carriage and pair now, and is a rising man—I mean out of doors. In his own single nook, I regret to say, he is hen-pecked—unmercifully hen-pecked. The gray mare is the better horse; and Mr. Blake submits to petticoat-government with that sublime good-nature your big man always manifests, and knocks meekly under at the first flash of Mistress Laura's bright eye—not that that lady is any less fond of Mr. Val than of yore. Oh, no! She thinks there is nobody like him in this little planet of ours; only she believes in husbands keeping their proper place, and acts up to this belief. She is becoming more and more literary every day—fearfully literary, I may say; and the first two fingers of the right hand are daily steeped to the bone in ink.

Mr. and Mrs. Wyndham are in New York, and are very busy. Charley Marsh was a frequent visitor at their house last winter, and says he never saw a happier and more loving husband and wife. Mr. Wyndham is high in the literary world; and Mrs. Wyndham is very much admired in society, as much, perhaps, for her gentleness and goodness as for her beauty. They are happy and at peace; and so we leave them.

Cherrie Nettleby (nobody thinks of calling her Mrs. Cavendish) is going to be married next week. The happy man is Sergeant O'Shaughnessy, a big Irishman, six feet four in his stockings, with a laugh like distant thunder, rosy cheeks, and curly hair. A fine-looking fellow. Sergeant O'Shaughnessy, with a heart as big as his body, who adores the ground Cherrie walks on.

And Charley is married, and happier than I can ever tell. He is rich and honored, and does a great deal of good, and is a great man in Speckport—a great and good man. And his wife—but you know her—and she is the same to-day, and will be the same unto death, as you have known her. Mrs. Marsh, Senior, lives with them, and reads as much as ever; and is waited on by Midge, who lives a life of luxurious leisure in Redmon kitchen, and queens it over the household generally.

There is a quiet little grave out in the country which Charles Marsh and his wife visit very often, and which they never leave without loving each other better, and feeling more resolute, with God's help, to walk down to

the grave in the straight and narrow path that leads to
salvation. They are only human. They have all erred,
and sinned, and repented ; and in that saving repentance
they have found the truth of the holy promise: "There
shall be light at the eventide."

THE END.